5TH EDITION

Managing and Using Information Systems

A Strategic Approach

KERI E. PEARLSON
KP Partners

CAROL S. SAUNDERS
University of Central Florida
Dr. Theo and Friedl Schoeller Research Center for Business and Society

WILEY
JOHN WILEY & SONS, INC.

To Yale & Hana

To Rusty, Russell & Kristin

VP & EXECUTIVE PUBLISHER:	Don Fowley
EXECUTIVE EDITOR:	Beth Lang Golub
ASSISTANT EDITOR:	Samantha Mandel
PROGRAM ASSISTANT:	Elizabeth Mills
MARKETING MANAGER:	Chris Ruel
MARKETING ASSISTANT:	Ashley Tomeck
DESIGNER:	Wendy Lai
ASSOCIATE PRODUCTION MANAGER:	Joyce Poh
PRODUCTION EDITOR:	Jolene Ling

This book was set in 10/12pt NewCaledonia by Thomson Digital and printed and bound by Courier Westford. The cover was printed by Courier Westford.

This book is printed on acid free paper.

Founded in 1807, John Wiley & Sons, Inc. has been a valued source of knowledge and understanding for more than 200 years, helping people around the world meet their needs and fulfill their aspirations. Our company is built on a foundation of principles that include responsibility to the communities we serve and where we live and work. In 2008, we launched a Corporate Citizenship Initiative, a global effort to address the environmental, social, economic, and ethical challenges we face in our business. Among the issues we are addressing are carbon impact, paper specifications and procurement, ethical conduct within our business and among our vendors, and community and charitable support. For more information, please visit our website: www.wiley.com/go/citizenship.

Library of Congress Cataloging-in-Publication Data
Pearlson, Keri.
  Managing and using information systems: a strategic approach/Keri E. Pearlson, Carol S. Saunders. – 5th ed.
    p. cm.
  Includes index.
  ISBN 978-1-118-28173-4 (pbk.)
  1. Knowledge management. 2. Information technology–Management. 3. Management information systems.
4. Electronic commerce. I. Saunders, Carol S. II. Title.
HD30.2.P4 2013
658.4'038011—dc23   2012015379

Printed in the United States of America
10 9 8 7 6 5 4 3 2 1

Preface

Information technology and business are becoming inextricably interwoven. I don't think anybody can talk meaningfully about one without the talking about the other.[1]

Bill Gates
Microsoft

I'm not hiring MBA students for the technology you learn while in school, but for your ability to learn about, use and subsequently manage new technologies when you get out.

IT Executive
Federal Express

Give me a fish and I eat for a day; teach me to fish and I eat for a lifetime.

Proverb

Managers do not have the luxury of abdicating participation in information systems decisions. Managers who choose to do so risk limiting their future business options. Information systems are at the heart of virtually every business interaction, process, and decision, especially when one considers the vast penetration of the Web in the last few years. Mobile and social technologies have brought information systems to an entirely new level within firms, and between individuals in their personal lives. Managers who let someone else make decisions about their information systems are letting someone else make decisions about the very foundation of their business. This is a textbook about managing and using information, written for current and future managers as a way of introducing the broader implications of the impact of information systems.

The goal of this book is to assist managers in becoming knowledgeable participants in information systems decisions. Becoming a knowledgeable participant means learning the basics and feeling comfortable enough to ask questions. It does not mean having all the answers nor having a deep understanding of all the technologies out in the world today. No text will provide managers with everything they need to know to make important information systems decisions. Some texts instruct on the basic technical background of information systems. Others discuss applications and their life cycle. Some take a comprehensive view of the management information systems (MIS) field and offer readers snapshots of current systems along with chapters describing how those technologies are designed, used, and integrated into business life.

This book takes a different approach. This text is intended to provide the reader with a foundation of basic concepts relevant to using and managing information. It is not intended to provide a comprehensive treatment on any one aspect of MIS, for certainly

---

[1] http://www.woopidoo.com/business quotes/authors/bill-gates-quotes.htm.

iii

each aspect is itself a topic of many books. It is not intended to provide readers with enough technological knowledge to make them MIS experts. It is not intended to be a source of discussion of any particular technology. This textbook is written to help managers begin to form a point of view of how information systems will help, hinder, and create opportunities for their organizations.

The idea for this text grew out of discussions with colleagues in the MIS area. Many faculties use a series of case studies, trade and popular press readings, and Web sites to teach their MIS courses. Others simply rely on one of the classic texts, which include dozens of pages of diagrams, frameworks, and technologies. The initial idea for this text emerged from a core MIS course taught at the business school at the University of Texas at Austin. That course was considered an "appetizer" course—a brief introduction into the world of MIS for MBA students. The course had two main topics: using information and managing information. At the time, there was no text like this one, hence students had to purchase thick reading packets made up of articles and case studies to provide them with the basic concepts. The course was structured to provide the general MBA with enough knowledge of the field of MIS that they could recognize opportunities to use the rapidly changing technologies available to them. The course was an appetizer to the menu of specialty courses, each of which went much deeper into the various topics. But completion of the appetizer course meant that students were able to feel comfortable listening to, contributing to, and ultimately participating in information systems decisions.

Today, many students are digital natives—people who have grown up using information technologies all of their lives. That means that students come to their courses with significantly more knowledge about things like tablets, apps, personal computers, smartphones, texting, the Web, social networking, file downloading, online purchasing, and social media than their counterparts in school just a few years ago. This is a significant trend that is projected to continue; students will be increasingly knowledgeable in personally using technologies. That knowledge has begun to change the corporate environment. Today's digital natives expect to find information systems in corporations that provide at least the functionality they have at home. At the same time, they expect to be able to work in ways that take advantage of the technologies they have grown to depend on for social interaction, collaboration, and innovation. This edition of the text has been completely edited with this new group of students in mind. We believe the basic foundation is still needed for managing and using information systems, but we understand that the assumptions and knowledge base of today's students is significantly different.

Also different today is the vast amount of information amassed by firms, sometimes called the "Big Data Problem." Not only have organizations figured out that there is a lot of data around their processes, their interactions with customers, their products, and their suppliers, but with the increase in communities and social interactions on the Web, there is an additional pressure to collect and analyze vast amounts of unstructured information contained in these conversations to identify trends, needs, and projections. We believe that today's managers face an increasing amount of pressure to understand what is being said by those inside and outside their corporations and to join the conversations as much as reasonable. That is significantly different from just a few years ago.

This book includes an introduction, twelve chapters of text and minicases, and a set of case studies and supplemental readings on a Web site. The introduction makes the argument introduced in this preface that managers must be knowledgeable participants in information systems decisions. The first few chapters build a basic framework of relationships between business strategy, information systems strategy, and organizational strategy and explore the links between these strategies. Readers will also find a chapter on how information systems relate to business transformation. Supplemental materials, including longer cases from all over the globe, can be found on the Web. Please visit http://www.wiley.com/college/pearlson for more information.

General managers also need some foundation on how IT is managed if they are to successfully discuss their next business needs with IT professionals who can help them. Therefore, the remaining chapters describe the basics of information architecture and infrastructure, the business of IT, the governance of the IS organization, the sourcing of information systems, project management, business intelligence, business analytics and knowledge management, and relevant ethical issues.

No text in the field of MIS is current. The process of writing the chapters, coupled with the publication process, makes a text somewhat out-of-date prior to delivery to its audience. With that in mind, this text is written to summarize the "timeless" elements of using and managing information. Although this text is complete in and of itself, learning is enhanced by coupling the chapters with the most current readings and cases. Students are encouraged to search the Web for examples and current events and bring them into the discussions of the issues at hand. The format of each chapter begins with a navigational guide, a short case study and the basic language for a set of important management issues. This is followed up with a set of managerial concerns related to the topic. The chapter concludes with a summary, a set of study questions, key words, and case studies.

This is the fifth edition of this text, and this version includes several significant additions and revisions. Each chapter now has a Social Business Lens, a textbox that calls out one topic related to the main chapter, but that is enabled or fundamental to using social tools in the enterprise. Most chapters also have a Geographic Lens box, a single idea from a global issue related to the topic of the main chapter. Gone are the "food for thought" sections in each chapter. Some have been incorporated into the main part of the chapter, and others have been moved to the companion Web site available to instructors using this text. Each chapter has been significantly revised, with newer concepts added, discussions of more current topics fleshed out, and old, outdated topics removed or at least their discussion shortened. And every chapter now has a navigation box to help the reader understand the flow and key topics of the chapter.

Who should read this book? General managers interested in participating in information systems decisions will find this a good reference resource for the language and concepts of IS. Managers in the information systems field will find this book a good resource for beginning to understand the general manager's view of how information systems affect business decisions. And IS students will be able to use the readings and concepts in this book as the beginning point in their journey to become informed and successful business people.

The information revolution is here. Where do you fit in?

Keri E. Pearlson and Carol S. Saunders

Acknowledgments

Books of this nature are written only with the support of many individuals. We would like to personally thank several individuals who helped with this text. Although we've made every attempt to include everyone who helped make this book a reality, there is always the possibility of unintentionally leaving some out. We apologize in advance if that is the case here.

Brandt Walker helped us with this edition by researching various topics, finding cases, and verifying examples from previous editions. We really appreciate his thoughtful efforts. We also appreciate the considerable efforts of Parul Acharya and Arturo Watlington III, students at the University of Central Florida who enthusiastically helped with proofreading, research and background checking of facts. Thank you also goes to Matthew Riley and Steve Kaplan of Presidio for help with the infrastructure and architecture concepts.

We also want to acknowledge and thank pbwiki.com. Without their incredible and free wiki, we would have been relegated to e-mailing drafts of chapters back and forth. For this edition, as with the fourth edition, we wanted to use Web 2.0 tools as we wrote about them. We found that having used the wiki for our previous edition, we were able to get up and running much faster than if we had to start over without the platform.

We have been blessed with the help of our colleagues in this and in previous editions of the book. They helped us by writing cases and reviewing the text. Our thanks continue to go out to Dennis Galletta, Jonathan Trower, Espen Andersen, Janis Gogan, Ashok Rho, Yvonne Lederer Antonucci, E. Jose Proenca, Bruce Rollier, Dave Oliver, Celia Romm, Ed Watson, D. Guiter, S. Vaught, Kala Saravanamuthu, Ron Murch, John Greenwod, Tom Rohleder, Sam Lubbe, Thomas Kern, Mark Dekker, Anne Rutkowski, Kathy Hurtt, Kay Nelson, John Butler, Philip Russell Saunders, Mihir Parikh, and Craig Tidwell. In addition, the students of the spring 2008 Technology Management and summer 2008 Information Resource Management classes at the University of Central Florida provided comments that proved helpful in writing some cases and making revisions. Though we cannot thank them by name, we also greatly appreciate the comments of the anonymous reviewers who have made a mark on this edition.

The book would not have been started were it not for the initial suggestion of a wonderful editor at John Wiley & Sons, Inc., Beth Lang Golub. Her persistence and patience have helped shepherd this book through many months of creation, modification, evaluation, and production, and she will shepherd it through translation into other languages. Special thanks go to Samantha Mandel, who very patiently helped us through the revision process. We also appreciate the help of all the staff at Wiley, who have made this edition a reality.

From Keri: Thank you to my husband, Dr. Yale Pearlson, and my daughter, Hana Pearlson. Once again, their patience with me while I worked on this edition was incredibly supportive. They understood my manic moments, and celebrated the victories and completion with as much joy as if they had written this book themselves. They also provided some ideas and examples, especially around the social business topics. I love you guys!

From Carol: Rusty, thank you for being my compass (always keeping me headed in the right direction) and my release valve (patiently walking me through stressful times— like writing revisions). I couldn't do it without you. Every year I love you more! I love you, Kristin, Russell, and Janel very much!

About the Authors

Dr. Keri E. Pearlson is president of KP Partners, an advisory services firm specializing in creating business leaders skilled in the strategic use of information systems and organizational design in the Web 2.0 world. Dr. Pearlson is an entrepreneur, teacher, researcher, consultant, and thought leader. She has held various positions in academia and industry. She was a member of the information systems faculty at the Graduate School of Business at the University of Texas at Austin, where she taught management information systems courses to MBAs and executives. She held positions at the Harvard Business School, CSC, nGenera (formerly the Concours Group), AT&T, and Hughes Aircraft Company. While writing this edition, she was also an Adjunct faculty member at Babson College, in Wellesley, MA, and elected the first President of the Austin Area Society of Information Management chapter.

She is co-author of *Zero Time: Providing Instant Customer Value—Every Time, All the Time* (John Wiley & Sons, 2000). Her work has been published in numerous places including *Sloan Management Review, Academy of Management Executive, and Information Resources Management Journal*. Many of her case studies have been published by Harvard Business School Publishing and are used all over the world. She currently writes a blog on issues at the intersection of IT and business strategy. It's available at www.kppartners.com.

Dr. Pearlson holds a Doctorate in Business Administration (DBA) in Management Information Systems from the Harvard Business School and both a Master's Degree in Industrial Engineering Management and a Bachelor's Degree in Applied Mathematics from Stanford University.

Dr. Carol S. Saunders is professor of Management at the University of Central Florida in Orlando, Florida, and Schoeller Senior Fellow (2012) at the University of Erlangen-Nuremberg. She served as General Conference Chair of the International Conference on Information Systems (ICIS) in 1999 and Telecommuting in 1996. She was the chair of the ICIS Executive Committee in 2000. For three years, she served as editor-in-chief of *MIS Quarterly*. She has received the Association of Information Systems (AIS) LEO award for lifetime accomplishments and is a Fellow of the AIS.

Her current research interests include the impact of information system on power and communication, overload, virtual teams, virtual worlds, time, sourcing, and inter-organizational linkages. Her research is published in a number of journals including *MIS Quarterly, Information Systems Research, Journal of MIS, Communications of the ACM, Academy of Management Journal, Academy of Management Review, Communications Research*, and *Organization Science*.

Contents

▶ **CHAPTER 12** Using Information Ethically   350

Glossary   377

Index   387

Introduction

This chapter introduces the perspectives that are used throughout this text. It begins by making the case for general manager participation in information systems decisions and the consequences that arise when managers do not participate in IS decisions. Basic assumptions about management, business, and information systems made by the authors are stated. The chapter concludes with a brief discussion about the difference between the economics of information versus things.

Why do managers need to understand and participate in the information decisions of their organizations? After all, most corporations maintain entire departments dedicated to the management of information systems (IS). These departments are staffed with highly skilled professionals devoted to the field of technology. Shouldn't managers rely on experts to analyze all the aspects of IS and to make the best decisions for the organization? The answer to that question is no.

Managing information is a critical skill for success in today's business environment. All decisions made by companies involve, at some level, the management and use of IS. Managers today need to know about their organization's capabilities and uses of information as much as they need to understand how to obtain and budget financial resources. The ubiquity of personal devices such as smart phones, laptops and tablets, and access to apps within corporations and externally over the Internet, highlights this fact because today's technologies form the backbone for virtually all business models. This backbone easily crosses the globe, adding the need for a global competency to the manager's skill set. Further, the proliferation of supply chain partnerships and the vast amount of technology available to individuals outside of the corporation has extended the urgent need for business managers to be involved in technology decisions. In addition, the availability of seemingly free (or at least very inexpensive) applications, collaboration tools and innovation engines in the consumer area has changed the landscape once again, increasing the integration of IS and business processes. A manager who does not understand the basics of managing and using information cannot be successful in this business environment.

The majority of U.S. adults own a smart phone, laptop, and access to online apps. According to the Pew Research Center, in 2011, 83% of U.S. adults had a cell phone of some kind, and of those who had a mobile phone, 42% had a smart phone.[1] Individuals now have to manage a virtual "personal IS" and make decisions about applications to purchase. Doesn't that give them insight into managing information systems in corporations? Students often think that because of their personal experience with technology, they also are experts in corporate IS. There is some truth in that perspective, but it's also a very dangerous perspective for managers to take. Certainly managing one's own

---

[1] Smartphone Adoption and Usage, July 2011, http://pewinternet.org/Reports/2011/Smartphones.aspx.

information systems gives some experience that is useful in the corporate setting such as knowing about interesting apps, being able to use a variety of technologies for different purposes, and being familiar with the ups and downs of networking. But in a corporate setting, information systems must be enterprise-ready. They must be scalable for large number of employees; they must be delivered in an appropriate manner for the enterprise; they must be managed with corporate guidelines, and sometimes governmental regulations, in mind. Issues like security, privacy, risk, and architecture take on a new meaning within an enterprise, and someone has to manage them. A similar phenomenon occurred in the early days of database applications. Individuals who used a personal computer version of a database assumed they understood databases, but they ran into issues when they try to integrate enterprise-level data from multiple users. That required a different architecture and skill set. Enterprise-level managing and using information systems require a unique perspective managers develop over time.

Consider the now-historic rise of companies such as Amazon.com, Google and Zappos. Amazon.com began as an online bookseller and rapidly outpaced traditional brick-and-mortar businesses like Barnes and Noble, Borders, and Waterstones. Management at the traditional companies responded by having their IS support personnel build Web sites to compete. But upstart Amazon.com moved on ahead, keeping its leadership position on the Web by leveraging its new business model into other marketplaces, such as music, electronics, health and beauty products, lawn and garden products, auctions, tools and hardware, and more. It cleared the profitability hurdle by achieving a good mix of IS and business basics: capitalizing on operational efficiencies derived from inventory software and smarter storage, cost cutting, and effectively partnering with such companies as Toys "R" Us Inc. and Target Corporation.[2] More recently Amazon.com changed the basis of competition in another market, but this time it was the Web services business. Amazon.com Web services offers clients the extensive technology platform used for Amazon.com, but in an on-demand fashion for developing and running the client's own applications. Shoe retailer Zappos.com challenged Amazon's business model, in part by coupling a social business strategy with exemplary service and sales, and they were so successful that Amazon.com bought them.

Likewise, Google played an important role in revolutionizing the way information is located, changing the playing field for advertising and publishing business models. Google began in 1999 as a basic search company but quickly learned that a unique business model was a critical factor for future success. The company changed the way people thought about Web content by making it available in a searchable format with an incredibly fast response time and in a host of languages. Further, Google's keyword-targeted advertising program revolutionized the way companies advertise. By 2001, Google announced its first quarter of profitability, solidifying the way the world finds information, publishes, and advertises.[3] More recently, Google expanded into a complete suite of Web-based applications, such as calendaring, e-mail, collaboration, shopping, and maps and then enhanced the applications by combining them with social

---

[2] Robert Hof, "How Amazon Cleared the Profitability Hurdle," *BusinessWeek Online* (February 4, 2002), http://www.businessweek.com/magazine/content/02_05/b3768079.htm (accessed on May 23, 2002).

[3] Adapted from information at www.google.com/corporate/history.html (accessed on June 17, 2005).

tools to increase collaboration. Further, like Amazon.com, Google also offers clients similar on-demand services.[4]

These and other online businesses are able to succeed where traditional companies have not, in part because their management understood the power of information, IS, and the Web. These exemplary online businesses did not succeed because their managers could build Web pages or assemble an IS network. Quite the contrary. The executives in these new businesses understood the fundamentals of managing and using information and could marry that knowledge with a sound, unique business vision to achieve domination of their intended market spaces.

The goal of this book is to provide the foundation to help the general business manager become a knowledgeable participant in IS decisions because any IS decision in which the manager does not participate can greatly affect the organization's ability to succeed in the future. This introduction outlines the fundamental reasons for taking the initiative to participate in IS decisions. Moreover, because effective participation requires a unique set of managerial skills, this introduction identifies the most important ones. These skills are helpful not just in making IS decisions, but all business decisions. We describe how managers should participate in the decision-making process and outline key topics to consider which develop this point of view. Finally, this introduction presents current models for understanding the nature of a business and an information system to provide a framework for the discussions that follow in subsequent chapters.

▶ THE CASE FOR PARTICIPATING IN DECISIONS ABOUT INFORMATION SYSTEMS

Experience shows that business managers have no problem participating in most organizational decisions, even those outside their normal business expertise. For example, ask a plant manager about marketing problems, and the result is likely to be a detailed opinion on both key issues and recommended solutions. Dialogue among managers routinely crosses all business functions in formal as well as informal settings, with one general exception: IS. Management continues to tolerate ignorance in this area relative to other specialized business functions. Culturally, managers can claim ignorance of IS issues without losing prestige among colleagues. On the other hand, admitting a lack of knowledge regarding marketing or financial aspects of the business earns colleagues' contempt.

These attitudes are attributable to the historic role that IS played in businesses. For many years, technology was regarded as a support function and treated as administrative overhead. Its value as a factor in important management decisions was minimal. It often took a great deal of technical knowledge to understand even the most basic concepts.

However, in today's business environment, maintaining this back-office view of technology is certain to cost market share and could ultimately lead to the failure of the organization. Technology has become entwined with all the classic functions of

---

[4] For more information on the latest services by these two companies, see http://www.amazon.com and http://www.google.com/enterprise/cloud/.

Reasons

IS must be managed as a critical resource
IS enable change in the way people work together
IS are part of almost every aspect of business
IS enable or inhibit business opportunities and new strategies
IS can be used to combat business challenges from competitors

FIGURE I-1 Reasons why business managers should participate in information systems decisions.

business—operations, marketing, accounting, finance—to such an extent that under-standing its role is necessary for making intelligent and effective decisions about any of them. Furthermore, a general understanding of key IS concepts is possible without the extensive technological knowledge required just a few years ago. Most managers today have personal technology such as a smart phone or tablet that is more functional than many corporate-supported personal computers provided by enterprises just a few years ago. In fact, the proliferation of personal technologies makes everyone a "pseudo-expert." Each individual must manage applications on smart phones, make decisions about applications to purchase, and procure technical support when the systems fail. Finally, with the robust number of consumer applications available on the Web, many decisions historically made by the IS group are increasingly being made by individuals outside the IS, sometimes at the detriment of corporate objectives.

Therefore, understanding basic fundamentals about using and managing informa-tion is worth the investment of time. The reasons for this investment are summarized in Figure I-1 and are discussed next.

A Business View

Information technology (IT) is a critical resource for today's businesses. It both supports and consumes a significant amount of an organization's resources. Just like the other three major types of business resources—people, money, and machines—it needs to be managed wisely.

IT spends a significant portion of corporate budgets. Worldwide IT spending topped $3.7 trillion in 2011, a jump of almost 8% from the previous year. It's projected to continue to increase.[5] More than 350 companies each plan to invest more than $1 billion in IT, particularly in cloud, social, mobile and big data. Companies in a Gartner study reported that cloud services will grow five times faster than overall IT enterprise spending annually through 2015.

These resources must return value, or they will be invested elsewhere. The business manager, not the IS specialist, decides which activities receive funding, estimates the risk associated with the investment, and develops metrics for evaluating the performance of the

---

[5] http://www.gartner.com/technology/research/it-spending-forecast/ (accessed on February 12, 2012).

investment. Therefore, the business manager needs a basic grounding in managing and using information. On the flip side, IS managers need a business view to be able to explain how the technology will impact the business and what the tradeoffs are.

People and Technology Work Together

In addition to financial issues, a manager must know how to mesh technology and people to create effective work processes. Collaboration is increasingly common, especially with the rise of social networking. Companies are reaching out to individual customers using social technologies such as Facebook, Twitter, YouTube and numerous other tools. In fact, the term **Web 2.0** describes the use of World Wide Web (the Internet) applications that facilitate, information sharing, user-centered design, interoperability and collaboration among users. Technology facilitates the work that people do and the way they interact with each other. Appropriately incorporating IS into the design of a business model enables people to focus their time and resources on issues that bear directly on customer satisfaction and other revenue- and profit-generating activities.

Adding a new IS to an existing organization, however, requires the ability to manage change. The skilled business manager must balance the benefits of introducing new technology with the costs associated with changing the existing behaviors of people in the workplace. There may be choices of technology solutions each with different impact and a decision must incorporate a clear understanding of the consequences. Making this assessment does not require detailed technical knowledge. It does require an understanding of what the short-term and long-term consequences are likely to be, how to mitigate the risks associated with and why adopting new technology may be more appropriate in some instances than in others. Understanding these issues also helps managers know when it may prove effective to replace people with technology at certain steps in a process.

Integrating Business with Information Systems

IS are integrated with almost every aspect of business and have been for quite some time. For example, as former CEO of Walmart Stores International, Bob Martin described IS's role, "Today technology plays a role in almost everything we do, from every aspect of customer service to customizing our store formats or matching our merchandising strategies to individual markets in order to meet varied customer preferences."[6] IS place information in the hands of Walmart associates so that decisions can be made closer to the customer. IS help simplify organizational activities and processes such as moving goods, stocking shelves, or communicating with suppliers. For example, handheld scanners provide floor associates with immediate and real time access to inventory in their store and the ability to locate items in surrounding stores, if necessary.

---

[6] "The End of Delegation? Information Technology and the CEO," *Harvard Business Review* (September–October 1995), 161.

Rapid Change in Technology

The proliferation of new technologies creates a business environment filled with opportunities. The changing demographics of the workforce and the integration of "**digital natives**," individuals who have grown up completely fluent in the use of personal technologies and the Web, also increase the rate of adoption of new technologies beyond the pace of traditional organizations. Even today, new uses of the Internet produce new types of online businesses that keep every manager and executive on alert. New business opportunities spring up with little advance warning. The manager's role is to frame these opportunities so that others can understand them, to evaluate them against existing business needs and choices, and finally to pursue those that fit with an articulated business strategy. The quality of the information at hand affects the quality of both the decision and its implementation. Managers must develop an understanding of what information is crucial to the decision, how to get it, and how to use it. They must lead the changes driven by IS.

Competitive Challenges

Competitors come from both expected and unexpected places. General managers are in the best position to see the emerging threats and utilize IS effectively to combat ever-changing competitive challenges. Further, general managers are often called on to demonstrate a clear understanding of how their own technology programs and products compare with those of their competitors. A deep understanding of the capabilities of the organization coupled with existing IS can create a competitive advantage and change the competitive landscape for the entire industry.

Customer Pull

With the emergence of social networks such as Facebook and Renren, social microblogs such as Sina Weibo and Twitter, social media and the Web, businesses have had to redesign their existing business models to account for the change in power now yielded by customers and others in their communities. Social media have given powerful voices to customers and communities and businesses must listen. Redesigning the customer experience when interacting with a company is top of mind for many managers and the key driver is IS. Social IT enable new and often deeper relationships with a large number customers and companies are learning how to integrate and leverage this capability into existing and new business models.

▶ WHAT IF A MANAGER DOESN'T PARTICIPATE?

Decisions about IS directly affect the profits of a business. The basic formula Profit = Revenue − Expenses can be used to evaluate the impact of these decisions. Adopting the wrong technologies can cause a company to miss business opportunities and any revenues those opportunities would generate. Inadequate IS can cause a breakdown in servicing customers, which hurts sales. Poorly deployed social IT resources can badly damage the reputation of a strong brand. On the expense side, a miscalculated investment in technology can lead to overspending and excess capacity or under spending and restricted opportunity. Inefficient business processes sustained by ill-fitting IS also increase expenses. Lags in implementation or poor process adaptation each reduce profits and therefore growth. IS decisions can dramatically affect the bottom line.

Failure to consider IS strategy when planning business strategy and organizational strategy leads to one of three business consequences: (1) IS that fail to support business goals, (2) IS that fail to support organizational systems, and (3) a misalignment between business goals and organizational capabilities. These consequences are discussed briefly in the following section and in more detail in later chapters. The driving questions to consider are the potential effects on an organization's ability to achieve its business goals. How will the consequences impact the way people work? Will the organization still be able to implement its business strategy?

Information Systems Must Support Business Goals

IS represent a major investment for any firm in today's business environment. Yet poorly chosen IS can actually become an obstacle to achieving business goals. The results can be disastrous if the systems do not allow the organization to realize its goals. When IS lack the capacity needed to collect, store, and transfer critical information for the business, decisions can be impacted and options limited. Customers will be dissatisfied or even lost. Production costs may be excessive. Worst of all, management may not be able to pursue desired business directions that are blocked by inappropriate IS. Victoria's Secret experienced this problem when a Superbowl ad promoting an online fashion show generated so many inquiries to its Web site that it crashed. After spending large amount of money on the advertisement, it was wasted when potential customers could not access the site. Likewise, Toys "R" Us experienced such a calamity when its well-publicized Web site was unable to process and fulfill orders fast enough one holiday season. It not only lost those customers, but it also had a major customer relations issue to manage as a result.

Information Systems Must Support Organizational Systems

Organizational systems represent the fundamental elements of a business—its people, work processes, tasks, structure and control systems—and the plan that enables them to work efficiently to achieve business goals. If the company's IS fail to support its organizational systems, the result is a misalignment of the resources needed to achieve its goals. For example, it seems odd to think that a manager might add functionality to a corporate Web site without providing the training these same employees need to use the tool effectively. Yet, this mistake—and many more costly ones—occur in businesses every day. Managers make major IS decisions without informing all the staff of resulting changes in their daily work. For example, an enterprise resource planning (ERP) system often dictates how many business processes are executed and the organization systems must change to reflect the new processes. Deploying technology without thinking through how it actually will be used in the organization—who will use it, how they will use it, how to make sure the applications chosen actually accomplish what is intended—results in significant expense. In another example, a company may decide to block access to the Internet, thinking that they are prohibiting employees from accessing

Social Business Lens

In this edition of the text, we introduce a new feature, the Social Business Lens. The explosion of consumer-based technologies, coupled with applications such as Facebook, Renren, Sina Weibo, Twitter, LinkedIn, YouTube, Foursquare, Skype, Pinterest, and more have brought into focus the concept of a social business. Some call this trend the consumerization of technology a term used to mean that technologies targeted at individual, personal users such as social tools, mobile phones, and Web applications are entering the corporation and pressuring the enterprise in new and unexpected ways. At the same time, technologies intended for the corporation, like cloud computing, are being retooled and "consumerized" to appeal to individuals outside the corporation.

This phenomenon is permeating every facet of business. There are new business models based on a social IT platform, new ways of connecting with stakeholders, governing, collaborating, doing work, and measuring results. In this book, we are particular about the terminology we use. Social IT is the term we use for all technologies in this space. We define **social IT** as the technologies used for collaboration, networking, and the general interaction between people over the Web. These include social networks and other applications that provide for interaction between people. Enterprise use of social IT for business applications, activities and processes is called **social business**.

Many use the term **social media** as an overarching term for this space, but increasingly social media refers to the marketing and sales applications of social IT, and we use it that way. Social networks are a specific type of tool, like Facebook, Ning, and similar tools. **Social networking** is the use of these types of social IT tools in a community. As of the writing of this text, the social space is still like the wild west; there are no widely accepted conventions about the terms and their meanings or the uses and their impact. But we have enough experience with social IT that we know it's a major force bursting on the enterprise scene and it must be addressed in discussions of managing and using information systems.

Look for the box "Social Business Lens" in each chapter. In that space, we explore one topic related to that chapter from a social business perspective. We look through the lens of a social business.

offensive or unsecure sites. But that decision also means that employees can't access social networking sites, which may be useful for collaboration, or other Web-based applications that may offer functionality to make the business more efficient.

The general manager, who, after all, is charged with ensuring that company resources are used effectively, must guarantee that the company's IS support its organizational systems and that changes made in one system are reflected in the other. For example, a company that plans to allow workers to work remotely needs an information system strategy compatible with its organization strategy. Desktop PCs located within the corporate office are not the right solution for a telecommuting organization. Instead, laptop computers, applications that are accessible online anywhere and anytime, and networks that facilitate information sharing are needed. Workers may want to use tablets or smart phones remotely, too, and those entail a different set of IS processes. If the organization only allows the purchase of desktop PCs and only builds systems accessible from desks within the office, the telecommuting program is doomed to failure.

► SKILLS NEEDED TO PARTICIPATE EFFECTIVELY IN INFORMATION TECHNOLOGY DECISIONS

Participating in IT decisions means bringing a clear set of skills to the table. All managers are asked to take on tasks that require different skills at different times. Those tasks can be divided into visionary tasks, or tasks that provide leadership and direction for the group; informational/interpersonal tasks, or tasks that provide information and knowledge the group needs to have to be successful; and structural tasks, tasks that organize the group. Figure I-2 lists basic skills required of managers who wish to participate successfully in key IT decisions. Not only does this list emphasize understanding,

Managerial Role	Skills
Visionary	Creativity—the ability to transform resources and create something new to the organization. Curiosity—the ability to question and learn about new ideas, applications, technologies and business models. Confidence—the ability to believe in oneself and assert one's ideas at the proper time. Focus on business solutions—the ability to bring experience and insight to bear on current business opportunities and challenges. Flexibility—the ability to change rapidly and effectively, such as by adapting processes, shifting perspectives, or adjusting a plan to achieve a new goal.
Informational and Interpersonal	Communication—the ability to share thoughts through speech, writing, text and images. Listening—the ability to hear and reflect back what others are saying. Information gathering—the ability to gather thoughts of others through listening, reading, and observing. Interpersonal skills—the ability to cooperate and collaborate with others on a team, among groups, or across a change of command to achieve results.
Structural	Project management—the ability to plan, organize, direct and control company resources to effectively complete a project. Analytical skills—the ability to break down a problem into its elements for ease of understanding and analysis. Organizational skills—the ability to bring together distinct elements and combine them into an effective whole. Planning skills—the ability to develop objectives and to allocate resources to ensure objectives are met.

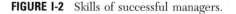

FIGURE I-2 Skills of successful managers.

organizing, planning, and solving the business needs of the organization, but it also is an excellent checklist for all managers' professional growth.

These skills may not look much different from those required of any successful manager, which is the main point of this book: General managers can be successful participants in IS decisions without an extensive technical background. General managers who understand a basic set of IS concepts and who have outstanding managerial skills, such as those listed in Figure I-2, are ready for the digital economy.

How To Participate in Information Systems Decisions

Technical wizardry is not required to become a knowledgeable participant in the IS decisions of a business. Managers need curiosity, creativity, and the confidence to ask questions in order to learn and understand. A solid framework that identifies key management issues and relates them to aspects of IS provides the background needed to participate.

The goal of this book is to provide that framework. The way in which managers use and manage information is directly linked to business goals and the business strategy that drive both organizational and IS decisions. Aligning business and IS decisions together is critical. Business, organizational, and information strategies are fundamentally linked in what is called the Information Systems Strategy Triangle, discussed in the next chapter. Failing to understand this relationship is detrimental to a business. Failing to plan for the consequences in all three areas can cost a manager his or her job. This book provides a foundation for understanding business issues related to IS from a managerial perspective.

Organization of the Book

To be a knowledgeable participant, managers must know about both using information and managing information. The first five chapters offer basic frameworks to make this understanding easier. Chapter 1 uses the Information Systems Strategy Triangle framework to discuss alignment of IS and the business. This chapter also provides a brief overview of relevant frameworks for business strategy and organizational strategy. It is provided as background for those who have not formally studied organization theory or business strategy. For those who have studied these areas, this chapter is a brief refresher of major concepts used throughout the remaining chapters of the book. Subsequent chapters provide frameworks and sets of examples for understanding the links between IS and business strategy (Chapter 2), links between IS and organizational strategy (Chapter 3), collaboration and individual work (Chapter 4), and business processes (Chapter 5).

The rest of the text looks at issues related to the business manager's role in managing IS itself. These chapters are the building blocks of an IS strategy. Chapter 6 provides a framework for understanding the four components of IS architecture: hardware, software, networks, and data. Chapter 7 discusses the business of IT, with a look at IS organization, funding models, portfolios, and monitoring options. Chapter 8 looks at the governance of IS resources. Chapter 9 explores sourcing and how companies provision IS resources. Chapter 10 focuses on project and change management. Chapter 11 dives into business intelligence, knowledge management, and analytics and provides an overview of how companies manage knowledge and create a competitive advantage using business analytics. Finally, Chapter 12 discusses the ethical use of information, privacy, and security.

▶ BASIC ASSUMPTIONS

Every book is based on certain assumptions, and understanding those assumptions makes a difference in interpreting the text. The first assumption made by this text is that managers must be knowledgeable participants in the IS decisions made within and affecting their organizations. That means that the general manager must have a basic understanding of the business and technology issues related to IS. Because technology changes rapidly, this text also assumes that the technology of today is different from the technology of yesterday, and most likely, the technology available to readers of this text today differs significantly from that available when the text was written. Therefore, this text focuses on generic concepts that are, to the extent possible, technology independent. It provides a framework on which to hang more current information, such as new uses of the Web, new social tools, or new networking technologies. It is assumed that the reader will seek out the most current sources to supplement the discussions of this text and to learn about the latest technology.

Although some may debate this next assumption, a second assumption is that the role of a general manager and the role of an IS manager are distinct and their skill sets differ. The general manager must have a basic knowledge of IS to make decisions that may have serious implications for the business. Whereas in addition to general business knowledge, the IS manager must have more in-depth knowledge of technology to manage IS and to partner with general managers who must use the information. As digital natives take on increasingly more managerial roles in corporations, this second assumption may have to be altered. But for this text, we assume a different skill set for the IS manager and we do not attempt to provide that here. Assumptions are also made about how business is done and what IS are in general.

Assumptions about Management

The classic view of management includes four activities performed by managers to reach organizational goals and each dependent on the others: planning, organizing, leading, and controlling (see Figure I-3). Conceptually, this simple model provides a framework

Planning	Managers think through their goals and actions in advance. Their actions are usually based on some method, plan, or logic, rather than a hunch or gut feeling.
Organizing	Managers coordinate the human and material resources of the organization. The effectiveness of an organization depends on its ability to direct its resources to attain its goals.
Leading	Managers direct and influence subordinates, getting others to perform essential tasks. By establishing the proper atmosphere, they help their subordinates do their best.
Controlling	Managers attempt to assure that the organization is moving toward its goal. If part of their organization is on the wrong track, managers try to find out why and set things right.

FIGURE I-3 Classic management model.
Source: Adapted from James A. F. Stoner, *Management*, 2nd ed. (Upper Saddle River, NJ: Prentice Hall, 1982).

of the key tasks of management, which is useful for both general business and IS management activities. Although many books have been written describing each of these activities, organizational theorist Henry Mintzberg offers a view that most closely details the perspective relevant to IS management.

Mintzberg's model describes management in behavioral terms by categorizing the three major roles a manager fills: interpersonal, informational, and decisional (see Figure I-4). This model is useful because it considers the chaotic nature of the environment in which managers actually work. Managers rarely have time to be reflective in their approaches to problems. They work at an unrelenting pace, and their activities are brief and often interrupted. Thus, quality information becomes

Type of Roles	Manager's Roles	IS Examples
Interpersonal	Figurehead	CIO greets touring dignitaries.
	Leader	IS manager puts in long hours to help motivate project team to complete project on schedule in an environment of heavy budget cuts.
	Liaison	CIO works with the marketing and human resource vice presidents to make sure that the reward and compensation system is changed to encourage use of new IS supporting sales.
Informational	Monitor	Division manager compares progress on IS project for the division with milestones developed during the project's initiation and feasibility phase.
	Disseminator	CIO conveys organization's business strategy to IS department and demonstrates how IS strategy supports the business strategy.
	Spokesperson	IS manager represents IS department at organization's recruiting fair.
Decisional	Entrepreneur	Division manager suggests an application of a new technology that improves the division's operational efficiency.
	Disturbance handler	Division manager, as project team leader, helps resolve design disagreements between division personnel who will be using the system and systems analysts who are designing it.
	Resource allocator	CIO allocates additional personnel positions to various departments based upon business strategy.
	Negotiator	IS manager negotiates for additional personnel needed to respond to recent user requests for enhanced functionality in a system that is being implemented.

FIGURE I-4 Manager's roles.
Source: Adapted from H. Mintzberg, *The Nature of Managerial Work* (New York: Harper & Row, 1973).

even more crucial to effective decision-making. The classic view is often seen as a tactical approach to management, whereas some describe Mintzberg's view as more strategic.

Assumptions about Business

Everyone has an internal understanding of what constitutes a business, which is based on readings and experiences in different firms. This understanding forms a model that provides the basis for comprehending actions, interpreting decisions, and communicating ideas. Managers use their internal model to make sense of otherwise chaotic and random activities. This book uses several conceptual models of business. Some take a functional view and others take a process view.

Functional View

The classical view of a business is based on the functions that people perform, such as accounting, finance, marketing, operations, and human resources. The business organizes around these functions to coordinate them and to gain economies of scale within specialized sets of tasks. Information first flows vertically up and down between line positions and management; after analysis it may be transmitted across other functions for use elsewhere in the company (see Figure I-5).

Process View

Michael Porter of Harvard Business School describes a business in terms of the primary and support activities that are performed to create, deliver, and support a product or service (see Figure I-6). The primary activities of inbound logistics, operations, outbound logistics, marketing and sales, and service are chained together in sequences that describe how a business transforms its raw materials into value-creating products. This value chain is supported by common activities shared across all the primary activities. For example, general management and legal services are distributed among the primary activities. Improving coordination among activities increases business profit. Organizations that effectively manage core processes across functional boundaries will be winners in the marketplace. IS are often the key to this process improvement and cross-functional coordination.

Both the process and functional views are important to understanding IS. The functional view is useful when similar activities must be explained, coordinated,

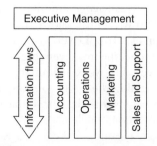

FIGURE I-5   Hierarchical view of the firm.

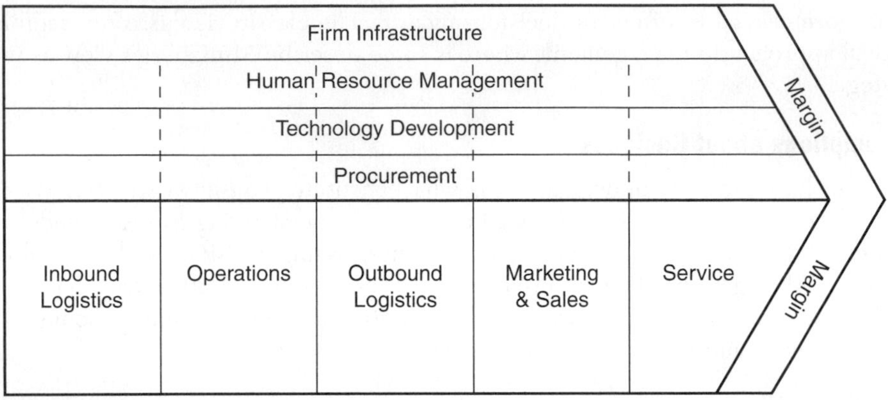

FIGURE I-6 Process view of the firm: the value chain.
Source: M. Porter, *Competitive Advantage: Creating and Sustaining Superior Performance* (New York: The Free Press, 1985, 1998).

executed, or communicated. For example, understanding a marketing information system means understanding the functional approach to business in general and the marketing function in particular. The process view, on the other hand, is useful when examining the flow of information throughout a business. For example, understanding the information associated with order fulfillment or product development or customer service means taking a process view of the business. This text assumes that both views are important for participating in IS decisions.

Assumptions about Information Systems

Consider the components of an information system from the manager's viewpoint, rather than from the technologist's viewpoint. Both the nature of information (hierarchy and economics) and the context of an information system must be examined to understand the basic assumptions of this text.

Information Hierarchy

The terms *data, information*, and *knowledge* are often used interchangeably, but have significant and discrete meanings within the knowledge management domain (and are more fully explored in Chapter 11). Tom Davenport, in his book *Information Ecology*, pointed out that getting everyone in any given organization to agree on common definitions is difficult. However, his work (summarized in Figure I-7) provides a nice starting point for understanding the subtle but important differences.

The information hierarchy begins with data, or simple observations, **data** are a set of specific, objective facts or observations, such as "inventory contains 45 units." Standing alone, such facts have no intrinsic meaning, but can be easily captured, transmitted, and stored electronically.

	Data	Information	Knowledge
Definition	Simple observations of the state of the world	Data endowed with relevance and purpose	Information from the human mind (includes reflection, synthesis, context)
Characteristics	• Easily structured • Easily captured on machines • Often quantified • Easily transferred • Mere facts	• Requires unit of analysis • Data that have been processed • Human mediation necessary	• Hard to structure • Difficult to capture on machines • Often tacit • Hard to transfer
Example	Daily inventory report of all inventory items sent to the CEO of a large manufacturing company	Daily inventory report of items that are below economic order quantity levels sent to inventory manager	Inventory manager knowing which items need to be reordered in light of daily inventory report, anticipated labor strikes, and a flood in Brazil that affects the supply of a major component.

FIGURE I-7 Comparison of data, information, and knowledge.
Source: Adapted from Thomas Davenport, *Information Ecology* (New York: Oxford University Press, 1997).

Information is data endowed with relevance and purpose.[7] People turn data into information by organizing it into some unit of analysis (e.g., dollars, dates, or customers). For example, a mashup of location data and housing prices adds something beyond what the data provides individually, and that makes it information. A **mashup** is the term used to for applications that combine data from different sources to create a new application on the Web. Deciding on the appropriate unit of analysis involves interpreting the context of the data and summarizing it into a more condensed form. Consensus must be reached on the unit of analysis.

To be relevant and have a purpose, information must be considered within the context that it is received and used. Because of differences in context, information needs vary across the function and hierarchical level. For example, when considering functional differences related to a sales transaction, a marketing department manager may be interested in the demographic characteristics of buyers, such as their age, gender, and home address. A manager in the accounting department probably won't be interested in any of these details, but instead wants to know details about the transaction itself, such as method of payment and date of payment.

Similarly, information needs may vary across hierarchical levels. These needs are summarized in Figure I-8 and reflect the different activities performed at each level. At

[7] Peter F. Drucker, "The Coming of the New Organization," *Harvard Business Review* (January–February 1988), 45–53.

	Top Management	Middle Management	Supervisory and Lower-Level Management
Time Horizon	Long: years	Medium: weeks, months, years	Short: day to day
Level of Detail	Highly aggregated Less accurate More predictive	Summarized Integrated Often financial	Very detailed Very accurate Often nonfinancial
Orientation	Primarily external	Primarily internal with limited external	Internal
Decision	Extremely judgmental Uses creativity and analytical skills	Relatively judgmental	Heavy reliance on rules

FIGURE I-8 Information characteristics across hierarchical level.

the supervisory level, activities are narrow in scope and focused on production or the execution of the business's basic transactions. At this level, information is focused on day-to-day activities that are internally oriented and accurately defined in a detailed manner. The activities of senior management are much broader in scope. Senior management performs long-term planning and needs information that is aggregated, externally oriented, and more subjective. The information needs of middle managers in terms of these characteristics fall between the needs of supervisors and senior management. Because information needs vary across levels, a daily inventory report of a large manufacturing firm may serve as information for a low-level inventory manager, whereas the CEO would consider such a report to be merely data. A report does not necessarily mean information. The context in which the report is used must be considered in determining if it is information.

Knowledge is information that is synthesized and contextualized to provide value. It is information with the most value. Knowledge consists of a mix of contextual information, values, experiences, and rules. For example, the mashup of locations and housing prices means one thing to a real estate agent, another thing to a potential buyer, and yet something else to an economist. It is richer and deeper than information and more valuable because someone thought deeply about that information and added his or her own unique experience, judgment, and wisdom. Knowledge also involves the synthesis of multiple sources of information over time.[8] The amount of human contribution increases along the continuum from data to information to knowledge. Computers work well for managing data, but are less efficient at managing information.

[8] Thomas H. Davenport, *Information Ecology* (New York: Oxford University Press, 1997), 9–10.

Some people think there is a fourth level in the information hierarchy, **wisdom**. In this context, wisdom is knowledge, fused with intuition and judgment that facilitates the ability to make decisions. Wisdom is that level of the information hierarchy used by subject matter experts, gurus, and individuals with a high level of experience who seem to "just know" what to do and how to apply the knowledge they gain. This is consistent with Aristotle's view of wisdom as the ability to balance different and conflicting elements together in ways that are only learned through experience.

▶ ECONOMICS OF INFORMATION VERSUS ECONOMICS OF THINGS

In their book, *Blown to Bits*, Evans and Wurster argued that every business is in the information business.[9] Even those businesses not typically considered to be information businesses have business strategies in which information plays a critical role. The physical world of manufacturing is shaped by information that dominates products as well as processes. For example, a high-end Mercedes automobile contains as much computing power as a midrange personal computer. Information-intensive processes in the manufacturing and marketing of the automobile include design, market research, logistics, advertising, and inventory management.

As our world is reshaped by information-intensive industries, it becomes even more important for business strategies to differentiate the timeworn economics of things from the evolving economics of information. Things wear out; things can be replicated at the expense of the manufacturer; things exist in a tangible location. When sold, the seller no longer owns the thing. The price of a thing is typically based on production costs. In contrast, information never wears out, though it can become obsolete or untrue. Information can be replicated at virtually no cost without limit; information exists in the ether. When sold, the seller still retains the information, but this ownership provides little value if the ability of others to copy it is not limited. Finally, information is often costly to produce,

Things	Information
Wear out	Doesn't wear out, can become obsolete or untrue
Are replicated at the expense of the manufacturer	Is replicated at almost zero cost without limit
Exist in a tangible location	Does not physically exist
When sold, possession changes hands	When sold, seller may still possess and sell again
Price based on production costs	Price based on value to consumer

FIGURE I-9 Comparison of the economics of things with the economics of information.

[9] Philip Evans and Thomas Wurster, *Blown to Bits* (Boston: Harvard Business School Press, 2000).

but cheap to reproduce. Rather than pricing it to recover the sunk cost of its initial production, its price is typically based on the value to the consumer. Figure I-9 summarizes the major differences between the economics of goods and the economics of information.

Evans and Wurster suggest that traditionally the economics of information has been bundled with the economics of things. However, in this Information Age, firms are vulnerable if they do not separate the two. The Encyclopedia Britannica story serves as an example. Bundling the economics of things with the economics of information made it difficult for Encyclopedia Britannica to gauge the threat posed by Encarta, the encyclopedia on CD-ROM that was given away to promote the sale of computers and peripherals. Britannica focused on its centuries-old tradition of providing information in richly bound tomes sold to the public through a well-trained sales force. Only when it was threatened with its very survival did Encyclopedia Britannica grasp the need to separate the economics of information from economics of things and sell bits of information online. Clearly, Encyclopedia Britannica's business strategy, like that of many other companies, needed to reflect the difference between the economics of things from the economics of information.[10]

System Hierarchy

An information system comprises three main elements: technology, people, and process (see Figure I-10). When most people use the term *information system*, they actually refer only to the technology element as defined by the organization's infrastructure. In this text the term **infrastructure** refers to everything that supports the flow and processing of information in an organization, including hardware, software, data, and network components, whereas **architecture** refers to the strategy implicit in these components. These ideas will be discussed in greater detail in Chapter 6. **Information**

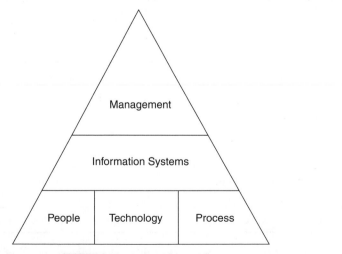

FIGURE I-10 System hierarchy.

[10] Ibid.

system (IS) is defined more broadly as the *combination* of technology (the "what"), people (the "who"), and process (the "how") that an organization uses to produce and manage information. In contrast, information technology (IT) focuses only on the technical devices and tools used in the system. We define **information technology** as all forms of technology used to create, store, exchange, and use information.

Above the information system itself is management, which oversees the design and structure of the system and monitors its overall performance. Management develops the business requirements and the business strategy that the information system is meant to satisfy. The system's architecture provides a blueprint that translates this strategy into components, or infrastructure.[11]

▶ SUMMARY

Aligning information systems and business decisions is no longer an option; it's an imperative for business. Every business operates as an information-based enterprise. In addition, the explosive growth of smart phones, tablets, social tools and Web-based businesses provides all managers with some experience in information systems, and some idea of the complexity involved in providing enterprise-level systems. This highlights the need for all managers to be skilled in managing and using IS.

It is no longer acceptable to delegate IS decisions to the management information systems (MIS) department alone. The general manager must be involved to both execute business plans and protect options for future business vision. IS and business maturity must be aligned to provide the right level of information resources to the business.

This chapter makes the case for general managers' full participation in strategic business decisions concerning IS. It outlines the skills required for such participation, and it makes explicit certain key assumptions about the nature of business, management, and IS that will underlie the remaining discussions. Subsequent chapters are designed to build on these concepts by addressing the following questions.

Frameworks and Foundations

- How should information strategy be aligned with business and organizational strategies? (Chapter 1)
- How can a business achieve competitive advantages using its IS? (Chapter 2)
- How do organizational decisions impact IS decisions? (Chapter 3)
- How is the work of the individual in an organization affected by decisions concerning IS? (Chapter 4)
- How are information systems integrated with business processes? (Chapter 5)

IS Management Issues

- What are the components of an IS architecture? (Chapter 6)
- How is the IT organization managed and funded? (Chapter 7)
- How are IS decisions made? (Chapter 8)

[11] Gordon Hay and Rick Muñoz, "Establishing an IT Architecture Strategy," *Information Systems Management* 14 (Summer 1997), 67–69.

- What source should provide IS services? (Chapter 9)
- How are IS projects managed and risks from change management mitigated? (Chapter 10)
- How is business intelligence managed within an organization? (Chapter 11)
- What ethical and moral considerations bind the uses of information in business? (Chapter 12)

▶ KEY TERMS

architecture (p. 18)	information	social IT (p. 8)
data (p. 14)	technology (p. 19)	social media (p. 8)
digital natives (p. 6)	infrastructure (p. 18)	social networking (p. 8)
information (p. 14)	knowledge (p. 16)	Web 2.0 (p. 5)
information	mashup (p. 15)	wisdom (p. 16)
system (p. 18)	social business (p. 8)	

▶ DISCUSSION QUESTIONS

1. Why is it important for a general manager to be knowledgeable about information technology?
2. Indicate whether each of the following is information, data, or knowledge:
   a. A daily sales report of each sales transaction that is sent to the chief operating officer
   b. A daily sales report of each sales transaction over $100,000 that is sent to the division marketing manager
   c. A monthly production report that is sent to shop floor supervisors who don't use the report because they believe the figures reported are outdated and inaccurate
   d. An exception report of all accounts that are more than 90 days past-due, which is sent to the Accounts Receivable Manager
   e. A list of Social Security numbers
   f. The contact list in an individual's LinkedIn account
3. Why, in your opinion, did the term Web 2.0 emerge? What is different in the way the Web is used today from the "Web 1.0" world? What do you predict Web 3.0 will mean?

CASE STUDY I-1

TERRY CANNON, MBA[12]

Terry Cannon, a typical MBA, was about to receive an MBA from a leading Business School, fueling a desire to change the world while growing a significant savings account. Terry was debating among three job opportunities, each of which would be a big step up the professional ladder from the associate's job held when working for Impressive Consulting Group (ICG) prior to returning to school to get an MBA. Terry wasn't sure which job to take.

Terry started business school after four years of experience at Impressive Consulting Group (ICG), a global consulting organization with practices in virtually every major city in the world. Terry worked in the Dallas office as an associate right out of undergraduate school, with a degree in business with a concentration in marketing. Terry had worked on a number of interesting strategic

---

[12] The names in this case are fictitious. This case is written to highlight administrative issues relevant to general managers, and any resemblance to real individuals or organizations is coincidental.

marketing projects while at ICG. The last one, before returning to school, involved monitoring Twitter for a large client, to make sure all mentions of the client were known to the client.

Terry was completing a standard MBA program after two years of full-time study and a summer working for MFG Corporation, a large manufacturing company in the Midwest. The internship at MFG Corporation involved working with the new Web marketing group, which Terry chose to see just how a company like MFG takes advantage of the Web. At the same time, Terry hoped to become more proficient in using Web and Internet technologies. The experience at MFG's Web marketing group, however, only made Terry more anxious, highlighting how much more was involved in information systems and the Web than Terry had previously thought. Terry returned to business school in the fall of the second year wondering just how much information systems knowledge would be needed in future jobs. Further, Terry felt that becoming a knowledgeable participant in information decisions was critical to success in the fast-paced Internet-based business world waiting after graduation.

Terry had three job offers as graduation closed in, and wondered just what type of information systems knowledge was needed for each of them. All three jobs involved a competitive salary, a signing bonus, and stock/retirement benefits, so the decision came down to the knowledge needed to be successful on the job. The three jobs are summarized as follows.

1. **Return to ICG as a consultant**. This job was attractive to Terry because it meant returning to a former employer. Terry had left in good standing and liked the company that rewarded innovation and supported learning and growth among consultants. Terry figured a partnership was possible in the future. As a consultant, Terry could live anywhere and travel to the client site four days a week. The fifth day each week, Terry would be able to work at home, or if desired, in a company office. As a consultant, Terry initially thought engagements in strategic marketing would be the most interesting. ICG had a strong programming group that was brought into each engagement to do the programming and systems analysis work. The consultant role involved understanding client concerns and assisting in building a marketing strategy. Virtually all the projects would have some social IT component and might involve actually building and managing communities for clients. This challenge interested Terry, but based on the summer job experience, Terry wondered just how much technical skill would be required of the consultants in this arena.

2. **Join start-up InfoMicro**. Several of Terry's friends from business school were joining together to form a new start-up company on the Web. This business plan for this company projected that InfoMicro would be one of only two start-ups in their marketplace, giving the company a good position and great opportunity for growth. The business plan showed the company intending to go public through an IPO as early as three years after inception, and Terry believed they could do it. Terry would join as VP of marketing, supplementing the other three friends who would hold president, VP of finance, and VP of operations positions. The friends who would be president and finance VP were just completing a techno-MBA at Terry's school and would provide the technical competence needed to get InfoMicro on the Web. Terry would focus on developing customers and setting marketing strategy, eventually building an organization to support that operation as necessary. Because InfoMicro was a Web-based business and because social IT was critical to successful marketing efforts, Terry felt a significant amount of information systems knowledge would be required of a successful marketing executive to both understand the company's business and to talk with customers about how to use InfoMicro's products.

3. **Return to MFG Corporation**. The job would be to join the marketing department as a manager responsible for new customer development. Many of MFG Corporation's customers were older, established companies like MFG Corporation itself, but new customers were likely to be start-ups and up-and-coming companies, or highly successful younger companies like Google or Zappos.

Terry felt that some knowledge of information systems would be necessary simply to provide innovative interaction mechanisms such as customer Web-based communities. Terry knew that discussions with the MFG information systems group would be necessary to build these new interfaces. How knowledgeable must Terry be on information systems issues to hold this job?

As spring break approached, Terry knew a decision had to be made. Recruiters from all three companies had given Terry a deadline of the end of break week, and Terry wasn't at all sure which job to take. All sounded interesting, and all were reasonable alternatives for Terry's next career move.

Discussion Questions

1. For each position Terry is considering, what types of information systems knowledge do you think Terry would need?
2. How could Terry be a knowledgeable participant in each of the three jobs? What would it mean to be a knowledgeable participant in each job? Give an example for each job.
3. As a marketing major and an MBA, is Terry prepared for the work world awaiting? Why or why not?

CASE STUDY I-2

ANYGLOBAL COMPANY INC.[13]

Memo

To: Chris Bytemaster, CIO
From: Hazel Hasslefree, CEO

The Board of Directors has been discussing an old article they found in *The Harvard Business Review* (May 2003) titled "IT Doesn't Matter" by Nicholas Carr. What particularly caught their attention was this quote:

> "Given the rapid pace of technology's advance, delaying IT investments can be another powerful way to cut costs—while also reducing a firm's chance of being saddled with buggy or soon-to-be-obsolete technology. . . Some managers may worry that being stingy with IT dollars will damage their competitive positions. But studies of corporate IT spending consistently show that greater expenditures rarely translate into superior financial results. . . The key to success, for the vast majority of companies, is no longer to seek advantage aggressively but to manage costs and risks meticulously."

I have been asked to prepare a short presentation about what the article means to our company and whether IT does, in fact, matter in our company. As you know, we have proposed a significant increase in our IT budget for next year and the Board is concerned about this investment. I'm not convinced that advantages from IT spending are no longer available.

Would you please prepare a short report, about a page, that I can use as a basis for my presentation to them? You can find the article in our library or online at Carr's blog:
                                      http://bit.ly/NCarrBlog
Thanks.

---

[13] We appreciate the suggestions provided to us by Ron Murch at the University of Calgary concerning this case.

CHAPTER 1

THE INFORMATION SYSTEMS STRATEGY TRIANGLE

The information systems strategy triangle highlights the alignment necessary between decisions of business strategy, information systems, and organizational design. This chapter reviews models of business strategy including Porter's generic strategies, and dynamic models such as hypercompetition. It suggests a model for creating a social business strategy and briefly discusses frameworks for designing organizational strategies including the Leavitt Business Diamond and the Managerial Levers model. It concludes with a simple framework for decoding information systems strategy.

Over the course of 87 news-filled days, the 2010 Deepwater Horizon oil spill became the largest marine oil spill in human history. The spill quickly became a public relations nightmare for BP, which quickly focused its efforts toward remedying its image by spearheading the cleanup. At one point, and estimated four million barrels per day flowed freely into the gulf waters, straining the marine ecosystem and threatening the shoreline from Texas to Florida.

After a lengthy investigation, BP concluded in its internal report that "a sequence of failures involving multiple companies and work teams" caused the explosion that subsequently allowed oil to spill freely into the gulf. While repeated failures to follow safety procedures were at the heart of the catastrophe, when looking at the timelines of the accident rather than focusing on who was to blame, one finds a series of IT failures coupled with organizational misalignments that ultimately catalyzed the accident.

This crisis highlighted the need for proper alignment of business strategy, information systems (IS) and organizational mechanisms and practices when designing the safety mechanism for an oilrig. When high pressure forced methane gas to the surface of the rig, causing it to ignite and explode, most workers evacuate by lifeboat. However, even with the lack of human control after the explosion, the rig's information systems and organizational control mechanisms should have both prevented the accident and the resulting spill of oil. Automated systems failed, including a key emergency disconnect system that failed to initialize, and would have prevented oil from escaping once the blowout preventer proved ineffective. But the early monitoring systems appeared to have worked. One indicated problems with oil flow almost an hour before the explosion, but an investigation indicated that managers and engineers on the rig may have ignored test results earlier that day. And the aftermath also highlighted issues in organizational culture, process, and leadership at BP.[1]

This case emphasizes the point made in the introduction: General managers *must* take a role in decisions about IS. Even though it is not necessary for a general manager to have a deep technical knowledge of their IS, it is necessary to aggressively seek to understand the consequences of using technologies relevant to the business's environment and to ask questions when it's not clear. General managers who leave IS decisions solely to their IS professionals often put themselves and their companies at a disadvantage. Although IS can facilitate the movement, exchange, and processing of information, an IS that is inappropriate for a given operating environment can actually inhibit and confuse things. This is especially true in crisis environments, such as the oil spill disaster at BP. The IS department is not an island within a firm. The IS department manages an infrastructure that is essential to the firm's functioning. Further, this case illustrates that a firm's IS must be aligned with the way it manages its employees and processes. In BP's case, it became clear that personnel policies needed to be adjusted to insure engineers and crew followed all procedures associated with monitoring results, and additional processes were needed to insure quality standards were appropriate and met from vendor-supplied systems.

This chapter introduces a simple framework for describing the alignment necessary with business systems and for understanding the impact of IS on organizations. This framework is called the **Information Systems Strategy Triangle** because it relates business strategy with IS strategy and organizational strategy. This chapter also presents key frameworks from organization theory that describe the context in which IS operate, as well as the business imperatives that IS support. Students with extensive background in organizational behavior and business strategy will find this a useful review of key concepts. The Information Systems Strategy Triangle presented in Figure 1.1 suggests three key points about strategy.

Successful firms have an overriding business strategy that drives both organizational strategy and IS strategy. The decisions made regarding the structure, hiring practices, vendor policies, and other components of the organizational strategy, as well as decisions

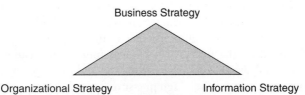

FIGURE 1.1 The Information Systems Strategy Triangle.

[1] Michael Krigsman, BP Oil Spill: Leadership and IT Failure, June 11, 2010 (accessed at http://www.enterpriseirregulars.com/19782/bp-oil-spill-leadership-and-it-failure/ on May 5, 2012); and Leo King, BP Oil Spill 'Slows' but Serious IT Failures Come to Surface, May 28, 2010 (accessed at http://www.cio.com/article/595620/BP_Oil_Spill_Slows_but_Serious_IT_Failures_Come_to_Surface on May 5, 2012).

regarding applications, hardware, and other IS components, are all driven by the firm's business objectives, strategies, and tactics. Successful firms carefully balance these three strategies—they purposely design their organization and their IS strategies to complement their business strategy.

IS strategy can itself affect and is affected by changes in a firm's business and organizational strategies. To perpetuate the balance needed for successful operation, changes in the IS strategy must be accompanied by changes in the organizational strategy and must accommodate the overall business strategy. If a firm designs its business strategy to use IS to gain strategic advantage, the leadership position in IS can only be sustained by constant innovation. The business, IS, and organizational strategies must constantly be adjusted.

IS strategy always involves consequences—intended or not—within business and organizational strategies. Avoiding harmful unintended consequences means remembering to consider business and organizational strategies when designing IS deployment. For example, deploying and expecting employees to use iPads or tablets without an accompanying set of changes to job descriptions, process design, compensation plans, and business tactics will fail to produce the anticipated productivity improvements. Success can only be achieved by specifically designing all three components of the strategy triangle.

In the BP case discussed earlier, the IS Strategy Triangle was out of alignment at the time of the explosion. The organizational strategy (e.g., personnel policies about responding to monitoring tests, and safety policies and practices) did not support the IS strategy (e.g., dispersed network of systems that monitored, managed, and aborted automated drilling processes in a crisis situation). Both of these strategies did not adequately support their purported business strategy (creating profits though, in part, drilling in environmental-sensitive areas without disrupting the ecosystem while also protecting their reputation).

Of course, once a firm is out of alignment, it does not mean that it has to stay that way. To correct the misalignment described earlier, BP replaced CEO Tony Hayward with American Bob Dudley, changed its processes regarding monitoring and test systems, restructured its upstream business into three separate divisions to provide increased visibility into operations, risk management, standards, processes, and "human and technical capability."[2] Further, it changed its culture to make sure checks and balances are in place. The new systems realign people, process, and technology to decrease the risk of deep water drilling and most closely align with the business's goals of environmental sustainability and oil/energy production.

What does alignment mean? A book entitled *Winning the 3-Legged Race* defines alignment as the situation in which a company's current and emerging business strategy is enabled, supported, and unconstrained by technology. The authors suggest that although alignment is good, there are higher states, namely synchronization and convergence, toward which companies should strive. With synchronization, technology not only enables current business strategy but also anticipates and shapes future business strategy. Convergence goes one step further by exhibiting a state in which

---

[2] BP Web site, http://www.bp.com/sectiongenericarticle800.do?categoryId=9036149&contentId=7066886 (accessed on December 30, 2011).

business strategy and technology strategy are intertwined and the leadership team members operate almost interchangeably. Although we appreciate the distinction and agree that firms should strive for synchronization and convergence, *alignment* in this text means any of these states, and it pertains to the balance between organizational strategy, IS strategy, and business strategy.[3]

A word of explanation is needed here. This chapter and subsequent chapters address questions of IS strategy squarely within the context of business strategy. Studying business strategy alone is something better done in other texts and courses. However, to provide foundation for IS discussions, this chapter and the next summarize several key business strategy frameworks and organizational theories. Studying IS alone does not provide general managers with the appropriate perspective. To be effective, managers need a solid sense of how IS are used and managed within the organization. Studying details of technologies is also outside the scope of this text. Details of the technologies are relevant, of course, and it is important that any organization maintain a sufficient knowledge base to plan for and adequately align with business priorities. However, because technologies change so rapidly, keeping a text current is impossible. Therefore, this text takes the perspective that understanding what questions to ask and having a framework for interpreting the answers are skills more fundamental to the general manager than understanding any particular technology. This text provides readers with an appreciation of the need to ask questions, a framework from which to derive the questions to ask, and a foundation sufficient to understand the answers received. The remaining book chapters build on the foundation provided in the Information Systems Strategy Triangle.

▶ BRIEF OVERVIEW OF BUSINESS STRATEGY FRAMEWORKS

A **strategy** is a coordinated set of actions to fulfill objectives, purposes, and goals. The essence of a strategy is setting limits on what the business will seek to accomplish. Strategy starts with a mission. A **mission** is a clear and compelling statement that unifies an organization's effort and describes what the firm is all about (i.e., its purpose). For example, Mark Zuckerberg, the CEO of Facebook, noted that he initially built Facebook as a product but what ended up "after we started hiring more people and building out the team is I began to get an appreciation that a company is a great way to get a lot of people involved in a mission you're trying to push forward. Our mission is getting people to connect."[4]

In a few words the mission statement sums up what is unique about the firm. Figure 1.2 demonstrates that even though Zappos, Amazon, and L.L. Bean are all in the retail industry, they view their missions quite differently. For example, Zappos' focus is on customer service, Amazon is about customer sets, and L.L. Bean is about the merchandise and treating people the right way. It's interesting to note that while Zappos

---

[3] F. Hogue, V. Sambamurthy, R. Zmud, T. Trainer, and C. Wilson, *Winning the 3-Legged Race* (Upper Saddle River, NJ: Prentice Hall, 2005).

[4] Shayndi Raice, "Is Facebook Ready for the Big Time?" *Wall Street Journal* (January 14–15, 2012), B1.

Company	Mission Statement
Zappos	To provide the best customer service possible. Internally we call this our WOW philosophy.[a]
Amazon	We seek to be Earth's most customer-centric company for three primary customer sets: consumer customers, seller customers and developer customers.[b]
L.L. Bean	Sell good merchandise at a reasonable profit, treat your customers like human beings and they will always come back for more.[c]

[a] http://about.zappos.com (accessed on February 19, 2012).
[b] http://www.amazon.com, Mission Statement on Amazon Investor Relations page (accessed on February 19, 2012).
[c] http://www.llbean.com/customerService/aboutLLBean/company_values.html (accessed on February 19, 2012).

FIGURE 1.2 Mission statements of three retail businesses.

was purchased by Amazon, part of their agreement was to keep Zappos running independently. (In 2009, all the stockholders of Zappos agreed to sell their stock to Amazon, but the agreement included clauses to keep Zappos independent, and it has remained so both culturally and physically. Zappos is located near Las Vegas, NV while Amazon is in Seattle, WA.)

Are these companies accomplishing their missions? It is hard to determine whether Zappos customers are receiving the "best customer service." That is why Zappos, like other firms, sets measurable objectives and performance targets. Once the objectives and performance targets are set, the measurable objectives and performance targets can help ensure that a firm is accomplishing its mission. And then the firm needs to decide on a business strategy to meet its objectives and performance targets.

A **business strategy** is a plan articulating where a business seeks to go and how it expects to get there. It is the means by which a business communicates its goals. Management constructs this plan in response to market forces, customer demands, and organizational capabilities. Market forces create the competitive context for the business. Some markets, such as those faced by delivering packages, manufacturers of laptop computers, and issuers of credit cards, are characterized by many competitors and a high level of competition such that product differentiation becomes increasingly difficult. Other markets, such as those for airlines and automobiles, are similarly characterized by high competition, but product differentiation is better established. Customer demands comprise the wants and needs of the individuals and companies who purchase the products and services available in the marketplace. Organizational capabilities include the skills and experience that give the corporation a currency that can add value in the marketplace.

Consider Dell, originally a personal computer company. Initially Dell's business strategy was to sell personal computers directly to the customer without going through a middleman. Reaching customers in this way was less expensive and time consuming than selling the computers in retail stores. The Internet, combined with Dell's well-designed IS infrastructure, allowed customers to electronically contact Dell, who then designed a PC for a customer's specific needs. Dell's ordering system was integrated with its production system and shared information automatically with each supplier of PC components. This IS enabled the assembly of the most current computers without the expense of storing large inventories. Cost savings were passed on to the customer, and the direct-to-customer model allowed Dell to focus its production capacity on building only the most current products. With small profit margins and new products arriving quickly to replace existing products, this creative use of IS aligned with Dell's business strategy. The strategic use of IS ultimately results in cost savings, reflected in the price of systems. In addition, Dell executives achieve a strategic advantage in reducing response time, building custom computers for one of the industry's lowest costs, and eliminating inventories that could become obsolete before they are sold. Thus, this business strategy was consistent with Dell's mission of delivering the best customer experience in the markets it serves.

But things aren't always as they seem. If the direct-to-customer strategy was so effective, why is Dell now also selling its computers at major retail outlets such as Walmart, Staples, and Best Buy? It is likely that the sales figures and profit margins were not measuring up to Dell's stated objectives and performance targets. Consequently, Dell adjusted its business strategy and we can expect to see changes in their organization design and information systems to reflect their altered direction.

The classic, well-accepted model developed by Michael Porter still frames most discussions of business strategy. We review the Porter generic strategies framework, as well as dynamic environment strategies.[5] The end of this section introduces key questions a general manager must answer to understand the strategy of the business.

The Generic Strategies Framework

Companies sell their products and services in a marketplace populated with competitors. Michael Porter's framework helps managers understand the strategies they may choose to build a competitive advantage. In his book *Competitive Advantage*, Porter claims that the "fundamental basis of above-average performance in the long run is sustainable competitive advantage."[6] Porter identified three primary strategies for achieving competitive advantage: (1) cost leadership, (2) differentiation, and (3) focus. These advantages derive from the company's relative position in the marketplace, and they depend on the strategies and tactics used by competitors. Figure 1.3 summarizes these three strategies for achieving competitive advantage.

Cost leadership results when the organization aims to be the lowest-cost producer in the marketplace. The organization enjoys above-average performance by minimizing costs. The product or service offered must be comparable in quality to those offered by others in the industry so that customers perceive its relative value. Typically, only one cost leader exists within an industry. If more than one organization seeks an advantage

---

[5] Another popular model by Michael Porter, the value chain, provides a useful model for discussing internal operations of an organization. Some find it a useful model for understanding how to link two firms together. This framework is used in Chapter 5 to examine business process design. For further information, see M. Porter, *Competitive Advantage* (New York: The Free Press, 1985).

[6] M. Porter, *Competitive Advantage: Creating and Sustaining Superior Performance* (New York: The Free Press, 1985, 1998).

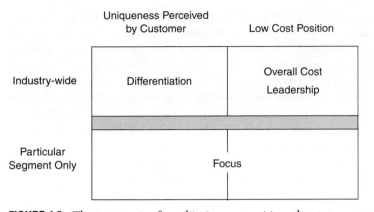

FIGURE 1.3 Three strategies for achieving competitive advantage.
Source: M. Porter, *Competitive Advantage: Creating and Sustaining Superior Performance* (New York: Free Press, 1985, 1998).

with this strategy, a price war ensues, which eventually may drive the organization with the higher cost structure out of the marketplace. Through mass distribution, economies of scale, and IS to generate operating efficiencies, Walmart epitomizes the cost-leadership strategy.

Through **differentiation**, the organization qualifies its product or service in a way that allows it to appear unique in the marketplace. The organization identifies which qualitative dimensions are most important to its customers and then finds ways to add value along one or more of those dimensions. For this strategy to work, the price charged customers by the differentiator must seem fair relative to the price charged by competitors. Typically, multiple firms in any given market employ this strategy. Progressive Insurance is able to differentiate itself from other automobile insurance companies by breaking out of the industry mold. Its representatives are available 24/7 (i.e., 24 hours a day, 7 days a week) to respond to accident claims. They arrive at an accident scene shortly after the accident with powerful laptops, intelligent software, and the authority to settle claims on the spot. This strategy spurred Progressive's growth and widened its profit margins.

Focus allows an organization to limit its scope to a narrower segment of the market and tailor its offerings to that group of customers. This strategy has two variants: (1) *cost focus*, in which the organization seeks a cost advantage within its segment, and (2) *differentiation focus*, in which it seeks to distinguish its products or services within the segment. This strategy allows the organization to achieve a local competitive advantage, even if it does not achieve competitive advantage in the marketplace overall. As Porter explains how the focuser can achieve competitive advantage by the way it focuses exclusively on certain market segments:

> Breadth of target is clearly a matter of degree, but the essence of focus is the exploitation of a narrow target's differences from the balance of the industry. Narrow focus in and of itself is not sufficient for above-average performance.[7]

[7] M. Porter, *Competitive Advantage: Creating and Sustaining Superior Performance* (New York: The Free Press, 1985, 1998).

Marriott International demonstrates focus in the business and related IS strategies of two of its hotel chains. To better serve its business travelers and cut operational expenses, Marriott properties have check-in kiosks that interface with their Marriott Rewards loyalty program. A guest can swipe a credit card or Marriott Rewards card at the kiosk in the lobby and receive a room assignment and keycard from the machine. She can also print airline boarding passes at the kiosks. Further, the kiosks help the Marriott chain implement its cost focus. The kiosk system is integrated with other systems such as billing and customer relationship management (CRM) to generate operating efficiencies and enhanced corporate standardization.

In contrast, stand-alone kiosks in the lobby would destroy the feeling that the Ritz-Carlton chain, acquired by Marriott in 1995, creates. To the Ritz-Carlton chain, CRM means capturing and using information about guests, such as their preference for wines, a hometown newspaper, or a sunny room. Each Ritz-Carlton employee is expected to promote personalized service by identifying and recording individual guest preferences. To demonstrate how this rule could be implemented, a waiter, after hearing a guest exclaim that she loves tulips, could log the guest's comments into the Ritz-Carlton CRM system called "Class." On her next visit to a Ritz-Carlton hotel, tulips could be placed in the guest's room after querying Class to learn more about her as her visit approaches. Class, the CRM, is instrumental in implementing the differentiation-focus strategy of the Ritz-Carlton chain.[8] Its strategy allows the Ritz-Carlton chain to live up to its very unique motto (mission): "We are ladies and gentlemen serving ladies and gentlemen."[9]

For example, airline JetBlue adopted a differentiation strategy based on low-costs coupled with unique customer experience. It might be called a "value-based strategy." It is not the lowest cost carrier in the airline industry; at 9.80 cents per passenger seat mile, JetBlue has one of the lowest costs but Virgin America, Spirit, and Allegient had lower per-seat mile costs in 2011. But JetBlue does manage its operational costs carefully, making decisions that keep its per passenger costs among the lowest in the business such as a limited number of airplane models in its fleet, gates at less congested airports, paperless cockpit and for other operations, and snacks instead of meals on flights. JetBlue has one of the longest stage length averages in the industry and the longer the flight the lower the unit costs. Network carriers, often larger competitors, may have different pay scales from having been in the business longer and with a different composition of staff, and higher maintenance costs for their fleets, which may be older and more diverse. Should its plans for growth be fully realized, while maintaining its low cost structure, JetBlue could move from its cost focus based on serving a limited, but growing, number of market segments to a cost leadership strategy.[10]

While sustaining a cost focus, JetBlue's chairman believes that JetBlue can compete on more than price and that is part of its unique differentiation strategy. It is why the airline continually strives to keep customers satisfied with frills such as extra leg room,

---

[8] Scott Berinato, "Room for Two," *CIO.com* (May 15, 2002), http://www.cio.com/archive/051502/two_content.html.

[9] http://corporate.ritzcarlton.com/en/About/GoldStandards.htm (accessed on February 13, 2008).

[10] http://www.oliverwyman.com/airline_analysis_2011.htm (accessed on December 26, 2011).

leather seats, prompt baggage delivery, DirectTV, and movies. It has been recognized with many awards for customer satisfaction in the North American airlines industry.

Dynamic Environment Strategies

Porter's generic strategies model is useful for diagnostics, or understanding how a business seeks to profit in its chosen marketplace, and for prescriptions, or building new opportunities for advantage. It reflects a careful balancing of countervailing competitive forces posed by buyers, suppliers, competitors, new entrants, and substitute products and services within an industry. As is the case with many models, they offer managers useful tools for thinking about strategy.

However, the Porter model was developed at a time when competitive advantage was sustainable because the rate of change in any given industry was relatively slow and manageable. Since the late 1980s when this framework was at the height of its popularity, newer models were developed to take into account the increasing turbulence and velocity of the marketplace. One example, the hypercompetition model, offers managers an especially useful tool for conceptualizing their organization's strategy in turbulent environments. Organizations need to be able to respond instantly and change rapidly, which requires dynamic structures and processes.

Discussions of hypercompetition take a perspective different from the previous model. Porter's model focus on creating competitive advantage, whereas **hypercompetition** models suggest that the speed and aggressiveness of the moves and counter-moves in any given market create an environment in which advantages are rapidly created and eroded. Trying to sustain a specific competitive advantage can be a deadly distraction, since the environment and the marketplace change rapidly. To manage the rapid speed of change, firms focus on their capability to dynamically adjust their organizational resources, valuing agility itself as the competitive advantage. Business strategies based on hypercompetition still focus on customer satisfaction, profit maximization, and other goals consistent with the business's values and beliefs, but build in components of business intelligence. These components include the ability to predict new opportunities, organizational designs that can sense, restructure and respond quickly, and strategic signaling and actions that both surprise and confuse competitors.

Since the 1990s a competitive dynamic has emerged in the marketplace that is characterized by wider gaps between industry leaders and laggards, more concentrated "winner-take-all" environments, and greater churn among sector rivals. This pattern of turbulent "creative destruction" was first predicted over 60 years ago by the economist Joseph Schumpeter. Coincidentally (or maybe not), the accelerated competition has occurred concomitantly with sharp increases in the quality and quantity of information technology (IT) investment. The changes in competitive dynamics are particularly striking in sectors that spend the most on IT.[11]

An application of these dynamic models is the *destroy your business* (DYB) (i.e., "creative destruction") approach to strategic planning that was implemented by leadership guru Jack Welch at General Electric (GE). Welch recognized that GE could only

---

[11] Andrew McAfee and Erik Brynjolfsson, "Investing in the IT That Makes a Competitive Difference," *Harvard Business Review* (July 2008), http://harvardbusinessonline.hbsp.harvard.edu.

sustain its competitive advantage for a limited time as competitors attempted to outmaneuver GE. He knew that if GE didn't identify its weaknesses, its competitors would relish doing so. DYB is an approach that places GE employees in the shoes of their competitors.[12] Through the DYB lenses, GE employees develop strategies to destroy GE's competitive advantage. Then, in light of their revelations, they apply the grow your business (GYB) strategy to find fresh ways to reach new customers and better serve existing ones. The goal of the DYB planning approach is the complete disruption of current practices, so that GE can take actions to protect its business before competitors hone in on its weaknesses. The implicit assumption underlying DYB is that GE would not be able to sustain its position in the marketplace over the long term.

A similar strategy of cannibalizing their own products was used by Apple and Gillette. Steve Jobs, the founder and CEO of Apple, felt strongly that if a company was not willing to cannibalize their own products, someone else will come along and do it for them. That was evident in the way Apple introduced the iPhone while iPod sales were brisk, and the iPad while its Macintosh sales were strong.[13] Apple continues to exhibit this strategy with subsequent releases of new models of all of its products. Likewise Gillette, known for its innovative razors and shaving products, is famous for introducing new razors while their current products are in demand. While the Mach3 razor was selling well, Gillette introduced the Fusion, and spent resources to convince customers to upgrade to the newer and more expensive product.

Why Are Strategic Advantage Models Essential to Planning for Information Systems?

A general manager who relies solely on IS personnel to make IS decisions may not only give up any authority over IS strategy, but also may hamper crucial future business decisions. In fact, business strategy should drive IS decision making, and changes in business strategy should entail reassessments of IS. Moreover, changes in IS potential should trigger reassessments of business strategy—as in the case of the Internet, where companies that failed to understand or consider its implications for the marketplace were quickly outpaced by competitors who had. For the purposes of our model, the Information Systems Strategy Triangle, understanding business strategy means answering the following questions:

1. What is the business goal or objective?

2. What is the plan for achieving it? What is the role of IS in this plan?

3. Who are the crucial competitors and partners, and what is required of a successful player in this marketplace?

4. What are the industry forces in this marketplace?

---

[12] M. Levinson, "GE Uses the Internet to Grow Business," *CIO Magazine* (October 15, 2001), http://www.cio.com/article/30624/HOT_TOPIC_E_BUSINESS_GE_Uses_the_Internet_to_Grow_Business_ (accessed on May 5, 2012).

[13] Walter Isaacson, *Steve Jobs* (New York: Simon and Schuster, 2011).

Strategic Approach	Key Idea	Application to Information Systems
Porter's generic strategies	Firms achieve competitive advantage through cost leadership, differentiation, or focus	Understanding which strategy is chosen by a firm is critical to choosing IS to complement the strategy
Dynamic environment strategies	Speed, agility, and aggressive moves and countermoves by a firm create competitive advantage	IS are critical to achieving the speed needed for moves and countermoves. IS are in a constant state of flux or development.

FIGURE 1.4 Summary of strategic approaches and IT applications.

Porter's generic strategies framework and the dynamic framework (summarized in Figure 1.4) are revisited in the next few chapters. They are especially helpful in discussing the role of IS in building and sustaining competitive advantages (Chapter 2) and for incorporating IS into business strategy. The next section of this chapter establishes a foundation for understanding organizational strategies.

▶ BRIEF OVERVIEW OF ORGANIZATIONAL STRATEGIES

Organizational strategy includes the organization's design as well as the choices it makes to define, set up, coordinate, and control its work processes. The organizational strategy is a plan that answers the question: "How will the company organize to achieve its goals and implement its business strategy?" A few of the many models of organizational strategy are reviewed in this section.

A classic framework for understanding the design of an organization is the business diamond, introduced by Harold Leavitt.[14] Shown in Figure 1.5, the **business diamond** identifies the crucial components of an organization's plan as its

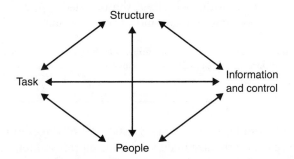

FIGURE 1.5 The Leavitt Business Diamond.
Source: Adapted from H. J. Leavitt, *Managerial Psychology* (University of Chicago Press, 1958, p. 286).

[14] H. J. Leavitt, *Managerial Psychology* (University of Chicago Press, 1958, p. 286).

Social Business Lens: Building a Social Business Strategy

Some companies use social IT as point solutions for business opportunities, but others build a social business strategy that looks at the application of social IT tools and capabilities to solve business opportunities holistically. A **social business strategy** is a plan of how the firm will use social IT, aligned with organization strategy and IS strategy. It includes a vision of how the business would operate if it seamlessly and thoroughly incorporated social and collaborative capabilities throughout the business model. It answers the same type of questions of what, how, and who, as any other business strategy.

Most of the social business opportunities fall into one of three categories:

Collaboration—using social IT to extend the reach of stakeholders, both employees and those outside the enterprise walls. Social IT such as social networks enable individuals to find and connect with each other to share ideas, information, and expertise.

Engagement—using social IT to involve stakeholders in the traditional business of the enterprise. Social IT such as communities and blogs provide a platform for individuals to join in conversations, create new conversations, offer support to each other, and other activities that create a deeper feeling of connection to the company, brand, or enterprise.

Innovation—using social IT to identify, describe, prioritize, and create new ideas for the enterprise. Social IT offer the community members a "super idea box" where individuals suggest new ideas, comment on other ideas, and vote for their favorite idea, giving managers a new way to generate and decide on products and services.

National Instruments (ni.com) is an example of a company that has embraced social IT and created a social business strategy. Managers developed a branded community consisting of a number of social IT tools like Facebook, Twitter, blogs, forums, and more. Thinking holistically about all of the ways customers and employees might interact with each other, the branded community has become the hub of collaboration, engagement and idea generation.

Source: Adapted from Keri Pearlson, "Killer Apps for a Social Business" (February 17, 2011), http://instantlyresponsive.wordpress.com/2011/02/27/killer-apps-for-a-social-business/ (accessed on May 5, 2012).

information/control, people, structure, and tasks. All of the components are interrelated. Over the years, there have been variations on this model, substituting terms like business processes, culture, and management systems for Leavitt's original terms. This simple framework is useful for designing new organizations and for diagnosing organizational troubles. For example, organizations that try to change their people but fail to change the way they manage and control cannot be effective, since all of these components impact each other.

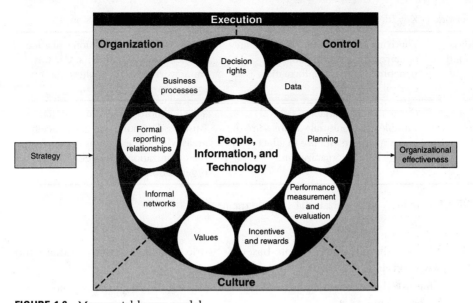

FIGURE 1.6 Managerial levers model.
Source: J. Cash, R. G. Eccles, N. Nohria, and R. L. Nolan, *Building the Information Age Organization* (Homewood, IL: Richard D. Irwin, 1994).

A complementing framework to the business diamond for organizational design can be found in the book by Cash, Eccles, Nohria, and Nolan, *Building the Information Age Organization*.[15] This framework, shown in Figure 1.6, suggests that the successful execution of a business's organizational strategy comprises the best combination of organizational, control, and cultural variables. Organizational variables include decision rights, business processes, formal reporting relationships, and informal networks. Control variables include the availability of data, the nature and quality of planning, and the effectiveness of performance measurement and evaluation systems, and incentives to do good work. Cultural variables comprise the values of the organization. These organizational, control, and cultural variables are **managerial levers** used by decision makers to effect changes in their organizations. These managerial levers are discussed in detail in Chapter 3.

Our objective is to give the manager a set of frameworks to use in evaluating various aspects of organizational design. Using these frameworks, the manager can review the current organization and assess which components may be missing and what options are available looking forward. Understanding organizational strategy means answering the following questions:

1. What are the important structures and reporting relationships within the organization?

2. Who holds the decision rights to critical decisions?

---

[15] James I. Cash, Robert G. Eccles, Nitin Nohria, and Richard L. Nolan, *Building the Information Age Organization* (Homewood, IL: Richard D. Irwin, 1994).

Framework	Key Idea	Usefulness in IS Discussions
Business Diamond	There are four key components to an organization's design: people, structure, tasks, and information/control.	Using IS in an organization will affect each of these components. Use this framework to identify where these impacts are likely to occur.
Managerial levers	Organizational variables, control variables, and cultural variables are the levers managers can use to affect change in their organization.	This is a more detailed model than the Business Diamond and gives specific areas where IS can be used to manage the organization and to change the organization.

FIGURE 1.7 Summary of organizational strategy frameworks.

3. What are the important people-based networks (social and informational) and how can we use them to get work done better?

4. What are the characteristics, experiences, and skill levels of the people within the organization?

5. What are the key business processes?

6. What control systems (management and measurement systems) are in place?

7. What are the culture, values, and beliefs of the organization?

The answers to these questions inform the assessment of the organization's use of IS. Chapters 3, 4, and 5 use the organizational strategy frameworks, summarized in Figure 1.7, to assess the impact of information systems (IS) on the firm. Chapters 7 and 8 use this same list to understand the business and governance of the IS organization.

▶ BRIEF OVERVIEW OF INFORMATION SYSTEMS STRATEGY

IS strategy is the plan an organization uses to provide information services. IS allows a company to implement its business strategy. JetBlue's vice president for people explains it nicely: "We define what the business needs and then go find the technology to support that."[16]

Business strategy is a function of competition (What does the customer want and what does the competition do?), positioning (In what way does the firm want to compete?), and capabilities (What can the firm do?). IS help determine the company's capabilities. An entire chapter is devoted to understanding key issues facing general managers concerning IT architecture, but for now a more basic framework is used to understand the decisions related to IS that an organization must make.

---

[16] F. Hogue, V. Sambamurthy, R. Zmud, T. Trainer, and C. Wilson, *Winning the 3-Legged Race* (Upper Saddle River NJ: Prentice Hall, 2005), 111.

	What	Who	Where
Hardware	List of physical components of the system	System users and managers	Physical location of components (cloud, datacenter, etc.)
Software	List of programs, applications, and utilities	System users and managers	What hardware it resides on and physical location of hardware
Networking	Diagram of how hardware and software components are connected	System users and managers; company that provides the service	Where the nodes are located, and where the wires and other transport media are located
Data	Bits of information stored in the system	Owners of data; data administrators	Where the information resides

FIGURE 1.8 IS strategy matrix.

The purpose of the matrix in Figure 1.8 is to give the manager a high-level view of the relation between the four IS infrastructure components and the other resource considerations that are keys to IS strategy. Infrastructure includes hardware, such as desktop units and servers. It also includes software, such as the programs used to do business, to manage the computer itself, and to communicate between systems. The third component of IS infrastructure is the network, which is the physical means by which information is exchanged among hardware components, such as through a modem and dial-up network (in which case, the service is actually provided by a vendor such as AT&T), or through a private digital network (in which case the service is probably provided by an internal unit). Finally, the fourth part of the infrastructure is the data. The data includes the bits and bytes stored in the system. In current systems, data are not necessarily stored alongside the programs that use them; hence, it is important to understand what data are in the system and where they are stored. Many more detailed models of IS infrastructure exist, and interested readers may refer to any of the dozens of books that describe them. For the purposes of this text, the matrix will provide sufficient information to allow the general manager to assess the critical issues in information management.

▶ SUMMARY

The Information Systems Strategy Triangle represents a simple framework for understanding the impact of IS on businesses. It relates business strategy with IS strategy and organizational strategy and implies the balance that must be maintained in business planning. The Information Systems Strategy Triangle suggests the following management principles.

Business Strategy

Business strategy drives organizational strategy and IS strategy. The organization and its IS should clearly support defined business goals and objectives.

- Definition: A well-articulated vision of where a business seeks to go and how it expects to get there
- Models: Porter's generic strategies model; dynamic environment models

Organizational Strategy

Organizational strategy must complement business strategy. The way a business is organized either supports the implementation of its business strategy or it gets in the way.

- Definition: The organization's design, as well as the choices it makes to define, set up, coordinate, and control its work processes
- Models: Business Diamond; managerial levers

IS Strategy

IS strategy must complement business strategy. When IS support business goals, the business appears to be working well. IS strategy can itself affect and is affected by changes in a firm's business and organizational strategies. Moreover, IS strategy always has consequences—intended or not—on business and organizational strategies.

- Definition: The plan the organization uses in providing information systems and services
- Models: A basic framework for understanding IS decisions relating architecture (the "what") and the other resource considerations ("who" and "where") that represent important planning constraints

Strategic Relationships

Organizational strategy and information strategy must complement each other. They must be designed so that they support, rather than hinder each other. If a decision is made to change one corner of the triangle, it is necessary to evaluate the other two corners to ensure that balance is preserved. Changing business strategy without thinking through the effects on the organizational and IS strategies will cause the business to struggle until balance is restored. Likewise, changing IS or the organization alone will cause an imbalance.

▶ KEY TERMS

▶ DISCUSSION QUESTIONS

1. Why is it important for business strategy to drive organizational strategy and IS strategy? What might happen if business strategy was not the driver?

2. Suppose managers in an organization decided to hand out tablets (iPad) to all salespeople without making any other formal changes in organizational strategy or business strategy. What might be the outcome? What unintended consequences might occur?

3. Consider a traditional manufacturing company that wanted to build a social business strategy. What might be a reasonable business strategy, and how would organizational and IS strategy need to change? How would this differ for a restaurant chain? A consumer-products company? A non-profit?

4. This chapter describes key components of an IS strategy. Describe the IS strategy of a consulting firm using the matrix framework.

5. What does this tip from *Fast Company* mean: "The job of the CIO is to provide organizational and strategic flexibility"?[17]

CASE STUDY 1-1

LEGO

Lego has long been an industry leader in children's toys with its simple, yet unique building block-style products. The privately held company was founded in 1932 by a Danish carpenter whose family still owns Lego today. But by 2004, the company found itself close to extinction, losing $1 million a day. A new CEO was brought in, and five years later, sales were strong, profits were up, and naysayers who felt the new strategy was going to fail were proved wrong.

With the advent of high-tech forms of entertainment such as the iPod and PlayStation Lego found itself more antique than cutting edge in the toy world. When new CEO Jorgen Vig Knudstorp, a father and former McKinsey consultant, took over, the company struggled with poor performance, missed deadlines, long development times, and poor deliver record. The most popular toys would run out and Lego was unable to ship enough products or manage production of its more complicated sets. Retail stores were frustrated, and that translated into reduced shelf space and ultimately to business losses.

Knudstorp changed all of that. He reached out to top retailers, cut costs, and added missing links to the supply chain. For example, prior to the new strategy, 90% of the components were used in just one design. Designers were encouraged to reuse components in their new products, which resulted in a reduction from about 13,000 different Lego components to 7,000. Since each component's mold could cost up to 50,000 euros on average to create, this reduction saved significant expense.

Lego was known for their traditional blocks and components that would allow children to build just about anything their imagination could create. The new strategy broadened the products, targeting new customer segments. Lego managers created products based on themes of popular

---

[17] "20 Technology Briefs: What's New? What's Next? What Matters," *Fast Company* (March 2002), http://www.fastcompany.com/online/56/fasttalk.html.

movies, such as Star Wars and Indiana Jones. They moved into video games, which featured animated Lego characters sometimes based on Hollywood movies. They created a product strategy for adults and engaged the communities who had already set up thousands of Web sites and blogs featuring Lego creations. They embraced the community who thought of Lego as a way to create art, rather than simply a building toy. And they designed a line of Legos aimed at girls, since the majority of their products had primarily targeted boys.

The culture of Lego changed to one where nonperformance was unacceptable. The company's past showed a tendency to focus on innovation and creativity, often at the expense of profits. But that changed. "Knudstorp made it clear that results, not simply feeling good about making the best toys, would be essential if Lego was to succeed. . . Its business may still be fun and games, but working here isn't," describes the current culture at Lego.

Some of the most drastic changes came from within Lego's organizational structure. After racking up massive losses in 2004, Lego switched its employee pay structure, offering incentives for appropriate product innovation and sales. Key Performance Indicators encourage product innovation that catalyzed sales while decreasing costs. Development time dropped by 50% and some manufacturing and distribution functions were moved to less expensive locations, but the focus on quality remained. The creation of reusable parts alleviated some of the strain on Lego's supply chain, which in turn helped its bottom line.

Lego also expanded into the virtual world, extending into video gaming and virtual-interaction games on the Internet. Thinking outside their previous product concepts cut costs while encouraging real-time feedback from customers across a global market. Additionally, Lego created brand ambassadors who organized conventions across the world to discuss product innovation and building communities of fellow customers. With increased revenue, Lego managers considered entering the movie-making business—a risky proposition for a toy company. However, Lego's success with Hollywood-type action figures fueled its interest in a movie-making endeavor.

The growth put strains on the information systems supporting the business. Order management and fulfillment were particularly affected, resulting in the inability to meet customer demands. Employee management systems were stretched as new employees were added to support the growth and additional locations. Product design and development, especially the virtual and video games, required new technology, too.

To solve some of these problems, Lego managers used the same approach they used for their blocks. They created a modularized and standardized architecture for their information systems, making it possible to expand more quickly and add capacity and functionality as it was needed. They implemented an integrated enterprise system that gave them new applications for human capital management, operations support, product life cycle management, and data management. The new systems and services, purchased from vendors such as SAP and IBM, simplified the IT architecture and the management processes needed to oversee the IS.

One manager at Lego summed it up nicely, "The toy world moves onwards constantly, and Lego needs to re-invent itself continuously. Significant corporate re-shaping introduced new energy to the company." He went on to say that simplifying Lego's IT systems and implementing an efficient product development process that was able to maintain quality and cost favorably positioned Lego to respond to the fast changing pace of the toy industry.

Discussion Questions

1. How did the information systems and the organization design changes implemented by Knudstorp align with the changes in business strategy?

2. Which of the generic strategies does Lego appear to be using based on this case? Provide support for your choice.

3. Are the changes implemented by Knudstorp an indication of hypercompetition? Defend your position.

4. What advice would you give Knudstorp to keep Lego competitive, growing, and relevant?

Sources: Adapted from http://www.nytimes.com/2009/09/06/business/global/06lego.html; Brad Wieners, "Lego is for Girls," *Bloomberg Businessweek* (December 19, 2011), pp. 68–73; and http://www-01.ibm.com/software/success/cssdb.nsf/CS/STRD-85KGS6?OpenDocument.

CASE STUDY 1-2

GOOGLE

Started in the late 1990s, Google grew rapidly to become one of the leading companies in the world. Google's mission is "to organize the world's information and make it universally accessible and useful." It is operating on a simple but innovative business model of attracting Internet users to its free search services and earning revenue from targeted advertising. In the winner-takes-all business of Internet search, Google has captured considerably more market share than its next highest rival, Yahoo!. This has turned Google's Web pages into the Web's most valuable real (virtual) estate. Through its two flagship programs, AdWords and AdSense, Google has capitalized on this leadership position to capture the lion's share in advertisement spending. AdWords enables businesses to place ads on Google and its network of publishing partners for as low as 25 cents per thousand impressions. On the other hand, it uses AdSense to push advertisements on publishing partners' Web sites targeting specific audience and share ad revenue with the publishing partner. This creates a win–win situation for both advertisers and publishers and developed Google into one giant sucking machine for ad revenue.

Even as a large company, Google continues to take risks and expand into new markets. It currently offers over 120 products or services. Sergey Brin and Larry Page, the founders, declared in Google's IPO prospectus, "We would fund projects that have a 10% chance of earning a billion dollars over the long term. . . We place smaller bets in areas that seem very speculative or even strange. As the ratio of reward to risk increases, we will accept projects further outside our normal areas." They further add that they are especially likely to fund new types of projects when the initial investment is small.

Google promotes a culture of creativity and innovation in a number of ways. IT encourages innovation in all employees by allowing them to spend 20% of their time on a project of their own choosing. In addition, it offers benefits such as free meals, on-site gym, on-site dentist, and even washing machines at the company for busy employees.

Despite open and free work culture, a rigid and procedure-filled structure is imposed for making timely decisions and executing plans. For example, when designing new features, the team and senior managers meet in a large conference room. They use the right side of the conference room walls to digitally project new features and the left side to project any transcribed critique with a timer clock giving everyone 10 minutes to lay out ideas and finalize features. Thus, Google utilizes rigorous, data-driven procedures for evaluating new ideas in the midst of a chaotic innovation process.

Google's vice president for search products and user experience, Marissa Mayer, outlines nine notions of innovations embedded in the organizational culture, processes, and structure of Google[18]:

1. "Innovation; not perfection": Google employees can take a good idea and experiment to improve upon it.
2. "Ideas come from everywhere": All Google employees can innovate.
3. "A license to pursue dreams": To help promote innovation, Google employees get one "free" day each week to work on their pet ideas.
4. "Morph projects, don't kill them": Google employees should always to find something salvageable in projects that aren't pursued
5. "Share everything you can": Google employees have a lot of collective knowledge. To encourage sharing, each employee writes an e-mail on Monday with five to seven bullet points of what they learned earlier and Google then consolidates this information and makes it available to the employees.
6. "Users, users, users": Google will be successful if we can please the users; advertisers (and their money) will follow the users.
7. "Data is apolitical": Design is a science at Google. Good ideas must be supported with evidence.
8. "Creativity loves constraints": Google employees work best when they are challenged and have to think outside the box.
9. "You're brilliant? We're hiring": Google likes to hire really smart people—even if they may not have a lot of experience.
10. Worry about usage and users, not money: Provide something simple to use and easy to love. The money will follow.

Keeping up with the organizational strategy of Google, its IT department provides free and open access to IT for all employees. Rather than keeping tight control, Google allows employees to choose from several options for computer and operating systems, download software themselves, and maintain official and unofficial blog sites. Google's intranet provides employees information about every piece of work at any part of Google. In this way employees can find and join hands with others working on similar technologies or features.

In building the necessary IT infrastructure, Google's IT department balances buying and making its own software depending on its needs and off-the-shelf availability. For example, it uses Oracle's accounting software, whereas it built its own customer relationship management (CRM) software, which it then integrated with its ad systems. It also supports open source projects both by extensively using open source software within the organization and by paying college students to contribute to them through programs like Summer of Code. In addition, Google also develops generic applications such as GoogleApps for both internal and external use.

Given the nature of business, security of information resources is critical for Google. For instance, its master search algorithm is considered a more valuable secret formula than Coca-Cola's. However, rather than improving IT security by stifling freedom through preventive policy controls, Google puts security in the infrastructure and focuses more on detective and corrective

[18] Chuck Slater, "Marissa Mayer's Nine Principles of Innovations," *Fast Company* (February 19, 2008), http://www.fastcompany.com/article/marissa-mayer039s-9-principles-innovation (accessed on April 12, 2012).

controls. Its network management software tools combined with 150 security engineers constantly look for viruses and spyware, as well as strange network traffic patterns associated with intrusion.

Discussion Questions

1. How is Google's mission statement related to its business strategy?
2. How does Google's information systems strategy support its business strategy?
3. How does Google's organizational strategy support its business strategy?
4. Which of Porter's three generic strategies does Google appear to be using based on this case? Provide a rationale for your response.
5. Analyze Google's strategy and the type of market disruption it has created using a dynamic environment perspective.

Sources: The Google Case is adapted from Michelle Colin, *"Champions of Innovation," BusinessWeek* (June 19, 2006), Issue 3989, 18–26; and Vauhini Vara, "Pleasing Google's Tech-Savvy Staff," *Wall Street Journal* (March 18, 2008), B6.

CHAPTER 2

STRATEGIC USE OF INFORMATION RESOURCES

This chapter introduces the concept of building competitive advantages using information systems-based applications. It begins with a discussion of the eras showing how the use of information resources has been historically viewed. It then looks at information resources as strategic tools, discussing information technology (*IT*) assets and IT capabilities. Michael Porter's Five Competitive Forces model then provides a framework for discussing strategic advantage, and his Value Chain model addresses tactical ways organizations link their business processes to create strategic partnerships. The Resource-Based View is then introduced to underpin the discussion of maintaining competitive advantage through information and other resources of the firm. The chapter concludes with a brief discussion of strategic alliances, co-opetition, risks of strategic use of IT, and co-creating IT and business strategy.

Zara, a global retail and apparel manufacturer based in Arteixo, Spain, needed a dynamic business model to keep up with the ever-changing demands of their customers and their industry. At the heart of their model was a set of business processes and an information system that linked demand to manufacturing and manufacturing to distribution. The strategy at Zara stores was simply to have a continuous flow of new products that were typically in limited supply. As a result, regular customers visited their stores often—on an average of 17 times a year, whereas most stores only enticed their customers inside on an average of four times a year. When customers saw something they liked, they bought it on the spot because they knew it would probably be gone the next time they visited the store. The result was a very loyal and satisfied customer base and a wildly profitable business model.

How did they do it? It was possible, in part, because Zara aligned its information system strategy with its business strategy. The Zara corporate Web site gave some insight:

Zara's approach to design is closely linked to our customers. A non-stop flow of information from stores conveys shoppers' desires and demands, inspiring our 200-person strong creative team.[1]

[1] Inditex Web site, http://www.inditex.com/en/who_we_are/concepts/zara (accessed on February 20, 2012).

The entire process from factory to shop floor is coordinated from Zara's headquarters using information systems. The point-of-sale (POS) system records the information from each sale, and the information is transmitted to headquarters at the end of each business day. Using a handheld device, the Zara shop managers also report back daily to the designers at headquarters to let them know what has sold and what the customers wanted but couldn't find. The information is used to determine which product lines and colors should be kept and which should be altered or dropped. The designers communicate directly with the production staff to plan for the incredible number of designs—more than 30,000—that will be manufactured every year.[2]

The shop managers have the option of ordering new designs twice a week using handheld computers. Before ordering, they can use their handheld computers to check out the new designs. Once an order is received at the manufacturing plant at headquarters, a large computer-controlled piece of equipment calculates how to position patterns to minimize scrap and cut up to 100 layers of fabric at a time. The cut fabric is then sent from Zara factories to external workshops for sewing. The completed products are sent to distribution centers, where miles of automated conveyor belts are used to sort the garments and recombine them into shipments for each store. Zara's Information Systems (IS) department wrote the applications controlling the conveyors, often in collaboration with vendors of the conveyor equipment.

As the Zara example illustrates, innovative use of a firm's information resources can provide companies with substantial and sustainable advantages over competitors. Every business depends on IS, making its use a necessary resource every manager must consider. But IS can create a strategic advantage for firms who bring creativity, vision, and innovation to their IS use. The Zara case is an example. This chapter uses the business strategy foundation from Chapter 1 to help general managers visualize how to use information resources for competitive advantage. This chapter highlights the difference between simply using IS and using IS strategically, and explores the use of information resources to support the strategic goals of an organization.

The material in this chapter can enable a general manager to understand the linkages between business strategy and information strategy on the Information Systems Strategy Triangle. General managers want to find answers to questions such as: Does using information resources provide a sustainable and defendable competitive advantage? What tools are available to help shape strategic use of information? What are the risks of using information resources to gain strategic advantage?

▶ EVOLUTION OF INFORMATION RESOURCES

The Eras model shows how organizations have used IS over the past decades. Figure 2.1 summarizes this view and provides a road map for a general manager to use in thinking strategically about the current use of information resources within the firm.

IS strategy from the 1960s to the 1990s was driven by internal organizational needs. First came the need to lower existing transaction costs. Next was the need to provide

[2] Shenay Kentish, Zara (October 18, 2011), http://unilifemagazine.com.au/special-interest/zara/ (accessed on April 10, 2012).

	Era I 1960s	Era II 1970s	Era III 1980s	Era IV 1990s	Era V 2000s	Era VI 2010+
Primary role of IT	Efficiency	Effectiveness	Strategic	Strategic	Value creation	Value extension
	Automate existing paper-based processes	Solve problems and create opportunities	Increase individual and group effectiveness	Transform industry/ organization	Create collaborative partnerships	Community and social business
Justify IT expenditures	ROI	Increasing productivity and better decision quality	Competitive position	Competitive position	Adding value	Creating relationships
Target of systems	Organization	Organization/ group	Individual manager/group	Business processes ecosystem	Customer/ supplier ecosystem	Customer/ employee/ supplier ecosystem
Information models	Application specific	Data-driven	User-driven	Business-driven	Knowledge-driven	People-driven (or relationship-driven)
Dominate technology	Mainframe, "centralized intelligence"	Minicomputer, mostly "centralized intelligence"	Microcomputer, "decentralized intelligence"	Client Server, "distributed intelligence"	Internet, global "ubiquitous intelligence"	Social platforms, social networks, mobile, cloud
Basis of value	Scarcity	Scarcity	Scarcity	Plentitude	Plentitude	Plentitude
Underlying economics	Economics of information bundled with economics of things	Economics of information bundled with economics of things	Economics of information bundled with economics of things	Economics of information separated from economics of things	Economics of information separated from economics of things	Economics of relationships bundled with economics of information

FIGURE 2.1 Eras of information usage in organizations.

support for managers by collecting and distributing information, followed by the need to redesign business processes. As competitors built similar systems, organizations lost any advantages they held from their IS, and competition within a given industry once again was driven by forces that existed prior to the new technology. Most recently, enterprises found that social IT platforms and capabilities drove a new evolution of applications, processes, and strategic opportunities.

As each era begins, organizations adopt a strategic role for IS to address not only the firm's internal circumstances but its external circumstances as well. Thus, in the value-creation era, companies seek those applications that again provide them with an advantage over competition. They also seek applications that keep them from being outgunned by start-ups with innovative business models or traditional companies entering new markets. For example, a plethora of "dot-coms" challenged all industries and traditional businesses by entering the marketplace armed with Internet-based innovative systems.

The Information System Strategy Triangle introduced in Chapter 1 reflects the link between IS strategy and organizational strategy and the internal requirements of the firm. The link between IS strategy and business strategy focuses on the firm's external requirements. Maximizing the effectiveness of the firm's business strategy requires that the general manager be able both to identify and use information resources. This chapter looks at how information resources can be used strategically by general managers.

▶ INFORMATION RESOURCES AS STRATEGIC TOOLS

Crafting a strategic advantage requires the general manager to cleverly combine all the firm's resources, including financial, production, human, and information resources, and to consider external resources such as the Internet and opportunities in the global arena. Information resources are more than just the infrastructure. This generic term, **information resources**, is defined as the available data, technology, people, and processes within an organization to be used by the manager to perform business processes and tasks. Information resources can either be assets or capabilities. An **IT asset** is anything, tangible or intangible, that can be used by a firm in its processes for creating, producing, and/or offering its products (goods or services). An **IT capability** is something that is learned or developed over time for the firm to create, produce, or offer its products. An IT capability makes it possible for a firm to use its IT assets effectively.[3]

An *IS infrastructure* (a concept that is discussed in detail in Chapter 6) is an IT asset. It includes each of an information resource's constituent components (i.e., data, technology, people, and processes). The infrastructure provides the foundation for the delivery of a firm's products or services. Another IT asset is an *information repository*, which is logically related data that is captured, organized, and retrievable by the firm. Some information repositories are filled with internally oriented information designed to improve the firm's efficiency. Other repositories tap the external environment and contain significant knowledge about the industry, the competitors, and the customers. Although most firms have these types of information repositories, not all firms use them effectively.

In the continually-expanding **Web 2.0** space, the view of IT assets is broadening to include potential resources that are available to the firm, but that are not necessarily owned by the firm. These additional information resources are often available as a

---

[3] G. Piccoli and B. Ives, "IT-Dependent Strategic Initiatives and Sustained Competitive Advantage: A Review and Synthesis of the Literature," *MIS Quarterly* (2003), 29(4), 747–776.

service, rather than as a system to be procured and implemented internally. For example, Internet-based software (also called Software as a Service, or SAAS) such as SalesForce.com offers managers the opportunity to find new ways to manage their customer information with an externally based IT resource. Social networking systems such as Facebook or LinkedIn offer managers the opportunity to find expertise or an entire network of individuals ready to participate in the innovation processes of the corporate using relatively little capital or expense.

The three major categories of IT capabilities are technical skills, IT management skills, and relationship skills. *Technical skills* are applied to designing, developing, and implementing information systems. *IT management skills* are critical for managing the IS department and IS projects. They include an understanding of business processes, the ability to oversee the development and maintenance of systems to support these processes effectively, and the ability to plan and work with the business units in undertaking change. *Relationship skills* can either be externally focused or span across departments. An externally focused relationship skill includes the ability to respond to the firm's market and to work with customers and suppliers. The relationship between a firm's IS managers and its business managers is a spanning relationship skill and includes the ability of IS to manage partnerships with the business units. Even though it focuses on relationships in the firm, it requires spanning beyond the IS department. Relationship skills develop over time and require mutual respect and trust. They, like the other information resources, can create a unique advantage for a firm. Figure 2.2 summarizes the different types of information resources and provides examples of each.

Committing and developing information resources require substantial financial resources. A general manager evaluating an information resource might consider the following questions to better understand the type of advantage the information resource can create:[4]

- *What makes the information resource valuable?* In Eras I through III, the value of information was tied to the physical delivery mechanisms. In these eras, value was derived from scarcity reflected in the cost to produce the information. Information, like diamonds, gold, and MBA degrees, was more valuable because it was found in limited quantities. However, the networked economy beginning in Era IV drives a new model of value—value from plenitude. **Network effects** offer a reason for value derived from plenitude; the value of a network node to a person or organization in the network increases when others join the network. For example, an e-mail account has no value without another e-mail account that could receive the e-mail. As e-mail accounts become relatively ubiquitous, the value of having an e-mail account increases as its potential for use increases. Further, copying additional people on an e-mail is done at a very low cost (virtually zero). As the cost of producing an additional copy of an information product within a network becomes trivial, the value of that network increases.

---

[4] Adapted from David J. Collis and Cynthia A. Montgomery, "Competing on Resources: Strategy in the 1990s," *Harvard Business Review* (July–August 1995), reprint no. 95403.

Type of Information Resource	Definition	Example
IT ASSET	Anything that can be used by a firm in its processes for creating, producing, and/or offering its products (goods or services).	
IT infrastructure	Base foundation of the IT portfolio shared through the firm[5]	Hardware, software, network, data components, proprietary technology, Web-based services
Information repository	Data that is logically related and organized in a structured form accessible and usable for decision making purposes.	Critical information about customers that can be used to gain strategic advantage. Much of this information is increasingly available on the Web.
IT CAPABILITY	Something that is learned or developed over time and used by the firm to create, produce, or offer its products using IT assets.	
Technical skill	Ability applied to designing, developing, and implementing information systems	Proficiency in systems analysis and design; programming skills
IT management skills	Ability to manage IT function and IT projects	Being knowledgeable about business processes and managing systems to support them; evaluating technology options; envisioning creative IT solutions to business problems
Relationship skills	Ability of IS specialists to work with parties outside the IS department.	*Spanning:* having a good relationship between IT and business managers. *Externally focused:* have a good relationship with an outsourcing vendor.

FIGURE 2.2 Information resources.

Source: Adapted from G. Piccoli and B. Ives, "IT-Dependent Strategic Initiatives and Sustained Competitive Advantage: A Review and Synthesis of the Literature," *MIS Quarterly* (2003), 29(4), 755.

Therefore, rather than using production *costs* to guide the determination of price, information products might be priced to reflect their *value* to the buyer.[5]

- *Who appropriates the value created by the information resource?* Determining where a resource's value lies and how it can be improved in a firm's favor is part of the analysis of determining the value. The attributes of information resources

[5] Adapted from M. Broadbent, P. Weill, and D. St. Clair. "The Implications of Information Technology Infrastructure for Business Process Redesign," *MIS Quarterly*, (1999), 23(2), 163.

that impact the value make it possible to create and sustain competitive advantage. For example, at Zara, the speed of information sharing is the source of the value to the firm. Information from the retail shops is quickly sent and analyzed by designers to identify future products.

- *Is the information resource equally distributed across firms now and in the future?* At the beginning of the life cycle of a new technology, early adopters may experience a competitive advantage from using an information resource. For example, a manager who has mastered the value from internal wikis may find uses for them that give his or her firm a momentary advantage. However in the longer term, these resources become more common and others are able to gain similar benefits. But the *experience* gained when using the information resource may cause inequities between firms. Within an industry, firms likely have different experiences with a resource, and that difference creates value because it can create strategic advantage. In addition, in some industries, the value of information mushrooms under conditions of information asymmetries. Finally, the possessor of information may use it against, or sell it to, companies or individuals who are not otherwise able to access the information.

- *Is the information resource highly mobile?* A reliance on the individual skills of IT professionals exposes a firm to the risk that key individuals will leave the firm, taking their experience with them. Developing unique knowledge-sharing processes and creating an organizational memory can help reduce the impact of the loss of a mobile employee. Recording the lessons learned from all team members after the completion of each project and using social technologies to record interactions and activity streams are two examples of ways to lower this risk. At Zara, customer information is compiled centrally, so any one store's experience, while valuable, is not likely to provide the same information as the consolidated information seen by the designers who analyze data from thousands of stores.

- *How quickly does the information resource become obsolete?* While information itself does not "wear out" like physical things, information can become obsolete. In the highly dynamic environment, information becomes obsolete much faster than ever before since like most other assets, information resources lose value over time. A general manager must understand the rate of decline of value, as well as factors that may speed or slow it. Consider, for example, a database of customer information. How long, on average, is the current address of each customer valid? What events in the economy might change their purchasing pattern and reduce the forecasting capability of the current information? Are the trends derived from analyzing past sales valid to predict future sales patterns?

Information resources exist in a company alongside other resources. The general manager is responsible for organizing all resources so that business goals are met. Understanding the nature of the resources at hand is a prerequisite to using them effectively. By aligning IS strategy with business strategy, the general manager maximizes its profit potential. Meanwhile, the firm's competitors are working to do the same.

In this competitive environment, how should the information resources be organized and applied to enable the organization to compete most effectively?

▶ HOW CAN INFORMATION RESOURCES BE USED STRATEGICALLY?

The general manager confronts many elements that influence the competitive environment of his or her enterprise. Overlooking a single element can bring about disastrous results for the firm. This slim tolerance for error requires the manager to take multiple views of the strategic landscape. Three such views can help a general manager align IS strategy with business strategy. The first view uses the five competitive forces model by Michael Porter to look at the major influences on a firm's competitive environment. Information resources should be directed strategically to alter the competitive forces to benefit the firm's position in the industry. The second view uses Porter's value chain model to assess the internal operations of the organization and partners in its supply chain. Information resources should be directed at altering the value-creating or value-supporting activities of the firm. We extend this view further to consider the value chain of an entire industry to identify opportunities for the organization to gain competitive advantage. The third view specifically focuses on the types of IS resources needed to gain and sustain competitive advantage. These three views provide a general manager with varied perspectives from which to identify strategic opportunities to apply the firm's information resources.

Using Information Resources to Influence Competitive Forces

Porter provides the general manager with a classic view of the major forces that shape the competitive environment of a firm. These five competitive forces are shown in Figure 2.3, along with some examples of how information resources can be applied to influence each force. This view reminds the general manager that competitive forces result from more than just the actions of direct competitors. Each force now will be explored in detail from an IS perspective.

Potential Threat of New Entrants

Existing firms within an industry often try to reduce the threat of new entrants to the marketplace by erecting barriers to entry. Barriers to entry help the firm create a stronghold by offering products or services that are difficult to displace in the eyes of customers based on apparently unique features. Such barriers include controlled access to limited distribution channels, public image of a firm, and government regulations of an industry. Information resources also can be used to build barriers that discourage competitors from entering the industry. For example, Google's search algorithm is a source of competitive advantage for the search company, and it's a barrier of entry for new entrants, who would have to create something better to compete against Google. Walmart, another example, effectively blocked competition with their inventory control system, which helped them drive down expenses and ultimately offer low costs to customers. Any company entering Walmart's marketplace would have to spend millions of dollars to build the inventory control system and IS required to provide its operations with the same competitive advantage. Therefore, the system at Walmart may be a barrier

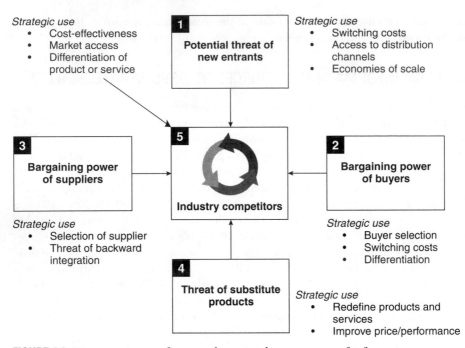

Strategic use
- Cost-effectiveness
- Market access
- Differentiation of product or service

1 Potential threat of new entrants

Strategic use
- Switching costs
- Access to distribution channels
- Economies of scale

3 Bargaining power of suppliers

5 Industry competitors

2 Bargaining power of buyers

Strategic use
- Selection of supplier
- Threat of backward integration

4 Threat of substitute products

Strategic use
- Buyer selection
- Switching costs
- Differentiation

Strategic use
- Redefine products and services
- Improve price/performance

FIGURE 2.3 Five competitive forces with potential strategic use of information resources. Sources: Adapted from M. Porter, *Competitive Strategy* (New York: The Free Press, 1998); and Lynda M. Applegate, F. Warren McFarlan, and James L. McKenney, *Corporate Information Systems Management: The Issues Facing Senior Executives*, 4th ed. (Homewood, IL: Richard D. Irwin, 1996).

to entry for new companies. Twitter is another example of a company that has erected a barrier to entry for new microblogging sites in the United States. Individuals wanting to tweet with the largest number of others will gravitate to Twitter, making it difficult for another U.S. microblogging site to enter the industry. Facebook has erected similar barriers in the social networking marketplace.

Bargaining Power of Buyers

Customers often have substantial power to affect the competitive environment. This power can take the form of easy consumer access to several retail outlets to purchase the same product or the opportunity to purchase in large volumes at superstores like Walmart. Information resources can be used to build switching costs that make it less attractive for customers to purchase from competitors. Switching costs can be any aspect of a buyer's purchasing decision that decreases the likelihood of "switching" his or her purchase to a competitor. Such an approach requires a deep understanding of how a customer obtains the product or service. For example, Amazon.com's One Click encourages return purchases by making buying easier. Amazon.com stores buyer information, including contact information and credit card numbers, so that it can be accessed with one click, saving consumers the effort of data reentry. Similarly, Apple's iTunes simple-to-use interface and proprietary software on the iPod make it difficult for customers to use other formats and technologies than the iPod, effectively reducing the power of the buyers, the customers.

Another good example of the power of buyers occurred at Facebook. When Facebook announced a new service, called Beacon, press releases from Facebook shouted that "users gain ability to share their actions from 44 participating sites with their friends on Facebook." The concept was called "Social Distribution" and gave Facebook information from the participating sites that would be posted on the Facebook customer's page. Customers erupted in protest, and one month later, CEO Mark Zuckerberg, personally issued an apology for the way Facebook handled the new feature. "We simply did a bad job with this release, and I apologize for it. While I'm disappointed with our mistakes, we appreciate all the feedback we have received from our users. I'd like to discuss what we have learned and how we have improved Beacon." [6] Zuckerberg continued by sharing why they built Beacon in the first place (to let people share with their friends a lot of information across sites) and why it was designed the way it was (to be as easy to use as possible and so users "didn't have to touch it to make it work"). But the blogosphere quickly lit up with issues of privacy, control, and security as well as general dislike of the strategy, forcing the company to respond. The power of the buyer community, the users of Facebook, banded together to force a change in the firm's activity.

Bargaining Power of Suppliers

Suppliers' bargaining power can reduce a firm's options and ultimately its profitability. Suppliers often strive to "lock in" customers through the use of systems (and other mechanisms). For example, there are many options for individuals to back up their laptop data, including many service options. The power of any one supplier is low, since there are a number of options. But when Apple's operating system makes it simple to back up to their iCloud, their power increases. Customers find it easy to use the iCloud and they do.

This force is strongest when a firm has few suppliers from which to choose, the quality of supplier inputs is crucial to the finished product, or the volume of purchases is insignificant to the supplier. For example, steel firms lost some of their bargaining power over the automobile industry because car manufacturers developed technologically advanced quality control systems. Manufacturers can now reject steel from suppliers when it does not meet the required quality levels.

Through the Internet, firms continue to provide information for free as they attempt to increase their share of visitors to their Web sites and gather information about them. This decision reduces the power of information suppliers and necessitates finding new ways for content providers to develop and distribute information. Many Internet firms are integrating backward or sideways within the industry by creating their own information supply and reselling it to other Internet sites. Well-funded firms simply acquire these content providers, which is often quicker than building the capability from scratch. One example is eBay's acquisition of PayPal, the system used to transact payment for goods and services all over the Web. Another is Amazon.com's acquisition of Zappos, the shoe retailer.

---

[6] http://www.facebook.com/blog/blog.php?post=7584397130 posted on December 5, 2007 (accessed on June 3, 2012).

Threat of Substitute Products

The potential of a substitute product in the marketplace depends on the buyers' willingness to substitute, the relative price-to-performance of the substitute, and the level of switching costs a buyer faces. Information resources can create advantages by reducing the threat of substitution. For example, Internet auction site eBay used innovative IT to create a set of services for their small businesses, a major source of revenue for the online auctioneer. At a time when customers were beginning to complain, sellers were wondering about the fees, and competition was trying to lure them both away, eBay brought out ProStores, a service to help all sellers build their own Web site. eBay managers noticed that many sellers did not have any Web presence other than eBay, and the move was another way to lock in these customers to the eBay environment. "The more those sellers are locked into an eBay environment, the less likely they will work with rivals," according to one Web site.[7] It seemed to work. One seller, a Tennessee-based, wholesale distributor of ball bearings and chains, reportedly doubled its eBay sales four months after its ProStores site was launched.[8] For competitors to be successful, they need to offer not just a substitute, but also a better service to these sellers. So far none has.

Substitutes that cause a threat come from many sources. Internal innovations can cannibalize existing revenue streams for a firm. For example, new iPhones motivate current customers to upgrade, essentially cannibalizing the older product line revenue. Of course, this is also a preemptive move to keep customers in the iPhone product family, rather than switch to another competitor's product. The threat might come from potentially new innovations that make the previous product obsolete. Some argue that the iPad is a substitute for laptops and personal computers. Consider how digital cameras have made film (and the cameras that use them) obsolete. CDs and more recently digitally based MP3 files have made vinyl records (and the record players that play them) obsolete. Free Web-based applications are a threat to software vendors who charge for their products and who do not have Web-based delivery. Managers must watch for potential substitutes from many different sources to fully manage this competitive threat.

Industry Competitors

Rivalry among the firms competing within an industry is high when it is expensive for a firm to leave the industry, the growth rate of the industry is declining, or products have lost differentiation. Under these circumstances, the firm must focus on the competitive actions of a rival to protect market share. Intense rivalry in an industry ensures that competitors respond quickly to any strategic actions. Facebook enjoys a competitive advantage in the social networking industry. Other sites have tried to compete with Facebook by offering a different focus, either a different type of interface, or additional features. Competition is fierce and many start-ups hope to "be the next Facebook."

---

[7] Evan Shumann, StorefrontBacktalk.com (June 26, 2005), http://storefrontbacktalk.com/securityfraud/ebay-pushes-to-be-everything-for-its-sellers/.

[8] Gwen Moran, "The Pros of Opening an eBay ProStore" (March 24, 2006), http://www.entrepreneur.com.

However Facebook continues to lead the industry, in part by continued innovation and in part by its huge customer base, which continues to raise the bar for competitors.

The processes firms use to manage their operations, and lower costs or increase efficiencies, can provide an advantage for cost-focus firms. However as firms within an industry begin to implement standard business processes and technologies—often using enterprise-wide systems such as those of SAP and Oracle—the industry becomes more attractive to consolidation through acquisition. Standardizing IS lowers the coordination costs of merging two enterprises and can result in a less-competitive environment in the industry.

One way competitors differentiate themselves with an otherwise undifferentiated product is through creative use of IS. Information provides advantages in such competition when added to an existing product. For example, the iPod, iPhone, and iPad are each differentiated in part because of the iTunes store and the applications available only to users of these devices. Competitors offer some of the same information services, but Apple was able to take an early lead by using information systems to differentiate their products.

The competitive forces identified by Porter's model are each acting on firms at all times, but perhaps to a greater or lesser degree. There are forces from potential new entrants, buyers, sellers, substitutes and competitors at all times, but their threat varies. Consider Zara, the case discussed in at the beginning of this chapter. Figure 2.4 summarizes these five forces working simultaneously at the retailer and manufacturer.

General managers can use the five competitive forces model to identify the key forces currently affecting competition, to recognize uses of information resources to influence forces, and to consider likely changes in these forces over time. The changing forces drive both the business strategy and IS strategy, and this model provides a way to think about how information resources can create competitive advantage for a business unit and, even more broadly, for the firm. They also can reshape a whole industry—compelling general managers to take actions to help their firm gain or sustain competitive advantage.

Consider an example of a large grocery retailer. Because of many factors, including the number of items on the shelves of the store, the complexity of managing customers, and the logistics necessary to keep inventory moving and reordered as necessary, these retailers are no longer are able to compete without information systems. The basis of competition has changed in part because of the innovative use of information systems by industry leaders. Keeping track of inventory is a given, but large chains must also intimately know their customers and find new ways to provide innovative services to keep their loyalties. The entire industry has changed from one of locally providing groceries to one of managing information about every aspect of their business. The alternative perspective presented in the next section provides the general manager with an opportunity to select the proper mix of information resources and to apply them to achieve strategic advantage by altering key activities.

Using Information Resources to Alter the Value Chain

The value chain model addresses the activities that create, deliver, and support a company's product or service. Porter divided these activities into two broad categories,

Competitive Force	IT Influence on Competitive Force
Threat of New Entrant	Zara's IT supports its tightly knit group of designers, market specialists, production managers, and production planners. New entrants are unlikely to provide IT to support relationships that have been built over time. Further, it has a rich information repository about customers that would be hard to replicate.
Bargaining Power of Buyers	With its constant infusion of new products, buyers are drawn to Zara stores. Zara boasts more than 30,000 new designs a year, whereas competitors typically offer only 2,000 to 4,000. Further, because of the low inventory that the Zara stores stock, the regular customers buy products they like when they see them because they are likely to be gone the next time they visit the store. More recently, Zara has employed laser technology to measure 10,000 women volunteers so that it can add the measurements of "real" customers into its information repositories. This means that the new products will be more likely to fit Zara customers. These are all strategies to reduce the bargaining power of Zara's buyers.
Bargaining Power of Suppliers	Its computer-controlled cutting machine cuts up to 1,000 layers at a time. It then sends the cut materials to suppliers who sew the pieces together. The suppliers' work is relatively simple, and many suppliers can do the sewing. Thus, the pool of suppliers is expanded, and Zara has greater flexibility in choosing the sewing companies. Further, because Zara dyes 50% of the fabric in its plant, it is less dependent on suppliers and can respond more quickly to midseason changes in customer color preferences. Hence, the bargaining power of Zara's suppliers is reduced.
Industry Competitors	Industry competitors long marketed the desire of durable, classic lines. Zara focuses on meeting customer preferences for trendy, low-cost fashion. It has the highest sales per square foot of any of its competitors. It does so with virtually no advertising and only 10% of stock is unsold. It keeps its inventory levels very low and offers new products at an amazing pace for the industry (i.e., 15 days from idea to shelves). Zara has extremely efficient manufacturing and distribution operations.
Threat of Substitute Products	IT helps Zara offer extremely fashionable lines that are only expected to last for approximately ten wears. IT enables Zara to offer trendy, appealing apparel at hard-to-beat prices, making substitutes difficult.

FIGURE 2.4 Application of five competitive forces model for Zara.

as shown in Figure 2.5: support and primary activities. Primary activities relate directly to the value created in a product or service, whereas support activities make it possible for the primary activities to exist and remain coordinated. Each activity may affect how other activities are performed, suggesting that information resources should not be applied in isolation. For example, more efficient IS for repairing a product may increase the possible number of repairs per week, but the customer does not receive any value

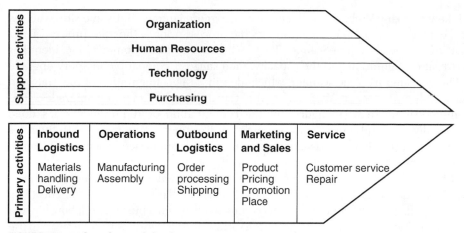

	Inbound Logistics	Operations	Outbound Logistics	Marketing and Sales	Service
	Materials handling Delivery	Manufacturing Assembly	Order processing Shipping	Product Pricing Promotion Place	Customer service Repair

FIGURE 2.5 Value chain of the firm.

Source: Adapted from Michael Porter and Victor Millar, "How Information Gives You Competitive Advantage," *Harvard Business Review* (July–August 1985), reprint no. 85415.

unless his or her product is repaired, which requires that the spare parts be available. Changing the rate of repair also affects the rate of spare parts ordering. If information resources are focused too narrowly on a specific activity, then the expected value increase may not be realized, as other parts of the chain are not adjusted.

The value chain framework suggests that competition stems from two sources: lowering the cost to perform activities and adding value to a product or service so that buyers will pay more. To achieve true competitive advantage, a firm requires accurate information on elements outside itself. Lowering activity costs only achieves an advantage if the firm possesses information about its competitors' cost structures. Even though reducing isolated costs can improve profits temporarily, it does not provide a clear competitive advantage unless a firm can lower its costs below a competitor's. Doing so enables the firm to lower its prices as a way to grow its market share.

Adding value can be used to gain strategic advantage only if a firm possesses accurate information regarding its customer. Which product attributes are valued, and where can improvements be made? Improving customer service when its products fail was a goal behind Otis Elevator's Otisline system, a classic story about value-added customer service. The customer's elevator service call is automatically routed to the field technician with the skill and knowledge to complete the repair. Otis Elevator managers know that customers value a fast response to minimize the downtime of the elevator. This goal is achieved by using information resources to move the necessary information between activities. When customers call for service, their requests are automatically and accurately entered and stored in the customer service database and communicated to the technician linked to that account. This technician is then contacted immediately over the wireless handheld computer network and told of the problem. That way the service technician can make sure he or she has both the parts and knowledge to make repairs. This approach provides Otis with an advantage because the response is fast, and the technician arrives at the job properly prepared to fix the problem.

Likewise, many Web sites sell memory to upgrade laptops. But some sites, such as crucial.com, have an option that automates the process prior to the sales process. Their site has the "Crucial System Scanner Tool," which scans the customer's Mac, identifies the current configuration and the capacity, then suggests compatible memory upgrade kits. The customer uses the scanner, which identifies the configuration of the Mac, and automatically opens up a Web page with the appropriate memory upgrades. The customer does not have to figure out the configuration or requirements; it's done automatically. By combining a software program like their configurator, with the sales process, crucial.com has added value to the customer's experience by automating a key part of the customer service process.

Although the value chain framework emphasizes the activities of the individual firm, it can be extended, as in Figure 2.6, to include the firm in a larger value system. This value system is a collection of firm value chains connected through a business relationship and through technology. From this perspective, a variety of strategic opportunities exist to use information resources to gain a competitive advantage. Understanding how information is used within each value chain of the system can lead to new opportunities to change the information component of value-added activities. It can also lead to shakeouts within the industry, as the firms that fail to provide value are forced out and as new business models are adopted by the surviving firms.

Opportunity also exists in the transfer of information across value chains. For example, sales forecasts generated by a manufacturer such as a computer or automotive company and linked to supplier systems, creates an order for the manufacture of the

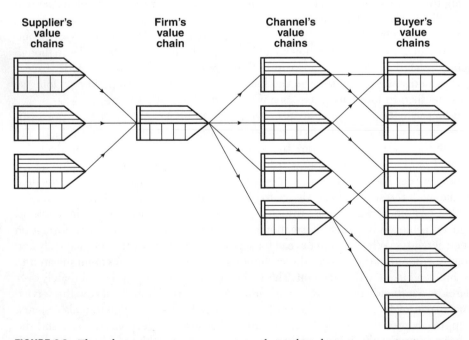

FIGURE 2.6 The value system: interconnecting relationships between organizations.

necessary components for the computer or car. Often this coupling is repeated from manufacturing company to vendor/supplier for several layers, linking the value chains of multiple organizations. In this way, value is added by each member of the supply chain by directly linking the elements of their value chains together.

Optimizing a company's internal processes, such as their supply chain, operations, and customer relationship processes, can be another source of competitive advantage. Tools such as **supply chain management** (SCM), an approach to how companies source materials for operations, **enterprise resource planning** (ERP) systems, a tool that automates functions of the operations activities of the value chain, and **customer relationship management** (CRM) systems, a tool to optimize the processing of customer information are routinely used to automate the internal operations of a firm's value chain. These systems are discussed in more detail in Chapter 5.

In an application of the value chain model to the Zara example discussed earlier in the chapter, Figure 2.7 describes the value added to primary and support activities provided by information systems at Zara. The focus in Figure 2.7 is on value added to Zara's processes, but suppliers and customers in its supply chain also realize the value added by information systems. Most notably, the customer is better served as a result of the information systems. For example, the stores place orders twice a week over personal digital assistants (PDAs). Each night, managers use their PDAs to learn about newly available garments. The orders are received and promptly processed and delivered. In this way Zara can be very timely in responding to customer preferences.

Unlike the five competitive forces model, which focuses on industry dynamics, the focus of the value chain is on the firm's activities. Yet, in applying the value chain, competitive forces may be affected to the extent that the proposed technology may add value to suppliers, customers, or even competitors and potential new entrants.

Using the Resource-Based View (RBV)

The third framework, the **resource-based view (RBV)**,[9] is useful in determining whether a firm's strategy has created value by using IT. Unlike Porter's competitive forces framework, this view maintains that competitive advantage comes from the information and other resources of the firm. On the other hand, Porter's competitive forces framework argues that aspects of the firm's industry create sources of competitive advantage that remain relatively stable. Like the value chain model, the resource-based view concentrates on areas that add value to the firm. Whereas the value chain model focuses on a firm's activities, the resource-based view focuses on the resources that it can manage strategically in a rapidly changing competitive environment.

[9] The resource-based view was originally proposed by management researchers, most prominently Jay Barney, "Firm Resources and Sustained Competitive Advantage," *Journal of Management* (1991), 17(1), 99–120; J. Barney, "Is the Resource-Based 'View' a Useful Perspective for Strategic Management Research? Yes," *Academy of Management Review* (2001), 26(1), 41–56; and M. Wade and J. Hulland, "Review: The Resource-Based View and Information Systems Research: Review, Extension and Suggestions for Future Research," *MIS Quarterly* (2004), 28(1), 107–142, reviewed its application in the MIS literature and derived a framework to better understand its application to IS resources.

Activity	Zara's Value Chain
PRIMARY ACTIVITIES	
Inbound Logistics	IT-enabled Just-in-Time (JIT) strategy results in inventory being received when needed. Most dyes are purchased from its own subsidiaries to better support JIT strategy and reduce costs. Many suppliers are located near its production facilities.
Operations	Information systems support decisions about the fabric, cut, and price points. Cloth is ironed and products are packed on hangers so they don't need ironing when they arrive at stores. Price tags are already on the products. Zara produces 60% of its merchandise in-house. Fabric is cut and dyed by robots in 23 highly automated Spanish factories.
Outbound Logistics	Clothes move on miles of automated conveyor belts at distribution centers and reach stores within 48 hours.
Marketing and Sales	Limited inventory allows low percentage of unsold inventory (10%); POS at stores linked to headquarters to track how items are selling; customers ask for what they want, and this information is transmitted daily from stores to designers over handheld computers.
Service	No focus on service on products
SUPPORT ACTIVITIES	
Organization	IT supports tightly knit collaboration among designers, store managers, market specialists, production managers, and production planners.
Human Resources	Managers are trained to monitor what's selling and report data to designers every day. The manager is key to making customers feel listened to, and to communicating with headquarters to keep each store and the entire Zara clothing line at the cutting edge of fashion.
Technology	Technology is integrated to support all primary activities. Zara's IT staff works with vendors to develop automated conveyor to support distribution activities.
Purchasing	Vertical integration reduces amount of purchasing needed.

FIGURE 2.7 Application of value chain model to Zara.

The RBV has been applied in the area of IS to help identify two types of information resources: those that enable a firm to *attain* competitive advantage and those that enable a firm to *sustain* the advantage over the long term. From the IS perspective,[10] some

---

[10] http://www.minonline.com/best_of_web/Best-of-the-Web-CommunitySocial-Networking_10185.html (accessed on January 1, 2012).

types of resources are better than others for creating attributes that enable a firm to attain (i.e., value, rarity) competitive advantage while other resources are better for creating attributes to sustain competitive value (i.e., low substitutability, low mobility, low imitability).

Resources to Attain Competitive Advantage

Valuable and rare resources that firms must leverage to establish a superior resource position help companies attain competitive advantage. A resource is considered valuable when it enables the firm to become more efficient or effective. It is rare when other firms do not possess it. For example, many banks today would not think of doing business without ATMs. ATMs are very valuable to the banks in terms of their operations. A bank's customers expect it to provide ATMs in many convenient locations. However, because many other banks also have ATMs, they are not a rare resource, and they do not offer a strategic advantage. Some call them *table stakes* or resources required just to be in the business. Many systems in Eras I and II, and especially Era III, were justified on their ability to provide a rare and valuable resource. In some cases these very systems have become table stakes.

Other examples of initially rare and valuable resources are the communities many companies implemented using social IT. People joined a community because they had a common interest with others and early on, they had only one or possibly a few communities to choose from. These communities were a valuable resource for the firms that sponsored them. For example, Rodale, Inc. Men's Health for Belly Off! Club won an award in 2009 for demonstrating that online communities can enhance a traditional franchise when they offered readers a diet supplemented with a program that included user-generated content, profiles progress reports, and additional tools for managing user goals. The program attracted 20,000 members, which was double the goal, and members provided positive, encouraging and goal-driven comments to each other, giving Rodale a valuable resource. At the time, no other community offered such a valuable service.

Resources to Sustain Competitive Advantage

Many firms who invested in systems learned that gaining a competitive advantage does not automatically mean that you can sustain it over the long term. The only way to do that is to continue to innovate and to protect against resource imitation, substitution, or transfer. For example, Walmart's complex logistics management is deeply embedded in both its own and its supplier's operations that imitations by other firms is unlikely. It was not easy for eBay customers to find a substitute for ProStores, discussed earlier in this chapter. The Oakland A's use of information systems propelled them to victory, as depicted in the movie "Moneyball," but as soon as other teams learned about the secret success Oakland was having with information systems, they, too began to use similar techniques, reducing the advantage Oakland initially enjoyed. Finally, to sustain competitive advantage, resources must be difficult to transfer or replicate, or relatively immobile. Some resources such as computer hardware and software can be easily bought and sold. However, technical knowledge, especially that relates to the firm's operation, a gung-ho company culture, and managerial experience in the firm's environment is less easy to obtain and, hence, considered harder to transfer to other firms.

Some IT management skills are general enough in nature to make them easier to transfer and imitate relationship skills. Although it clearly is important for IS executives to manage internally oriented resources such as IS infrastructure, systems development, and running cost-effective IS operations, these skills can be acquired in many different forums. They are basic IT management skills possessed by virtually all good IS managers. Other skills, however, are unique to a firm and require considerable time and resources to develop. For example, it takes time to learn how the firm operates and to understand critical processes and socially complex working relationships. However, the message posed by the resource-based view is that IS executives must look beyond their own IS shop and concentrate on cultivating resources that help the firm understand changing business environments and allow them to work well with all their external stakeholders. Even when considering internally oriented information resources, there are differences in the extent to which they add value. Many argue that IS personnel are willing to move, especially when offered higher salaries by firms needing these skills. Yet, some technical skills, such as knowledge of a firm's use of technology to support business processes and technology integration skills are not easily moved to another firm. Further, hardware and many software applications can be purchased or outsourced, making them highly imitable and transferrable. Because it is unlikely that two firms will have exactly the same strategic alternatives, resources at one firm have only moderate substitutability in the other firm.

Zara and RBV

Figure 2.8 indicates the extent to which the attributes of each information resource may add value to Zara, discussed earlier in the chapter. Zara's advantage did not come from the specific hardware or software technologies it employed. Its management spent five to ten times less than its rivals on technology. Zara skillfully uses the POS equipment, handheld computers, automated conveyors, and the large computer-controlled equipment to cut patterns, but Zara could eventually be purchased or imitated by competitors. The IT infrastructure in terms of value creation (i.e., value and rarity) has a moderate rating. It is easy to imitate and transfer and only moderately difficult to substitute considering the automated conveyors; hence Zara's infra-structure would not be a particularly good resource for maintaining strategic value. In contrast, Zara has created considerable value from the other information asset—its valuable information repository with customers' preferences and body types. The information about customer preferences that the store managers communicate daily is captured and saved in Zara's information repository. That information is easily retrievable by the designers, market specialists, procurement planners, and produc-tion managers. It would be a challenge for other companies to develop and apply the rich information not only because of the volume of data, but also because of the working relationships that leverage its use. Thus, the information repository has great value to Zara and is relatively rare because of its integration with Zara's operations and

	VALUE CREATION		VALUE SUSTAINABILITY		
	Value	Rarity	Imitation	Substitution	Transfer
IT ASSET					
IT Infrastructure	M	M	H	M	H
Information Repository	H	M	M	L	M
IT CAPABILITY					
Technical Skills	M	L	M	M	M
IT Management Skills	H	H	L	L	M
Relationship Skills—*Externally Focused*	H	M	L	M	L-M
Relationship Skills—*Spanning*	H	H	L	L	L

FIGURE 2.8 Information resources at Zara, by attribute. (L = low; M = medium; H = high). Source: Based on M. Wade and J. Hulland, "The Resource-Based View and Information Systems research: Review, Extension and Suggestions for Future Research," *MIS Quarterly* (2004), 28(1), 107–142.

personnel. It would be relatively difficult to imitate or transfer and extremely difficult to substitute.

In terms of information capability, much of Zara's value creation is from its valuable and rare IT management skills. Zara's technical skills, while not exceptionally valuable or rare, may offer some sustainable value because they are used to integrate across Zara's range of systems, and would thus not be overly easy to imitate, substitute or transfer. However, its IT management skills are strong to the extent that they can leverage the use of IT resources, a skill that is not easily replicable, transferrable, or substitutable. Zara's relationship skills also serve as a tool for value creation and sustainablitility. The spanning capabilities demonstrated by the tight-knit teams at headquarters are very unusual and are not easy to replicate, imitate, or purchase in the market place. They allow Zara the ability to correctly interpret and quickly respond to customers' needs. IT is integrally involved in supporting the spanning. Zara is also able to maintain and sustain external relationships with their suppliers. The externally focused relationships Zara maintains with manufacturers in Europe allow for a turnaround time of under five weeks from conception to distribution. Overall, Zara is able to create high value from its IT management and relationship skills. It would be moderately to extremely difficult to substitute, imitate, or transfer them.

Most firms don't really have a choice of creating competitive advantage by manipulating industry forces either through their use of information resources or IT-enhanced activities. Yet, like Zara, they can leverage the IT resources they do have to create and sustain strategic value for their firms.

Social Business Lens: Social Capital

A management theory that is gaining in popularity as a tool in understanding a social business is Social Capital Theory. **Social capital** is the sum of the actual and potential resources embedded within, available through, and derived from the network of relationships possessed by an individual or social unit. Relationships associated with networks have the potential of being a valuable resource for businesses. The focus on the theory is not on managing individuals, but rather managing relationships.

The value from networks may be derived in one of three interrelated ways: structural, relational, and cognitive. The *structural* dimension is concerned with the pattern of relationships in the network—who is connected to whom. The *relational* dimension looks at the nature of relationships among members in the network (i.e., respect, friendship)—how do the connected people interact. The third *cognitive* dimension looks at the way people think about things in the network, in particular whether they have a shared language, system of meanings or interpretations—how do the connected people think. The unusual thing about social capital is that no one person owns it. Rather it is owned jointly by the people in the relationship. Thus, it can't be traded easily, but it can be used to do certain things more easily. In particular, in social business applications, social capital may make it easier to get the information needed to perform a task or connect with certain key people. In information systems development teams it may improve the willingness and ability of team members to coordinate their tasks in completing a project.

Source: J. Nahapiet and S. Ghosal, "Social Capital, Intellectual Capital and the Organizational Value," *Academy of Management Review* (1998), 23(2), 242–266.

▶ STRATEGIC ALLIANCES

The value chain helps a firm focus on adding value to the areas of most value to its partners. The resource-based view suggests adding value using externally oriented relationships skills. The most recent eras of information usage evolution emphasized the importance of collaborative partnerships and relationships. The increasing number of Web applications focused on collaboration and social networking only foreshadow even more emphasis on alliances. These relationships can take many forms, including joint ventures, joint projects, trade associations, buyer–supplier partnerships, or cartels. Often such partnerships use information technologies to support strategic alliances and integrate data across partners' information systems. A **strategic alliance** is an interorganizational relationship that affords one or more companies in the relationship a strategic advantage. An example was the strategic alliance between game-maker Zynga and Facebook. As documented in Facebook's IPO filing in January 2012, the relationship is a mutually beneficial one. Zynga developed some of the most popular games on Facebook, including Mafia Wars, Farmville, and WordsWithFriends. Facebook got exclusive rights to Zynga's games many of which generated thousands of new members of Facebook. The alliance generated significant revenue for both parties. Zynga accounted for 12% of Facebook's revenue in 2011, according to the IPO documents, since players of these games purchase virtual goods with real money and Zynga purchases significant advertising space from Facebook to promote its games. Zynga benefits from the revenue resulting from its gamers on Facebook community.[11]

IS can be the platform upon which a strategic alliance functions. Technology can help produce the product developed by the alliance, share information resources across the partners' existing value systems, or facilitate communication and coordination among the partners. For example, Delta formed a strategic alliance with e-Travel Inc., a travel service software company that targets large corporations, to promote Delta's online reservations system. The alliance was strategic because it helped Delta reduce agency reservation fees and offered e-Travel new corporate leads. As introduced earlier, linking value chains through SCM is another way firms build an IT-facilitated strategic alliance.

Co-opetition

Clearly, not all strategic alliances are formed with suppliers or customers as partners. Rather, co-opetition is an increasingly popular alternative model. As defined by Brandenburg and Nalebuff in their book of the same name, **co-opetition** is a strategy whereby companies cooperate and compete at the same time with companies in its value net.[12] The value net includes a company and its competitors and complementors, as well as its customers and suppliers, and the interactions among all of them. A complementor is a company whose product or service is used in conjunction with a particular product or service to make a more useful set for the customer. For example, Goodyear is a complementor to Ford and GM because tires are a complementary product to automobiles. Likewise, Amazon is a complementor to Apple in part because the Amazon reading application, the Kindle, named after the reading tablet Amazon sells, is one of the most popular apps for the iPad.

Co-opetition, then, is the strategy for creating the best possible outcome for a business by optimally combining competition and cooperation. It frequently creates competitive advantage by giving power in the form of information to other organizations or groups. For example, Covisint, the auto industry's e-marketplace, grew out of a consortium of competitors General Motors, Ford, and DaimlerChrysler, Nissan, and Renault. By addressing multiple automotive functional needs across the entire product life cycle, Covisint offers support for collaboration, supply chain management, procurement, and quality management. Thus, co-opetition as demonstrated by Covisint, not only streamlines the internal operations of its backers, but also has the potential to transform the automotive industry.

---

[11] Adapted from N. Wingfield, "Virtual Products, Real Profits," *Wall Street Journal* (September 9, 2011), A1, 16; L. B. Baker, Zynga's sales soar on Facebook connection, http://news.yahoo.com/zynga-shares-soar-facebook-connection-172923796.html; and Jackie Cohen, "So Much For The Facebook Effect: Zynga Sees $978.6 Million Loss In 2011" (February 14, 2012), http://www.allfacebook.com/facebook-zynga-eps-2012-02 (accessed on February 20, 2012).

[12] A. Brandenburg and B. Nalebuff, *Co-opetition* (New York: Doubleday, 1996).

▶ RISKS

As demonstrated throughout this chapter, information resources may be used to gain strategic advantage, even if that advantage is fleeting. When information systems are chosen as the tool to outpace their firm's competitors, executives should be aware of the many risks that may surface. Some of theses risks include the following:

- *Awaking a sleeping giant.* A firm can implement IS to gain competitive advantage, only to find that it nudged a larger competitor with deeper pockets into implementing an IS with even better features. FedEx offered its customers the ability to trace the transit and delivery of their packages online. FedEx's much larger competitor, UPS, rose to the challenge. UPS not only implemented the same services, but also added a new set of features eroding some of the advantages FedEx enjoyed, and causing FedEx to update its offerings. Both the UPS and FedEx sites passed through multiple Web site iterations as the dueling delivery companies continue to struggle for competitive advantage.

- *Demonstrating bad timing.* Sometimes customers are not ready to use the technology designed to gain strategic advantage. For example, Grid Systems created the GRiDPAD in 1989. It was a tablet computer designed for businesses to use in the field, and was well reviewed at its time. But it didn't get traction. Three decades later, in 2010, Apple introduced the iPad, and tablet computing took off.

- *Implementing IS poorly.* Stories abound of information systems that fail because they are poorly implemented. Typically these systems are complex and often global in their reach. Web snafus plagued Virgin America's implementation of its online reservation system. It had turned to Sabre Holdings Corp, an industry standard, to develop a reservations system to interface with other airlines and handle its future growth. But apparently, its other systems aren't compatible with Sabre's and systems problems still exist four months after the installation was supposed to be completed. During the lengthy installation period, customers were unable to book or modify their flights, check-in on-line. These created a huge amount of problems for Virgin America's customers during the busy flying periods over the Thanksgiving and Christmas holidays.[13]

  Another implementation fiasco took place at Hershey Foods, when it attempted to implement its supply and inventory system. Hershey developers brought the complex system up too quickly and then failed to test it adequately. Related systems problems crippled shipments during the critical Halloween shopping season, resulting in large declines in sales and net income. More recently, in 2012, more than 100,000 Austin Energy customers received incorrect utility bills due to problems with their vendor-supplied bill collection system.

---

[13] "Virgin America Still Having Major System Problems More Than a Month After System Changes," *The Cranky Flier*, http://crankyflier.com/2011/12/20/virgin-america-still-having-major-system-problems-more-than-a-month-after-system-changes/; and J. Nicas, "Jet-Lagged: Web Glitches Still Plague Virgin America," *Wall Street Journal* (November 23, 2011), B1.

Some customers went months without a bill, others were incorrectly billed. Some businesses that owed $3,000 were billed $300,000. Still others tried to pay their bill online, only to be told it wasn't recorded when it was. The utility calculated that the problems cost it more than $8 million.[14]

- *Failing to deliver what users want.* Systems that do not meet the needs of the firm's target market are likely to fail. For example, in 2011, Netflix leadership divided the company into two, calling the DVD-rental business Qwikster, and keeping the streaming business under Netflix. But customers complained, and worse, closed their accounts, and less than a month later, Qwikster was gone. Netflix reunited both businesses under the Netflix name.[15]

- *Mobile-based alternative removes advantages.* With increasingly more applications moving to mobile-based platforms, managers must consider the risk of losing any advantage obtained by a Web-based information resource that later becomes available as a service on mobile platforms. The mobile-based alternative may be much simpler to use, be more easily available, and include a similar set of advantages. An example was iHeartRadio launched by Clear Channel Communications, a mobile application that streamed live radio broadcasts from more than 800 radio stations from all over the country on mobile devices. It allowed listeners to build customized channels of just the music or programming they like, and to share them with friends. It also had the ability to suggest new music the listener might like based on predictive software routines. These features outweighed advantages local radio stations enjoyed. Likewise, mobile phones were able to stream videos from YouTube and movie sites like Netflix, offering advantages such as portability and watching videos any place and any time.

- *Running afoul of the law.* Using IS strategically may promote litigation if the IS results in the violation of laws or regulations. Years ago, American Airlines' reservation system, Sabre, was challenged by American Airlines' competitors on the grounds that it violated antitrust laws. More recently, in 2010, Google said it was no longer willing to adhere to Chinese censorship. The Chinese government responded by banning searching via all Google search sites (not only google.cn but all language versions, e.g. google.co.jp. google.com.au, etc.), including Google Mobile. Google then created an automatic re-direct to Google Hong Kong, which stopped June 30, 2010 so that Google would not lose its license to operate in China. Today, Google, Inc. is acting in compliance with the Chinese government's censorship laws and Chinese users of Google.cn see filtered results as before.

[14] Marty Toohey, "More than 100,000 Austin Energy customers hit by billing errors from $55 million IBM system" (February 18, 2012), http://www.statesman.com/news/local/more-than-100-000-austin-energy-customers-hit-2185031.html (accessed on February 20, 2012).

[15] Qwikster = Gonester (October 10, 2011), http://www.breakingcopy.com/netflix-kills-qwikster (accessed on February 20, 2012).

Geographic Box: Mobile-Only Internet Users Dominate Emerging Countries

More than 25% of mobile Web users in emerging markets connect to the Internet solely through mobile devices. This is the case for 70% of mobile Web users in Egypt, 59% in India and 50% in Nigeria, but only for 25% of U.S. and 22% of U.K. mobile Web users. Malaysia is emerging as a test case for mobile-only Internet. It has rolled out a next-generation, high-speed broadband network that covers most of its population. This infrastructure makes it possible to make video calls with Apple's FaceTime application in locations throughout the country using a tiny pocket router that accesses a WiMAX wireless-broadband network set up by a local conglomerate, YTL Corp. Bhd. To further encourage the spread of Internet, Malaysia's leaders have pledged not to censor the Internet.

Sources: G. Dunaway, "Mobile-Only Internet Users Dominate Emerging Markets" (October 24, 2011), http://www.adotas.com/201w1/10/mobile-only-internet-users-dominate-emerging-markets/; and J. Hookway, "Broadband in the tropics," *Wall Street Journal* (September 21, 2011), B6.

Every business decision has risks associated with it. However, with the large expenditure of IT resources needed to create sustainable, strategic advantages, the manager will want to carefully identify and then design a mitigation strategy to manage the associated risks.

► CO-CREATING IT AND BUSINESS STRATEGY

This chapter has discussed the alignment of IT strategy with business strategy. Certainly they must be carefully choreographed to ensure that maximum value is achieved from IT investments and the maximum opportunity to achieve the business strategy. However in the fast-paced business environment where information is increasingly a core component of the product or service offered by the firm, managers must co-create IT and business strategy. That is to say that IT strategy *is* business strategy; one cannot be created independent of the other. In many cases they are now one in the same.

For companies whose main product is information, such as financial services companies, it's clear that how information is managed is the core of the business strategy itself. How an investment firm manages the clients' account, how their clients interact with the company, and how investments are made are all done through the management of information. A financial services company must co-create business and IT strategy.

But consider a company like FedEx, most well known as the package delivery company. Are customers paying to have a package delivered or to have information about that package's delivery route and timetable? One could argue that they are one in the same, and that increasingly the company's business strategy **is** its IS strategy. Certainly there are components of the operation that are more than just information.

There are actual packages to be loaded on actual trucks and planes, which are then actually delivered to their destinations. However, to make it all work, the company must rely on IS. Should the IS go down, FedEx would be unable to do business. A company like this must co-create IT strategy and business strategy.

This was not true a few years ago. Companies could often separate IS strategy from business strategy, in part because their products or services did not have a large information component. For example, a few years ago, should the IS of a trucking company stop working, the trucks would still be able to take their shipments to their destination and pick up new shipments. It might be slower or a bit more chaotic, but the business wouldn't stop. Today, that's not the case. Complicated logistics are the norm, and IS are the foundation of the business, such as seen at FedEx.

With the increasing number of IS applications on the Web and on mobile devices, firm will increasingly need to co-create business and IT strategy. Managers who think they can build a business model without considering the opportunities and impact of information systems, both the resources owned by the firm and those available on the Web will find they have significant difficulties creating business opportunities as well as sustainable advantage in their marketplace.

▶ SUMMARY

- Information resources include data, technology, people, and processes within an organization. Information resources can be either assets or capabilities.

- IT infrastructure and information repositories are IT assets. Three major categories of IT capabilities are technical skills, IT management skills, and relationship skills.

- Using IS for strategic advantage requires an awareness of the many relationships that affect both competitive business and information strategies.

- The five competitive forces model implies that more than just the local competitors influence the reality of the business situation. Analyzing the five competitive forces—new entrants, buyers, suppliers, industry competitors, and substitute products—from both a business view and an information systems view helps general managers use information resources to minimize the effect of these forces on the organization.

- The value chain highlights how information systems add value to the primary and support activities of a firm's internal operations, as well as to the activities of its customers, and other components of its supply chain.

- The resource-based view (RBV) helps a firm understand the value created by their strategy. RBV maintains that competitive advantage comes from the information resources of the firm. Resources enable a firm to attain and sustain competitive advantage.

- IT can facilitate strategic alliances. Supply chain management (SCM) is a mechanism that may be used for creating strategic alliances.

- Co-opetition is the complex arrangement through which companies cooperate and compete at the same time with other companies in its value net.

- Numerous risks are associated with using information systems to gain strategic advantage: awaking a sleeping giant, demonstrating bad timing, implementing poorly, failing to deliver what customers want, avoiding mobile-based alternatives, and running afoul of the law.

► KEY TERMS

co-opetition (p. 65)

customer relationship
  management
  (CRM) (p. 59)

enterprise resource planning
  (ERP) (p. 59)

information resources (p. 47)

IT asset (p. 47)

IT capability (p. 47)

network effects (p. 48)

resource-based view
  (RBV) (p. 59)

strategic alliance (p. 64)

supply chain management
  (SCM) (p. 59)

Web 2.0 (p. 47)

► DISCUSSION QUESTIONS

1. How can information itself provide a competitive advantage to an organization? Give two or three examples. For each example, describe its associated risks.

2. Use the five competitive forces model as described in this chapter to describe how information technology might be used to provide a winning position for each of these businesses:

    a. A global airline

    b. A local dry cleaner

    c. A mobile phone company

    d. A bank

    e. A Web-based wine retailer

3. Using the value chain model, describe how information technology might be used to provide a winning position for each of these businesses:

    a. A global airline

    b. A local dry cleaner

    c. A mobile phone company

    d. A bank

    e. A Web-based wine retailer

4. Use the resource-based view as described in this chapter to describe how information technology might be used to provide and sustain a winning position for each of these businesses:

    a. A global airline

    b. A local dry cleaner

    c. A mobile phone company

    d. A bank

    e. A Web-based wine retailer

5. Some claim that no sustainable competitive advantages can be gained from IT other than the capability of the IS organization itself. Do you agree or disagree? Defend your position.

6. Cisco Systems has a network of component suppliers, distributors, and contract manufacturers that are linked through Cisco's extranet. When a customer orders a Cisco product at Cisco's Web site, the order triggers contracts to manufacturers of printed circuit board assemblies when appropriate and alerts distributors and component suppliers. Cisco's contract manufacturers are aware of the order because they can log on to Cisco's extranet and link with Cisco's own manufacturing execution systems. What are the advantages of Cisco's strategic alliances? Does this Cisco example demonstrate SCM? Why or why not?

GROUPON

Groupon, Inc. raised $700 million at its IPO in the fall of 2011, instantly providing a valuation of almost $13 billion for a company that was only 3 years old at the time. Some question the value claiming Groupon has no sustainable competitive advantage. Others see Groupon as an innovative company with high potential.

Groupon sells Internet coupons for events, services, and other popular items customers might want to buy. Customers sign up for daily emails targeted to their local market. The daily deal, offered for one-day only and only if a pre-determined minimum number of customers buy it, gives customers 50% off the "retail" price. For example, a $100 3-month health club membership would sell for $50 on Groupon. The customer pays $50 to Groupon and prints a certificate to redeem at the health club. Groupon keeps 50% of the revenue, or $25 in this case, and gives the rest to the health club. Effectively, retailers are offering 75% off, with the customer saving 50% and Groupon taking the rest.

Groupon pays the retailer when the coupon is redeemed, making money both on the float between the time revenue is collected and the time the retailer is paid, and on the certificates that are never redeemed at all, which the industry calls "breakage." Retailers make money in the long run by introducing customers to their products, selling them additional products and services when they come in to redeem their coupons, and turning them into repeat customers. And retailers benefit from the buzz created when their business is on Groupon.

In August 2010, Groupon launched its first national deal, a coupon worth $50 of Gap apparel and accessories for $25. Over 440,000 coupons were sold, netting Groupon and the Gap close to $11 million. But not all vendors are the size of the Gap, and smaller vendors have been overwhelmed with too many coupons. One local business owner said they lost $8,000 on their Groupon promotion when too many coupons were issued. In fact a study of 150 retailers showed that only 66% found their deals profitable.

Around the time of the IPO, the analysts and observers alike claimed that Groupon's business model was not sustainable. In addition to the large number of retailers who found their deals unprofitable, observers noted that Groupon does not produce anything of value, and they are not adding value to the retailers. Further, there are no barriers to entry to stop competitors. In May 2011, there were over 450 competitors who offer discounts and deals including LivingSocial, another daily deal site, restaurant.com, a site for restaurant gift certificates at a deep discount, overstock.com and woot.com, sites offering discounted merchandise, not to mention deep-pocketed competitors like Amazon.com.

But Groupon added to its business strategy with mobile capability and new services. In February 2012, they purchased Kima Labs, a mobile payment specialist, and Hyperpublic, a company that builds databases of local information. In May 2011, in a few cities, the company launched GrouponNow, a time-based local application that gives customers instant deals at merchants nearby using location-based software. CEO Andrew Mason told Wall Street analysts in February 2012 that he saw significant growth potential, including working on new features that will help customers personalize offers and avoid deals they don't want.

Discussion Questions

1. How does information technology help Groupon compete?

2. Do you agree or disagree with the statement that "Groupon has no sustainable competitive advantage?" Please explain your point of view.

3. How does Groupon add value to the companies whose offers are sold on the site?

4. What impact, if any, will Groupon Now have on Groupon's competitive position? Explain.

5. What would you advise Groupon leaders to consider as their next application?

6. Apply the Resource-Based View to Groupon's business model to show how information resources may be used to gain and sustain competitive advantage.

Sources: Adapted from http://mashable.com/2010/08/19/gap-groupon/ (accessed on February 21, 2012); http://www.forbes.com/sites/petercohan/2011/06/06/memo-to-sec-groupon-has-no-competitive-advantage-stop-its-ipo/ (accessed on February 21, 2012); http://blogs.wsj.com/venturecapital/2010/09/29/rice-university-study-groupon-renewal-rate-not-so-hot/ (accessed on February 21, 2012); http://articles.chicagotribune.com/2011-05-18/business/ct-biz-0519-groupon-now-20110518_1_groupon-chief-executive-andrew-mason-first-phase (accessed on February 21, 2012); and http://www.reuters.com/article/2012/02/09/us-groupon-idUSTRE81727B20120209 (accessed on February 21, 2012).

CASE STUDY 2-2

ZIPCAR

Zipcar was an answer for customers who want to rent a car for a few hours in their home city, rather than for a few days from a traditional rental agency. Car reservations were for a specific pick-up time and location around the city, often in neighborhoods so the customers need only to walk to pick up their reserved car. Customers applied for a Zipcard, which enabled them to reserve a car online and unlock their car when they arrive at the car's location.

The company operated with a very small staff compared to traditional rental agencies. Very little human interaction was required between the customer and Zipcar for a transaction. A customer reserved a car online, entered into the reserved car by waving the RFID-enabled Zipcard against the card reader mounted behind the windshield on the driver side, returned the car to the same location, and was billed on the credit card already on file. The customer could check all rental records and print receipts from the online reservation system. The system also had a color-coded time chart showing availability and location of all rental cars in the vicinity. This transparent information exchange allows a customer to pick the car he or she wants, if available, or delay the reservation until the car was returned by another customer. Zipcar also created and installed a GPS-enabled wireless device in each car, which allowed members to find and reserve a nearest vehicle using a cell phone. Customers also can use an iPhone or Android app on their iPhone or Android mobile device to find and reserve a Zipcar on a 24/7 basis. Zipcar sends text alerts near the end of the rental period and customers can text back if they want to extend their rental time.

All the cars were outfitted with patented wireless technology. Their proprietary IT platform carried information flow between customers, vehicles, and the company. It was used to monitor car security, fulfill reservations, record hourly usage, and maintain mileage information. It also relayed vital technical information such as battery voltage and fuel level. It even informed the central system if a customer forgot to turn off headlights, which can quickly drain battery power.

This business model provided unique advantages over traditional car rentals. The customer did not have to stand in line or fill out papers to rent a car. The customer knew exactly which make and model he or she would be getting. Unlike most off-airport rental agency locations, which were only open during business hours, Zipcar locations were open 24 hours. The Zipcar rates also included the cost of gas and insurance, as well as reserved parking spots at some locations.

Additionally, the company used social networking technologies to develop an online community of Zipcar members—Zipsters. It encouraged Zipsters to talk about their Ziptrips (i.e., share their personal experiences with Zipcar).

Thus, information technology was not only the key enabler of this business model but also was a facilitator in creating a buzz and encouraging community development around the concept. Zipcar changed the rules of the rental car industry by bringing the new Web 2.0 mind-set of focusing on automation, customer empowerment, transparency, and community. Zipcar has been very successful, with over 200,000 paying members and renting over 5,000 vehicles in 50 markets in the United States, Canada, and the United Kingdom.

Discussion Questions

1. Analyze the business model of Zipcar using Porter's five forces model.
2. Discuss the synergy between the business strategy of Zipcar and information technology.
3. What *network effects* are part of the strategy of Zipcar? How do they add value?
4. As the CEO of Zipcar, where is your most threatening competition? What would you do to sustain a competitive advantage?

Sources: Adapted from Paul Boutin, "A Self-Service Rental Car," *BusinessWeek* (May 4, 2006); Mary K. Pratt, "RFID: A Ticket to Ride," *ComputerWorld* (December 18, 2006); and "Zipcar: Our technology downloaded," http://www.zipcar.com/how/technology.

CHAPTER 3

ORGANIZATIONAL STRATEGY AND INFORMATION SYSTEMS

In order for Information Systems to support an organization in achieving its goals, they must reflect the business strategy and be coordinated with the organizational strategy. This chapter focuses on linking and coordinating the IS strategy with the three components of organizational strategy:

- organizational design (decision rights, formal reporting relationships and structure, informal networks)
- management control systems (planning, data collection, performance measurement, evaluation, incentives, and rewards)
- organizational culture (organizational, national)

Started in 1994, Cognizant Technology Solutions grew fast to become a $1.45 billion revenue company providing IS outsourcing services. However, growing at such a break-neck speed, it had to reinvent its organization structure many times to make sure that it facilitated the flow of information which was supported by the development of IS and the delivery of IS services. Initially, its India-centric structure located the managers of each group in India along with software engineers. Employees at customer locations worldwide reported to the managers. As the company grew and its focus shifted from simple, cost-based solutions to complex, relationship-based solutions, this model had to be changed to be more customer-oriented. Under the redesigned reporting structure, the managers were moved to customer locations, while software engineers remained in India. This change improved customer relations but brought in new headaches on the technical side. Under the new arrangement, managers had to spend their days with customers and unexpectedly ended up spending their nights with software engineers to clarify customer requirements and fix bugs. This created a tremendous strain on managers, who threatened to quit. It also hampered systems development. Thus, neither of these organizational structures was working well. Neither structure was well-aligned with the business strategy and the IS strategy.

However, Cognizant found that despite these problems some groups were working and performing well. Upon an extensive analysis of those groups, the company decided to

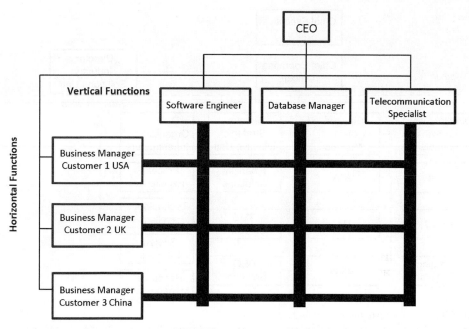

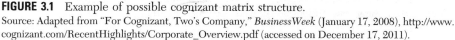

FIGURE 3.1 Example of possible cognizant matrix structure.
Source: Adapted from "For Cognizant, Two's Company," *BusinessWeek* (January 17, 2008), http://www.cognizant.com/RecentHighlights/Corporate_Overview.pdf (accessed on December 17, 2011).

adopt a matrix structure of co-management throughout the company. In this matrix structure, each project has two managers equally responsible for the project. One manager is in India and the other is at the client site. They work out among themselves how and when to deal with issues. And both managers are equally responsible for customer satisfaction, project deadlines, and group revenue. The new structure, demonstrated in Figure 3.1, enables Cognizant to "establish extremely close partnerships that foster continuous operational improvements and better bottom-line results for clients." That is, the new matrix structure makes it possible to build IS that the customers wanted.

During the same time period in 2008, the largest outsourcing company and software exporter in India, Tata Consultancy Services (TCS), chose a different organization structure designed to focus on customers and boost revenue growth (see Figure 3.2), "As we scale up over 100,000 employees, TCS needs a structure that allows us to build a nimble organization to capture new growth opportunities," said then TCS CEO and Managing Director S. Ramadorai.[1] That structure, which was modified in 2011 by the new TCS CEO N. Chandrasekaran, adds a new layer of leaders to oversee the businesses and free up his time to work on strategy.[2]

---

[1] "Reinvented Blog by Prashanth Rai," *CIO* (March 19, 2008), http://cio-reinvented.typepad.com/cioreinvented/2008/03/tcs---new-organ.html (accessed on December 19, 2011).

[2] N. Shivapriya, "TCS CEO N Chandrasekaran creates new layer to oversee verticals," *India Times* (May 25, 2011), http://articles.economictimes.indiatimes.com/2011-05-25/news/29581999_1_tcs-ceo-n-chandrasekaran-tcs-spokesperson-structure (accessed on December 19, 2011).

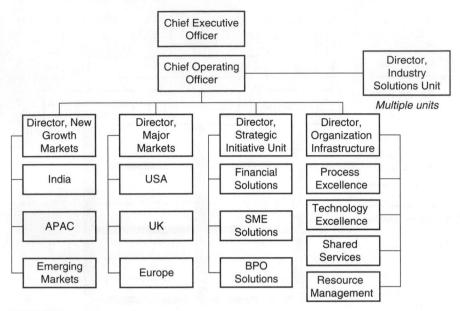

FIGURE 3.2 Tata Consultancy Services.
Source: "TCS plans new organizational structure," *The Financial Express* (February 12, 2008), http://www.financialexpress.com/printer/news/272100/ (accessed on December 19, 2011).

Both Cognizant and TCS are large Indian outsourcing companies that found they needed to reorganize to respond to problems resulting from growth. Cognizant's main problem was its lack of necessary information flows between the software engineers in India and the customer service managers on the client location. Its complex problems resulted in a correspondingly complex matrix structure. Its focus is on the delivery to its customers of information systems that reflect refined technical solutions to their problems. Its organization structure both improves customer responsiveness and necessary information flows. It focuses on system development and delivery and seeks to address a problem that Cognizant experienced in buliding systems.

In contrast, TCS's organization chart reflects a focus not only on current customers but also on future markets. That is why it added major units called "New Growth Markets" and "Strategic Initiative Unit." The Business Process Outsourcing and Small and Medium Enterprise solutions in this later major unit indicate the strategic directions TCS wants to take. The organization structure is designed to emphasize these new growth areas and facilitate information flows along these lines in the organization. Its focus is on building an ever bigger market for the IS that it builds and the IS services that it provides.

The point is that different organizational structures reflect different organizational strategies that are used by organizations to implement their business strategies and accomplish organizational goals. These organizational strategies should be in agreement with IS strategies. When used appropriately, IS leverage human resources, capital, and materials to create an organization that optimizes performance. Companies that design organizational strategy without considering IS strategies run into problems like those Cognizant experienced. A synergy results from designing organizations with IS strategy in mind—a synergy that cannot be achieved when IS strategy is just added on.

Chapter 1 introduced a simple framework for understanding the role of IS in organizations. The Information Systems Strategy Triangle relates business strategy with IS strategy and organizational strategy. In an organization that operates successfully, an overriding business strategy drives both organizational strategy and information strategy. The most effective businesses optimize the interrelationships between the organization and IS, maximizing efficiency and productivity.

Variable	Description
Organizational variables	
Decision rights	Authority to initiate, approve, implement, and control various types of decisions necessary to plan and run the business.
Business processes	The set of ordered tasks needed to complete key objectives of the business.
Formal reporting relationships	The structure set up to ensure coordination among all units within the organization; reflects allocation of decision rights.
Informal networks	Mechanism, such as ad hoc groups, which work to coordinate and transfer information outside the formal reporting relationships.
Control variables	
Data	The facts collected, stored, and used by the organization.
Planning	The processes by which future direction is established, communicated, and implemented.
Performance measurement and evaluation	The set of measures that are used to assess success in the execution of plans and the processes by which such measures are used to improve the quality of work.
Incentives	The monetary and nonmonetary devices used to motivate behavior within an organization.
Cultural variables	
Values	The set of implicit and explicit beliefs that underlies decisions made and actions taken; reflects aspirations about the way things should be done.

FIGURE 3.3 Organizational design variables.
Source: James I. Cash, Robert G. Eccles, Nitin Nohria, and Richard L. Nolan, *Building the Information Age Organization* (Homewood, IL: Richard D. Irwin, 1994).

Organizational strategy includes the organization's design, as well as the managerial choices that define, set up, coordinate, and control its work processes. As discussed in Chapter 1, many models of organizational strategy are available, such as the business diamond that identifies four primary components of an organization: tasks, structures (or organizational design), people (and their culture), and information/control. Figure 3.3 summarizes complementary design variables from the managerial levers framework. Optimized organizational designs support optimal business processes, and they, in turn, reflect the firm's values and culture. Organizational strategy may be considered as the coordinated set of actions that leverages the use organizational design, management control systems and organizational culture to make the organization effective by achieving the organization's objectives. The organizational strategy works best when it meshes well with the IS strategy.

This chapter builds on the managerial levers model. Of primary concern is the ways in which IS impacts the three types of managerial levers: organizational, control, and cultural. This chapter looks at organizational designs that incorporate IS to define the flow of information throughout the organization, explores how IS can facilitate management control at the organizational and individual levels, and concludes with some ideas about how culture impacts IS and organizational performance. It focuses on organizational-level issues related to strategy. The next two chapters complement it with a discussion of new approaches to work and organizational processes.

▶ INFORMATION SYSTEMS AND ORGANIZATIONAL DESIGN

This section examines the first type of managerial lever–organizational. It focuses on how IS may be reflected in the design of an organization's physical structure. Ideally an organization structure is designed to facilitate the communication and work processes necessary for it to accomplish the organization's goals. The organization structures of Cognizant and TCS, while very different, reflect and support the goals of each company. This section expands the discussion of organization structures by describing decision rights that underlie formal structures, formal reporting relationships, and informal networks. Oranizational processes are another important organizational variable that are studied in more detail in Chapter 5.

Decision Rights

Decision rights indicate who in the organization has the responsibility to initiate, supply information for, approve, implement, and control various types of decisions. Ideally the individual who has the most information about a decision and who is in the best position to understand all of the relevant issues should be the person who has the decision right for the decision. But this may not happen, especially in organization designs where senior leaders make most decisions. Much of the discussion of IT governance and accountability in Chapter 8 is based upon who has the decision right for critical IS decisions. When talking about accountability, one has to start with the person who is responsible for the decision—that is, the person who has the decision right for the decision. Organizational design is all about making sure that decision rights are properly allocated—and reflected in the structure of formal reporting relationships. IS support decision rights by making it easier to receive information needed to make the decision by the person holding the decision right and to transmit information from the decision maker to the people who will implement the decision. In some cases, IS enables a centralized decision maker to pass information that has been gathered from operations and stored centrally down through the organization. If information systems deliver the wrong information to the person who holds the decision rights, or if the right information isn't delivered to the the person with the decision rights, poor decision making is bound to occur.

Consider the case of Zara from the last chapter. Each of its 1,000 stores orders clothes in the same way, using the same digital form, using the same type of handheld devices, following a rigid weekly timetable for ordering. Most other large retailers use forecasting and inventory control models to determine what clothes should be sent to the stores. That is, the ordering decisions are made at headquarters. However, with Zara, the decision rights for ordering have been moved to the Zara store managers. By giving them the decision rights for ordering, Zara store managers can place orders that reflect the tastes and preferences of customers in their localized areas. Using handheld devices that are linked directly to the company's design rooms in Spain, store managers can make daily reports with information what the customers want. However, the store managers do not have decision rights for order fulfullment because they have no way of knowing the consolidated demand of stores in their area. The decision rights for order fulfillment lay with the commercial team in headquarters, since it is the team that knows about overall demand, overall supply, and store performance in their assigned area. The information from the commercial team then flows directly to the designers and production people to respond quickly to customer preferences, and in so doing offers Zara a distinct strategic advantage over its competitors because of its designation of decision rights and its use of IS to make sure those who make the decisions have the information necessary to make the best decision.[3]

Formal Reporting Relationships and Organization Structures

Organization structure is the way of designing an organization so that decision rights are correctly allocated. The structure of reporting relationships typically reflects the flow of communication and decision making throughout the organization. Traditional organization structures are hierarchical, flat, or matrix. The networked structure is a newer organizational form. A comparison of these four types of organization structures may be found in Figure 3.4.

Hierarchical Organization Structure

As business organizations entered the twentieth century, they found themselves growing and needing to devise systems for processing and storing information. A new class of

[3] Andrew McAfee and Erik Brynjolfsson, "Investing in the IT that makes a Competitive Difference," *Harvard Business Review*, http://harvardbusinessonline.hbsp.harvard.edu; and James Surowiecki, *The Wisdom of Crowds* (New York: Anchor Books, 2005).

	Hierarchical	Flat	Matrix	Networked
Description	Bureaucratic form with defined levels of management	Decision making pushed down to the lowest level in the organization	Workers assigned to two or more supervisors in an effort to make sure multiple dimensions of the business are integrated	Formal and informal communication networks that connect all parts of the company
Characteristics	Division of labor, specialization, unity of command, formalization	Informal roles, planning and control; often small and young organizations	Dual reporting relationships based on function and purpose	Known for flexibility and adaptability
Type of Environment Best Supported	Stable Certain	Dynamic Uncertain	Dynamic Uncertain	Dynamic Uncertain
Basis of Structuring	Primarily function	Very loose	Functions and purpose (i.e., location, product, customer)	Networks
Power Structure	Centralized	Decentralized	Distributed (matrix managers)	Distributed (network)

FIGURE 3.4 Comparison of organizational structures.

worker—the clerical worker—flourished. From 1870 to 1920 alone, the number of clerical workers mushroomed from 74,200 to more than a quarter of a million.[4]

Factories and offices structured themselves using the model that Max Weber observed when studying the Catholic Church and the German army. This model, called a bureaucracy, was based on a hierarchical organization structure.

Hierarchical organization structure is an organizational form based on the concepts of division of labor, specialization, spans of control, and unity of command. Decision rights are highly specified and centralized. When work needs to be done, orders typically come from the top and work is subjected to the division of labor. That means it is segmented into smaller and smaller pieces until it reaches the level of the business in which it will be done. Middle managers do the primary information processing and communicating, telling their subordinates what to do and telling senior managers the outcome of what was done. Jobs within the enterprise are specialized and

[4] Frances Cairncross, *The Company of the Future* (London: Profile Books, 2002).

often organized around particular functions, such as marketing, accounting, manufacturing, and so on. Spans of control indicates the number of direct reports. The new TCS CEO, N. Chandrasekaran, revised the organization structure to lower his span of control by inserting a new layer with only a few leaders reporting directly to him. Unity of command means that each person has a single supervisor, who in turn has a supervisor, and so on. A number of rules are established to handle the routine work performed by employees of the organization. When in doubt about how to complete a task, workers turn to rules. If a rule doesn't exist to handle the situation, workers turn to the hierarchy for the decision. Key decisions are made at the top and filter down through the organization in a centralized fashion. Hierarchical structures, which are sometimes called vertical structures, are most suited to relatively stable, certain environments where the top-level executives are in command of the information needed to make critical decisions. This allows them to make decisions quickly.

IS are typically used to store and communicate information along the lines of the hierarchy and to support the information needs of managers throughout the organization. IS convey the decisions of top managers downward and provide a hierarchy of reports to support organizational operations. Data from the operations is sent upward through the hierarchy using IS. Hierarchical structures are also very compatible with efforts to organize and manage data centrally. The data from operations that have been captured at lower levels and conveyed through IS increasingly need to be consolidated, managed and made secure at a higher level. The data is integrated into databases that are designed so that employees at all levels of the organization can see the information that they need when they need it.

Flat Organization Structure

In contrast to the hierarchical structure, the **flat, or horizontal, organization structure** has less well-defined chain of command. You often don't see an actual organization chart for a flat organization because the relationships are so fluid and the jobs are so ill-defined. That is, drawing an organization chart for a flat organization is like trying to tie a ribbon around a puddle. If you do see an organization chart, you probably won't see many middle managers in it. In flat organizations, everyone does whatever needs to be done in order to complete business. For this reason, flat organizations can respond quickly to dynamic, uncertain environments. Entrepreneurial organizations, as well as smaller organizations, often use this structure because they typically have fewer employees, and even when they grow they initially build on the premise that everyone must do whatever is needed. Teamwork is important in flat organizations. To increase flexibility and innovation, decision rights may not be clearly defined. Hence, the decision making is often decentralized since it is spread across the organization to where the decisions are made. It is also time consuming. As the work grows, new individuals are added to the organization, and eventually a hierarchy is formed where divisions are responsible for segments of the work processes. Many companies strive to keep the "entrepreneurial spirit," but in reality work gets done in much the same way as with the hierarchy described previously. Flat organizations often use IS to off-load certain routine work in order to avoid hiring additional workers. As a hierarchy develops, the IS become the glue tying together parts of the organization that otherwise would not communicate. IS also enable flat organizations to respond quickly to their environment.

Matrix Organization Structure

The third popular form, which Cognizant ultimately adopted, is the **matrix organization structure**. It typically assigns workers to two or more supervisors in an effort to make sure multiple dimensions of the business are integrated. Each supervisor directs a different aspect of the employee's work. For example, a member of a matrix team from marketing would have a supervisor for marketing decisions and a different supervisor for a specific product line. The team member would report to both, and both would be responsible in some measure for that member's performance and development. That is, the marketing manager would oversee the employee's development of marketing skills and the product manager would make sure that the employee develops skills related to the product. Thus, decision rights are shared between the managers. The matrix structure allows organizations to concentrate on both functions and purpose. The matrix structure allows the flexible sharing of human resources and achieves the coordination necessary to meet dual sets of organizational demands. It is suited for complex decision making and dynamic and uncertain environments. IS reduce the operating complexity of matrix organizations by allowing information sharing among the different managerial functions. For example, a saleswoman's sales would be entered into the information system and appear in the results of all of the managers to whom she reports.

Cognizant probably moved to the matrix structure (see Figure 3.1) from a hierarchical structure based on purpose because the complexity of its projects had increased. "As part of the structure of a Cognizant engagement, we always pair our technologists with people who have business context experience," says Raj Mamodia, who was then the Assistant Vice President of Cognizant's Consumer Goods business unit. The purpose of these formally structured relationships is to meet the customer's needs, and not just focus on "how beautiful the technology is in and of itself."[5]

The matrix organization structure carries its own set of weaknesses. Though theoretically each boss has a well-defined area of authority, the employees often find the matrix organization structure frustrating and confusing since they are frequently subjected to dual authority. Consequently working in a matrix organization stucture can be time-consuming since confusion must be dealt with through frequent meetings and conflict resolution sessions. Matrix organizations often make it difficult for managers to achieve their business strategies because they flood managers with more information than they can process.

Networked Organization Structure

Made possible by advances in IT, a fourth type of organization structure emerged: the **networked organization structure**. Networked organizations characteristically

---

[5] Cognizant Computer Goods Technology, "Creating A Culture Of Innovation: 10 Steps To Transform The Consumer Goods Enterprise" (October 2009), 6, http://www.cognizant.com/InsightsWhitepapers/Cognizant_Innovation.pdfm (accessed on April 8, 2012).

feel flat and hierarchical at the same time. An article published in the *Harvard Business Review* describes this type of organization: "Rigid hierarchies are replaced by formal and informal communication networks that connect all parts of the company. . . [This type of organizational structure] is well known for its flexibility and adaptiveness."[6] It is particularly suited to dynamic, unstable environments.

Networked organization structures are those that rely on highly decentralized decision rights and utilize distributed information and communication systems to replace inflexible hierarchical controls with controls based in IS. Networked organizations are defined by their ability to promote creativity and flexibility while maintaining operational process control. Because networked structures are distributed, many employees throughout the organization can share their knowledge and experience, and participate in making key organizational decisions. IS are fundamental to process design; they improve process efficiency, effectiveness, and flexibility. As part of the execution of these processes, data are gathered and stored in centralized data warehouses for use in analysis and decision making. In theory at least, decision making is more timely and accurate because data are collected and stored instantly. The extensive use of communication technologies and networks also renders it easier to coordinate across functional boundaries. In short, the networked organization is one in which IT ties together people, processes, and units.

The organization feels flat when IT is used primarily as a communication vehicle. Traditional hierarchical lines of authority are used for tasks other than communication when everyone can communicate with everyone else, at least in theory. The term used is *technological leveling,* because the technology enables individuals from all parts of the organization to reach all other parts of the organization.

At least portions of Zara's organization structure appear networked. Because it is networked, the store managers can use technology to communicate directly with designers. Zara uses the technology-supported structure to coordinate the actions and decisions of tens of thousands of its employees so that they can focus their attention on the same goal of making and selling clothes that people want to buy.

Other Organizational Structures

An organization is seldom a pure form of one of the four structures described above. It is much more common to see a hybrid structure in which different parts of the organization use different structures depending on their information needs and desired work processes. For example, the IS department may use a hierarchical structure that allows more control over data warehouses and hardware, whereas the R&D department may employ a networked structure to capitalize on knowledge sharing. In the hierarchical IS department, information flows from top to bottom, whereas in the networked R&D department, all researchers may be connected to one another.

---

[6] L. M. Applegate, J. I. Cash, and D. Q. Mills, "Information Technology and Tomorrow's Manager," *Harvard Business Review* (November–December 1988), 128–136.

Further, IS are enabling even more advanced organization forms such as the adaptive organization and the zero time organization.[7] Common to these advanced forms is the idea of agile, responsive organizations that can configure their resources and people quickly. These organizations are flexible enough to sense and respond to changing demands. The zero time organization, for example, describes the concept of instant "customerization," or the ability to respond to customers immediately. It can respond quickly only if it masters five key principles: instant value alignment, instant learning, instant involvement, instant adaptaion, and instant execution. Building in the capability to respond instantly means designing the organization so that each of the key structural elements are able to respond instantly.

Informal Networks

The organization chart reflects the authority derived from formal reporting relationships in the organization's formal structure. However, informal relationships also exist and can play an important role in an organization's functioning. Informal networks, in addition to formal structures, are important for alignment with the organization's business strategy. Some informal relationships are designed by management. For example, when working on a special project, an employee might be asked to let the manager in another department know what is going on. This is considered an informal reporting relationship. Or a company may have a job rotation program that provides employees with broad-based training by allowing them to work a short time in a variety of areas. Long after they have moved on to another job, employees on job rotations may keep in touch informally with former colleagues, or call upon their past co-workers when a situation arises where their input may be helpful. Hewlett Packard's Decision Support and Analytics Servies unit encouraged the development of work-related informal networks when they established focused interest group/forums known as Domain Excellence Platforms (DEPs). An IT-enabled DEP allows at least five people who hold a common interest related to the business to form a team to share their knowledge on a topic (e.g., cloud computing, Web analytics). For non-business related topics, the employees can join conferences to talk about the topic and get to know one another better. The hope is that they will start thinking beyond their work silos.[8]

However, not all informal relationships are a consequence of a plan by management. Some networks unintended by management develop for a variety of other factors including work proximity, friendship, shared interests, family ties, etc. The employoyss can make friends with employees in another department when they play together on the company softball team, share the same lunch period in the company cafeteria, or see one another repeatedly at family gatherings. Informal networks can also arise for political reasons. Employees can cross over departmental, functional, or divisional lines in an effort to create political coalitions to further their goals. Some informal networks even cross organizational boundaries. As computer and information technologies facilitate

---

[7] For more information on zero time organizations, see R. Yeh, K. Pearlson, and G. Kozmetsky, *ZeroTime: Providing Instant Customer Value Everytime, All the Time* (Hoboken, NJ: John Wiley and Sons, 2000).

[8] T. S. H. Teo, R. Nishant, M. Goh, and S. Agarwal "Leveraging Collaborative Technologies to Build a Knowledge Sharing Culture at HP Analytics," *MIS Quarterly Executive* (March 2011), 10(1), 1–18.

Social Business Lens: Social Networks

Social networks are a form of informal networks. They even have begun to supplement and possibly replace organization charts in enterprises. A **social network** is an IT-enabled network that links individuals together in ways that enable them to find experts, get to know colleagues, and see who has relevant experience for projects across traditional organization lines. Much like the networked organization, a social network provides an IT backbone linking all individuals in the enterprise, regardless of their formal title or position. Some might regard a social network as a "super-directory" that provides not only the name of the individuals, but also their role in the company, their title, their contact information, and their location. It might even list details such as their supervisor (and their direct reports and peers), the project(s) they are currently working on, and personal information specific to the enterprise.

What differentiates a social network from previous IT solutions to connect individuals is that it is integrated with the work processes themselves. Conversations can take place, work activities can be recorded, and information repositories linked or just represented within the structure of the social network.

IBM is a good example of how a social network permeates an organization, changing its culture, structure, and collaboration processes. With over 400,000 employees, IBM has a flurry of social activity, with more than 17,000 individual blogs, 1 million daily page views of internal wikis and Web sites, and 400,000 employee profiles on IBM Connections, its social network that allows employees to share status updates, collaborate on internal systems, and share files. There have been 15 million downloads of employee-generated videos and podcasts so far. Employees can find experts and have created a number of topic-specific networks to expose people to new topics and ways of work, and to surface expertise.

Source: Is Social Business the Same as Social Media (December 9, 2011), http://www.forbes.com/sites/haydnshaughnessy/2011/12/09/is-social-business-the-same-as-social-media/ (accessed on April 5, 2012).

collaboration across distances, social networks and virtual communities are formed. Many of these prove useful in getting a job done, even if not all of the members of the network belong to the same organization. LinkedIn is an example of a tool that enables large, global informal networks.

► INFORMATION SYSTEMS AND MANAGEMENT CONTROL SYSTEMS

Controls are the second type of managerial lever. Not only does IS change the way organizations are structured, it also profoundly affects the way managers control their organizations. Management control is concerned with how planning is performed in organizations and how people and processes are monitored, evaluated, and compensated or rewarded. Ultimately it means that senior leaders make sure the things that are supposed to happen actutally happen.

Management control systems are similar to room thermostats. Thermostats register the desired temperature. A sensing device within the thermostat determines if the temperature in the room is within a specified range of the desired temperature. If the temperature is beyond the desired range, a mechanism is activated to adjust the temperature. For instance, if the thermostat is set at 78 and the temperature in the room is 76, then the heater can be activated (if it is winter) or the air conditioning can be turned off (if it is summer). Similarly management control systems must respond to the goals established through planning. Measurements must be taken periodically and if the variance is too great, adjustments must be made to organizational processes or practices. For example, operating processes might need to be changed to achieve the desired goals.

IS offer new opportunities for collecting and organizing data for three management control processes:

1. *Data Collection*: IS enable the collection of information that helps managers determine if they are satisfactorily progressing toward realizing the organization's mission as reflected in its stated goals.

2. *Evaluation*: IS facilitate the comparison of actual performance with the desired performance that is established as a result of planning.

3. *Communication*: IS speed the flow of information from where it is generated to where it is needed. This allows an anlaysis of the situation and a determination about what can be done to correct for problematic situations.

When managers need to control work, IS can play a crucial role. IS provide decision models for scenario planning and evaluation. For example, the airlines routinely use decision models to study the effects of changing routes or schedules. IS collect and analyze information from automated processes, and they can be used to make automatic adjustments to the processes. For example, a paper mill uses IS to monitor the mixing of ingredients in a batch of paper and to add more ingredients or change the temperature of the boiler as necessary. IS collect, evaluate, and communicate information, leaving managers with more time to make decisions.

Planning and Information Systems

In the first chapter the importance of aligning organizational strategy with the business strategy was discussed. An output of the strategizing process is a plan to guide in achieving the strategic objectives. IS can play a role in planning in four ways:

• IS can provide the necessary data to develop the strategic plan. They can be especially useful in collecting data from organizational units and integrating the data in a fashion that they are transformed into information for the strategic decision makers.

• IS can provide scenario and sensitivity analysis through simulation and data analysis.

• Some IS automate the planning process.

• In some instances, an information system is a major component of a strategic plan. That is, as discussed in Chapters 1 and 2, information systems can be used to gain strategic advantage.

Data Collection and Information Systems

In addition to focusing on organizational-level planning and control, the next three subsections in this section focus on the individual level. An important part of management control lies in making sure that individuals perform appropriately. At the individual level, IS can streamline the process of data collection (i.e., monitoring), and support performance measurement and evaluation, as well as compensation through salaries, incentives, and rewards.

Monitoring work can take on a completely new meaning with the use of information technologies. IS make it possible to collect such data as the number of keystrokes, the precise time spent on a task, exactly who was contacted, and the specific data that passed through the process. For example, a call center that handles customer service telephone calls is typically monitored by an information system that collects data on the number of calls each representative received and the length of time each representative took to answer each call and then to respond to the question or request for service. Managers at call centers can easily and nonintrusively collect data on virtually any part of the process. In contrast, a manager of field representatives might also use IS to monitor work, but the use may be more obvious, and, thus, more intrusive. For example, having field sales personnel complete documents detailing their progress adds work for them.

The organizational design challenge in data collection is twofold: (1) to embed monitoring tasks within everyday work, and (2) to reduce the negative impacts to workers being monitored. Workers perceive their regular tasks as value-adding, but have difficulty in seeing how value is added by tasks designed to provide information for management control. Often these tasks are avoided, or worse, data recorded are inaccurate, falsified, or untimely. Collecting monitoring data directly from work tasks—or embedding the creation and storage of performance information into software used to perform work—renders them more reliable.

A large number of software products are available for companies to monitor employees. Software monitoring products are installed by companies to get specific data about what employees are doing. This information can help ensure that work is being perfromed correctly. It can also be used to avoid barriers to employee productivity from "cyberslacking" and "cyberslouching."[9] While the intention may seem both ethical and in the best interest of business, in practice the reverse may actually be true. In many cases employees are not informed that they are being monitored or that the information gleaned is being used to measure their productivity. In these cases, monitoring violates both privacy and personal freedoms. To protect their freedom and to gain their acceptance, employees should be informed when they are monitored, and their bonuses or other rewards should be linked to an increase in productivity derived from the monitoring. In summary, managers need to take into account employee privacy rights and try to balance their right to privacy against the needs of the business to have surveillance mechanisms in place.

---

[9] Bernd Carsten Stahl, "The Impact of the UK Human Rights Act 1008 on Privacy Protection in the Workplace," *Computer Security, Privacy and Politics: Current Issues, Challenges and Solutions*, (Hershey, PA: Idea Group Publishing, 2008), 55–68.

However, prior notice about monitoring may heighten employee stress levels and the control that employers exert over their employees. As employees become aware of monitoring activities, productivity and morale may fall. Also, tracking job performance in terms of discrete, measurable tasks may disconnect workers from the larger business process in which they are involved, giving them less opportunity to broaden their skills and advance in the organization. Breaking down jobs into simple tasks counters an organizational philosophy that seeks to empower individuals to make significant contributions to the company as a whole. While the side effects of monitoring may seem peripheral or trivial, its importance can only increase as technology further intrudes into the workplace and shapes working conditions. Today's managers must be concerned with creating a work atmosphere that is amenable to IS and responsive to employees' needs.

Performance Measurement, Evaluation, and Information Systems

IS make it possible to evaluate actual performance data against reams of standard or historical data, often using models and simulations. Thus, managers can more easily and completely understand work progress and performance. In fact, the ready availability of so much information catches some managers in "analysis paralysis": analyzing too much or too long. In our example of the call center, a manager can compare a worker's output to that of colleagues, to earlier output, and to historical outputs reflecting similar work conditions at other times. Even though evaluation constitutes an important use of IS, how the information is used has significant organizational consequences. Information collected for evaluation may be used to provide feedback so that the worker can improve personal performance; it also can be used to determine rewards and compensation. The former use—for improvement in performance—is nonthreatening and generally welcome.

Using the same information for determining compensation or rewards, however, can be threatening. Suppose the call center manager is evaluating the number and duration of calls service representatives answer on a given day. The manager's goal is to make sure all calls are answered quickly, and he or she communicates that goal to his or her staff. Now think about how the evaluation information is used. If the manager simply provides the workers with information about numbers and duration, then the evaluation is not threatening. Typically, each worker will make his or her own evaluation and respond by improving call numbers and duration. A discussion may even occur in which the service representative describes other important dimensions, such as customer satisfaction and quality. Perhaps the representative takes longer than average on each call because of the attention devoted to the customer. On the other hand, if the manager uses the information about number of calls and duration to rank workers so that top workers are rewarded, then workers may feel threatened by the evaluation and respond accordingly. The representative who is not on the top of the list may shorten calls or deliver less quality, consequently decreasing customer satisfaction. The lesson for managers is to pay attention to what is monitored and how the information is used. Metrics for performance must be meaningful in terms of the organization's broader goals, but these metrics are harder to define when work is decentralized and monitored electronically.

How feedback is communicated in the organization plays a role in affecting behavior. Some feedback can be communicated via IS themselves. A simple example is the feedback built into an electronic form that will not allow it to be submitted until it is properly filled out. For more complex feedback, IS may not be the appropriate vehicle. For example, no one would want to be told they were doing a poor job via e-mail or voice mail. Negative feedback of significant consequence often is best delivered in person.

IS can allow for feedback from a variety of participants who otherwise could not be involved. Many companies provide "360-degree" feedback, in which the individual's supervisors, subordinates, and co-workers all provide input. IS make it relatively easy to solicit feedback from anyone who has access to the system and report it anonymously. Because that feedback is received more quickly, improvements can be made faster.

Incentives and Rewards and Information Systems

Incentives and rewards are the ways organizations encourage good performance. A clever reward system can make employees feel good without paying them more money. IS can affect these processes, too. Some organizations use their Web sites to recognize high performers, giving them electronic badges that are displayed on the social network to identify them as award recipients. Others reward them with new technology. At one organization, top performers get new computers every year, while lower performers get the "hand-me-downs."

IS make it easier to design complex incentive systems, such as shared or team-based incentives. IS make it easier to keep track of contributions of team members and, in conjunction with qualitative inputs, allocate rewards according to complex formulas. For example, in the call center example, tracking metrics, such as "average time per call" and "number of calls answered," allows the manager to monitor agents' performance. This quantitative data makes comparisons easier, but it cannot account for qualitative variables: for example, agents who spend more time handling calls may be providing better customer service. Agents who know they will be evaluated by the volume of calls they process may rush callers and provide poorer service in order to maximize their performance according to the narrow metric. Agents providing the poorest service could in fact be compensated best if the firm's performance evaluation and compensation strategy is linked only to such metrics. The manager must consider both the metrics and qualitative data in assigning compensation and rewards.

▶ INFORMATION SYSTEMS AND CULTURE

The third managerial lever of organizational strategy is culture. Culture is playing an increasingly important role in information system development and use. Since information systems development and use is complicated by human factors, it is important to consider culture's impact on information systems. **Culture** is defined as the set of "shared values and beliefs" that a group holds and that determines how the group perceives, thinks about, and appropriately reacts to its various environments.[10]

---

[10] A. Kinicki, *Organizational Behavior: Core Concepts* (Boston, MA: McGraw-Hill Irwin, 2008), 183.

It is a "collective programming of the mind" that distinguishes not only societies (or nations) but also industries, professions, and organizations.[11] **Beliefs** are the perceptions that people hold about how things are done in their community, while **values** reflect the community's aspirations about the way things should be done. Culture is something of a moving target since it evolves over time as the group solves problems adapting to the environment and internal operations.

Culture has been compared to an iceberg because, like an iceberg, only part of the culture is visible from the surface. In fact, it is necessary to look below the surface to understand the deep-rooted aspects of culture that aren't visible. That is, culture may be thought of in terms of layers: observable artifacts, values, and assumptions. **Observable artifacts** are the most visible level. They include such physical manifestations as traditional dress, symbols in art, acronyms, awards, myths and stories told about the group, rituals, and ceremonies and so on. **Espoused values** are the explicitly stated preferred organizational values. Ideally, they should be consistent with the **enacted values**, which are the values and norms that are actually exhibited or displayed in employee behaviaor. For example, if an organization says that it believes in a a good work-life balance for its employees, but actually requires them to work ten-hour days and on weekends, the enacted values don't match with the espoused ones. The deepest layer of culture is the underlying assumption layer, or the fundamental part of every culture that helps discern what is real and important to the group. **Assumptions** are unobserveable since they reflect organizational values that have become so taken for granted that they guide organizational behavior without any of the group members thinking about them.[12]

Levels of Culture and IT

Culture can vary depending upon which group you are studying. Culture can be found in countries, organizations, or even within organizations. IS development and use can be impacted by culture at all these levels. IS can even play a role in promoting it. For instance, Cognizant used IT to implement "10/10/10," a program designed to keep its associates focused on innovation. On the tenth workday of each month at 10 a.m., everyone's computer screen is frozen, allowing the entire Cognizant workforce to spend ten minutes thinking about and sharing innovative ideas.[13]

A within-organizational level example of culture is when IS developers have values that differ from the clients in the same organization for whom they are developing systems. Clients may favor computer-based development practices that encourage reusability of components that allow flexibility and fast turnaround. Developers, on the other hand, may prefer a development approach that favors stability and control, but tends to be slower. In another example, engineers and operators showed different ways of resisting to the adoption of certain new technologies.

---

[11] G. J. Hofstede, *Culture's Consequences: Comparing Values, Behaviors, Institutions, and Organizations Across Nations*, 2nd ed. (Thousand Oaks, CA: Sage Publications, 2001).

[12] E. Schein, *Organizational Change and Leadership*, 4th ed., (San Francisco, CA: Jossey-Bass, 2010).

[13] Cognizant Computer Goods Technology, "Creating a Culture of Innovation: 10 Steps to Transform the Consumer Goods Enterprise" (October 2009), 1–6.

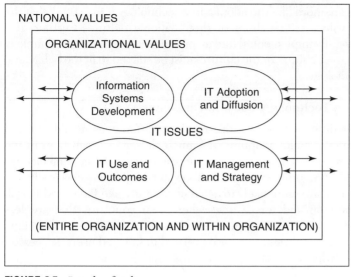

FIGURE 3.5 Levels of culture.
Source: Adapted from Leidner and Kayworth (2006), p. 372, Figure 1.

Both national and organizational cultures can affect the IT issues and vice versa. Differences in national culture may affect IT in a variety of ways impacting information systems development, technology adoption and diffusion, system use and outcomes, and management and strategy. We have shown the relationships in Figure 3.5 and described these impacts below. The model and the discussion of the impact culture on IT issues draws heavily from the work of Leidner and Kayworth.[14]

Culture and Information Systems Development

Variation across national cultures may lead to differing perceptions and approches to IS development. In particular, systems designers may have different perceptions of the end users and how the systems would be used. For example, Danish designers who had more socialist values were more concerned about people-related issues when compared to Canadian designers with more capitalist values. The Canadian designers were more interested in technical issues. National culture may also affect the perceptions of project risk and risk management behaviors. At the organizational level, cultural values can affect the features of then new software and the way it is implemented.

Culture and Information Technology Adoption and Diffusion

National cultures that are more willing to accept risk appear to be more likely to adopt new technologies Those cultures that are less concerned about power differences among people (i.e., have low power distance) are more likely to adopt technologies that help

[14] D. Leidner and T. Kayworth, "A Review of Culture in Information Systems Research: Toward a Theory of Information Technology Culture Conflict," *MIS Quarterly* (2006), 30(2), 357–399.

promote equality. People are more likely to adopt a new technology if they think that the technology's embedded values match those of their national culture. Further, if a technology is to be successfully implemented into an organization, either the technology must fit with the organization's culture or the culture must be shaped to fit the behavioral requirements of the technology.

Culture and Information Technology Use and Outcomes

Research has shown that differences in culture result in differences in the use and outcomes of IT. For example, email adoption was much slower in Japan than in the United States. Japanese prefer richer forms of communication such as meeting face-to-face. The lean email couldn't accommodate the symbols in their language as easily as a fax. Further, in countries that are more likely to avoid uncertainty like Japan and Brazil, IT is used often for planning and forecasting, whereas in countries that are less concerned about risk and uncertainty, IT is more often used for maintaining flexibility. At the organizational level, cultural values are often related to satisfied users, successful IS implementations or knowledge management success.

Culture and Information Technology Management and Strategy

Culture affects planning, governance, and perceptions of service quality at the national and organizational levels. For example, having planning cultures at the top levels of an organization typically signal that strategic systems investment is important.

National Cultural Dimensions and Their Application

Certainly one of the best-known (and prolific) researchers in the area differences in the values across national cultures is Geert Hofstede. Most studies about the impact of national cultures on IS have used Hofstede's dimensions of national culture. Hofstede[15] originally identified four major dimensions of national culture: power distance, uncertainty avoidance, individiualism-collectivism, and masculinity-feminity. To correct for a possible bias toward Western values, a new dimension, Confusian Work Dynamism, also refered to "short-term vs. long-term orientation," was later added.[16] Many others have used, built upon, or tried to correct problems related to Hofstede's four dimensions. One notable project is the GLOBE (Global Leadership and Organizational Behavior Effectiveness) research program, which is a team of 150 researchers who have collected data on cultural values and practices and leadship attributes from over 18,000 managers in 62 countries. The GLOBE project has uncovered nine cultural dimensions, six of which have their origins in Hofstede's pioneering work. The Hofstede dimensions and their relationship to the GLOBE dimensions are summarized in Figure 3.6.

Even though the world may be becoming "flatter," cultual differences have not totally disappeared. But some leadership traits are seen as universally acceptable across

---

[15] G. Hofstede, *Culture's Consequences: International Differences in Work-Related Values* (London: Sage, 1980).

[16] G. Hofstede and M. H. Bond, "The Confucius Connection: from cultural roots to economic growth," *Organizational Dynamics* (1988), 16, 4021.

Hofstede Dimensions (Related GLOBE Dimensions)	Description[a]	Examples of Effect on IT[b]
Uncertainty Avoidance (Uncertainty Avoidance)	Extent to which a society tolerates uncertainty and ambiguity; extent to which members of an organization or society strive to avoid uncertainty by reliance on social norms, rituals, and bureaucratic practices to alleviate the unpredictability of future events.	Countries with high uncertainty avoidance are less likely to adopt new IT and have higher perceptions of project risk than countries with low uncertainty avoidance.
Power Distance (Power Distance)	Degree to which members of an organization or society expect and agree that power should be equally shared.	Individuals from high power distance countries are found to be less innovative and less trusting of technology than individuals from low power distance countries.
Individualism/ Collectivism (Societal and In-Group Collectivism)	Degree to which individuals are integrated into groups; extent to which organizational and societal institutional practices encourage and reward collective distribution of resources and collective action.	Invidualistic cultures are more predisposed than collectivistic cultures to report bad news on troubled IT projects; companies in collectivist societies are more likely than individualistic societies to fill IS position from within the company.
Masculinity/Femininity (General Egalitarianism and Assertiveness)	Degree to which emotional roles are distributed between the genders; extent to which an organization or society minimizes gender role differences and gender discrimination; often focuses on caring and assertive behaviors.	Australian groups (high masculinity) generated more conflict and relied less on conflict resolution strategies than Singaporean groups (low masculinity).
Confucian Work Dynamism (Future Orientation)	Extent to which society rewards behaviors related to long- or short-term orientations; degree to which individuals in organizations or societies engage in future-oriented behaviors such as planning, investing in the future, and delaying gratification.	When considering future orientation studies found differences in the use of Executive Information Systems and the evaluation of service quality across countries.

FIGURE 3.6 National cultural dimensions.

[a] Adapted from R. House, M. Javidan, P. Hanges, and P. Dorfman, "Understanding cultures and implicit leadership theories across the globe: an introduction to project GLOBE," *Journal of World Business* (2002), 37(1), 3–10; and G. Hofstede and G. J. Hofstede, Dimensions of National Culture, http://www.geerthofstede. nl/culture/dimensions-of-national-cultures.aspx.

[b] D. Leidner and T. Kayworth, "A Review of Culture in Information Systems Research: Toward a Theory of Information Technology Culture Conflict," *MIS Quarterly* (2006), 30(2), 357–399.

Geographic Lens: Does National Culture Affect Firm Investment in IS Training?

In a massive study of 6,000 firms in 21 countries, Hilla Peretz and Zehava Rosenblatt found that differences along Hofstede's cultural dimensions do affect employee training. In particular, firms in countries that embrace low power distance (i.e., Germanic countries, Anglo-American countries, the Netherlands, and Israel) tend to invest more in training than firms in countries with high power distance (i.e., some Asian, Latin America, and Middle Eastern countries).

Why might this be the case? Perhaps firms in high power distance societies view investment in training as less favorable because it might narrow the power gaps by making a higher level of skills available across all levels of the organization. Those in power might not want to see a leveling of power throughout the organization.Peretz and Rosenblatt also discovered that firms in countries that had a high future orientation (i.e, some Asian countries) were more likely to invest in training than firms in countries with a low future orientation (i.e., some Anglo-American countries). The researchers think this might be so because training is all about helping employees develop so that they can perform better in the future. Better trained employees help the firm's competitive prospects down the line. Finally, the researchers found that firms in countries with high uncertainty avoidance (i.e., some Hispanic cultures, Japan, South Korea, Israel, and Russia) spend more on training than countries with low uncertainty avoidance (i.e., the United Kingdom, Ireland, Hong Kong, and Singapore)—maybe because employee training may be seen as a way to reduce uncertainty.

While the study was about training in general, the findings are even more likely to hold for IS training. Since IS change so quickly, IS professionals need considerable training to stay current and do their jobs well.

Source: H. Peretz and Z. Rosenblatt, "The role of societal cultural practices in organizational investment in training: a comparative study in 21 countries," *Journal of Cross-Cultural Psychology* (2011), 42(5), 817–831.

cultures such as being trustworthy, just and honest; having foresight and planning ahead; being positive, dynamic encrouaging, and motivational; and being communicative and informed.[17]

The generally accepted view is that the national culture predisposes citizens of a nation to act in a certain way along a Hofstede or GLOBE dimension, such as in an individualistic way in England or in a collectivist way in China. Yet, the extent of the influence of a national culture may vary among individuals, and culturally based

[17] Mansour Javidan and R. J. House, "Cultural Acumen for the Global Manager," *Organizational Dynamics* (2001), 29(4), 289–305.

idiosyncrasies may surface based upon the experiences that shape each person's ultimate orientation on a dimension. Having an understanding and appreciation for cultural values, practices and subtleties can help in smoothing the challenges that occur in dealing with this idiosyncrasies. An awareness of the Hofstede or GLOBE dimensions may help improve communications and reduce conflict.

Effective communication means listening, framing the message in a way that is understandable to the receiver, and responding to feedback. Effective cross-cultural communication involves all of these plus searching for an integrated solution that can be accepted and implemented by members of diverse cultures. This may not be as simple as it sounds. For instance, typical American managers, noted for their high-performance orientation, prefer direct and explicit language full of facts and figures. However, managers in lower performance-oriented countries like Russia or Greece tend to prefer indirect and vague language that encourages the exploration of ideas.[18] Communication differences surfaced when one of this book's authors was designing a database in Malaysia. She asked questions that required a "yes" or "no" response. In trying to reconcile the strange set of responses she received, the author learned that Malaysians are hesitant to ever say "No." Communication in meetings is also subject to cultural differences. In countries with high levels of uncertainty avoidance such as Switzerland and Austria, meetings should be planned in advance with a clear agenda. The managers in Greece or Russia who come from a low uncertainty avoidance culture often shy away from agendas or planned meetings.

Knowing that a society tends to score high or low on certain dimensions helps a manager anticipate how a person from that society might react. However, it only provides a starting point, because each person is different. Importantly, without being aware of cultural differences, it is unlikely that IS will be developed or used effectively.

▶ SUMMARY

- Organizational strategy reflects the use of the managerial levers of organization's design, organizational culture and management control systems that coordinate and control work processes.

- Organizational designers today must have a working knowledge of what information systems can do and how the choice of information system will affect the organization itself.

- Organization structures can facilitate or inhibit information flows.

- Organizational design should take into account decision rights, organization structure and informal networks.

- Structures such as flat, hierarchical, matrix and networked organizations are being enhanced by information technology. Increasingly information technology enables and supports networked organizations that can better respond to dynamic, uncertain organizational environments.

- Information technology affects managerial control mechanisms: planning, data, performance measurement and evaluation, incentives and rewards.

[18] Ibid.

- Management control at the individual level is concerned with monitoring (i.e., data collection), evaluating, providing feedback, compensating, and rewarding. It is the job of the manager to ensure the proper control mechanisms are in place and the interactions between the organization and the information systems do not undermine the managerial objectives.

- Organizational and national culture should be taken into account when designing and using IS.

▶ KEY TERMS

assumptions (p. 90)
beliefs (p. 90)
culture (p. 89)
decision rights (p. 78)
enacted values (p. 90)
espoused values (p. 90)

flat organization
   structure (p. 81)
hierarchical organization
   structure (p. 80)
matrix organization
   structure (p. 82)

networked organization
   structure (p. 82)
observable artifacts (p. 90)
organizational
   strategy (p. 78)
social network (p. 85)
values (p. 90)

▶ DISCUSSION QUESTIONS

1. How might IS change a manager's job?

2. Is monitoring an employee's work on a computer a desirable or undesirable activity from a manager's perspective? From the employee's perspective? Defend your position.

3. Consider the brief description of the zero time organization. What is an example of a control system that would be critical to manage for success in the zero time organization? Why?

4. Mary Kay, Inc., sells facial skin care products and cosmetics around the globe. The business model is to provide one-on-one, highly personalized service. More than 500,000 Independent Beauty Consultants (IBCs) sell in 43 markets worldwide. Each IBC runs his or her own business by developing a client base, and then providing services and products for sale to those clients. Recently the IBCs were offered support through an e-commerce system with two major components: mymk.com and Mary Kay InTouch. Mymk.com allows IBCs to create instant online sites where customers can shop anytime directly with their personal IBC. Mary Kay InTouch streamlines the ordering process by automatically calculating discounts, detecting promotion eligibility, allowing the IBCs to access up-to-date product catalogs, and providing a faster way to transact business with the company.[19]

   a. How would the organizational strategy need to change to respond to Mary Kay's new business strategy?

   b. What changes would you suggest Mary Kay, Inc. managers make in their management systems order to realize the intended benefits of the new systems? Specifically, what types of changes would you expect to make in the evaluation systems, the reward systems, and feedback systems?

---

[19] Adapted from "Mary Kay, Inc.," Fortune, Microsoft supplement (November 8, 1999).

THE MERGER OF AIRTRAN BY SOUTHWEST AIRLINES: WILL THE ORGANIZATIONAL CULTURES MERGE?

Southwest's merger with AirTran, valued at over US$3 billion, makes Southwest the fourth largest American carrier. The merger increases Southwest's presence in a number of major cities, most notably New York (LaGuardia) and Washington D.C. (Ronald Reagan National Airport). Thanks to AirTran, it now flies into the coveted Atlanta's Hartsfield-Jackson Atlanta International, the world's busiest airport, along with a number of international vacation destinations such as Aruba, Puerto Rico and the Bahamas.

Southwest has grown organically, acquiring only two other smaller carriers—Morris Air and Muse Air in the 1980s. This has made it easier to maintain its quirky identity. On the other hand, AirTran was created from several airlines, including the former ValuJet, a little over 10 years ago. It is known mostly as a low-cost, on-time carrier. The Company Culture page on AirTran's Web site prior to the merger claimed that "loyal crew members keep AirTran airways customers soaring" who have a "timely and accommodating demeanor." AirTran's values included a total commitment to safety, technical excellence, continuous learning, fun and profit.[21]

Southwest, headquartered at Love Field in Dallas, uses the ticker symbol LUV and they use all kinds of ways to show that the "Luv" their customers. Southwest has cultivated a corporate culture that focuses on employees and customers having a good time while flying. They carefully select their employees using interviews that involve creative activities and or even asking the recruits to wear tutus. Their training program with karaoke and amusing challenges is designed to socialize the new recruits into Southwest's fun-loving culture. According to its Web site, its cultural values are "A Warrior Spirit, A Servant's Heart, A Fun-Luving Attitude."[22]

"Southwest's whole business model is built on a particular approach to managing employees. It's a big bet they are making that they can swallow AirTran. . . This is a very different approach, taking thousands of AirTran employees, dumping them into the system and hoping it works. It's a pretty risky move," says Peter Capelli, a Wharton management professor in 2010. Cappelli adds that airline mergers are always difficult because integration has to take place while a carrier continues to carry out complex operations. Thousands of employees can't easily be put through an orientation program in the merger's short time frame and the information systems supporting the complex operations of two airlines can't be easily changed.[23]

In November 2011, Southwest Airlines' more than 6,000 pilots and AirTran Airways' 1,700 pilots overwhelmingly approved a plan to combine the seniority lists of the two carriers, with five

---

[20] Written by Parul Acharya.

[21] (www.airtran.com (accessed on April 2011).

[22] Southwest Airlines, http://www.southwest.com/html/about-southwest/careers/culture.html (accessed on January 27, 2012).

[23] "By Acquiring AirTran, Will Southwest Continue to Spread the LUV?" Knowledge@Wharton (October 13, 2010), http://knowledge.wharton.upenn.edu/article.cfm?articleid=2614 (accessed on April 12, 2012); and B. Snyder, "How the Southwest-AirTran Merger Creates a Labor Problem, Published in CBS Money," CBS News (October 5, 2010), http://www.cbsnews.com/8301-505123_162-43642550/how-the-southwest-airtran-merger-creates-a-labor-problem/ (accessed on April 12, 2012).

out of six pilots voting in favor.[24] The personnel systems have to be modified to reflect the new seniority and pay systems.

The disparate cultures of Southwest and AirTran are also posing problems for the merger of their online reservation systems. Southwest currently is planning to switch from Sabre or Amadeus to better accommodate merchandising and international flights. AirTran's reservations system vendor is Navitaire.[25] AirTran and Southwest have diametrically opposed views on distribution through online travel agencies. Southwest usually sells its tickets via telephone or through its Web site whereas AirTran prefers online reservation systems such as Orbitz and Expedia.[26] It will likely take several years after to figure out how to blend the two different reservations systems. Will the cultures of Southwest and Airtran come together? People are optimistic but the real answer lies in the future.

Discussion Questions

1. Discuss the layers of culture that are evident in this case.
2. What are the similarities and dissimilarities between the cultures, values and beliefs of Southwest and AirTran airlines?
3. What problems could arise due to the different perspectives of both airlines towards online reservation systems? What do you recommend the managers do to solve these problems?
4. What would you recommend managers to do insure a smooth integration of the information systems, given the culture differences?

CASE STUDY 3-2

THE FBI

The Federal Bureau of Investigation of the U.S. government, the FBI, was forced to scrap its $170 million virtual case file (VCF) management system. Official reports blamed numerous delays, cost overruns, and incompatible software. But a deeper examination of the cause of this failure uncovered issues of control, culture, and incompatible organizational systems.

Among its many duties, the FBI is charged with the responsibility to fight crime and terrorism. To do so requires a large number of agents located within the Unites States and around the world. That means agents must be able to share information among themselves within the bureau, and with other federal, state, and local law enforcement agencies. But sharing information has never been standard operating procedure for this agency. According to one source, "agents are accustomed to holding information close to their bulletproof vests and scorn the idea of sharing information." This turned

[24] T. Maxon, "Southwest Airlines, AirTran pilots overwhelming approve plan to combine seniority lists," Aviationblog, Dallas News (November 7, 2011), http://aviationblog.dallasnews.com/archives/mergers-consolidation/ (accessed on November 7, 2011); and B. Snyder, "How the Southwest-AirTran Merger Creates a Labor Problem, Published in CBS Money." CBS News (October 5, 2010), http://www.cbsnews.com/8301-505123_162-43642550/how-the-southwest-airtran-merger-creates-a-labor-problem/ (accessed on April 12, 2012).

[25] D. Schall, "Distribution questions loom following US approval of Southwest-AirTran merger," tnooz.com (April, 27, 2011), http://www.tnooz.com/2011/04/27/news/distribution-questions-loom-following-us-approval-of-southwest-airtran-merger/ (accessed on April 12, 2012).

[26] J. Brancatelli, "The Fight Stuff: Why the Airlines Are Fighting Travel Sites," Portfolio.com (January 5, 2011), http://www.portfolio.com/business-travel/2011/01/05/why-legacy-airlines-are-warring-with-expedia-and-orbitz/ (accessed on November 7, 2011).

out to be a real problem in an investigation of DarkMarket, an Internet forum that connected buyers and sellers so that they could exchange stolen information such as bank details and credit card numbers. When both the FBI and Secret Service agents were investigating each other as criminals, it took their British colleagues, who knew the secrets of both agencies, to avert a crisis.

Enter the FBI's efforts to modernize its infrastructure, codenamed "Trilogy." The efforts included providing agents with 30,000 desktop PCs, high-bandwidth networks to connect FBI locations around the world, and the VCF project to facilitate sharing of case information worldwide. The FBI Director explained to Congress that VCF would provide "an electronic means for agents to globally send field notes, documents, pieces of intelligence and other evidence so they could hopefully act faster on leads." It was designed to replace a paper-intensive process with an electronic, Web-based process. With such a reasonable goal, why didn't it work?

The CIO of the FBI offered one explanation. He claimed that the FBI needed to change its culture. "If the Bureau is ever going to get the high-tech analysis and surveillance tools it needs to. . . fight terrorism, we must move from a decentralized amalgam of 56 field offices. . . to a seamlessly integrated global intelligence operation capable of sharing information and preventing crimes in real-time." He added that they were also very distrustful of the technology, as well as others not only in other organizations, but also within the FBI.

A former project manager at the FBI further explained, "They work under the idea that everything needs to be kept secret. But everything doesn't have to be kept secret. To do this right, you have to share information."

The VCF system has been shut down, but the CIO is working on a new approach. He is busy trying to win buy-in from agents in the field so that the next case management system will work. In addition, he is working to establish a portfolio management plan that will cover all of the FBI's IT projects, even those begun in decentralized offices. His team has been designing an enterprise architecture that will lay out standards for a bureauwide information system. The Director of the FBI has helped too. He reorganized the governance of IT, taking IT budget control away from the districts and giving total IT budget authority to the CIO.

The FBI is building a new case management system called Sentinel in four phases. The first two phases have been deployed and, according to the Federal IT dashboard, the project is on schedule and on budget. The new system, according to the CIO, will include workflow, document management, record management, audit trails, access control, and single sign-on. It will provide enhanced information sharing, search, and analysis capabilities to FBI agents and also facilitate information sharing with members of the law enforcement and intelligence communities. To manage the expectations of the agents, the CIO plans to communicate often and significantly increase the training program for the new system. The CIO commented, "We want to automate those things that are the most manually cumbersome for the agents so they can see that technology can actually enhance their productivity. That is how to change their attitudes."

Discussion Questions

1. What do you think were the real reasons why the VCF system failed?
2. What were the points of alignment and misalignment between the Information Systems Strategy and the FBI organization?
3. What do you think of the CIO's final comment about how to change attitudes? Do you think it will work? Why or why not?
4. If you were the CIO, what would you do to help the FBI modernize and make better use of information technology?

Sources: Adapted from Allan Holmes, "Why the G-Men Aren't IT Men," *CIO Magazine* (June 15, 2005), 42–45; and Federal IT dashboard: FBI Sentinnel, http://www.itdashboard.gov/investment?buscid=441.

CHAPTER 4

INFORMATION SYSTEMS AND THE DESIGN OF WORK

IT has drastically changed the way we work. A Work Design Framework is used to explore how IT can be used effectively to support these changes and help make workers more effective. The framework answers the "What," "Who," "Where," and "When" of these changes. In particular, the chapter discusses technologies to support communication and collaboration, new types of work, new ways of doing traditional work, new challenges in managing workers, issues in working remotely, and virtual teams. It concludes with a section on change management.

Best Buy, the leading U.S. retailer in electronics, completely transformed its view of the ordinary workday. Once known for killer hours and herd-riding bosses, it ushered in a new approach to work: Results-Only Work Environment (ROWE). ROWE was the brainchild of two passionate employees who thought that Best Buy managers were mired in analog-age inertia and did not recognize that employees could use technology to perform work from a variety of places. The ROWE developers thought implementing a flextime program "stigmatizes those who use it. . . and keeps companies acting like the military (fixated on schedules) when they should behave more like MySpace (social networks where real-time innovation can flourish)."[1]

ROWE is a program that allows limitless flexibility when it comes to work hours. Employees can choose where and when they will do their work—as long as project goals are satisfied. IS enhance the flexibility of ROWE programs because they make it possible for workers to be away from the office but still connected when needed. Employee decisions about working hours and location are framed by 13 guideposts—the most surprising of which is "Every meeting is optional."

How can Best Buy's approach work? Since the program's implementation, average voluntary turnover has fallen by 45%,[2] whereas productivity is up an average 35% in departments that have switched to ROWE. Overall employee satisfaction is up

---

[1] M. Conlin, "Smashing the Clock," *BusinessWeek* (December 11, 2006), www.businessweek.com/print/magazine/content/06_50/b4013001.htm?chan=gl.

[2] John Hollon, "Weekly Wrap: Best Buy and ROWE—Yes, Flex Work Works, at Least For Them," *TLNT* (March 8, 2011), http://www.tlnt.com/2011/04/08/weekly-wrap-best-buy-and-rowe-yes-flex-work-works-at-least-for-them/ (accessed on February 2, 2012).

as well.[3] This is credited to the greater flexibility in handling the balance between their work and personal lives—a flexibility that would not be possible without IT to keep them connected. Best Buy clearly has adopted one of the most accommodating approaches to work hours, but 79% of employers now allow their employees some flexibility. A third or more of IBM and AT&T employees have no official office, and Sun Microsystems Inc. calculates that it has saved over $400 million in real estate costs by allowing nearly half of its employees to work anywhere they want.[4]

The Best Buy example illustrates how the nature of work is changing before our eyes—and information technology is supporting, if not propelling, the changes. In preindustrial societies, work was seamlessly interwoven into everyday life. Activities all revolved around nature's cyclical rhythms (i.e., the season, day and night, the pangs of hunger) and the necessities of living. The Industrial Revolution changed this. With the advent of clocks and the ability to divide time into measurable, homogeneous units for which they could be paid, people started to separate work from other spheres of life. Their workday was distinguished from family, community, and leisure time by punching a time clock or responding to the blast of a factory whistle. Work was also separated into space as well as time as people started going to a particular place to work.[5]

Technology has now brought the approach to work full circle in that the time and place of work are increasingly blended with other aspects of living. People now can do their work in their own homes at times that accommodate home life and leisure activities. They are able to enter cyberspace—a virtually unlimited space full of opportunities.[6] Paradoxically, however, they want to create a sense of belonging within that space. That is, they wish to create a sense of "place," which is a bounded domain in space that structures their experiences and interactions with objects that they use and others that they meet in this "place." People learn to identify with these places, or locations in space, based on a personal sharing of experiences with others within the space. Over time visitors to the place associate with it a set of appropriate behaviors.[7] Increasingly places are being constructed in space with Web 2.0 tools that encourage collaboration, allowing people to easily communicate on an ongoing basis.

The Information Systems Strategy Triangle, discussed in Chapters 1 and 3, suggests that changing IS results in altered organizational characteristics. Significant changes in IS and the work environments in which they function are bound to coincide with significant changes in the way that companies are structured and how people experience work in their daily lives. Chapter 3 explores how IT influences organizational design. This chapter examines how IT is related to changing the nature of work, the rise of new work environments, and IT's impact on different types of workers where and when they

---

[3] Fpolom's Blog, "ROWE Program at Best Buy" (March 7, 2010), http://fpolom.wordpress.com/2011/03/07/rowe-program-at-best-buy/ (accessed on February 2, 2012).

[4] "Finding Freedom at Work," *Time* (May 30, 2008), http://www.time.com/time/printout/0,8816,1810690,00.html (accessed on June 25, 2008).

[5] S. Barley and G. Kunda, "Bringing Work Back In," *Organizational Science* (2001), 12(1), 76–95.

[6] S. Harrison and P. Dourish, "Re-Place-ing Space: The Roles of Place and Space in Collaborative Systems," *CSCW Proceedings* (1996), 1–11.

[7] C. Saunders, A. F. Rutkowski, M. van Genuchten, D. Vogel, and J. M. Orrega, "Virtual Space and Place: Theory and Test," *MIS Quarterly* (2011), 35(4), 1079–1098.

do their work, and how they work with one another. This chapter looks at how IT enables and facilitates a shift toward collaborative work. The terms *IS* and *IT* are used interchangeably in this chapter, and only basic details are provided on technologies used. The point of this chapter is to look at the impact of IT on the way work is done by individuals and teams. This chapter should help managers understand the challenges in designing technology-intensive work and develop a sense of how to address these challenges and overcome resistance to IT in our rapidly changing world.

▶ WORK DESIGN FRAMEWORK

As the place and time of work becomes less distinguishable from other aspects of people's lives, the concept of "jobs" is changing and being replaced by the concept of work. Prior to the Industrial Revolution, a job meant a discrete task of a short duration with a clear beginning and end.[8] By the mid-20th century the concept of job had evolved into an ongoing, often unending stream of meaningful activities that allowed the worker to fulfill a distinct role. More recently organizations are moving away from organization structures built around particular jobs to a setting in which a person's work is defined in terms of what needs to be done.[9] In many organizations it is no longer appropriate for people to establish their turfs and narrowly define their jobs to only address specific functions. Yet, as jobs "disappear," IT can enable workers to better perform their roles in tomorrow's workplace; that is, IT can help workers function and collaborate in accomplishing work that more broadly encompasses all the tasks that need to be done.

In this chapter a simple framework is used to assess how emerging technologies may affect work. As is suggested by the Information Systems Strategy Triangle (in Chapter 1), this framework links the organizational strategy with IS decisions. This framework is useful in designing key characteristics of work by asking key questions and helping identify where IS can affect how the work is done. Consider the following questions:

- *What work will be performed?* Understanding what tasks are needed to complete the process being done by the worker requires an assessment of specific desired outcomes, inputs, and the transformation needed to turn inputs into outcomes. Many types of work are based upon recurring operations such as those found in manufacturing plants or service industries. The value chain helps understand the workflow for key tasks that are performed (i.e., purchasing, materials handling, manufacturing, customer service, repair). Increasingly work involves managing knowledge, which typically displays different patterns of tasks. Understanding changes in tasks helps better understand changes in the nature of work.

- *Who is going to do the work?* Sometimes the work can be automated. However, if a person is going to do the work, who should that person be? What skills are needed? From what part of the organization should that person come? If a team is going to do the work, many of these same questions need to be asked. However, they are asked within the context of the team: Who should be on the team? What skills do the team members need? What parts of the organization need to be represented by the team? Will the team members be dispersed?

---

[8] William Bridges, *JobShift: How to Prosper in a Workplace without Jobs* (New York: Addison-Wesley, 1995).
[9] Ibid.

- *Where will the work be performed?* With the increasing availability of networks, Web 2.0 tools, and the Internet, managers can now design work for workers who are not physically near them. Does the work need to be performed locally at a company office? Can it be done remotely at home? On the road?

- *When will the work be performed?* In many parts of the world, a job between 9-5 is an anomaly. Increasingly we are seeing companies adopting flexible scheduling such as Best Buy did. The reality of modern technologies is that they often tether employees to a 24 hours a day/7 days a week (24/7) schedule where they always have to respond to their mobile.

- *How can IT increase the effectiveness of the workers doing the work?* How can IT help workers communicate with other workers to get the work done? How can IT support collaboration? What can be done to increase the acceptance of IT-induced change? In this text the overarching questions are how to leverage IT to help improve work and how to keep IT from inhibiting work. Sometimes this means automating certain tasks. For example, computers are much better at keeping track of inventory, calculating compensation, and many other repetitive tasks that are opportunities for human error. On the other hand, ITs provide increasing support for communication and collaboration tasks among workers.

Figure 4.1 shows how these questions can be used in a framework to incorporate IS into the design of work. Although it is outside the scope of this chapter to discuss the current research on either work or job design, the reader is encouraged to read these rich literatures.

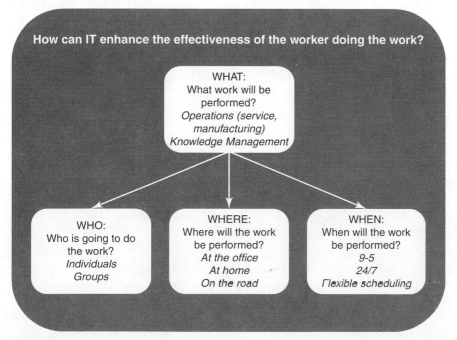

FIGURE 4.1 Framework for work design.

▶ HOW INFORMATION TECHNOLOGY SUPPORTS COMMUNICATION AND COLLABORATION

Though it may seem like putting the cart before the horse, the discussion will respond to the last question in Figure 4.1 first. This is because many of the changes that are described in later sections of this chapter have been supported, if not propelled, by IT. Some of these technologies such as social networking and blogs seem to have been introduced into the workplace by digital natives when they started their first full-time jobs. However, businesses are still trying to get a handle on how these technologies can be applied to work-related applications. Figure 4.2 describes major technologies that have affected communications in today's work environment.

The IT support for communication is considerable and growing. It includes technologies such as e-mail, intranets, instant messaging, VoIP, video teleconferencing, unified communications, RSS, virtual private networks, and file transfer.

In addition to communication, collaboration also is a key task in many work processes. IS greatly changed how collaboration is done. It is important for an organization's survival. Thomas Friedman, the author of the popular *The World is Flat*, and other books, argues that collaboration is the way that small companies can "act big" and flourish in today's flat world. The key to success is for such companies "to take advantage of all the new tools for collaboration to reach farther, faster, wider and deeper."[10] Collaboration tools include social networking sites, virtual worlds, Web logs (blogs), wikis, and groupware. They often leverage collaboration by increasing available connections. The major collaboration tools also are described in Figure 4.2.

▶ HOW INFORMATION TECHNOLOGY CHANGES THE NATURE OF WORK

Advances in IT provide an expanding set of tools that make individual workers more productive and broaden their capabilities. They transform the way work is performed—and the nature of the work itself. This section examines three ways in which new IT alters employee life: by creating new types of work, by enabling new ways to do traditional work, and by supporting new ways to manage talent.

Creating New Types of Work

IT often leads to the creation of new jobs or redefines existing ones. The high-tech field emerged in its entirety over the past 60 years and has created a wide range of positions in the IT sector, such as programmers, analysts, IT managers, hardware assemblers, Web site designers, software sales personnel, social media specialists, and IT consultants. A study based on the Bureau of Labor Statistics places the number of IT workers in the United States at an all-time high of 4.1 million workers.[11] Even within traditional non-IT

---

[10] Thomas L. Friedman, *The World is Flat* (New York: Farrar, Straus and Giroux, 2005), 145.

[11] Association of Information Technology Professionals, "IT Employment reaches an all-time high" (February 8, 2012), http://www.aitp.org/news/news.asp?id=83261&hhSearchTerms=statistics (accessed on April 10, 2012).

IT	Description
COMMUNICATION	
E-mail (electronic mail)	*Means of transmitting messages over communication networks.* It was one of the first uses of the Internet and still constitutes a good portion of Internet traffic.
Intranet	*Network that looks and acts like the Internet, but it is comprised of information used exclusively with a company and unavailable to the general public via the Internet.* It is a password-protected set of interconnected nodes that is under the company's administrative control.
Instant messaging (IM)	*Internet protocol (IP)–based application that provides real-time text-based communication between people using a variety of different device types, including computer-to-computer and mobile devices.* It can identify which "buddies" have a "presence" and are able to receive messages at the moment.
Voice over Internet Protocol (VoIP)	*Method for taking analog audio signals (i.e., those used in phone calls) and turning them into digital data that can be transmitted over the Internet.* It is rapidly gaining in popularity because of the free VoIP software that is available with proprietary systems such as Skype. It allows people to make free Internet phone calls without using the phone company.
Video teleconference (also called videoconference)	*Set of interactive telecommunication technologies that simultaneously allows two or more locations to interact via two-way video and audio transmissions.* It can be analog, digital, or use Internet Protocol (Web conference).
Unified communications (UC)	*Suite of products that provides a consistent unified user interface and user experience across multiple devices and media types.* Unified communications offer a streamlined interface in which such technologies as cell phones, fax machines, personal computers, VoIP, instant messaging, file transfers, collaborative workspaces, teleconferencing, e-mail, and videoconferencing meld together to form a collaborative communications environment.
Virtual private network (VPN)	*Network that primarily uses a public telecommunication infrastructure, such as the Internet, to provide remote offices or traveling users access to a central organizational network.* With a VPN, users at remote sites are treated as if they were on a local network. If the various sites of the VPN are owned by a single company, they are often referred to as a corporate intranet. However, if they are owned by different companies, the VPN may be called an extranet.

FIGURE 4.2 IT tools for communication and collaboration.

Really Simple Syndication or RSS (also called Web feeds)	*Structured file format for porting data from one platform or information system to another.* RSS allows the user to aggregate frequently updated data such as news, blog entries, changing stock prices, and recent changes on wiki pages into one easily manageable location, as well as to receive regular data updates at timely intervals.
File Transfer	*Means of transferring a copy of a file from one computer to another on the Internet.* The most common procedure, file transfer protocol (FTP), allows entire files—even large ones—to be transferred over the Internet more quickly and securely than with e-mail.

COLLABORATION

Social Networking Site	*Web-based service that allows its members to create a public profile with their interests and expertise, post text and pictures and all manner of data, list other users with whom they share a connection, and view and communicate openly or privately with their list of connections and those made by others within the system.* These sites are particularly useful for forming ad hoc groups, networking, locating potential business allies, or searching for jobs.
Virtual World	*Electronic environment that visually mimics complex three-dimensional physical spaces, where people can interact with each other and with virtual objects, and where people are represented by animated characters called avatars.* Most virtual worlds are characterized by creativity, interactivity, collaboration, and three-dimensionality. They allow users to collaborate virtually by having their avatars meet and talk on the screen.
Web Logs (blogs)	*On-line journals that link together into a very large network of information sharing.* Blogs discuss a wide range of topics and provide news and information to potentially thousands of individuals connected with an event or situation.
Wiki	*Software that allows users to work collaboratively to create, edit, and link Web pages easily.* Wikis are especially good for supporting multimedia content, keeping track of multiple revisions of a document, and for collaboration on writing a document. The best-known wiki effort is the collaborative encyclopedia Wikipedia.
Groupware	*Software that enables group members to work together on a project, even from remote locations, by supporting group decision making, information processing, and simultaneous file access.* Calendars, documents, e-mail messages, databases, decision-making tools, and meetings are popular applications.

FIGURE 4.2 (Continued)

organizations, the growing reliance on IS creates new types of jobs, such as knowledge managers who manage firms' knowledge systems (see Chapter 11 for more on knowledge management), community managers who manage the firm's online communities, and communications managers, who manage the use of communication technologies for the business. IS departments also employ individuals who help create and manage the technologies, such as systems analysts, database administrators, network administrators, and network security advisors. The Internet has given rise to many other types of jobs, such as Web masters and site designers. Virtually every department in every business has someone who "knows the computer" as part of their job.

New Ways to Do Traditional Work

Changing the Way Work Is Done

IT has changed the way work is done. Many traditional jobs are now done by computers. For example, computers can check spelling of documents, whereas traditionally that was the job of an editor or writer. Jobs once done by art and skill are often greatly changed by the introduction of IT. Workers at one time needed an understanding of not only what to do, but also how to do it; now their main task often is to make sure the computer is working because the computer does the task for them. Sadly, many cashiers no longer seem to be able to add, subtract, or take discounts because they have grown so used to letting the computer in POS terminal do the calculations for them. Workers once were familiar with others in their organization because they passed work to them; now they may never know those co-workers because the computer routes the work. In sum, the introduction of IT into an organization can greatly change the day-to-day tasks performed by the workers in the organization.

In her landmark research, Shoshana Zuboff describes a paper mill, where papermakers' jobs were radically changed with the introduction of computers.[12] The papermakers mixed big vats of paper and knew when the paper was ready by the smell, consistency, and other subjective attributes of the mixture. For example, one worker could judge the amount of chlorine in the mixture by sniffing and squeezing the pulp. They were masters at their craft, but they were not able to explicitly describe to anyone else exactly what was done to make paper. The company, in an effort to increase productivity in the papermaking process, installed an information and control system. Instead of the workers looking at and personally testing the vats of paper, the system continuously tested parameters and displayed the results on a panel located in the control room. The papermakers sat in the control room, reading the numbers, and making decisions on how to make the paper. Many found it much more difficult, if not impossible, to make the same quality paper when watching the control panel instead of personally testing, smelling, and looking at the vats. The introduction of the information system resulted in different skills needed to make paper. Abstracting the entire process and displaying the results on electronic readouts required skills to interpret the measurements, conditions, and data generated by the new computer system.

[12] Shoshana Zuboff, *In the Age of the Smart Machine: The Future of Work and Power* (New York: Basic Books, 1988), 211.

In another example, salespeople at a snack company have portable terminals that not only keep track of inventory, but also help them in the selling function. Prior to the information system, the salespeople used manual processes to keep track of inventory in their trucks. When visiting customers, it was only possible to tell them what was missing from their shelves and to replenish any stock they wanted. With IT, the salespeople have become more like marketing and sales consultants, helping the customers with models and data of previous sales, floor layouts, and replenishment as well as forecasting demand based on analysis of the data histories stored in the IS. The salespeople need to do more than just be persuasive. They now must also do data analysis and floor plan design, in addition to using the computer. Thus, the skills needed by the salespeople, as well as the workflow, have greatly changed with the introduction of IT.

One of the biggest changes in workflow has been in the area of data entry. In the past the workflow included capturing the data, keying it into the system, rekeying it to check its accuracy, and then processing it. The workflow is now changed to capture the data directly when it is entered by the user in a variety of ways including on the Web, with a GPS signal, or by reading the RFID code. A program may check its accuracy when it is captured and then it is processed. Thus, the steps in the workflow are drastically reduced and the process is much faster.

The Internet enables changes in many types of work. For example, within minutes, financial analysts can download an annual report from a corporate Web site to their smartphones and check what others have said about the company's growth prospects. They can automatically receive RSS Web feeds for stock updates from Google every few seconds. Librarians can check the holdings of other libraries online and request that particular volumes be routed to their own clients, or download the articles from a growing number of databases. Marketing professionals can pretest the reactions of consumers to potential products in virtual worlds. Sales jobs are radically changing to complement online ordering systems. Technical support agents diagnose and resolve problems on client computers using the Internet and software from Motive Communications. The cost and time required to access information has plummeted, increasing personal productivity and giving workers new tools. It is hard to imagine a job today that doesn't have a significant information systems component.

Changing Communication Patterns

All one has to do is observe people walking down a busy downtown street or a college campus to note changes in communication patterns over a period as short as the last decade. Some people are talking on their cell phones, but even more are texting or using apps for all kinds of reasons such as checking out game scores, specials at nearby restaurants, or movie times. Or observe what happens when a plane lands. It is possible that as many as half the people on the plane whip out their portable devices or cell phones as soon as the plane touches down. They are busy making arrangements to meet the people who are picking them up at the airport or checking to see the calls they missed while in flight. Finally, consider meeting a friend at a busy subway station in Hong Kong. It is virtually impossible, without the aid of a cell phone, to locate one another.

Applications (Apps) such as Skype, Twitter, and Sina Weibo (Chinese Twitter) have changed how people communicate. Traditionally, people found each other in person to have a conversation. With the telephone, people called each other. Along came e-mail, which rapidly became the communication technology of choice since it decoupled the time the sender sends the message from the time the recipient receives it. Today, people have an array of communications technology and once again IT is changing communication patterns. Some rely on texting, others on Skype, still others on social networks such as Facebook or Renren for their primary communications channel. The challenge created by the large number of choices is that it's now much more difficult to communicate with others. Individuals now have to have a presence in numerous platforms in order to ensure they can be contacted. Worse still is that one must not only know how to contact someone, but the preferred medium might change during the day, week, or month. For example, while during normal business hours, an employee might prefer to receive an e-mail or a phone all. After hours, he might prefer a text, and late at night, while surfing the Web, he may prefer a chat line, or Facebook message, or even Skype. Without knowledge of the recipients' preferences for how to receive the message, the sender is likely to be unsuccessful in communicating with the recipient over the proper channel. If a sender doesn't know which medium the recipient prefers, he might use one medium (e.g., e-mail) to see if the recipient minds using another medium (e.g., phone).

Similarly, IT is changing the communication patterns of workers. There are still some workers who do not need to communicate with other workers for the bulk of their workday—however that workday is defined. For example, many truck drivers do not interact with others in their organization. But consider the example of a Walmart driver who picks up goods dropped off by manufacturers at the Walmart distribution center and then delivers those goods in small batches to each of the Walmart stores. Walmart has connected its drivers with radios and satellites so that they can pick up goods from manufacturers on the return trip after they have dropped off their goods at the Walmart stores. In this way, Walmart saves the delivery charges from that manufacturer and conserves energy in the process. Walmart drivers use IT to save money by enhancing their communications with suppliers.[13]

Changing Organizational Decision Making and Information Processing

IT changes not only organizational decision-making processes, but also the information used in making those decisions. Data processed to create more accurate and timely information are being captured earlier in the process. Through technologies such as RSS Web feeds, information that they need to do their job can be pushed to them.

IT can change the amount and type of information available to workers. For example, salespeople can use technology to get quick answers to customer questions. Further, Web 2.0 tools allow salespeople to search for best practices on a marketing topic over a social network and to benefit from blogs and wikis written by informed employees in their company. Furthermore, organizations now maintain large historical

---

[13] Thomas L. Friedman, *The World is Flat* (New York: Farrar, Straus and Giroux, 2005), 145.

business databases, called data warehouses, which can be mined by using tools to analyze patterns, trends, and relationships in the data warehouses. We discuss data management in Chapter 11.

In their classic 1958 *Harvard Business Review* article, Leavitt and Whisler boldly predicted that IT would shrink the ranks of middle management by the 1980s.[14] Because of IT, top-level executives would have access to information and decision-making tools and models that would allow them to easily assume tasks previously performed by middle managers. Other tasks clearly in the typical job description of middle managers at the time would become so routinized and programmed because of IT that they could be performed by lower-level managers. As Leavitt and Whisler predicted, the 1980s saw a shrinking in the ranks of middle managers. This trend was partly attributable to widespread corporate downsizing. However, it was also attributable to changes in decision making induced by IT. Since the 1980s, IT has become an even more commonly employed tool of executive decision makers. IT has increased the flow of information to these decision makers and provided tools for filtering and analyzing the information.

Changing Collaboration

Whereas decision making in organizations is often viewed as deliberate and distinct acts, an increasing amount of work being performed by teams is definitely more fluid.[15] Teams have learned to collaborate by continually structuring and restructuring their work—constantly adjusting their highly entwined actions—to respond to their ever-evolving environments.

IT helps make work more team-oriented and collaborative. Technologies such as blogs, virtual worlds, wikis, social networking, and video teleconferencing provide collaborative applications that facilitate creating groups that form around a large number of goals at a rate much faster than ever before. Workers can more easily share information with their teammates. They can send documents over computer networks to others, and they can more easily ask questions using e-mail or instant messaging.

The president of a New York-based marketing firm, CoActive Digital, decided to implement a wiki to have a common place where 25 to 30 people could go to share a variety of documents ranging from large files to meeting notes and PowerPoint presentations.[16] An added benefit is that the wiki is encrypted, protected, and used with a VPN. The president recognized that the challenge for implementing the wiki would be to change a culture in which e-mail had long been the staple for communication. Consequently, he decided to work closely with the business leader of the business development group. This group handles inquiries from customers and coordinates how the work (i.e., marketing campaigns) gets done internally. The group has lots of meetings and lots of work that needs to be shared. He populated the wiki site with documents that had been traded over e-mail, such as meeting notes, and with relevant documents and

---

[14] Harold Leavitt and Thomas Whisler, "Management in the 1980s," *Harvard Business Review* (November–December 1958), 41–48.

[15] S. Barley and G. Kunda, "Bringing Work Back In," *Organizational Science* (2001), 12(1), 76–95.

[16] C. G. Lynch, "How a Marketing Firm Implemented an Enterprise Wiki," *CIO.com*, http://www.cio.com/article/print/413063 (accessed on July 9, 2008).

asked the business leader to encourage her group members to use the wikis. It took some effort, but eventually the group learned to appreciate the benefits of the wiki for collaboration.

Verifone's company culture is one that encourages information sharing. A story is told of a new salesperson who was trying to close a particularly big deal. He was about to get a customer signature on the contract when he was asked about the competition's system. Being new to the company, he did not have an answer, but he knew he could count on the company's information network for help. He asked his customer for 24 hours to research the answer. He then sent a note to everyone in the company asking the questions posed by the customer. The next morning, he had several responses from others around the company. He went to his client with the answers and closed the deal. What is interesting about this example is that the "new guy" was treated as a colleague by others around the world, even though they did not know him personally. He was also able to collaborate with them instantaneously. It was standard procedure, not panic time, because of the culture of collaboration in this company. With increased use of social networks and other social tools, instantaneous collaboration is commonplace.[17]

The Internet greatly enhances collaboration. Beyond sharing and conversation, teams can also use the Internet and Web 2.0 to create something together. An example here is the well-known Web-based site Wikipedia. Further, teams can undertake collective action that creates a situation for its members to share something and make something happen For example, IBM's ThinkPlace, is an open intranet forum for presenting, developing, and implementing ideas throughout the company. Once an idea is posted on ThinkPlace, it is immediately available for comments and suggestions by other employees. Since the third quarter of 2005 when it was launched, more than 160,000 users introduced over 18,000 ideas. Of the more than 350 ideas that were already adopted, savings of over $500 million were generated. Typically the ideas start small and morph into inexpensive implementable ideas. For instance, in response to a question about recapturing third-party software licenses that had been lost when employees left the company, a formal license tracking process was proposed that led to the transfer of licenses to employees who could use them. Further discussion led to an implementation as a mashup, or combination of data, presentation, or functionality from two or more sources, which was sponsored by an IBM director responsible for the Situational Applications Environment.[18]

Changing the Ways to Connect

Probably one of the biggest changes that people are experiencing as a result of new technologies is that they are always connected. In fact, many feel tethered to their mobile phones or laptop to the extent that they must be available at all times to respond to requests from their boss or customers. As a result the boundaries between work and play are being blurred and people often struggle with work-life balance.

---

[17] Hossam Galal, Donna Stoddard, Richard Nolan, and Jon Kao, "VeriFone: The Transaction Automation Company," Harvard Business School case study 195–088.

[18] A. Majchrzak, L. Cherbakov, and B. Ives, "Harnessing the Power of the Crowds with Corporate Social Networking Tools: How IBM Does It," *MIS Quarterly* (2009), 8(2), 103–108.

Businesses are still trying to get their arms around the technological advances that are becoming so commonplace. Many in the workforce find that their technology at home differs from that at work. Whereas many use social media tools on their iPads, laptops, or smartphones during the weekend at home, they find themselves on Monday mornings staring into a black screen with green letters on a monitor attached to a desktop that has little Internet connectivity.[19] They find this quite bothersome. In fact, a recent Cisco Systems survey of young professionals and college students found that one in three believes the Internet is as important as air, water, food, and shelter and two in five say they would accept a lower-paying job that had more flexibility with regard to device choice, social media access, and mobility over a higher-paying job with less flexibility.[20] In commenting on the survey findings, Marie Hattar, vice president, Enterprise Marketing, Cisco, stated:

> "The results of the Cisco Connected World Technology Report should make businesses re-examine how they need to evolve in order to attract talent and shape their business models. Without a doubt, our world is changing to be much more Internet-focused, and becomes even more so with each new generation."

Hattar believes this has implications for CIOs:

> "CIOs need to plan and scale their networks now to address the security and mobility demands that the next generation workforce will put on their infrastructure, and they need to do this in conjunction with a proper assessment of corporate policies."[21]

CIOs have the ability to drastically improve productivity by making available directories of knowledge holders with these newer social media tools. Consider IBM's SmallBlue—an opt-in social network analysis tool that maps the knowledge and the connections of IBM employees. SmallBlue can be used to find employees with specific knowledge or skills, display employee networks on particular topics, validate a person's expertise based on their corporate profile, and display a visualization of an employees' personal social networks. IBM claims that SmallBlue has promoted innovation, effectiveness, and efficiency.[22]

The preceding examples show how IS are a key component in the design of work. IS can greatly change the day-to-day tasks, which in turn change the skills needed by workers. The examples show that adding IS to a work environment change the way work is done.

[19] Cognizant, "The Future of Work has Arrived: Time to Re-Focus IT" (February 2011), 1–15, http://www.cognizant.com/approach/SiteDocuments/The_Future_of_Work_next-generation_solutions.pdf (accessed on April 8, 2012)

[20] Cisco Connected World Technology Report, 2011 Findings, http://www.cisco.com/en/US/netsol/ns1120/index.html#~2011 (accessed on February 4, 2012).

[21] "Air, Food, Water, Internet—Cisco Study Reveals Just How Important Internet and Networks Have Become as Fundamental Resources in Daily Life," http://newsroom.cisco.com/press-release-content?type=webcontent&articleId=474852 (accessed on February 4, 2012).

[22] A. Majchrzak, L. Cherbakov, and B. Ives, "Harnessing the Power of the Crowds with Corporate Social Networking Tools: How IBM Does It," MIS Quarterly (2009), 8(2), 103–108.

Social Business Lens: Activity Streams

An activity stream is a list of activities on a Web site that, in a brief manner, highlight what the individuals connected to that stream are doing. Activity streams can include posts by individuals who share what they are doing or thinking and posts directly by other programs, which deposit an update about what an individual is doing. By collecting all of these posts in a single feed, the activity stream gives the reader a good sense of what is happening in a community.

An example of an activity stream is the news feed in Facebook, or Chatter offered by Salesforce.com. One company that implemented an activity stream inside its business is SAS, the international statistical software company based in North Carolina. They have about 11,800 employees and a Web-based collaboration space for internal wikis and about 600 blogs. They added an activity stream to spark conversations that link the other resources with individuals who need them. It created an internal company activity stream that mimics the news feed on a Facebook user's home page. It also links to the company's identity-management and document-management systems. When combined with the other social IT tools used by SAS, employees can easily share, comment on, or 'like' a Web page they find in their system or on the larger Web, and it will show up in the company's activity stream.

Companies who incorporate activity streams in their social business platform report that teams using it have fewer in person meetings, reduced e-mail, faster information flows, better collaboration, and increased responsiveness.

Source: David F. Carr, "SAS Creates Internal Facebook with Socialcast," *InfoWeek* (April 29, 2011), http://www.informationweek.com/thebrainyard/news/social_networking_private_platforms/229402527/sas-institute-creates-internal-facebook-with-socialcast (accessed on April 5, 2012).

New Challenges in Managing People

New working arrangements create new challenges in how workers are supervised, evaluated, compensated, and even hired. When most work was performed individually in a central location, supervision and evaluation were relatively easy. A manager could directly observe the employee who spent much of his or her day in an office. It was fairly simple to determine whether or not the employee was present and productive.

Modern organizations often face the challenge of managing a workforce that is spread across the world, working in isolation from direct supervision, and working more in teams. Rather than working in a central office, many salespeople labor remotely and rely on laptop computers, Web 2.0, and smart phones to link them to customers and their office colleagues. The technical complexity of certain products, such as enterprise software, necessitates a team-based sales approach combining the expertise of many individuals; it can be difficult to say which individual closed a sale, making it difficult to apportion individual-based rewards.

	Traditional Approach: Subjective Observation	Newer Approach: Objective Assessment
Supervision	Personal and informal. Manager is usually present or relies on others to ensure employee is present and productive.	Electronic or assessed by deliverable. As long as the employee is producing value, he does not need formal supervision.
Evaluation	Focus is on process through direct observation. Manager sees how employee performs at work. Subjective (personal) factors are very important.	Focus is on output by deliverable (e.g., produce a report by a certain date) or by target (e.g., meet a sales quota). As long as deliverables are produced and/or targets achieved, the employee is meeting performance expectations adequately. Subjective factors may be less important and are harder to gauge.
Compensation and Rewards	Often individually based.	Often team-based or contractually spelled out.
Hiring	Personal with little reliance on computers. Often more reliance on clerical skills.	Often electronic with recruiting Web sites and electronic testing. More information-based work that requires a higher level of IT skills.

FIGURE 4.3 Changes to supervision, evaluations, compensation, and hiring.

One technological solution, electronic employee monitoring (introduced in Chapter 3), replaces direct supervision by automatically tracking certain activities, such as the number of calls processed, e-mail messages sent, or time spent surfing the Web. Direct employee evaluation can be replaced, in part, by pay-for-performance compensation strategies that reward employees for deliverables produced or targets met, as opposed to subjective factors such as "attitude" or "teamwork." These changes are summarized in Figure 4.3.

The introduction of ROWE at Best Buy illustrates the need to change from an approach where managers watch employees and count the hours they spend at their desks, to one that focuses instead on the work they actually do. Best Buy's Senior Vice President, John "J.T." Thompson admitted, "For years I had been focused on the wrong currency. I was always looking to see if people were here. I should have been looking at what they were getting done."[23] He changed his mind when he realized that the benefits the ROWE program offered—and the managerial changes that it commanded.

[23] M. Conlin, "Smashing the Clock," *BusinessWeek* (December 11, 2006), www.businessweek.com/print/magazine/content/06_50/b4013001.htm?chan=gl.

Hiring is also different because of IT for four reasons. First, in IT-savvy firms, workers must either know how to use the technologies that support the work of the firm before they are hired, or they must be trainable in the requisite skills. Hiring procedures incorporate activities that determine the skills of applicants. For example, a company may ask a candidate to sit at a computer to answer a basic questionnaire, take a short quiz, or simply browse the Web to evaluate the applicant's skill level, or they may only accept applications submitted to a Web site.

Second, IT utilization affects the array of non-technical skills needed in the organization. Certain functions—many clerical tasks, for example—can be handled more expeditiously, so fewer workers adept in those skills are required. IT-savvy companies can eliminate clerical capabilities from their hiring practices and focus resources on more targeted skills.

Third, IT has become an essential part of the hiring process for many firms. Advertisements for positions are posted on the Web, and applicants send their resumes over the Web, complete applications on-line, or send potential employers to their Web sites. Companies, when researching candidates, often look at their Facebook pages (and in many cases, they do not like what they see). Social networking also involves informal introductions and casual conversations in cyberspace. Virtual interviews can be arranged in virtual worlds or via teleconferencing to reduce recruiting costs. A face-to-face interview is usually eventually required, but recruiters can significantly increase their chances of finding the right applicant with initial virtual interviews.

Fourth, companies increasingly realize that hiring is changing and that recruiting efforts should reflect the new approaches people are using to look for jobs. Tech-savvy job applicants are now using business-oriented social networks such as LinkedIn to seek out contacts for jobs and online job search engines like Monster.com and CareerBuilder.com to find job listings. A new Facebook app, BeKnown, provides a profile detailing an individual's work experience, a news feed for contact updates and actions, a search tool to locate people and connect with them, a way to recommend other users or display badges earned for completing certain professional goals. The app also is integrated with Monster.coms job listings.[24]

The design of the work needed by an organization is a function of the skill mix required for the firm's work processes and of the flow of those processes themselves. Thus, a company that infuses technology effectively and employs a workforce with a high level of IT skills designs itself differently from another company that does not. The skill mix required by an IT-savvy firm reflects greater capacity for using the technology itself. It requires less of certain clerical and even managerial skills that are leveraged by technical capacity. It may also deploy skills according to different ratios in central and local units.

New IT also challenges employee skills. Employees who cannot keep pace are increasingly unemployable. As many lower-level service or clerical jobs become partially automated, only those workers able to learn new technologies and adapt to changing work practices can anticipate stability in their long-term employment.

---

[24] Kristin Burnham, "Monster.com bring professional social networking to Facebook," CIO.com (July 15, 2011), http://blogs.cio.com/print/16406 (accessed on February 2, 2012).

Firms institute extensive training programs to ensure their workers possess the skills to use IT effectively.

As workforce demographics shift, so do the IT needs and opportunities to change work. Digital natives, those employees who have grown up using computers, social networking sites, texting, and the Web as a normal, integrated part of their daily lives, are finding new and innovative ways to do their work. There are all sorts of impacts from the skills these employees bring to their work, including how to do their work in a new, and often more efficient, manner.

IT has drastically changed the landscape of work today. As a result of IT, many new jobs were created. In the next section, we examine how IT can change where work is done, when it is done, and who does it.

▶ HOW INFORMATION TECHNOLOGY CHANGES WHERE AND WHEN WORK IS DONE AND WHO DOES IT

This section examines another important effect of IT on work: the ability of some workers to work anywhere, at any time. At the individual level, we focus on tele-commuters and mobile workers. At the group level we focus on virtual teams.

Telecommuting and Mobile Work

The terms *telecommuting* and *mobile worker* are often used to describe flexible work arrangements. **Telecommuting**, sometimes called teleworking, refers to work arrangements with employers that allow employees to work from home, at a customer site, or from other convenient locations instead of coming into the corporate office. The term *telecommute* is derived from combining "telecommunications" with "commuting," hence these workers use telecommunications instead of commuting to the office. **Mobile workers** are those who work from wherever they are. They are outfitted with the technology necessary for access to coworkers, company computers, intranets, and other information sources. We use the term "remote workers" when we are referring to both telecommuters and mobile workers.

Factors Driving Use of Telecommuting

Telecommuting has been around since the 1970s, but since the late 1990s it has steadily been gaining popularity. In 2008, according to World at Work, more than 17.2 million Americans and 33.7 million people worldwide telecommuted. This number of American telecommuters is expected to increase by an additional 29 million telecommuters, or 43% or the workforce, in 2016 as more work is performed from remote locations.[25] One poll of 11,300 employees in 22 countries found that one out of six telecommute worldwide. Several factors that drive this trend are shown in Figure 4.4.

[25] The actual statistics for the number of telecommuters is hard to find. The figures were obtained from Suite Commute, http://www.suitecommute.com/research-and-statistics/statistics/of-telecommuters-in-us (accessed on February 2, 2012 and February 13, 2012); and Smart Planet, http://www.smartplanet.com/blog/business-brains/one-sixth-of-the-worlds-employees-now-telecommute-survey/21616 (accessed on February 14, 2012).

Geographic Lens: How Do People Around the World Feel About Working Remotely?

A recent survey by Cisco found marked national differences about how professionals viewed their ability to be productive when working remotely. While on average 39% of the 1,303 professionals in 13 countries surveyed answered "yes" when asked if it was necessary for them to be in the office to make decisions more effectively and efficiently (i.e., nothing replaces daily in-person interaction), only 7% answered "yes" in India, whereas 56% and 57% answered "yes" in Japan and Germany, respectively. That is, a large percentage of people in Japan and Germany thought they had to come into the physical office to be productive. This wasn't the case at all in India. A very small percentage of Indians felt they had to be tethered to a desk in a physical office. They could do their work by staying connected to their workplaces through a variety of devices including their laptops, tablets, and smartphones.

Source: *The Cisco Connected World Report* (October 2010), http://newsroom.cisco.com/dlls/2010/ekits/ccwr_final.pdf (accessed on February 4, 2012).

First, work is increasingly knowledge based. The United States and many other world economies continue to shift from manufacturing to service industries. Equipped with the right IT, employees can create, assimilate, and distribute knowledge as effectively at home as they can at an office. The shift to knowledge-based work thus tends to minimize the need for a particular locus of activity.

Second, telecommuters often time-shift their work to accommodate their lifestyles. For instance, parents modify their work schedules to allow time to take their children to school and extracurricular activities. Telecommuting provides an attractive alternative

Driver	Effect
Shift to knowledge-based work	Eliminates requirement that certain work be performed in a specific place.
Changing demographics and lifestyle preferences	Provides workers with geographic and time-shifting flexibility.
New technologies with enhanced bandwidth	Makes remotely performed work practical and cost effective.
Reliance on Web	Provides workers with the ability to stay connected to co-workers and customers, even on a 24/7 basis.
Energy concerns	Reduces the cost of commuting (for telecommuters), energy costs associated with real estate (for companies), and travel costs (for companies and for people on virtual teams).

FIGURE 4.4 Driving factors of telecommuting and virtual teams.

for parents who might otherwise decide to take leaves of absence from work for child rearing. Telecommuting also enables persons housebound by illness, disability, or the lack of access to transportation to join the workforce.

Telecommuting also may provide employees with enormous geographic flexibility. The freedom to live where one wishes, even at a location remote from one's corporate office, can boost employee morale and job satisfaction. As a workplace policy, it may also lead to improved employee retention. For example, Best Buy workers use the ROWE program as part of its recruiting pitch. Further, productivity and employee satisfaction for those on the ROWE program are markedly higher, and voluntary turnover is down. Many employees can be more productive at home, and they actually work more hours than if they commuted to an office. Furthermore, such impediments to productivity as traffic delays, canceled flights, bad weather, and mild illnesses become less significant. Companies enjoy this benefit, too. Those who build in telecommuting as a standard work practice are able to hire workers from a much larger talent pool than those companies who require geographical presence.

The third driving factor of telecommuting is that the new technologies, which make work in remote locations viable, are becoming better and cheaper. For example, prices of personal computers continue to drop, and processing power roughly doubles every 18 months.[26] The drastic increase in capabilities of portable technologies makes mobile work more effective and productive. Telecommunication speeds are increasing exponentially at the same time that the costs for connectivity are plummeting. The Web offers an easy-to-use "front-end" to sophisticated "back-office" applications used by major corporations, such as those that run on mainframe computers.

A fourth driving factor is the increasing reliance on Web-based technologies by all generations, but especially the younger generations, such as Generation Y and the Millennials. The younger generations are at ease with Web-based social relationships and are adept at using social networking tools to grow these relationships. Web-based tools allow them to stay connected with their co-workers and customers. Further, as more and more organizations turn to flexible working hours such as the ROWE program implemented by Best Buy and as 24/7 becomes the norm in terms of service, the Web becomes the standard platform to allow workers to respond to customers' increasing demands.

A fifth factor is the mounting emphasis on conserving energy. As the cost of gasoline continues to skyrocket, employees are looking for ways to save money. Telecommuting is quite appealing in such a scenario, especially when public transportation is not readily available. Companies can also experience lower energy costs from telecommuting. SAP reduced its global greenhouse footprint by encouraging employees to shift their commuting behavior. As a result of SAP's ongoing efforts, emissions from employees' commutes dropped by 14% in 2010. In addition to telecommuting and encouraging the use of mass transit and carpooling, SAP also began providing employees with

---

[26] Gordon Moore, head of Intel, observed that the capacity of microprocessors doubled roughly every 12 to 18 months. Even though this observation was made in 1965, it still holds true. Eventually, it became known in the industry as Moore's law.

information on their carbon footprint from commuting through a new internal dash-board aimed at ensuring greater transparency and accountability.[27]

Many workers no longer need to be tied to official desks. Thus, real estate needs of their employers are shrinking. Further, energy is no longer needed to heat or cool these office spaces. Companies are realizing that they can comply with the Clean Air Act and be praised for their "green computing" practices at the same time they are reaping considerable cost savings.

Disadvantages of Telecommuting

Telecommuting also has some disadvantages. Remote work challenges managers in addressing performance evaluation and compensation. Managers of telecommuters must evaluate employee performance in terms of results or deliverables. Virtual offices make it more difficult for managers to appreciate the skills of the people reporting to them, which in turn make performance evaluation more difficult. For the many telecommuting tasks that do not produce well-defined deliverables or results, or those where managerial controls typically prove inadequate, managers must rely heavily on the telecommuter's self-discipline. As a result, managers may feel they are losing control over their employees, and some telecommuting employees do, in fact, abuse their privileges. Managers accustomed to traditional work models in which they are able to exert control more easily may strongly resist telecommuting. In fact, managers are often the biggest impediment to implementing telecommuting programs. Of course, if they can also be one of the biggest drivers if they support the telecommuting programs.

Workers who go to an office or who must make appearances at customer locations have a structure that gets them up and out of their home. Telecommuters, on the other hand, must exert a high level of self-discipline to ensure they get the work done. Working from home, in particular, is full of distractions such as personal phone calls, visitors, and inconvenient family disruptions. A telecommuter must carefully set up a home-work environment and develop strategies to enable quality time for the work task.

Telecommuters often opt for the increased flexibility in work hours that remote work offers them. They are lured by the promise of being able to work around the schedules of their children or other family members. Paradoxically, because of their flexible work situation, it is often difficult for them to separate work from their home life. Consequently, they may work many more hours than the standard nine-to-five worker, or experience the stress of trying to separate work from play. As a matter of fact, one of the reasons higher-ups at Best Buy were not immediately informed about the ROWE experiment is because employees were concerned that overbearing bosses would expect them to always be working, and middle of the night phone calls would become routine.[28]

[27] SAP Sustainability Report, Greenhouse Gas Footprint, http://www.sapsustainabilityreport.com/greenhouse-gas-footprint (accessed on February 2, 2012).
[28] M. Conlin, "Smashing the Clock," *BusinessWeek* (December 11, 2006), www.businessweek.com/print/magazine/content/06_50/b4013001.htm?chan=gl.

Working remotely can disconnect employees from their company's culture and make them feel isolated. The casual, face-to-face encounters that take place in offices transmit extensive cultural, political, and other organizational information. These encounters are lost to an employee who seldom, if ever, works at the office. Consequently, telecommuters need to undertake special efforts to stay connected. They must engage in forms of conversation to replace "water cooler" talk. This could take the form of instant messaging, telephone calls/conferences, e-mail, blogs, or even video conferencing or unified communications. They should also schedule regular visits to the office.

Not all jobs are suitable for telecommuting. Some jobs may require the worker to be at the work location. Basically only those job aspects that can be performed independently at remote locations are the most suitable for telecommuting. Further, the employees selected to staff telecommuting jobs must be self-starters. They must be responsible for completing work tasks without being in the corporate office. New employees who need to be socialized into the organization's practices and culture are not good candidates for mobile or remote work.

Virtual work also raises the specter of **offshoring,** or foreign outsourcing of software development and computer services. Once a company establishes an infrastructure for remote work, the work often can be performed abroad as easily as domestically. U.S. immigration laws limit the number of foreigners who may work in the United States since the terrorist attacks in New York City and Washington, D.C., on September 11, 2001. However, no such limitations exist on work performed outside this country by workers who then transmit their work to the United States electronically. Because such work is not subject to minimum wage controls, companies may have a strong economic incentive to outsource work abroad. Companies find it particularly easy to outsource clerical work related to electronic production, such as data processing and computer programming. Benefits and potential problems associated with telecommuting are summarized in Figure 4.5.

Employee Advantages of Telecommuting	Potential Problems
Reduced stress due to increased ability to meet schedules and less work-related distractions	Increased stress from inability to separate work life from home life
Higher morale; lower absenteeism	Harder to evaluate performance
Geographic flexibility	Employee may become disconnected from company culture
Higher personal productivity	Telecommuters are more easily replaced by offshore workers
Housebound individuals can join the workforce	Not suitable for all jobs or employees

FIGURE 4.5 Advantages and disadvantages of telecommuting.

Managerial Issues in Remote Work

Remote work requires managers to undertake special planning, staffing, and supervising activities. In terms of planning, business and support tasks must be redesigned to support remote workers. Everyday business tasks such as submitting employee expense reports in person (as is common when an original signature is needed on the form) and attending daily progress meetings are inappropriate if most of the workers are remote. Support tasks such as fixing computers by dispatching someone from the central IS department may not be feasible if the worker is in a hotel in a remote city. Basic business and support processes must be designed with both the remote worker and the worker remaining in the office in mind. Because remote workers may not be able to deal with issues requiring face-to-face contact, office (non-remote) workers may find that they are asked to assume additional tasks. Training should be offered to remote workers and office workers alike so that they can anticipate and understand the new work environment.

Managers must find new ways to evaluate and supervise those employees without seeing them every day in the office. Typically this means judging their work on the basis of targeted output, and not based on how remote workers do the work. They must also work to coordinate schedules, ensure adequate communication among all workers, establish policies about use of different technologies to support communications, and help their organizations adapt by building business processes to support remote workers.

Security is another issue for remote workers. Typically it is a "BYOD" (Bring Your Own Device) world where remote workers have their own computers in the location where they work that may or may not have been issued by their employers. Remote workers pose a threat to office workers because if they come into the office with an infected computer and plug into the network, perimeter security technology is unable protect all the other workers connected to the network. Further, as demonstrated by the Department of Veterans Affairs (VA) employee whose laptop carrying unencrypted, sensitive personal information on more that 2.2 million active-duty military personnel was stolen from the employee's home, remote workers can be the source of security breaches.[29] It is impossible for organizations to make remote workers totally secure. However, managers need to get more involved in assessing the areas and severity of risk and take appropriate steps, via policies, education, and technology, to reduce the risks and make those remote workers as secure as possible.

The development, posting, and enforcement of remote worker policies are vital in a world where security breaches are commonplace. These policies should incorporate such simple rules as never store sensitive information on a laptop, encrypt all information once it leaves the office and only systems with virus detection software can be used on company networks. If an organization does not wish to adhere to these strict guidelines, then it at least needs to develop remote workers' policies that define

[29] Robert Lemos, "VA Data Theft Affects Most Soldiers," *Security Focus* (June 7, 2006), http://www.securityfocus.com/brief/224 (accessed on May 7, 2012).

what software is allowed on the home-based computer and what data can be stored on the computer. Further, employees must be made aware of the policies through a well-planned education program.[30]

One approach to make sure that remote workers understand the security policy, and to make them accountable, is to have them sign an agreement with employers on exactly how their computers are to be used and maintained. In addition, antivirus and antispyware software should be deployed on computers used by remote workers and a desktop firewall and SSL (Security Socket Layer) for authentication should be added. Many government-issued computers are even equipped with Absolute Software's Computrace—"the LoJack of computer hardware" to trace the location of a missing or stolen computer.[31] But IS leaders are aware that even with the best policies and tools available, breaches occur. The IS organizations typically has many levels of security to sense and respond to threats.

Virtual Teams

Employees are not only working remotely on an independent basis, but also with remote members on virtual teams. **Virtual teams** are defined as two or more people who (1) work together interdependently with mutual accountability for achieving common goals, (2) do not work in either the same place and/or at the same time, and (3) must use electronic communication technology to communicate, coordinate their activities, and complete their team's tasks. Initially, virtual teams were seen as the opposite of conventional teams that meet face-to-face. However, it is now realized that it is simplistic to view teams as either meeting totally face-to-face or totally virtually. Rather, teams may reflect varying degrees of virtuality, depending on some combination of points 2 and 3. Thus, virtual team members may be in different locations, organizations, time zones, or time shifts. Further, virtual teams may have distinct, relatively permanent membership, or they may be relatively fluid as they evolve to respond to changing task requirements and as members leave and are replaced by new members.

Virtual teams are thought to have a life cycle.[32] Their lifecycle, shown in Figure 4.6, is noteworthy because it highlights the cyclical nature of virtual teams and the importance of team development. Teams are formed, their work is completed, and the team is disbanded. But in this cycle, team members learn to work not only with specific individuals, but also how to work in virtual teams. So, the concept of disbanding and then forming new teams with the same people or new ones make the concept of team development very important.

---

[30] Mary J. Culnan, Ellen R. Foxman, and Amy W. Ray, "Why IT Executives Should Help Employees Secure Their Home Computers," *MIS Quarterly Executive* (March 2008), 7(1), 49–56, http://test.misqe.org/ojs/index.php/misqe/article/view/161.

[31] Cara Garretson, "Heightened Awareness, Reinforced Products Advance Teleworker's Security," *Network World* (February 20, 2007), http://www.networkworld.com/news/2007/022007-heightened-awareness.html?ap1=rcb (accessed on May 7, 2012).

[32] G. Hertel, S. Geister, and U. Konradt, "Managing virtual teams: a review of current empirical research," *Human Resource Management Review* (2005), 15, 69–95.

Phase	Preparation	Launch	Performance Management	Team Development	Disbanding
Key Activities	Mission statement Personnel selection Task design Rewards system Technology selection and installment	Kick-off meetings Getting acquainted Goal clarification Norm development	Leadership Communication Conflict resolution Task accomplishment Motivation Knowledge management Norm enforcement and shaping	Assessment of needs/deficits Individual and/or team training Evaluation of training effects Trust building	Recognition of achievements Re-integration of team members

FIGURE 4.6 Key activities in the life cycle of virtual teams.

Factors Driving Use of Virtual Teams

The same drivers that apply to telecommuting, listed in Figure 4.4, can also be applied to virtual teams. Virtual teams clearly offer advantages in terms of expanding the knowledge base through team membership. Thanks to new and ever-emerging communication and information technologies, managers can draw team members with needed skills or expertise from around the globe, without having to commit to huge travel expenses. That is, difficulties in getting relevant stakeholders together physically are relaxed. Further, virtual teams can benefit from *following the sun*. In an example of following the sun, London team members of a virtual team of software developers at Tandem Services Corporation initially code the project and transmit their code each evening to U.S. team members for testing. U.S. members forward the code they tested to Tokyo for debugging. London team members start their next day with the code debugged by their Japanese colleagues, and another cycle is initiated.[33] Increasingly, growing pressure for offshoring has resulted in systems development by global virtual teams whose members are located around the world.

Disadvantages and Challenges of Virtual Teams

There are some clear disadvantages to virtual teams. For example, different time zones, although helpful when following the sun, can work against virtual team members when they are forced to stay up late or work in the middle of the night to communicate with team members in other time zones. Further, security is harder to ensure with distributed workers. There also are a considerable number of challenges, that if not correctly

[33] Marie-Claude Boudreau, Karen Loch, Daniel Robey, and Detmar Straub, "Going Global: Using Information Technology to Advance the Competitiveness of the Virtual Transnational Organization," *Academy of Management Executive* (1998), 12(4), 120–128.

managed could turn into disadvantages. A summary of these challenges in comparison with more traditional teams can be found in Figure 4.7.

Virtual teams face major communication challenges by because they primarily have to communicate electronically via e-mail, teleconferences, or messaging systems.

Challenges	Virtual Teams (VT)	Traditional Teams
Communication	• Multiple time zones can lead to greater efficiencies when leveraged, but can also create communication difficulties in terms of scheduling meetings and interactions. • Communication dynamics such as facial expressions, vocal inflections, verbal cues, and gestures are altered.	• Teams are collocated in same time zone. Scheduling is less difficult. • Teams may use richer communication media, including face-to-face discussions.
Technology	• Team members must have proficiency across a wide range of technologies; VT membership may be biased toward individuals skilled at learning new technologies. • Technology offers an electronic repository that may facilitate building an organizational memory. • Work group effectiveness may be more dependent on the ability to align group structure and technology with the task environment.	• Technology is not critical for group processes. Technological collaboration tools, while possibly used, are not essential for communications. Team members may not need to possess these skills. • Electronic repositories are not typically used. • Task technology fit may not be as critical.

Team Diversity	• Members typically come from different organizations and/or cultures. This makes it:
	  • Harder to establish a group identity
	  • Necessary to have better communication skills
	  • More difficult to build trust, norms, and shared meanings about roles, because team members have fewer cues about their teammates' performance
	  • More likely that they have different perceptions about time and deadlines
		• Because members are more homogeneous, group identity is easier to form.
		• Because of commonalities, communications are easier to complete successfully.

FIGURE 4.7 Comparison of challenges facing virtual teams and traditional teams.

Electronic media allow team members to transcend the limitations of space and even store messages for future reference. But electronic communications may not allow team members to convey the nuances that are possible with face-to-face conversations. Thus, conflict may be more likely to erupt in virtual environments, and trust may be slower to form. In addition, virtual teams differ from traditional teams in terms of technological and diversity challenges. For example, traditional teams, unlike virtual ones, may not have to deal with the hassles of learning new technologies or selecting the technology that is most appropriate for the task at hand. Perhaps the greatest challenges that virtual teams face in comparison to their more traditional counterparts arise from the diversity of the team members. Virtual teams enable members to come from many different cultures and nations. Even though this diversity allows managers to pick team members from a wider selection of experts, global virtual teams are more likely than more traditional teams to be stymied by team members who have different native languages and cultures.

Managerial Issues in Virtual Teams

Managers cannot manage virtual teams in the same way that they manage more traditional teams. The differences in management control activities are particularly pronounced. Leaders of virtual teams cannot easily observe the behavior of virtual team members. Thus, monitoring of behavior is likely to be more limited than in traditional teams. As is the case with remote workers, performance is more likely to be evaluated in terms of output than on displays of behavior. Because the team members are dispersed, providing feedback is especially important—not just at the end of a team's project, but throughout the team's life. To encourage the accomplishment of the team's goal, compensation should be based heavily on the team's performance, rather than just on individual performance. Compensating team members for individual performance may result in "hot-rodding" or lack of cooperation among team members. Organizational reward systems must be aligned with the accomplishment of desired team goals. This alignment is especially difficult when virtual team members belong to different organizations, each with their own unique reward and compensation systems. Each compensation system may affect individual performance in a different way. Managers need to be aware of differences and discover ways to provide motivating rewards to all team members. Further, policies about the selection, evaluation, and compensation of virtual team members may need to be enacted.

Looking beyond these management control activities, we see that prescriptions for managing the communications and information technologies in virtual team environments are limited. The rest of this section is devoted to managing the challenges highlighted in Figure 4.7: communication, technology, and diversity.

Communication Challenges

Considerable research has focused on ways to overcome communication challenges. Because the distances are often great, managers clearly need to keep the channels of communication open to allow team members to get their work done. Some communication tasks lend themselves to certain technologies. This means that they must have the necessary technological support. For instance, if a team leader wants to have a meeting of team members but has neither the budget nor the lead time to plan for extensive travel to the meeting, video teleconferencing may be a viable alternative. SAP claimed a drop of 425kTons of greenhouse gas emission in the first quarter after asking their employees to consider alternatives to business flights.[34] E-mails and texts are excellent for short messages to one or all group members. Team leaders may decide to initiate a team's activity with a face-to-face meeting so that the seeds of trust can be planted and team members feel as if they know one another on a more personal basis.

Face-to face meetings also appear to be the heartbeat of successful global virtual teams.[35] An in-depth study of three global virtual teams, found that the two effective teams created a rhythm organized around regularly scheduled face-to-face meetings. Before each meeting there was a flurry of communication and activity as team members prepared for the meeting. After the meeting there were a considerable number of follow-up messages and tasks. The ineffective team did not demonstrate a similar pattern. Since not all teams can meet face-to-face, well-managed synchronous meetings using video teleconferencing, or possibly in a virtual world, can activate the heartbeat.

Because team leaders cannot always see what their team members are up to or if they are experiencing any problems, frequent communications are important. If team members are quiet, the team leader must reach out to them to encourage their participation and to ensure that they feel their contributions are appreciated. Further, team leaders can scrutinize the team's asynchronous communications and team's repository to evaluate and give feedback about each team member's contributions. Even though a majority of team members are in one location, the team leader should rotate meeting times to alternate the convenience among team members. Further, in the event that there is a larger group of team members in one or several places, the team leader should encourage these subgroups to have all their discussions online so remote members will not feel isolated.

Technology Challenges
Having the needed communication and information technologies available, mean that all team members have the same or compatible technologies at their locations. The support staff to maintain and update the systems must be in place. Managers must ensure that seamless telephone transfers to the home office, desktop support, network connectivity, and security support are provided to the remote workers. Team members (like telecommuters) must have access to the files and applications they need to do their work. The importance of security for remote work cannot be overstated.

---

[34] SAP Sustainability Report, "Greenhouse Gas Footprint," http://www.sapsustainabilityreport.com/greenhouse-gas-footprint (accessed on March 2, 2012).

[35] M. L. Maznevski and K. Chudoba, "Bridging Space Over Time: Global Virtual Team Dynamics and Effectiveness," *Organization Science* (2000), 11(5), 373–392.

Further, managers must also provide the framework for using the technology. Policies and norms, or unwritten rules, need to be established about how the team members should use the technology to work with one another.[36] These should include norms about telephone, e-mail, and videoconferencing etiquette (i.e., how often to check for messages, the maximum time to wait to return e-mails, warning team members about absences or national holidays), work to be performed, and so on. Such norms are especially important when team members are not in the same office and cannot see when team members are unavailable.

Diversity Challenges

Managers may also seek to provide technologies to support diverse team member characteristics. For example, team members from different parts of the globe may have different views of time.[37] Team members from Anglo-American cultures (i.e., United States, United Kingdom, Canada, Australia, New Zealand) may view time as a continuum from past, to present and future. For such team members, each unit of time is the same, and thus they can be interchanged with one another or used as a basis for pay. These team members are likely to be concerned with deadlines and often prefer to complete one task before starting another (i.e., monochronous). For team members who are conscious of deadlines, planning and scheduling software may be especially useful. In contrast, team members from India often have a cyclical view of time. They do not get excited about deadlines and there is no hurry to make a decision because it is likely to cycle back—at which time the team member may be in a better position to make the decision. Many people from India tend to be polychronous. Team members who are polychronous and prefer to do several activities at one time may want to have instant messaging or Skype (a voice-over-IP support system) available to them so that they can communicate with their teammates and still work on other tasks.

In addition to providing the appropriate technologies, managers with team members who have different views of time need to be aware of the differences and try to develop strategies to motivate those who are not concerned with deadlines to deliver their assigned tasks on time. Or the managers may wish to assign these team members to do tasks that are not sensitive to deadlines.

Of course, views of time are only one dimension of diversity. Other dimensions of diversity are discussed in Chapter 3. Although diversity has been demonstrated to lead to more creative solutions, it also makes it harder for team members to learn to trust one another, to communicate, and to form a group identity. Through open communications, managers may be able to uncover and deal with other areas of diversity that negatively affect the team. Managers may establish an expertise directory at the start of the team's life or encourage other ways of getting team members to know more about one another.

---

[36] C. Saunders, C. Van Slyke, and D. R. Vogel, "My Time or Yours? Managing Time Visions in Global Virtual Teams," *Academy of Management Executive* (2004), 18(1), 19–31.

[37] Ibid.

▶ GAINING ACCEPTANCE FOR IT-INDUCED CHANGE

The changes described in this chapter no doubt alter the frames of reference of organizational employees and may be a major source of concern for them. Employees may resist the changes if they view the changes as negatively affecting them. In the case of a new information system that they do not fully understand or are not prepared to operate, they may resist in several ways:

- They may deny that the system is up and running.
- They may sabotage the system by distorting or otherwise altering inputs.
- They may try to convince themselves, and others, that the new system really will not change the status quo.
- They may refuse to use the new system where its usage is voluntary.

Managing Change

To help avoid these resistance behaviors, John Kotter[38] builds upon Lewin's change model of unfreezing, changing, and refreezing. Kotter recommends eight specific steps in bringing about change. Kotter's steps are related to Lewin's changes and listed in Figure 4.8.

Managers should keep in mind these eight steps as they introduce change into their workplaces. Very importantly they need to make clear why the change is being made prior to the actual change and they must follow the change with reinforcement behaviors such as rewarding those employees who have successfully adopted new desired behaviors.

Technology Acceptance Model and Its Variants

To avoid the negative consequences of resistance to change, those implementing change must actively manage the change process and gain acceptance for new IS. To help explain how to gain acceptance for a new technology, Professor Fred Davis and his colleagues developed the Technology Acceptance Model (TAM). Many variations of TAM exist, but its most basic form is displayed on the right-hand side in Figure 4.9. TAM suggests that managers cannot get employees to use a system until they want to use it. To convince employees to want to use the system, managers may need to employ unfreezing tactics to change employee attitudes about the system. Employee attitudes may change if employees believe that the system will allow them to do more or better work for the same amount of effort (perceived usefulness), and that it is easy to use. Training, documentation, and user support consultants are external variables that may help explain the usefulness of the system and make it easier to use.

---

[38] John Kotter, *Leading Change* (Boston, MA: Harvard Business School Press, 1996).

Lewin's Stage	Unfreezing	Changing	Refreezing
Definition	*Creating motivation to change*	*Providing stakeholders with new information, systems, products, or services*	*Reinforcing change by integrating stakeholder's changed behaviors and attitudes into new operations resulting from change*
Kotter's Steps	1. Establish a sense of urgency: Create a compelling reason why change is needed. 2. Create the guiding coalition: Select a team with enough expertise and power to lead the change. 3. Develop a vision and strategy: Use the vision and strategic plan to guide the change process. 4. Communicate the change vision: Devise and implement a communication strategy to consistently convey the vision.	5. Empower broad-based action: Encourage risk-taking and creative problem solving to overcome barriers to change. 6. Generate short-term wins: Celebrate short-term improvements and reward contributions to change effort. 7. Consolidate gains and produce more change: Use credibility from short-term wins to promote more change so that change cascades throughout the organization.	8. Anchor new approaches in the culture: Reinforce change by highlighting areas where new behaviors and processes are linked to success.

FIGURE 4.8 Stages and steps in change management.

TAM has many variants. For example, one variant considers subjective norms,[39] whereas another adds attitudes toward behaviors.[40] The Unified Theory of Acceptance and Use of Technology makes a valiant effort to integrate the many fragmented findings about TAM.[41] Another attempt to integrate the many findings is TAM3.[42] A simplified version of TAM3 is shown in Figure 4.9. The left-hand side of Figure 4.9 provides the four categories of determinants of perceived usefulness and perceived ease of use.

[39] V. Venkatesh and F. D. Davis, "A Theoretical Extension of the Technology Acceptance Model: Four Longitudinal Field Studies," *Management Science* (2000), 45(2), 186–204.

[40] S. Taylor and P. Todd, "Assessing IT Usage: The Role of Prior Experience," *MIS Quarterly* (1995), 19(2), 561–570.

[41] V. Venkatesh, M. G. Morris, G. B. Davis, and F. D. Davis, "User acceptance of information technology: Toward a unified view," *MIS Quarterly* (2003), 27(3), 425–478.

[42] V. Venkatesh and H. Bala, "Technology Acceptance Model 3 and a Research Agenda on Interventions," *Decision Sciences* (2008), 39(2), 273–315.

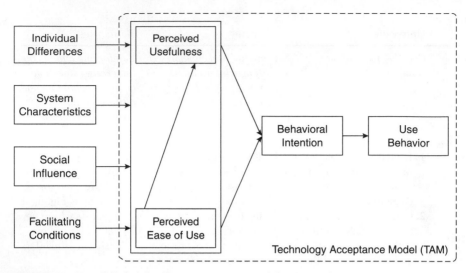

FIGURE 4.9 Simplified technology acceptance model 3 (TAM3).
Source: Viswanath Venkatest and Hillol Bala, "Technology Acceptance Model 3 and a Research Agenda on Interventions," *Decision Sciences* (2008), 39(2), 276.

Specifically, they are *individual differences* (e.g., gender, age), *system characteristics* (such things as output quality and job relevance that help individuals develop favorable or unfavorable views about the system), *social influence* (e.g., subjective norms), and *facilitating conditions* (e.g., top management support). The interrelationships described in UTAUT and TAM3 are very complex. For example, although social influences are important, they are likely to be important *only* for older works and women, and then *only* when they start using the system. The more complex models (UTAUT and TAM3) are useful for experts who are trying to take into account the nuances when trying to figure out the best way to implement systems. However, the parsimonious TAM model is clearly easier for practitioners trying to grasp the major issues involved in user acceptance.

TAM and all of these variants assume that system use is under the control of the individuals. When employees are mandated to use the system, they may use it in the short run, but over the long run the negative consequences of resistance may surface. Thus, gaining acceptance of the system is important, even in those situations where it is mandated.

▶ SUMMARY

- The nature of work is changing, and IT supports, if not propels, these changes.
- Communication and collaboration are becoming increasingly important in today's work. Technology to support communication includes e-mail, intranets, instant messaging (IM), Video conferences, Voice over Internet Protocol (VoIP), unified communications, RSS (Web feeds), virtual private networks (VPN), and file transfers. Technology to support

collaboration includes social networking sites, Web logs (blogs), virtual worlds, wikis, and groupware.

- IT affects work by creating new work, creating new working arrangements, and presenting new managerial challenges in employee supervision, evaluation, compensation, and hiring.

- Newer approaches to management reflect greater use of computer and information technology in hiring and supervising employees, a greater focus on output (compared to behavior), and a greater team orientation.

- The shift to knowledge-based work, changing demographics and lifestyle preferences, new technologies, growing reliance on the Web, and energy concerns all contribute to the growth in remote work.

- Companies find that building telecommuting capabilities can be an important tool for attracting and retaining employees, increasing worker productivity, providing flexibility to otherwise overworked individuals, reducing office space and associated costs, responding to environmental concerns about energy consumption, and complying with the Clean Air Act. Telecommuting also promises employees potential benefits: schedule flexibility, higher personal productivity, less commuting time and fewer expenses, and greater geographic flexibility.

- Disadvantages of telecommuting include difficulties in evaluating performance, greater feelings of isolation among employees, easier displacement by offshoring, and limitations of jobs and workers in its application.

- Virtual teams are defined as "two or more people who (1) work together interdependently with mutual accountability for achieving common goals, (2) do not work in either the same place and/or at the same time, and (3) must use electronic communication technology to communicate, coordinate their activities and complete their team's tasks." They are increasingly common organizational phenomenon and must be managed differently than more traditional teams.

- Managers of virtual teams must focus on overcoming the challenges of communication, technology, and diversity of team members.

- To gain acceptance of a new technology, potential users must exhibit a favorable attitude toward the technology. In the case of information systems, the users' beliefs about its perceived usefulness and perceived ease of use color their attitudes about the system. Kotter provides some suggested steps for change management that are related to Lewin's three stages of change: unfreezing, change, and refreezing.

▶ KEY TERMS

e-mail (p. 105)
file transfer (p. 106)
groupware (p. 106)
instant messaging (IM)
  (p. 105)
intranet (p. 105)
mobile workers (p. 116)
offshoring (p. 120)

RSS (Web feed) (p. 106)
social networking site
  (p. 106)
telecommuting (p. 116)
unified communications
  (p. 105)
video teleconference
  (p. 105)

virtual private network
  (VPN) (p. 105)
virtual teams (p. 122)
virtual world (p. 106)
Voice over Internet Protocol
  (VoIP) (p. 105)
Web logs (blogs) (p. 106)
wiki (p. 106)

▶ DISCUSSION QUESTIONS

1. Why might a worker resist the implementation of a new technology? What are some of the possible consequences of asking a worker to use a computer or similar device in his or her job?

2. How can IT alter an individual's work? How can a manager ensure that the impact is positive rather than negative?

3. What current technologies do you predict will show the most impact on the way work is done? Why?

4. Given the growth in telecommuting and other mobile work arrangements, how might offices physically change in the coming years? Will offices as we think of them today exist by 2020? Why or why not?

5. How is working at an online retailer different from working at a brick-and-mortar retailer? What types of jobs are necessary at each? What skills are important?

6. Paul Saffo, director of the Institute for the Future, noted, "Telecommuting is a reality for many today, and will continue to be more so in the future. But beware, this doesn't mean we will travel less. In fact, the more one uses electronics, the more they are likely to travel."[43] Do you agree with this statement? Why or why not?

7. The explosion of information-driven self-serve options in the consumer world is evident in the gas station, where customers pay, pump gas, and purchase a car wash without ever seeing an employee; in the retail store such as Walmart, Home Depot, and the local grocery, where self-service checkout stands mean customers can purchase a basket of items without ever speaking to a sales agent; at the airport, where customers make reservations and pay for and print tickets without the help of an agent; and at the bank, where ATMs have long replaced tellers for most transactions. But a backlash is coming, experts predict. Some say that people are more isolated than they used to be in the days of face-to-face service, and they question how much time people are really saving if they have to continually learn new processes, operate new machines, and overcome new glitches. Labor saving technologies were supposed to liberate people from mundane tasks, but it appears that these technologies are actually shifting the boring tasks to the customer. On the other hand, many people like the convenience of using these self-service systems, especially because it means customers can visit a bank for cash or order books or gifts from an online retailer 24 hours a day. Does this mean the end of "doing business the old-fashioned way?" Will this put a burden on the elderly or the poor when corporations begin charging for face-to-face services?[44]

CASE STUDY 4-1

TRASH AND WASTE PICKUP SERVICES, INC.

Martin Andersen is responsible for 143 of Trash and Waste Pickup Services, Inc.'s (TWPS's) garbage trucks. Trash and Waste Pickup Services is a commercial and household trash hauler. When a caller recently complained to Andersen that a brown and green Trash and Waste Pickup

---

[43] "Online Forum: Companies of the Future," http://www.msnbc.com/news/738363.asp (accessed on June 11, 2002).

[44] Stevenson Swanson, "Are Self-Serve Options a Disservice?" *Austin American Statesman* (May 8, 2005), Section H, p. 1. Reprinted from *Chicago Tribune*.

Services truck was speeding down Farm Route 2244, Andersen turned to the company's information system. He learned that the driver of a company front-loader had been on that very road at 7:22 a.m., doing 51 miles per hour (mph) in a 35 mph zone. The driver of that truck was in trouble!

The TWPS information system uses a global positioning system (GPS) not only to smooth its operations, but also to keep closer track of its workers, who may not always be doing what they are supposed to be doing during work hours. Andersen pointed out, "If you're not out there babysitting them, you don't know how long it takes to do the route. The guy could be driving around the world, he could be at his girlfriend's house."

Before TWPS installed the GPS system, the drivers of his 37 front-loaders clocked in approximately 250 hours a week of overtime at one and a half times pay. Once TWPS started monitoring the time they spent in the yard before and after completing their routes and the time and location of stops that they made, the number of overtime hours plummeted to 70 per week. This translated to substantial savings for a company whose drivers earn about $20 an hour.

TWPS also installed GPS receivers, which are the size and shape of cans of tuna, in salesmen's cars. Andersen was not surprised to learn that some of the company's salespeople frequented, The Zone, a local bar around 4 p.m. when they were supposed to be calling on customers. Andersen decided to set digital boundaries around the bar.

Understandably, the drivers and salespeople aren't entirely happy with the new GPS-based system. Ron Simon, a TWPS driver, admits: "It's kind of like Big Brother is watching a little bit. But it's where we're heading in this society. . . I get testy in the deli when I'm waiting in line for coffee, because it's like, hey, they're (managers) watching. I've got to go."

Andersen counters that employers have a right to know what their employees are up to: "If you come to work here, and I pay you and you're driving one of my vehicles, I should have the right to know what you're doing."

Discussion Questions

1. What are the positive and negative aspects of Andersen's use of the GPS-based system to monitor his drivers and salespeople?
2. What advice do you have for Andersen about the use of the system for supervising, evaluating, and compensating his drivers and salespeople?
3. As more and more companies turn to IS to help them monitor their employees, what do you anticipate the impact will be on employee privacy? Can anything be done to ensure employee privacy?

Source: This is a fictitious case. Any resemblance to an actual company is purely coincidental.

CASE STUDY 4-2

SOCIAL NETWORKING: HOW DOES IBM DO IT?

IBM's award-winning developerWorks site was established in 2000 as a technical resource for the company's global development community. Designed to share knowledge and skills related to IBM products and other key technologies, it has been a solid success. The site attracts about 4 million unique visitors a month—including students, professionals, and developers from almost all the world's countries-- who search its library of 30,000 articles, demos, podcasts and tutorials.

DeveloperWorks is available in 8 languages, including Russian, Chinese, and Spanish, and about 70% of visitors come from outside IBM.

My developerWorks, a social networking function built on the IBM Connections platform, was added in 2009 to allow developers to connect, communicate and collaborate on projects. Soon the network had added more than 600,000 user profiles, as well as numerous blogs and forums. In addition to allowing established business, start-ups and partners to collaborate, it has also helped users find answers to support questions that would otherwise go to IBM's call centers and help desks, thus saving the company an estimated $100 million.

Alice Chou, Director of IBM developerWorks, carefully monitored the number of My developerWorks profiles and the volume of traffic to the site. She looked at unique visitors, developer demographics, time spent on the site, and patterns of page views. She created a reward and recognition framework so that when users contributed a highly regarded article or blogpost to the site, "they got the kudos they deserve."

Discussion Questions

1. How does My developerWorks leverage changes in the way people work?
2. Why do you think Alice Chou carefully monitors the My developerWorks site? What would be an example of an insight she would gain from the data she's collecting?
3. Why do you think Alice Chou thinks a rewards program is necessary for My developerWorks given that so many profiles have already been developed. Do you agree that a reward would be necessary?

Sources: IBM Web site, www.ibm.com/developerworks (accessed on April 17, 2012); and Ellen Traudt and Richard Vancil, "Becoming a Social Business: The IBM Story," IDC White Paper #226706, January 2011, 1–14 (quote on p. 6).

5

INFORMATION SYSTEMS FOR MANAGING BUSINESS PROCESSES

Business processes, the cross-functional sets of activities that turn inputs into outputs, are at the heart of how businesses operate. In this chapter, business processes and the systems that support them are discussed. The chapter begins with a discussion of a functional versus process perspective of a firm, including agile and dynamic business processes. The chapter then focuses on the way managers change business processes, including incremental and radical approaches. Information systems (IS) that support and automate business processes follow, including workflow and business process management systems and enterprise systems. The chapter concludes by examining when IS drive business transformations and the complexities that arise from integrating systems between companies.

Business strategy at Sloan Valve Company,[1] a family-owned global manufacturer of plumbing products, had executives launching a range of new products every year. The new product development (NPD) process was both a core process and a strategic asset. But the process was complex, with over 16 functional units involved, and slow, taking 18–24 months to bring a new product to market. Sloan Valve's process of initiating and screening new product ideas was broken. More than 50% of the ideas that began the process didn't make it through, resulting in wasted resources. Further, no one was accountable for the process, making it difficult to get a handle on process management and improvement. Information flow was blocked in part because of the structure of the organization.

Management initially invested in an enterprise system to automate their internal processes, believing that the IS would provide a common language, database, and platform. Despite successful implementation, the communication and coordination problems continued. Further, the new system didn't provide an NPD process. Upon deeper analysis by a new CIO brought in to "fix things," management realized that the

---

[1] Adapted from S. Balaji, C. Ranganathan, and T. Coleman, "IT-Led Process Reengineering: How Sloan Valve Redesigned its New Product Development Process," *MIS Quarterly Executive* (June 2011), 10(2), 81–92.

enterprise system was working fine, but the underlying process was broken. Top management decided to redesign the process.

The NPD process redesign began with a process redesign team, led by an IT manager with considerable process experience and involving members from manufacturing, engineering, IT, finance, marketing, operations, and quality assurance. The Director of Design Engineering was made process owner, to provide oversight for the process changes. The team spent nine months assessing the current process and proposing a new end-to-end NPD process. The reengineered NPD process included six sub-processes: ideation, business case development, project portfolio management, product development, product and process validation, and launch. The underlying information system was the enterprise system, upgraded to include newer modules, which supported product life cycle management.

The quality, timing, and output of the NPD process greatly improved. The new NPD process reduced time-to-market to less than 12 months. New product ideas that were unlikely to work were filtered out early, eliminating problem of wasting resources. Synthesis of product and process information improved. Customer feedback was easier to access. And accountability increased, smoothing out responsibilities and workflow.

Not all IS enterprise system implementations are as successful as Sloan Valve. There are hundreds of stories of companies that ran into significant problems when automating and transforming their business processes, especially when an information system is at the heart of the change. Overstock.com's order tracking system failed for a full week when they rolled out a new enterprise system. By rushing to implement the new system, a glitch put the enterprise system out of sync with the accounting system, causing the company to have to restate more than five years of earnings, which showed lower revenue and higher losses. Clothing manufacturer Levi Strauss had similar problems with their new enterprise system, causing shipping errors and issues with their financial control systems. The latter was blamed for the company's 98% decrease in net income for the second quarter in 2008. Avis Europe attempted to implement an enterprise system, but project delays and cost overruns caused the company to cancel the project and write off £28 million on its books. With so much at risk, general managers must be informed and involved in these types of complex information systems that change business processes.[2]

IS can enable or impede business change. The right design coupled with the right technology can result in changes such as Sloan Valve experienced. The wrong business process design or the wrong technology, however, can force a company into operational, and sometimes financial, crisis as the Overstock.com, Levi Strauss, and Avis Europe examples show.

To a manager in today's business environment, an understanding of how IS enable business change is essential. The terms *management* and *change management* are used almost synonymously in today's business vocabulary: To manage effectively means to manage change effectively. As IS become ever more prevalent and more powerful, the speed and magnitude of the changes that organizations must address to remain

[2] Adapted from http://www.baselinemag.com/c/a/ERP/Five-ERP-Disasters-Explained-878312/ (accessed on February 24, 2012).

competitive continues to increase. To be a successful manager, one must understand how IS enable change in a business, one must gain a process perspective of business, and one must understand how to transform business processes effectively. This chapter provides the manager with a view of business process change. It provides tools for analyzing how a company currently does business and for thinking about how to effectively manage the inevitable changes that result from competition and the availability of IS. This chapter also describes an IT-based solution commonly known as enterprise IS (information systems).

A brief word to the reader is needed. The term *process* is used extensively in this chapter. In some instances, it is used to refer to the steps taken to change aspects of the business. At other times, it is used to refer to the part of the business to be changed: the business process. The reader should be sensitive to the potentially confusing use of the term *process*.

► SILO PERSPECTIVE VERSUS BUSINESS PROCESS PERSPECTIVE

When effectively linked with improvements to business processes, advances in IS enable changes that make it possible to do business in a new way, better and more competitive than before. On the other hand, IS can also inhibit change, which occurs when managers fail to adapt business processes because they rely on inflexible systems to support those processes. Finally, IS can also drive change, for better or for worse. Examples abound of industries that were fundamentally changed by advances in IS and of companies whose success or failure depended on the ability of their managers to adapt. This chapter considers IS as an enabler of business transformation, a partner in transforming business processes to achieve competitive advantages. We begin by comparing a process view of the firm with a functional view.

Transformation requires discontinuous thinking—recognizing and shedding outdated rules and fundamental assumptions that underlie operations. "Unless we change these rules, we are merely rearranging the deck chairs on the *Titanic*. We cannot achieve breakthroughs in performance by cutting fat or automating existing processes. Rather, we must challenge old assumptions and shed the old rules that made the business under perform in the first place."[3]

Functional (or Silo) Perspective

Many think of business by imagining a hierarchical structure organized around a set of functions. Looking at a traditional organization chart allows an understanding of what the business does to achieve its goals. A typical hierarchical structure, organized by function, might look like the one shown in Figure 5.1.

In a hierarchical structure, departments are organized on the basis of their core competencies. The structure allows them to focus on what they do best. For example, the operations department focuses on operations, the marketing department focuses on

[3] Michael Hammer, "Reengineering Work: Don't Automate, Obliterate," *Harvard Business Review* (July–August 1990), 4.

FIGURE 5.1 Hierarchical structure.

marketing, and so on. Each major function within the organization usually forms a separate department to ensure that work is done by groups of experts in that function. This functional structure is widespread in today's organizations and is reinforced by business education curricula, which generally follow functional structures—students take courses in functions (i.e., marketing, management, accounting), major in functions, and then are predisposed to think in terms of these same functions.[4]

Even when companies use the perspective of the value chain model (as discussed in Chapter 2), they still focus on functions that deliver their portion of the process and "throwing it over the wall" to the next group on the value chain. These **silos**, or self-contained functional units, are useful for several reasons. First, they allow an organization to optimize expertise and their training. For example, instead of having marketing people in a number of different groups, all the marketing people belong to the same department, which allows them to informally network and learn from each other and allows the business to leverage its resources. Second, the silos allow the organization to avoid redundancy in expertise by hiring one person who can be assigned to projects across functions on an as-needed basis instead of hiring an expert in each function. Third, with a functional organization, it is easier to benchmark with outside organizations, utilize bodies of knowledge created for each function, and easily understand the role of each silo. For example, it is clear that the marketing department produces and executes marketing plans, but it may not be clear what a customer-relationship department does. (It typically has some marketing, some sales, some services, and some accounting processes.)

On the other hand, silo organizations can experience significant sub-optimization. First, individual departments often recreate information maintained by other departments. Second, communication gaps between departments are often wide. Third, handoffs between silos are often a source of problems, such as finger-pointing and lost information, in business processes. Finally, silos tend to lose sight of the objective of the overall organization and operate in a way that maximizes their local goals.

A firm's work changes over time. In a functionally organized silo business, each group is primarily concerned with its own set of objectives. The executive officers jointly seek to ensure that these functions work together to create value, but the task of providing the "big picture" to so many functionally oriented personnel can prove

---

[4] Thomas Davenport and John Beck, *The Attention Economy* (Boston, MA: Harvard Business School Press, 2001), 173.

extremely challenging. As time passes and business circumstances change, new work is created that relies on more than one of the old functional departments. Departments that took different directions must now work together. They negotiate the terms of any new work processes with their own functional interests in mind, and the "big picture" optimum gets scrapped in favor of suboptimal compromises among the silos. These compromises then become repeated processes, they become standard operating procedures.

Losing the big picture means losing business effectiveness. After all, a business's main objective is to create as much value as possible for its shareholders and other stakeholders by satisfying its customers to the greatest extent possible. When functional groups duplicate work, when they fail to communicate with one another, when they lose the big picture and establish suboptimal processes, the customers and stakeholders are not being well served.

Process Perspective

A manager can avoid such sub-optimization—or begin to "fix" it—by managing from a process perspective. A **process perspective** keeps the big picture in view and allows the manager to concentrate on the work that must be done to ensure the optimal creation of value. A process perspective helps the manager avoid or reduce duplicate work, facilitate cross-functional communication, optimize business processes, and ultimately, best serve the customers and stakeholders.

In business, a **process** is defined as an interrelated, sequential set of activities and tasks that turns inputs into outputs, and includes the following:

- A beginning and an end
- Inputs and outputs
- A set of tasks (subprocesses or activities) that transform the inputs into outputs
- A set of metrics for measuring effectiveness

The term workflow, discussed later in this chapter, is often used to describe the sequence of activities that take place in a process.

Metrics are important because they focus managers on the critical dimensions of the process. Metrics for a business process are things like throughput, which is how many outputs can be produced per unit time; or cycle time, which is how long it takes for the entire process to execute. Some use measures are the number of handoffs in the process or actual work versus total cycle time. Other metrics are based on the outputs themselves, such as customer satisfaction, revenue per output, profit per output, and quality of the output.

Examples of business processes include customer order fulfillment, manufacturing planning and execution, payroll, financial reporting, and procurement. A procurement process might look like Figure 5.2. The process has a beginning and an end, inputs (requirements for goods or services) and outputs (receipt of goods, vendor payment), and subprocesses (filling out a purchase order, verifying the invoice). Metrics of the success of the process might include turnaround time and the number of paperwork errors.

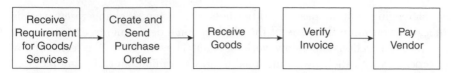

FIGURE 5.2 Sample procurement business process.

The procurement process in Figure 5.2 cuts across the functional lines of a traditionally structured business. For example, the requirements for goods might originate in the operations department based on guidelines from the finance department. Paperwork would likely flow through the administration department, and the accounting department would be responsible for making payment to the vendor.

Focus on the process by its very nature ensures focus on the business's goals (the "big picture") because each process has an "endpoint" that is usually a deliverable to a customer, supplier, or other stakeholder. A process perspective recognizes that processes are often cross-functional. In the diagram in Figure 5.3, the vertical bars represent functional departments within a business. The horizontal bars represent processes that flow across those functional departments. A process perspective requires an understanding that processes properly exist to serve the larger goals of the business, and that functional departments must work together to optimize processes in light of these goals.

For example, an order-fulfillment process might include payment, order delivery, implementation, and after-sales service tasks. This process would involve multiple functions, including operations, accounting, service, and sales, making it a cross-functional business process. The "sales order" would be the input for this process. A satisfied customer might be the output, and there are a number of metrics that can be used to measure success such as satisfaction of the customer, time to complete the order fulfillment process, number of defects (or other quality measure), etc.

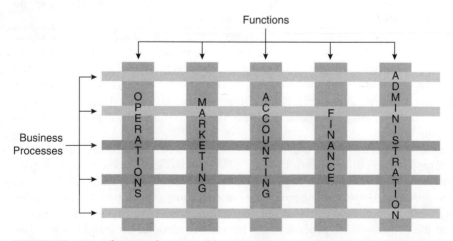

FIGURE 5.3 Cross-functional nature of business processes.

When managers take a process perspective, they are able to optimize the value that customers and stakeholders receive by managing the flow as well as the tasks. They begin to manage processes by:

- Identifying the customers of processes (who receives the output of the process?)
- Identifying these customers' requirements (what are the criteria for successful implementation of the process?)
- Clarifying the value that each process adds to the overall goals of the organization
- Sharing their perspective with other organizational members until the organization itself becomes more process focused

The differences between the silo and process perspective are summarized in Figure 5.4. Unlike a silo perspective, a process perspective recognizes that businesses operate as a set of processes that flow across functional departments. It enables a manger to analyze the business's processes in light of its larger goals, as compared to the functional orientation of the silo perspective. Finally, it provides a manager with insights into how those processes might better serve these goals.

Zara's Cross-Functional Processes

Consider Spanish clothing retailer Zara (introduced in Chapter 2). With over 1,600 stores in 78 countries around the world and a well-designed set of cross-functional processes, Zara often is able to design, produce, and deliver a garment within 15 days. For this to happen, Zara managers must regularly create and rapidly replenish small batches of goods all over the world. Zara's organization, operational procedures, performance measures, and even its office layout are all designed to make information transfer easy.

Zara's designers are co-located with the production team, including marketing, procurement, and production planners. Prototypes are created nearby, facilitating easy

	Silo Perspective	Business Process Perspective
Definition	Self-contained functional units such as marketing, operations, finance, and so on	Interrelated, sequential set of activities and tasks that turns inputs into outputs
Focus	Functional	Cross-functional
Goal Accomplishment	Optimizes on functional goals, which might be a suboptimal organizational goal	Optimizes on organizational goals, or "big picture"
Benefits	Highlighting and developing core competencies; functional efficiencies	Avoiding work duplication and cross-functional communication gaps; organizational effectiveness

FIGURE 5.4 Comparison of silo perspective and business process perspective.

discussion about the latest design. Large circular tables in the middle of the production process encourage impromptu meetings where ideas are readily exchanged among the designers, market specialists, and production planners. The speed and quality of the design process is greatly enhanced by the colocation of the entire team. That is because the designers can quickly check their ideas with others on their cross-functional teams. For example, the market specialists can quickly respond to their designs in terms of the style, color, and fabric, whereas the procurement and production planners can update them about manufacturing costs and available capacity.

Information technology provides a platform but does not preclude informal face-to-face conversations. Retail store managers are linked to marketing specialists through customized handheld computers but just as often use the telephone to share order data, sales trends, and customer reactions to a new style. Zara's cross-functional teams enable information sharing among everyone who "needs to know" and therefore creates the opportunity to change directions quickly to respond to new market trends.

▶ BUILDING AGILE AND DYNAMIC BUSINESS PROCESSES

To stay competitive and consistently meet changing customer demands, organizations build **dynamic business processes** or **agile business processes**; processes that iterate through a constant renewal cycle of design, deliver, evaluate, redesign, and so on. Agile processes are designed with the intention of simplifying redesign and reconfiguration. They are designed so they are flexible and easily adaptable to changes in the business environment and can be incrementally changed with little effort. Dynamic processes, on the other hand, reconfigure themselves as they "learn" and are utilized in the business.

For a process to be agile or dynamic necessitates a high degree of IT use. The more of the process that can be done with software, the easier it is to change, and the more likely it can be designed to be agile or dynamic.

Examples of agile process are often found in manufacturing operations, where production lines are reconfigured regularly to accommodate new products and technologies. For example, automobile production lines produce large quantities of cars, but very few are identical to the car before or after it on the production line. The design of the line is such that many changes in design, features, or options are just incorporated into the assembly of the car at hand.

Another common example is in software development. Agile software development methodologies underlie an incremental and iterative development process that is often used to rapidly and collaboratively create working and relevant software.

More recently, with the use of the Internet and social technologies, building agility into business processes is increasingly common. Processes run entirely on the Internet, such as order-management, service provisioning, software development, and human resource support are candidates for agile designs that take advantage of the latest innovations offered by the vendors on the Internet.

An example of a dynamic process is a network with changing flow of data. The network would have sensors built in to monitor the flow, and when flow is greater than the current network configuration can handle, the network automatically requisitions more capacity to handle the additional data and reconfigures itself to balance the flow over the new channels. Another example, with a more physical configuration, would be a call-center. Call center systems are designed to monitor the flow of calls coming into the center and the time it takes for agents to respond to the calls. These systems automatically reconfigure as volume increases. The system might add additional agents to the schedule or alert a supervisor of the increase and route calls to standby agents. Or should an agent be taking more time than expected for a call, the system would avoid sending a new call to that agent. Because the system helps manage the process, it can automatically redistribute incoming calls as necessary to respond to changes in the center.

Dynamic IT applications are required for dynamic business processes. When the underlying IT is not designed with this goal in mind, the business process itself cannot adapt as necessary to changing requirements of the business environment. The benefits of agile and dynamic business processes are operational efficiency gained by the ease of incrementally improving the process as necessary and the ability to create game-changing innovative processes more quickly.

Sloan Valve's new NPD was another example of a more flexible process. Previously seeped in the old way of doing things, and tied to legacy information systems, the redesigned NPD speeded up the process and had ways to listen and adapt to customer feedback, process problems, and team misalignments.

▶ CHANGING BUSINESS PROCESSES

Sloan Valve decided to do a complete redesign of their NPD process. After trying to incrementally change it with a new IS, and minor changes to the process, managers realized that a complete redesign was necessary.

Two techniques are used to transform business processes: (1) radical process, redesign, which is sometimes called **business process reengineering (BPR)** or simply reengineering, and (2) incremental, continuous process improvement, which includes **total quality management (TQM)** or simply quality management and Six Sigma. Radical and incremental improvement concepts are important; they continue to be different tools a manager can use to effect change in the way his or her organization does business. The basis of both approaches is viewing the business as a set of business processes, rather than using a silo perspective.

Incremental Change

At one end of the continuum, managers use incremental change approaches to improve business processes through small, incremental changes. This improvement process generally involves the following activities:

- Choosing a business process to improve
- Choosing a metric by which to measure the business process
- Enabling personnel involved with the process to find ways to improve it based on the metric

Personnel often react favorably to incremental change because it gives them control and ownership of improvements and, therefore, renders change less threatening. The improvements grow from their grassroots efforts. TQM is one such approach that incorporates methods of continuous process improvement. At the core of the TQM method is W. Edwards Deming's key principles to transform business processes, called Deming's 14 Points, which outline a set of activities for increasing quality and improving productivity.[5] TQM has lost some of its luster in the United States, but it continues to be very popular in Europe and Asia.

Six Sigma is another incremental approach to quality management. It is a data-driven approach and methodology for eliminating defects from a process. The term "Six Sigma" comes from the idea that if the quality of all output from a process were to be mapped on a bell-shaped curve, the tail of the curve, six sigma from the mean, would be where there were less than 3.4 defects per million. A process that has this low rate of defects would be close to perfect—close to zero defects. Six Sigma methodology is a very specific set of steps to be followed, called DMAIC and DMADV. The Six Sigma **DMAIC** process (define, measure, analyze, improve, control) is an improvement system for existing processes falling below specification and looking for incremental improvement. The Six Sigma **DMADV** process (define, measure, analyze, design, verify) is an improvement system used to develop new processes or products at Six Sigma quality levels.[6] Six Sigma methodology is carried out by experts, known as Green Belts and more experienced experts known as Black Belts, who have taken special Six Sigma training and worked on numerous Six Sigma projects. Motorola was one of the first companies in the United States to use Six Sigma, but GE made Six Sigma a part of their business culture driving significant and continuous improvement throughout their corporation. The GE Web site states, "Six Sigma is a highly disciplined process that helps us focus on developing and delivering near-perfect products and services."[7]

Radical Change

Incremental change approaches work well for tweaking existing silo processes. However, it tends to be ineffective for addressing cross-functional processes. More major changes usually associated with cross-functional processes require a different type of management tool. At the other end of the change continuum, radical change enables the organization to attain aggressive improvement goals (again, as defined by a set of metrics). The goal of radical change is to make a rapid, breakthrough impact on key metrics. Some businesses even have made radical process reconfiguration a core competency so that they can better serve customers whose demands are constantly changing.

---

[5] For more information about TQM, and Deming's 14 Point approach to quality management, see the ASQ (Formerly known as the American Society for Quality), a global community of experts on quality and the administrators of the Malcolm Baldrige National Quality Award program at http://asq.org/learn-about-quality/total-quality-management/overview/overview.html.

[6] "What is Six Sigma," iSixSigma, http://www.isixsigma.com/new-to-six-sigma/getting-started/what-six-sigma/ (accessed on February 24, 2012).

[7] http://www.ge.com/en/company/companyinfo/quality/whatis.htm (accessed on February 24, 2012).

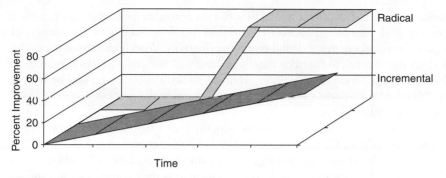

FIGURE 5.5 Comparison of radical and incremental improvement.

Sloan Valve is an example of a company that set aggressive improvement goals and reached them with a radical change approach. They set out to dramatically improve the time-to-market of new products and were able to reduce it from 18–24 months down to 12 months. They sought a less complex way to get the NPD process completed, and were able to restructure the governance from involving 16 functional units, to a dual strategic and process-level governance structure. They had no clear accountability for the NPD process, and after redesign, had well established process ownership.

The difference in the incremental and radical approaches over time is illustrated by the graph in Figure 5.5. The vertical axis measures, in one sense, how well a business process meets its goals. Improvements are made either incrementally or radically. The horizontal axis measures time.

Not surprisingly, radical change typically faces greater internal resistance than does incremental change. Therefore, radical change processes should be carefully planned and only used when major change is needed in a short time. Some examples of situations requiring radical change are when the company is in trouble, when it imminently faces a major change in the operating environment, or when it must change significantly to outpace its competition. Key aspects of radical change approaches include the following:

- The need for major change in a short amount of time
- Thinking from a cross-functional process perspective
- Challenging old assumptions
- Networked (cross-functional) organizing
- Empowerment of individuals in the process
- Measurement of success via metrics tied directly to business goals and the effectiveness of new processes (e.g., production cost, cycle time, scrap and rework rates, customer satisfaction, revenues, and quality)

▶ WORKFLOW AND MAPPING PROCESSES

Workflow is a way to look at a cross-functional process. In its most basic meaning, it's the series of connected tasks and activities done by people and computers that, together, form a business process. But the term workflow has come to also mean software products that document and automate processes. Workflow software facilitates the design of business processes and creates a digital workflow diagram. Workflow software lets the manager diagram answers to questions such as how will the process work, who does what, what the information system will do, what decisions will be made, and by whom. When combined with business process management modules, processes can be managed, monitored, and modified.

The tool used to understand a business process is a **workflow diagram**, which shows a picture, or map, of the sequence and detail of each process step. More than 200 products are available for helping managers diagram the workflow. The objective of process mapping is to understand and communicate the dimensions of the current process. Typically, process engineers begin the process mapping procedure by defining the scope, mission, and boundaries of the business process. Next, the engineer develops a high-level overview flowchart of the process and a detailed flow diagram of everything that happens in the process. The diagram uses active verbs to describe activities and identifies all actors, inputs, and outputs of the process. The engineer verifies the detailed diagram for accuracy with the actors in the process and adjusts it accordingly.

Business Process Management (BPM)

Thinking about the business as a set of processes has become commonplace for most organizations. Managing their processes is another story. Some claim that to have truly dynamic or agile business processes requires a well-defined and optimized set of IT processes, tools, and skills called **Business Process Management (BPM)**. In the 1990s, a class of systems emerged to help manage workflows in the business. They primarily helped track document-based processes where people executed the steps of the workflow. BPM systems go way beyond the document-management capabilities and include features that manage person-to-person process steps, system-to-system steps, and those processes that include a combination. Systems include process modeling, simulation, code generation, process execution, monitoring, and integration capabilities for both company-based and Web-based systems. The tools allow an organization to actively manage and improve its processes from beginning to end.

Enterprise Rent-a-Car, one of the largest car rental companies in the world with 7,000 locations and more than 65,000 employees worldwide used BPM to model, manage, and streamline its IT-based processes. It used BPM to build Request Online, the IT request services system through which employees requested laptops, software and applications, system access, reports, and other services available from the IS department. The prior system was mostly manual, not scalable as request volume increased, and not automatable. Not surprisingly, it was difficult to make improvements to that system. Using a BPM system, staff developed a model that copied the way service requests were already handled so the experience would be familiar, and added additional features slowly to enhance the experience. The result was a BPM-based system that provided better management capabilities, created a common platform for rapid change and capacity for future growth. That proved critical when Enterprise acquired National Car Rental and Alamo Rent A Car, creating much more demand for Request Online.

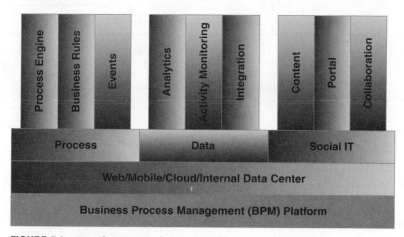

FIGURE 5.6 Sample BPM architecture.
Source: Adapted from www.appian.com.

Enterprise was able to shift development to less costly IT staff who could make process modifications directly through the BPM. Finally, the usability of the system was increased as the BPM facilitated the creation of customized interfaces based on characteristics of the specific users.[8]

BPM systems are a way to build, execute, and monitor automated processes that may go across organizational boundaries. Some of the functionality of a BPM may be found in enterprise applications such as ERP, CRM, and financial software because these systems also manage processes within a corporation. But BPM systems go outside a specific application to help companies manage across processes. Some BPM systems manage front office applications that are often person-to-person processes such as a sales or ordering process. These processes are people-centric and incorporate social IT. Other BPM systems support back-office processes that often are more system-to-system oriented and possibly extend outside the corporation to include Web-based components. Figure 5.6 contains a representative illustration of the components of a BPM system.

Enterprise's Request Online used a BPM system by Appian. Appian's BPM product includes components to help companies design, manage, and optimize core business processes. Appian has sophisticated features that combine social IT capabilities with process modeling, content management, data management, and integration with existing enterprise systems. SharePoint, one of the most popular collaboration environments, can be managed through Appian's suite, creating a one-stop-shop for managing business processes in an enterprise. Figure 5.7 summarizes the components of their system.

Two other common vendors for BPM are IBM and SoftwareAG's ARIS. ARIS has also come to mean an entire modeling approach. ARIS, which stands for Architecture of Integrated Information Systems, and structures four views of the enterprise, including an organizational view, a data view, a functional view, and a control view. Using ARIS,

---

[8] Adapted from www.appian.com.

Appian BPM Suite

Process	Process modeling platform to design, execute, manage, and optimize enterprise business processes
Rules	Audit policies, practices, and business rules can be managed, automatically monitored, and enforced and tracked for audits
Content	Documents, process contents and metrics stored and managed and integrated with other enterprise systems
Data Access	Enterprise data systems are included in the modeling capability and connected to processes as needed
Social and Collaboration	Using threaded discussion boards, targeted content, and content sharing, users monitor, discuss, and take action on business processes using social BPM feeds that combine real-time collaboration, key event monitoring, and direct action
Portal	Customizable user interface providing each user a personalized view of the content and applications in the suite
Analytics	Algorithms for analyzing real-time process performance data, creating customized dashboards, identifying bottlenecks in processes, and predicting future issues
Forms	Reports built dynamically and interactively
Mobile	Application interfaces available for mobile devices such as iPhone, iPad, Android, and Blackberry devices to allow monitoring, collaborating, alerts, and taking action
Service Oriented Architecture (SOA) and Integration	Users, enterprise data systems, and external services are integrated and managed with a set of pre-built connectors for common system interfaces and frameworks

FIGURE 5.7 Appian BPM suite.
Source: Adapted from www.appian.com.

managers can model the business, including its processes, using a common language and set of procedures.

▶ ENTERPRISE SYSTEMS

Information technology is a critical component of most every business process today because information flow is at the core of most every process. A class of IT applications called **enterprise systems** is a set of information systems tools that many organizations

Integration versus Standardization

Processes are the way organizations deliver goods and services to customers. Designing, building and executing processes is one of the roles of management. Dr. Jeanne Ross, Principal Research Scientist at MIT's Center for Information Research, suggested that the level of integration and standardization of business processes, another management decision, determines the role of IS. Ross pointed out that "Companies make two important choices in the design of their operations: (1) how standardized their business processes should be across operational units (business units, region, function, market segment) and (2) how integrated their business processes should be across those units." The resulting model defines important IT and business capabilities (see figure). The level of process integration and standardization defines the necessary IS capabilities and ultimately the investment the firm will need to make in IS.

Process Integration versus Standardization

		Business Process Standardization	
		Low	High
Business Process Integration	High	The business is focused on process integration, usually creating a single face to customers and suppliers, but doesn't usually impose process standards on operating units.	The business has a centralized design, with high needs for reliability, predictability and sharing data across business units creating a single view of the process.
	Low	The business has a decentralized design where business units make local decisions on processes to meet customer needs.	The business is focused on process standardization where tasks are done the same way with the same systems across business units, but the business units have little need to interact.

CEMEX, the multinational cement company based in Monterrey, Mexico, built a business based on high levels of process standardization, but low levels of process integration. CEMEX standardized on eight information systems-based business processes to cover logistics, manufacturing, accounting, planning, operations, procurement, finance and HR. Each of the CEMEX operating units used the same processes and create similar data, but the units run autonomously, rarely sharing data. CEMEX finds a competitive advantage from their standardized processes because it enables them to assimilate acquired companies quickly.

A company with a high degree of integration and low standardization is Merrill Lynch's Global Private Client business, which provides a wide range of financial services to clients across multiple channels such as financial advisory services, online services, and help-center support services. The key to their success is integration across processes to provide a single view of the customer, which can then be leveraged when new products and services are announced. At the same time, the company does not expect standardization across processes; each operating unit can create what they need, as long as they use a standardized technology platform that also supports the integrated design.

Source: J. Ross, *"Forget Strategy: Focus IT on Your Operating Model,"* MIT Center for Information Research, Research Briefing (December 2005), V(3C).

use to enable this information flow within and between processes across the organization. They help ensure integration and coordination across functions such as accounting, production, customer management, and supplier management. Some are designed to support a particular industry such as health care, retail, and manufacturing.

Computer systems in the 1960s and early 1970s were typically designed around a specific application. These early systems did not interface well with each other and often had their own version of data. When systems needed the same data, a second set of data was built into each system. The systems were designed to support a silo approach, and they did so very effectively.

Organizational computing groups were faced with the challenge of linking and maintaining the patchwork of loosely overlapping, redundant systems. In the 1980s and 1990s, software companies in a number of countries, including the United States, Germany, and the Netherlands, began developing integrated software packages that used a common database and cut across organizational systems. Some of these packages were developed from administrative systems (e.g., finance and human resources) and others evolved from materials resource planning (MRP) in manufacturing. These comprehensive software packages that incorporate all modules needed to run the operations of a business are called **Enterprise Information Systems (EIS)** or simply enterprise systems. Enterprise systems include Enterprise Resource Planning (ERP), Supply Chain Management (SCM), Customer Relationship Management (CRM), and Product Lifecycle Management (PLM) systems (see Figure 5.8). Some companies develop proprietary enterprise systems to support mission critical processes when they believe these processes give them an advantage and using a vendor-supplied system would jeopardize that advantage. Other enterprise systems may be developed specifically to integrate organizational processes.

Two of the largest vendors of enterprise systems are German-based SAP and California-based Oracle. Initially, SAP defined the ERP software space and Oracle was the database system supporting it. But in more recent history, SAP has moved to its own database system, and Oracle has acquired many other smaller vendors, creating their own suite of enterprise software solutions.

Sloan Valve, the case introduced at the beginning of this chapter, used SAP. Initially they implemented the ERP module, but as the design emerged for the new NPD process, the PLM module was key. It enabled the process owner to keep track of targets, look at efficiencies in the process, and understand process problems. It also helped track

Enterprise System	Sample Processes
Customer Relationship Management (CRM)	Marketing (resource management, brand management, campaign management, segmentation management) Lead management Loyalty program management Sales planning and forecasting Territory and Account management Quotes, Contract, order capture management Sales team performance management Customer service and support history Return and repair management Field service management Warranty and claim management Installation and maintenance management
Enterprise Resource Planning (ERP)	Financial Management (accounting, financial close, treasury management, Invoice to pay process, receivables management) Human Capital Management (talent management, Core HR, payroll, workforce management, succession planning) Operations Management (Procurement, logistics management, product development and manufacturing life cycle, requisition-invoice payment, parts inventory and logistics management)
Supplier Chain Management (SCM)	Supply chain design Order fulfillment Warehouse management Demand planning, forecasting Sales and operations planning Service parts planning Source-to-pay/procurement process Supplier lifecycle management Supply contract management
Product Lifecycle Management (PLM)	Innovation management (strategy and planning, idea capture and management, program/project management) Product development and management Product compliance management

FIGURE 5.8 Enterprise systems and the processes they automate.

and allocate resources for each new product idea and enabled coordination between all the cross-functional team members.

Enterprise Resource Planning (ERP)

ERPs are traditionally what first comes to mind when talking about enterprise information systems. They were designed to help large companies manage the fragmentation of information stored in hundreds of individual desktop, department, and business unit computers across the organization. They offered the IS department in many large organizations an option for switching from underperforming, obsolete mainframe systems to client-server environments designed to handle the changing business demands of their operational counterparts. The threat of the year 2000 problem (Y2K), a problem in which computers used two digits instead of four digits to represent the year, making it impossible to distinguish between years such as 2000 and 1900, pushed many senior managers to outside vendors who offered Y2K-compliant enterprise systems as the solution for their companies in the late 90s. In some cases, business processes were so untamed that managers thought installing an enterprise system would be a way to standardize processes across their businesses. These managers wanted to transform their business processes by forcing all to conform to a software package.

The next generation of enterprise system emerged, ERP II systems. Whereas an ERP makes company information immediately available to all departments throughout a company, ERP II makes company information immediately available to *external stakeholders*, such as customers and partners. ERP II enables e-business by integrating business processes between an enterprise and its trading partners. More recently, a move to better manage information systems using the cloud has again called into question the design of some business processes.

Today, ERP systems include all of the ERP II functionality plus social and collaboration features. SAP's ERP solution includes SAP ERP Financials, SAP ERP Human Capital Management, and SAP ERP Operations. Oracle's ERP solution, EnterpriseOne, offers these same functions. Both vendors have integrated their ERP solutions with their supply chain/logistics solutions, their CRM solutions, and several other modules that make them a one-stop-shop for software that provides the backbone of an enterprise.

Characteristics of ERP Systems

ERP systems have several characteristics:[9]

- *Integration*. ERP systems are designed to seamlessly integrate information flows throughout the company. ERP systems are configured by installing various modules, such as:
  - Manufacturing (materials management, inventory, plant maintenance, production planning, routing, shipping, purchasing, etc.)
  - Accounting (general ledger, accounts payable, accounts receivable, cash management, forecasting, cost accounting, profitability analysis, etc.)
  - Human resources (employee data, position management, skills inventory, time accounting, payroll, travel expenses, etc.)

---

[9] M. Lynne Markus and Cornelis Tanis, "The Enterprise System Experience—From Adoption to Success," in R. Zmud (ed.), *Framing the Domains of IT Management: Projecting the Future Through the Past* (Cincinnati, OH: Pinaflex Educational Resources, Inc., 2000), 176–179.

- Sales (order entry, order management, delivery support, sales planning, pricing, etc.)

- *Packages*. ERP systems are usually commercial packages purchased from software vendors. Unlike many packages, ERP systems usually require long-term relationships with software vendors because the complex systems must typically be modified on a continuing basis to meet the organization's needs.

- *Best practices*. ERP systems reflect industry best practices for generic business processes. To implement them, businesses often have to change their processes in some way to accommodate the software.

- *Some assembly required*. The ERP system is software that needs to be integrated with the organization's hardware, operating systems, databases, and network. Further, ERP systems often need to be integrated with proprietary legacy systems. It often requires that **middleware** (software used to connect processes running in one or more computers across a network) or "bolt-on" systems be used to make all the components operational. Vendor supplied ERP systems have a number of configurable components, too, which need to be setup to best fit with the organization. Rarely does an organization use it directly "out of the box" without configuration.

- *Evolving*. ERP systems were designed first for mainframe systems then client-server architectures and now for Web-enabled or cloud-based delivery.

Integrating ERP packages with other software in a firm is often a major challenge. For example, integrating internal ERP applications with supply chain management software seems to create issues. Making sure the linkages between the systems happen seamlessly is a challenge. One important problem in meeting this challenge is to allow companies to be both more flexible in sourcing from multiple (or alternative) suppliers, while also increasing the transparency in tightly coupled supply chains. A second problem is to integrate ERP's transaction-driven focus into a firm's workflow.[10]

Managing Customer Relationships

A type of software package that is increasingly considered an enterprise system is customer relationship management systems. **Customer relationship management (CRM)** is a set of software programs that support management activities performed to obtain, enhance relationships with, and retain customers. They include sales, support, and service processes. Today, CRM has come to mean the enterprise systems that support these processes and the term is used interchangeably with the set of activities.

CRM processes create ways to learn more about customers' needs and behaviors with the objective of to developing stronger relationships. CRM systems consist of technological components, as well as many pieces of information about customers, sales, marketing effectiveness, responsiveness, and market trends. Optimized CRM processes

---

[10] Amit Basu and Akhil Kumar, "Research Commentary: Workflow Management Issues in e-Business," *Information Systems Research* (March 2002), 13(1), 1–14.

Geographic Lens: Global vs. Local ERPs

ERP systems are usually designed around best practices—but whose best practices? SAP and Oracle, the leading vendors of ERP systems, have a decided Western bias. More specifically, best practices at the heart of their systems are based upon business processes that are found in successful companies in Germany and North America. However, when these systems are transplanted into Asian companies, problematic "misfits" have been found to occur.

Take, for example, the use of ERP systems designed for hospitals. Western health care models are decidely different from those used in Singapore. In Western countries, insurance enables patients to pay a fraction of their medical expenses themselves, while the government or private insurance covers the rest. Singapore has a completely different model. In Singapore, health care expenses are covered primarily by the individual. Government subsidies and other community support is minimal.

How does this affect processes embedded in ERP systems in hospitals? When ERP systems are designed for Western hospitals, they include modules that help manage the complexity of billing and collections that result from claims submissions and insurance verification. When the primary payment is from individuals paying at the time of service, or in installments, the collections process is significantly different. Further, "bed class" is a big deal in Singapore where patients in public hospitals can choose from a variety of plans ranging from one bed to six or more per room. The Western model is simpler since single-bedded rooms are more common.

Because of differences and "misfits," businesses in many non-Western companies are turning to local vendors that have developed systems reflecting local best practices. For example, local ERP vendors in Taiwan have developed ERP systems to support the majority of firms in the market space—small- to medium-sized Taiwaneses companies with sophisticated, adaptive logistic networks. The local ERP vendors have adopted a strategy of customization and are more willing to modify their systems to satisfy local needs than are their large, global competitors.

These examples suggest that another factor needs to be considered when designing and implementing and ERP. The ERP should not be implemented if the system is based on a cultural model that conflicts with the local customs and that can not easily be accommodated by the ERP.

Sources: C. Soh, S. K. Sia, and J. Tay-Yap, "Cultural Fits and Misfits: Is ERP a Universal Solution," *Communications of the ACM*, 2000, **43**(4), 47–51; and E. T. G. Wang, G. Kleing, and J. J. Jiang, "ERP Misfit: Country of Origin and Organizational Factors," *Journal of Management Information Systems* (2006), **23**(1), 263–292.

and systems can lead to better customer service, more efficient call centers, product cross-selling, simplified sales and marketing efforts, more efficient sales transactions, and increased customer revenues. The goal is a more effective interaction with customers and bringing together all information the company has on a customer.

Three common CRM systems are Oracle, SAP, and Salesforce.com. Oracle and SAP have CRM systems that integrate nicely with their other enterprise systems. Oracle's CRM system includes modules for pricing, sales force automation, sales order management, support activities, customer self-service, and service management. SAP's CRM system has similar modules plus marketing support such as resource and brand management, campaign management, real-time offer management, loyalty management, and e-marketing. There is also an e-commerce module that facilitates personalized interface and self-service applications for customers. Salesforce.com is a different type of CRM. Whereas Oracle and SAP came from the enterprise systems space and then created a CRM module, Salesforce.com started with a CRM solution. In addition, Oracle and SAP grew from an on-premise enterprise system and eventually built Web-based versions of their products, but Salesforce.com started as a Web-based cloud system. Managers who seek a CRM system for their organizations want to compare the features and delivery systems of these and other solutions provided by niche vendors who specialize in systems optimized for specific industry applications.

Of course, there are other players on the enterprise systems field. For example, Scribe Software Corporation offers data integration for CRM systems. One of its clients is Oil Purification Systems, Inc (OPS), a developer of a patented onboard fluid cleaning system that streamlines oil maintenance routines for large vehicles and industrial equipment. OPS wanted a more robust financial and operations management solution to fit its business processes. In particular, OPS had clear objectives about how information should flow from sales and orders through product shipment and invoicing. To meet these objectives it chose Scribe software as an integration solution between Microsoft Dynamics GP (an ERP system) and Dynamics CRM. OPS wanted its sales people to have certain customer account details at their fingertips, but did not want them to have direct access to the ERP system. That is, OPS wanted to control access to sensitive information and they also wanted an efficient, reliable, and seamless integration between the two enterprise systems.[11]

Social IT is increasingly integrated into CRM solutions. Providing software or Web applications that extend the brand, engage customers, allow customers to interact with each other and with employees, and provide service options all generate additional "touches" with customers. CRM systems record these touches. The information becomes an additional channel of data useful for building customer relationships. Salesforce.com recently teamed with Dun & Bradstreet to use Data.com, a cloud-based storehouse of company and customer contact information for use in CRM systems. Data. com uses a crowd-sourcing model to collect up-to-date information, with users of the serve contributing data and helping to keep that data accurate.

In Chapter 1 we described the Ritz-Carlton's CRM, Class, which captures information about guest preferences and enables providing enhanced customized service during future visits. Web sites collect information from customers who visit, make purchases, or request information. That information is stored in the company's CRM and used in many ways to better meet customer needs and enhance the customer

---

[11] Scribe Customer Case – OPS, Scribe Software Corporation, http://www.harvestsolutions.net/Portals/53955/docs/ops-casestudy.pdf (accessed on February 14, 2012).

experience. For example, movie site Netflix stores all the purchases and product reviews a customer makes in their CRM. Using that information, the site recommends additional films the customer might enjoy, based on analysis of the data in the CRM.

Managing Supply Chains

Another type of enterprise system in common use is the **supply chain management (SCM)** system, which manages the integrated supply chain. Business processes are not just internal to a company. With the help of information technologies, many processes are linked across companies with a companion process at a customer or supplier, creating an integrated supply chain. Technology, especially Web-based technology, allows the supply chains of a company's customers and suppliers to be linked through a single network that optimizes costs and opportunities for all companies in the supply chain. By sharing information across the network, guesswork about order quantities for raw materials and products can be reduced, and suppliers can make sure they have enough on hand if demand for their products unexpectedly rises.

The supply chain of a business is the process that begins with raw materials and ends with a product or service ready to be delivered (or in some cases actually delivered) to a customer. It typically includes the procurement of materials or components, the activities to turn these materials into larger subsystems or final products, and the distribution of these final products to warehouses or customers. But with the increase in information systems use, it may also include product design, product planning, contract management, logistics, and sourcing. Globalization of business and ubiquity of communication networks and information technology has enabled businesses to use suppliers from almost anywhere in the world. At the same time, this has created an additional level of complexity for managing the supply chain. Supply chain integration is the approach of technically linking supply chains of vendors and customers to streamline the process and to increase efficiency and accuracy.

Integrated supply chains have several challenges, primarily resulting from different degrees of integration and coordination among supply chain members.[12] At the most basic level, there is the issue of information integration. Partners must agree on the type of information to share, the format of that information, the technological standards they will both use to share it, and the security they will use to ensure that only authorized partners access it. Trust must be established so the partners can solve higher-level issues that may arise. At the next level is the issue of synchronized planning. At this level, the partners must agree on a joint design of planning, forecasting, and replenishment. The partners, having already agreed on what information to share, now have to agree on what to do with it. The third level can be described as workflow coordination—the coordination, integration, and automation of critical business processes between partners. For some supply chains, this might mean simply using a third party to link the procurement process to the preferred vendors or to communities of vendors who compete virtually for the business. For others it might be a more complex process of integrating order processing and

[12] Adapted from Hau Lee and Seungjin Whang, "E-Business and Supply Chain Integration," Stanford University Global Supply Chain Management Forum (November 2001).

payment systems. Ultimately, the integration of supply chains is leading to new business models, as varied as the visionaries who think them up. These business models are based on new ideas of coordination and integration made possible by the Internet and information-based supply chains. In some cases, new services have been designed by the partnership between supplier and customer, such as new financial services offered when banks link up electronically with businesses to accept online payments for goods and services purchased by the businesses' customers. In other cases, a new business model for sourcing has resulted, such as one in which companies list their supply needs, and vendors electronically bid to be the supplier for that business.

Demand-driven supply networks are the next step for companies with highly evolved supply chain capabilities. Kimberly Clark, the 135-year-old consumer products company, is one such example. Their vision is for a highly integrated suite of supply chain systems that provide end-to-end visibility of the supply processes in real time. Key processes in their demand-driven supply network are forecast-to-stock and order-to-cash. Using an integrated suite of systems allows their users to share the same information in as close to real time as possible, and to use the data in their systems for continually updating their supply chain, category management, and consumer insight processes. IS have allowed management to reduce the problems of handing off data from one system or process to another (because now everything is in one system), having workers work from different databases (because it's now one database), and of working off old data (because it's as real time as possible). This has improved their ability to see what's going on in the marketplace and evaluate the impact of promotions, production, and inventory much more quickly.

Integrated supply chains are truly global in nature. Thomas Friedman, in his book *The World is Flat*, describes how the Dell computer that he had ordered to write his book was developed from the contributions of an integrated supply chain that involved about four hundred companies in North America, Europe, and, primarily, Asia. However, the globalization of integrated supply chains faces a growing challenge from skyrocketing transportation costs. For example, Tesla Motors, a pioneer in electric-power cars, had originally planned the production of a luxury roadster for the American market based on an integrated global supply chain. The 1,000-pound battery packs for the cars were to be manufactured in Thailand, shipped to Britain for installation, and then shipped to the United States, where they would be assembled into cars. However, because of the extensive costs associated with shipping the batteries more than 5,000 miles, Tesla decided to make the batteries and assemble the cars near its headquarters in California. Darryl Siry, Tesla's senior vice president of global sales, marketing, and service explains: "It was kind of a no-brain decision for us. A major reason was to avoid the transportation costs, which are terrible." Economists warn managers to expect the "neighborhood effect" in which factories may be built closer to components suppliers and consumers to reduce transportation costs. This effect may apply not only to cars and steel, but also to chickens and avocados and a wide range of other items.[13]

---

[13] Larry Rohter, "Shipping Costs Start to Crimp Globalization," *New York Times* (August 3, 2008), 1, 10.

Product Lifecycle Management (PLM)

Another less well-known type of enterprise system is a Product Lifecycle Management (PLM) system. PLM systems automate the steps that take ideas for products and turns them into real products. PLM refers to the process that starts with the idea for a product and ends with the "end-of-life" of a product. It includes the innovation activities, new product development and management, design, and product compliance (if necessary). PLM systems contain all the information about a product such as design, production, maintenance, components, vendors, customer feedback, and marketing.

Benefits and Disadvantages of Enterprise Systems

The major benefit of an enterprise system is that all modules of the information system easily communicate with each other, offering enormous efficiencies over stand-alone systems. In business, information from one functional area is often needed by another area. For example, an inventory system stores information about vendors who supply specific parts. This same information is required by the accounts payable system, which pays vendors for their goods. It makes sense to integrate these two systems to have a single accurate record of vendors.

Because of the focus on integration, enterprise systems are useful tools for an organization seeking to centralize operations and decision making. One of the benefits of centralization is the effective use of organizational databases. Redundant data entry and duplicate data may be eliminated; standards for numbering, naming, and coding may be enforced; and data and records can be cleaned up through standardization. Further, the enterprise system can reinforce the use of standard procedures across different locations.

The obvious benefits notwithstanding, implementing an enterprise system represents an enormous amount of work. Using the same simple example as previously, if an organization has allowed both the manufacturing and the accounting departments to keep their own records of vendors, then most likely these records are kept in somewhat different forms (one department may keep the vendor name as "IBM," the other as "International Business Machines" or even "IBM Corp.," all of which make it difficult to integrate the databases). Such data inconsistencies must be addressed for the enterprise system to provide optimal advantage.

Moreover, even though enterprise systems are flexible and customizable to a point, most also require business processes to be redesigned to achieve optimal performance of the integrated modules. The flexibility in an enterprise system comes from being able to change parameters in a process, such as the type of part number the company will use. However, all systems make assumptions about how the business processes work, and at some level, customization is not possible. For example, one major Fortune 500 company refused to implement a vendor's enterprise system because the company manufactured products in lots of "one," and the vendor's system would not handle the volume this company generated. If they had decided to use the ERP, a complete overhaul of their manufacturing process in a way that executives were unwilling to do would have been necessary.

Organizations are expected to conform to the approach used in the enterprise system, arguably because the enterprise system represents a set of industry best practices. Implementing enterprise systems requires organizations to make changes in their organization structure and often in the individual tasks done by workers. Recall in Chapter 1, the Information Systems Strategy Triangle suggests that implementing an information system must be accompanied with appropriate organizational changes to be effective. Implementing an enterprise system is no different. For example, who will now be responsible for entering the vendor information that was formerly kept in two locations? How will that information be entered into the enterprise system? The answer to such simple operational questions often requires managers at a minimum to modify business processes and more likely to redesign them completely to accommodate the information system.

Furthermore, enterprise systems and the organizational changes they induce tend to come with a hefty price tag. In a study of the initial acquisition and implementation costs of ERP systems in primarily midsize companies (with $100 million to $1 billion in annual revenues), half of the responding 157 Chief Financial Officers (CFO) admitted spending *more than* $1 million for the license, service and first year's maintenance on their current ERP system. Nine out of ten respondents said they spent a minimum of $250,000. Unreported were additional hidden costs in the form of technical and business changes are likely to be necessary when implementing an enterprise system. These include project management, user training, and IT support costs.[14]

One of the reasons that enterprise (ERP) systems are so expensive is that they are sold as a suite, such as financials or manufacturing, and not as individual modules. Because buying modules separately is difficult, companies implementing ERP software often find the price of modules they won't use hidden in the cost of the suite.

Enterprise systems are also risky. The number of enterprise system horror stories demonstrates this risk. For example, Kmart wrote off its $130 million ERP investment. American LaFrance (ALF), the manufacturer of highly customized emergency vehicles and a spinoff from Freightliner, declared bankruptcy, blaming their IT vendor and their ERP implementation. The problems with the implementation kept ALF from being able to manufacture many preordered vehicles.[15] The Fort Worth Police Officers Association complained in December 2010 to officials working for the city of Fort Worth that officers were having problems with paychecks, managed by their new ERP system installed two months prior. Some officers had not been paid since the installation, and others were shortchanged in their paychecks, because the new system was not able to handle odd hours and shift work.

Oftentimes, installing an enterprise system means the business must reengineer its business processes. Because the enterprise system is an automation of the major business processes such as financial, manufacturing, and human resource management and because most enterprise systems are purchased from, it is rare that an off-the-shelf system is perfectly harmonious with an existing business process. More

---

[14] T. Wailgum, "Why CEOs and CFOs hate it: ERP," *CIO Magazine* (April 8, 2009), http://advice.cio.com/thomas_wailgum/why_cfos_and_ceos_hate_it_erp (accessed on February 14, 2012).

[15] For additional examples of IT failures in general, and enterprise systems failures in particular, please visit the blog written by Michael Krigsman, http://blogs.zdnet.com/projectfailures/.

typical is that either the software requires significant modification or customization to fit with the existing processes, or the processes must change to fit the software. In most installations of enterprise systems, both take place. The system is customized when it is installed in a business by setting a number of parameters, and in the worst case, by modifying the code itself. The business processes are changed, often through a radical change project, as described earlier in this chapter. Lumber Liquidators net income fell 45% in the third quarter of 2010, and managers blamed the weak performance on their new ERP system. Employees had difficulty using the new system, which structured many of their activities differently than they had been doing them. Many of these projects are massive undertakings, requiring formal, structured project management tools (as discussed in Chapter 10).

When the System Drives the Change

When is it appropriate to use the enterprise system to drive business process redesign, and when is it appropriate to redesign the process first, and then implement an enterprise system? While it may seem like the process should be redesigned first, then the information system aligned to the new design, there are times when it is appropriate to let the enterprise system drive business process redesign. First, when an organization is just starting out and processes do not yet exist, it is appropriate to begin with an enterprise system as a way to structure operational business processes. After all, most of the processes embedded in the "plain vanilla" enterprise system from a top vendor are based on the best practices of corporations who have been in business for years. Second, when an organization does not rely on its operational business processes as a source of competitive advantage, then using an enterprise system to redesign these processes is appropriate. Third, it is reasonable when the current systems are in crisis and there is not enough time, resources, or knowledge in the firm to fix them. Even though it is not an optimal situation, managers must make tough decisions about how to fix the problems. A business must have working operational processes; therefore, using an enterprise system as the basis for process design may be the only workable plan. It was precisely this situation that many companies faced with Y2K.

Likewise, it is sometimes inappropriate to let an enterprise system drive business process change. When an organization derives a strategic advantage through its operational business processes, it is usually not advisable to buy a vendor's enterprise system. Using a standard, publicly available information system that both the company and its competitors can buy from a vendor may mean that any competitive advantage is lost. For example, consider a major computer manufacturer that relied on its ability to process orders faster than its competitors to gain strategic advantage. It would not have been to that organization's benefit to use an enterprise system to drive the redesign of the order fulfillment system because doing so would force the manufacturer to restrict its process to that which is available from enterprise system vendors. More important, any other manufacturer could then copy the process, neutralizing any advantages. Furthermore, the manufacturer believed that relying on a third party as the provider of such a strategic system would be a mistake in the long run. Should the system develop a bug or need to be redesigned to accommodate unique aspects of

Social Business Lens: Crowdsourcing Changes Innovation Processes

One business process that has been radically changed by the use of social IT is the way innovation is managed using crowdsourcing. Enterprises have found ways to use a social IT platform to solicit, discuss, and prioritize new ideas. Anyone in the community can add an idea, then the entire community can discuss, comment, and rate the idea. Managers then have a wealth of ideas along with community input, to use as input into the innovation process.

One of the original examples of this is Dell's Ideastorm. Anyone in the community can access Ideastorm to view ideas posted by the community, post an idea for Dell products or services, vote on the ideas presented, and see what Dell managers have decided to do with the ideas presented. Ideas presented by the community range from suggestions for new features on existing systems, to new products and services Dell might offer. By allowing the community to comment and vote on ideas, managers get a sense of the importance and viability of implementing the innovation.

Similar social platforms have been implemented by numerous other companies including Starbucks's mystarbucksidea.com and Best Buy's IdeaX. Companies have also taken this idea inside the corporation to solicit ideas and innovations about processes, products and other enterprise issues. Dell's EmployeeStorm and the City of New York's Simplicity are two social IT examples of soliciting ideas to improve processes and efficiencies from employees.

Companies have also embraced the crowd for individual projects, such as Sam Adams, the beer company, who used a Facebook application for crowdsourcing the next flavor of beer. Their application let fans select the color, clarity, body, malt, hops, and yeast components of a recipe. For each component, the crowdsourcing application educated fans about the contribution each component made to the resulting beer. They collected the crowd's preferences, sharing them along the way for comment and discussion. The results not only gave Sam Adams managers information about preferences of their fans, but prioritized ideas about the next product to create with a high probability that it will have a large fan base to get it started.

Sources: http://www.ideastorm.com; http://gigaom.com/2011/01/19/new-york-city-crowdsourcing/; and http://www.facebook.com/SamuelAdams?sk=app_299970113373932 (accessed on January 19, 2012).

the business, the manufacturer would be forced to negotiate with the enterprise system vendor to get it to modify the enterprise system. With a system designed in-house, the manufacturer was able to ensure complete control over the IS that drives its critical processes.

Another situation in which it would be inappropriate to let an enterprise system drive business process change is when the features of available packages and the needs of the business do not fit. An organization may use specialized processes that cannot be accommodated by the available enterprise systems. For example, many ERPs were developed for discrete part manufacturing and do not support some processes in paper, food, or other process industries.[16]

A third situation would result from lack of top management support, company growth, a desire for strategic flexibility, or decentralized decision making that render the enterprise system inappropriate. For example, Dell stopped the full implementation of SAP R/3 after only the human resources module had been installed because the CIO did not think that the software would be able to keep pace with Dell's extraordinary growth. Enterprise systems were also viewed as culturally inappropriate at the highly decentralized Kraft Foods.

Challenges for Integrating Enterprise Systems Between Companies

With the widespread use of enterprise systems, the issue of linking supplier and customer systems to the business's systems brings many challenges. As with integrated supply chains, there are the issues of deciding what to share, how to share it, and what to do with it when the sharing takes place. There are also issues of security and agreeing on encryption or other measures to protect data integrity as well as to ensure that only authorized parties have access.

Some companies have tried to reduce the complexity of this integration by insisting on standards, either at the industry level or at the system level. An example of an industry-level standard is the bar coding used by all who do business in the consumer products industry. An example of a system-level standard is the use of SAP or Oracle as the ERP system used by both supplier and customer. And the increasing use of cloud-based systems with standard interfaces makes the integration easier.

► SUMMARY

- Most business processes today have a significant information systems component to them. Either the process is completely executed through software, or there is an important information component which complements the physical executing of the process.

- IS can enable or impede business process change. IS enables change by providing both the tools to implement the change and the tools on which the change is based on. IS can also impede change, particularly when the process flow is mismatched with the capabilities of the IS.

- To understand the role IS plays in business transformation, one must take a business process, rather than a functional, perspective. Business processes are a well-defined, ordered set of tasks characterized by a beginning and an end, a set of associated metrics, and cross-functional boundaries. Most businesses operate business processes, even if their organization charts are structured by functions rather than by processes.

---

[16] M. Lynne Markus and Cornelis Tanis, "The Enterprise System Experience—From Adoption to Success," in R. Zmud (ed.), *Framing the Domains of IT Management: Projecting the Future Through the Past* (Cincinnati, OH: Pinaflex Educational Resources, Inc., 2000), 176–179.

- Agile business processes are processes that are designed to be easily reconfigurable. Dynamic processes are designed to automatically update themselves as conditions change. Both types of processes require a high degree of information systems, which makes the task of changing the process a software activity, rather than a physical activity.

- Making changes in business processes is typically done through either incremental or radical change techniques. Incremental change such as with TQM techniques and six sigma tend to imply an evolutionary change, where processes are improved incrementally. Radical change as is found with BPR techniques, on the other hand, imply a more drastic objective and improvement. Both techniques can be disruptive to the normal flow of the business; hence strong project management skills are needed.

- BPM systems are used to help managers design, control, and document business processes and ultimately workflow in an organization.

- Enterprise systems are large information systems that provide the core functionality needed to run a business. These systems are typically implemented to help organizations share data between divisions. However, in some cases enterprise systems are used to affect organizational transformation by imposing a set of assumptions on the business processes they manage.

- ERP systems are a type of enterprise system used to manage resources including financial, human resources and operations.

- CRM systems are a type of enterprise system used manage the processes related to customers and the relationships developed with customers.

- An integrated supply chain is often managed using an SCM system, an enterprise system that crosses company boundaries and connects vendors and suppliers with organizations to synchronize and streamline planning and deliver products to all members of the supply chain.

- Information systems are useful as tools to both enable and manage business transformation. The general manager must take care to ensure that consequences of the tools themselves are well-understood and well-managed.

► KEY TERMS

agile processes (p. 142)
business process
  management
  (BPM) (p. 146)
business process
  reengineering
  (BPR) (p. 143)
customer relationship
  management
  (CRM) (p. 153)

DMADV (p. 144)
DMAIC (p. 144)
dynamic processes (p. 142)
Enterprise Information
  Systems (EIS) (p. 150)
enterprise resource planning
  (ERP) (p. 151)
enterprise systems (p. 148)
middleware (p. 153)
process (p. 139)

process perspective (p. 139)
silos (p. 138)
six sigma (p. 144)
supply chain management
  (SCM) (p. 156)
total quality management
  (TQM) (p. 143)
workflow (p. 145)
workflow diagram (p. 146)

► DISCUSSION QUESTIONS

1. Why was radical design of business processes embraced so quickly and so deeply by senior managers of so many companies? In your opinion, and using hindsight, was its popularity a benefit for businesses? Why or why not?

2. Off-the-shelf enterprise IS often forces an organization to redesign its business processes. What are the critical success factors to make sure the implementation of an enterprise system is successful?

3. ERP systems are usually designed around best practices. But whose best practices are the right ones? A western bias is common; practices found in North America or Europe are often the foundation. When transferred to Asia, however, the resulting systems may be problematic. Why do you think this is the case? What might be different in the way different countries use processes (besides the standard "language" difference)?

4. Have you been involved with a company doing a redesign of its business processes? If so, what were the key things that went right? What went wrong? What could have been done better to minimize the risk of failure?

5. What do you think the former CIO of Dell, Jerry Gregoire, meant when he said, "Don't automate broken business processes"?[17]

6. What might an integrated supply chain look like for a financial services company such as an insurance provider or a bank? What are the components of the process? What would the customer relationship management process look like for this same firm?

7. Tesco, the U.K. retail grocery chain, used their CRM system to generate annual incremental sales of £100 million. Using a frequent-shopper card, a customer got discounts at the time of purchase, and the company got information about their purchases, creating a detailed database of customer preferences. Tesco then categorized customers and customized discounts and mailings, generating increased sales and identifying new products to expand their offerings. At the individual stores, data showed which products must be priced below competitors, which products had fewer price-sensitive customers, and which products must have regular low prices to be successful. In some cases, prices are store-specific, based on the customer information. The information system has enabled Tesco to expand beyond groceries to books, CDs, DVDs, consumer electronics, flowers, and wine. The chain also offers services such as loans, credit cards, savings accounts, and travel planning. What can Tesco management do now that they have a CRM that they could not do prior to the CRM implementation? How does this system enable Tesco to increase the value provided to customers?

CASE STUDY 5-1

SANTA CRUZ BICYCLES

Bicycle enthusiasts not only love the ride their bikes provide, but they also are often willing to pay for newer technology especially when it will increase their speed or comfort. Innovating new technologies for bikes is only half the battle for bike manufacturers. Designing the process to manufacture the bikes is often the more daunting challenge.

Consider the case of Santa Cruz Bicycles. It digitally designs and builds mountain bikes and tests them under the most extreme conditions to bring the best possible product to their customers. A few years back, the company designed and patented the Virtual Pivot Point (VPP) suspension system, a means to absorb the shocks that mountain bikers encounter when

---

[17] "Technology: How Much? How Fast? How Revolutionary? How Expensive?" *Fast Company* 56, 62, http://www.fastcompany.com/online/56/fasttalk.html (accessed on May 30, 2002).

on the rough terrain of the off-road ride. One feature of the new design allowed the rear wheel to bounce 10 inches without hitting the frame or seat, providing shock absorption without feeling like the rider was sitting on a coiled spring.

The first few prototypes did not work well; in one case, the VPP joint's upper link snapped after a quick jump. The experience was motivation for a complete overhaul of the design and engineering process to find a way to go from design to prototype faster. The 25-person company adopted a similar system used by large, global manufacturers: product life cycle management (PLM) software.

The research and development team had been using computer-aided-design (CAD) software, but it took 7 months to develop a new design, and if the design failed, starting over was the only solution. This was not only a drain on the company's time but also on finances. The design team found a PLM system that helped them analyze and model capabilities in a much more robust manner. The team uses simulation capabilities to watch the impact of the new designs on rough mountain terrain. The software tracks all the variables the designers and engineers need so they can quickly and easily make adjustments to the design. The new system allows them to run a simulation in a few minutes, which is a very large improvement over their previous design software, which took 7 hours to run a simulation.

The software was just one component of the new process design. The company also hired a new master frame builder to build and test prototypes in-house and they invested in a van-size machine that can fabricate intricate parts for their prototypes, a process they used to outsource. The result was a significant decrease in their design-to-prototype process. What used to average about 28 months from start of design to shipping of the new bike now takes 12 to 14 months.

Discussion Questions

1. What, in your opinion, was the key factor in Santa Cruz Bicycles' successful process redesign? Why was that factor the key?
2. What outside factors had to come together for Santa Cruz Bicycles to be able to make the changes they did?
3. Why is this story more about change management that software implementation?

Source: Adapted from Mel Duvall, "Santa Cruz Bicycles," www.baselinemag.com (accessed on February 24, 2008).

CASE STUDY 5-2

BOEING 787 DREAMLINER

The first Boeing 787 Dreamliner was delivered to Japan's ANA in the third quarter of 2011, more than three years after the initial planned delivery date. Its complicated, unique design (including a one-piece fuselage that eliminated the need for 1,500 aluminum sheets and 50,000 fasteners and reduced the resulting weight of the plane proportionally), promise of 20% increase in fuel economy and reduction in 'out of service' maintenance time, and problems with early testing of the new design all contributed to the giant project's troubles.

Delivery of Boeing's 787 Dreamliner project was delayed, in part, because of their global supply chain network, which was touted to reduce cost and development time. In reality, this turned out to be a major cause for problems. Boeing decided to change the rules of the way large passenger aircraft were developed through its Dreamliner program; rather than simply relying on technological know-how, it decided to use collaboration as a competitive tool embedded into a new global supply chain process.

With the Dreamliner project, Boeing not only attempted to create a new aircraft through the innovative design and new material, but it also radically changed the production process. It built an incredibly complex supply chain involving over fifty partners scattered in 103 locations all over the world. The goal was to reduce the financial risks involved in a $10 billion-plus project for designing and developing a new aircraft and reduce the new product development cycle time. It tapped expertise of various firms in different areas such as composite materials, aerodynamics, and IT infrastructure to create a network in which partners' skills complement each other. This changed the basis of competition to skill set rather than the traditional basis of low cost. In addition, this was the first time Boeing had outsourced the production on the two most critical parts of the plane— the wings and the fuselage.

The first sign of problems showed up just six months into the trial production. Engineers discovered unexpected bubbles in the skin of the fuselage during baking of the composite material. This delayed the project a month. Boeing officials insisted that they made up the time and all things were under control. But next to fail was the test version of the nose section. This time a problem was found in the software programs, which were designed by various manufacturers. They failed to communicate with each other, leading to a breakdown in the integrated supply chain. Then problems popped up in the integration of electronics. The Dreamliner program entered the danger zone when Boeing declared that it was having trouble getting enough permanent titanium fasteners to hold together various parts of the aircraft. The global supply network did not integrate well for Boeing and left it highly dependent on a few suppliers.

This case clearly underscores the hazards in relying on an extensive supply chain in which information exchange problems may create extended problems and seriously compromise a company's ability to carry out business as planned. Creating a radically different process can mean encountering unexpected problems. In some cases, it would put a company so far behind their competition that they were doomed to fail. However, in this case, the major competitor to the Dreamliner, the Airbus 380 program, was also using a global supply-chain model, and its program was delayed by a couple of years. The result for Boeing was a much-anticipated plane with fuel economy and outstanding design that made the wait worth it, but the resulting design, a plane that holds up to 250 passengers, compared to the A380, which has a seating capacity between 525 and 853, was a major compromise.

Discussion Questions

1. Why did Boeing adopt the radical change approach for designing and developing the 787 Dreamliner? What were the risks? In your opinion, was it a good move? Defend your choice.

2. Using the Silo Perspective versus Business Process Perspective, analyze the Dreamliner program.

3. What are your conclusions about the design of the integrated supply chain? Give some specific ideas about what could have been done to integrate it better.

4. If you were the program manager, what would you have done differently to avoid the problems faced by the Dreamliner program?

Sources: Adapted from J. Lynn Lunsford, "Boeing Scrambles to Repair Problems with New Plane," *Wall Street Journal* (December 7, 2007), A1, 13; Stanley Holmes, "The 787 Encounters Turbulence," *BusinessWeek* (June 19, 2006), 38–40; and Zach Honig, "Boeing 787 review: ANA's Dreamliner flies across Japan, we join for the ride" (December 16, 2011), http://www.engadget.com/2011/12/16/boeing-787-review-anas-dreamliner-flies-across-japan-we-join/.

CHAPTER 6

ARCHITECTURE AND INFRASTRUCTURE

This chapter provides managers with an overview of IT architecture and infrastructure issues and designs. It begins by translating a business into IT architecture and then from the architecture into infrastructure. The manager's role is then discussed, and an example of a fictitious company, TennisUp, is used to show how strategy leads to infrastructure. The framework used to describe the basic components of architecture and infrastructure, introduced in Chapter 1, is revisited here, providing a language and structure for describing hardware, software, network, and data considerations. Common architectures are then presented, including centralized, decentralized and Web-based Services Oriented Architecture (SOA). Architectural principles are covered, followed by a discussion of enterprise architecture. Virtualization and cloud computing, two current architectural considerations, are reviewed. The chapter concludes with a discussion of managerial considerations that apply to any architecture.

Valero Energy, the North American oil and gas refiner, has experienced hypergrowth for the past ten years, mostly through acquisitions.[1] The company's revenue has grown from $29 billion to $90 billion, but with this growth came a mixture of different information technology (IT) systems and applications that were difficult and expensive to manage, and that did not easily integrate into their corporate enterprise resource planning (ERP) system and their business applications suite. Further, in the future, managers wanted to implement a self-service model where business units could create applications themselves in an easy, low-cost manner. For the managers to execute their business strategy, their IT architecture had to be redesigned and their infrastructure updated.

The architecture had to be flexible, able to grow with the company, and easily reused as new systems were needed. The IS organization decided to use an SOA (service-oriented architecture) design in which applications and computing resources were available as components. For example, an order management component might be used by both a customer service application and a profitability analysis application.

The infrastructure for the ERP and business applications suite was SAP's R/3 system. The newer components included a set of 90 services built on SAP's development

---

[1] Adapted from http://www.cioinsight.com—CIOInsight, Ziff Davis Enterprise Holdings Inc. (accessed on February 24, 2008).

environment. Further, these core services have been used to create 40 different composite applications, helping management attain their reusability goal and keeping application development costs down. For example, one of the new applications was designed to let wholesale clients view account information via the Internet. The infrastructure used SAP NewWeaver Portal interface to connect to the SAP R/3 CRM (customer relationship management) system data warehouse and to other non-SAP systems. This design gives users a single view into the integrated information.

The results were dramatic. Savings added up for Valero because they did not have to build interfaces between all the independent systems they inherited through the acquisitions. New applications made operations more efficient and effective. One application saved the company a half-million dollars in fees that are charged when a ship sits idle at the dock. Before this new application, the managers did not have a way to monitor tankers as they unloaded oil, and therefore sometimes ships had to wait to unload their cargo. The new application provides visibility to the tankers and communications with employees at the refineries in order to avoid scheduling conflicts and the ensuing costs.

So far, this text explored the organizational, tactical, and strategic importance of IS. As illustrated with the Valero story, this chapter examines the mechanisms by which business strategy is transformed into tangible IS architecture and infrastructure. The terms *architecture* and *infrastructure* are often used interchangeably in the context of IS. This chapter discusses how the two differ and the important role each plays in realizing a business strategy. Then this chapter examines some common architectural components for IS today.

▶ FROM VISION TO IMPLEMENTATION

As shown in Figure 6.1, architecture translates strategy into infrastructure. Building a house is similar: the owner has a vision of how the final product should look and function. The owner must decide on a strategy about where to live—in an apartment or in a house. The owner's strategy also includes deciding how to live in the house in terms of taking advantage of a beautiful view, having an open floor plan, or planning for special interests

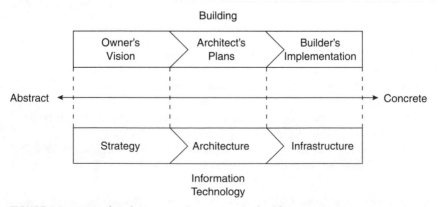

FIGURE 6.1 From the abstract to the concrete—building vs. IT.

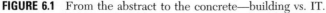

by designing such special areas as a game room, study, music room, or other amenities. The architect develops plans based on this vision. These plans, or blueprints, provide a guide—unchangeable in some areas, but subject to interpretation in others—for the carpenters, plumbers, and electricians who actually construct the house. Guided by past experience and by industry standards, these builders select the materials and construction techniques best suited to the plan. The plan helps them determine where to put the plumbing and wiring. When the process works, the completed house fulfills its owner's vision, even though he or she did not participate in the actual construction. As finishing touches, the owner adds window coverings, light fixtures, and furniture to make the new house livable.

An IT **architecture** provides a blueprint for translating business strategy into a plan for IS. An IT **infrastructure** is everything that supports the flow and processing of information in an organization, including hardware, software, data, and network components. It consists of components, chosen and assembled in a manner that best suits the plan and therefore best enables the overarching business strategy.[2] Infrastructure in an organization is similar to the plumbing, wiring, and furnishings in a house; it's the actual hardware, software, network, and data used to create the information system.

The Manager's Role

Even though he or she is not drawing up plans or pounding nails, the homeowner in this example needs to know what to reasonably expect from the architect and builders. The homeowner must know enough about architecture, specifically about styling and layout, to work effectively with the architect who draws up the plans. Similarly, the homeowner must know enough about construction details such as the benefits of various types of siding, windows, and insulation to set reasonable expectations for the builders.

Like the homeowner, the manager must understand what to expect from IT architecture and infrastructure to be able to make full and realistic use of them. The manager must effectively communicate his or her business vision to IT architects and implementers and, if necessary, modify the plans if IT cannot realistically create or support them. For without the involvement of the manager, IT architects could inadvertently make decisions that limit the manager's business options in the future.

For example, a sales manager for a large distribution company did not want to partake in discussions about providing sales force automation systems for his group. He felt that a standard package offered by a well-known vendor would work fine. After all it worked for lots of other companies, he rationalized, so it would be fine for his company. No architecture was designed, and no long-range thought was given to how the application might support or inhibit the sales group. After implementation, it became clear that the application had limitations and did not support the type of sales process in use at this company. He approached the IT department for help, and in the discussions that ensued, he learned that earlier infrastructure decisions now made it prohibitively expensive to implement the capability he wanted. Involvement with earlier decisions and the ability to convey his vision of what the sales group wanted to do might have resulted

[2] Gordon Hay and Rick Muñoz, "Establishing an IT Architecture Strategy," *Information Systems Management* (Summer 1997).

in an IT infrastructure that provided a platform for the changes the manager now wanted to make. Instead, the infrastructure lacked an architecture that met the business objectives of the sales and marketing management.

▶ THE LEAP FROM STRATEGY TO ARCHITECTURE TO INFRASTRUCTURE

The huge number of IT choices available, coupled with the incredible speed of technology advances, makes the manager's task of designing an IT infrastructure seem nearly impossible. However, in this chapter, the task is broken down into two major steps: first, translating strategy into architecture and, second, translating architecture into infrastructure. This chapter describes a simple framework to help managers sort through IT issues. This framework stresses the need to consider business strategy when defining an organization's IT building blocks. Although this framework may not cover every possible architectural issue, it does highlight major issues associated with effectively defining IT architecture and infrastructure.

From Strategy to Architecture

The manager must start out with a strategy, and then use the strategy to develop more specific goals, as shown in Figure 6.2. Then detailed business requirements are derived from each goal. In the Valero case, the strategy was to provide a single face to customers, and the goal was to integrate all the acquisitions. The business requirements were to integrate the information systems into a single, flexible system. By outlining the overarching business strategy and then fleshing out the business requirements associated with each goal, the manager can provide the architect with a clear picture of what IS must accomplish and the governance arrangements needed to ensure their smooth development, implementation, and use. The governance arrangements specify who in the company retains control of, and responsibility for, the IS. Preferably this is somebody at the top.

Of course, the manager's job is not finished here. Continuing with Figure 6.2, the manager must work with the IT architect to translate these business requirements into a more detailed view of the systems requirements, standards, and processes that shape an IT architecture. This more detailed view, the architectural requirements, includes consideration of such things as data and process demands, as well as security objectives. These are the architectural requirements. The IT architect takes the architectural requirements and designs the IT architecture.

From Architecture to Infrastructure

Valero's decision to use a service-oriented architecture led to the design of a number of services and composite applications. This illustrates the next step, translating the architecture into infrastructure. This task entails adding yet more detail to the architectural plan that emerged in the previous phase. Now the detail comprises actual hardware, data, networking, and software. Details extend to location of data and access procedures, location of firewalls, link specifications, interconnection design, and so on. This phase is also illustrated in Figure 6.2 where the architecture is translated into functional specifications. The functional specifications can be broken down into hardware specifications,

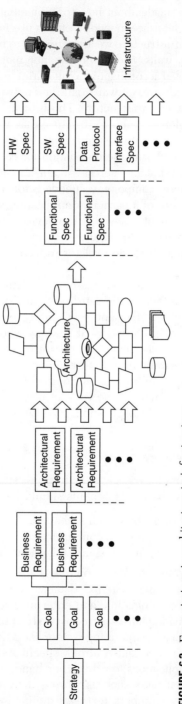

FIGURE 6.2 From strategy to architecture to infrastructure.

software specifications, storage specifications, interface specifications, network specifications, etc. Then decisions are made about how to implement these specifications; what hardware, software, storage, interface, network, etc. to use in the infrastructure.

When we speak about infrastructure we are referring to more than the components. Plumbing, electrical wiring, walls, and a roof do not make a house. Rather, these components must be assembled according to the blueprint to create a structure in which people can live. Similarly, hardware, software, data, and networks must be combined in a coherent pattern to have a viable infrastructure. This infrastructure can be considered at several levels. At the most global level infrastructure may focus on the enterprise and refer to the infrastructure for the entire organization. Infrastructure may also focus on the interorganizational level by laying the foundation for communicating with customers, suppliers, or other stakeholders across organizational boundaries. Sometimes infrastructure refers to those components needed for an individual application. When considering the structure of a particular application, it is important to consider databases and program components, as well as the devices and operating environments on which they run. The application-level infrastructure reflects decisions made at the enterprise level. The following discussion relates to infrastructure and architecture at the enterprise level.

Often when referring to an infrastructure, the underlying computer system is called the **platform**. A platform refers to the hardware and operating system on which applications run. For example, in the laptop/PC industry, technologists talk about a "windows platform," which refers to personal systems whose hardware supports the windows operating system. Another common platform is the "Mac platform," which refers to the latest operating system from Apple running on a Macintosh laptop or PC. In the smartphone industry, the "Android platform" and the "iPhone platform" are two examples frequently seen. Both may run the same applications from a user's perspective, but that is because the vendor of the applications has written two versions—one for each platform.

A Framework for the Translation

When developing a framework for transforming business strategy into architecture and then into infrastructure these basic components should be considered:

- *Hardware:* The physical components that handle computation, storage, or transmission of data (e.g., personal computers, servers, mainframes, hard drives, RAM, fiber-optic cabling, modems, and telephone lines).

- *Software:* The programs that run on the hardware to enable work to be performed (e.g., operating systems, databases, accounting packages, word processors, sales force automation, and enterprise resource planning systems). Software is usually divided into two groups: **system software** and **applications**. System software, such as an operating system like Microsoft's Windows, Apple's Lion, Linux, iPhone's iOS, and Android, specifies the platform on which the applications run. Applications, on the other hand, are software that automate business and personal tasks such as storing data, transferring files, creating documents, calculating numbers, texting, listening to music and playing games.

- *Network:* Software and hardware components, such as switches, hubs, and routers, that create a path for communication and data sharing according to a common protocol. Some networks are private, requiring credentials to connect. Others, like the Internet, are public.

- *Data:* The electronic representation of the numbers and text. Here, the main concern is the quantity and format of data, and how often it must be transferred from one piece of hardware to another or translated from one format to another.

The framework that guides the analysis of these components was introduced in the first chapter, in Figure 1.8. This framework is simplified to make the point that initially understanding an organization's infrastructure is not difficult. Understanding the technology behind each component of the infrastructure and the technical requirements of the architecture is a much more complex task. The main point is that the general manager must begin with an overview that is complete and that delivers a big picture.

This framework asks three types of questions that must be answered for each infrastructure component: what, who, and where. The "what" questions are those most commonly asked and that identify the specific type of technology. The "who" questions seeks to understand what individuals, groups, and departments are involved. In most cases, the individual user is not the owner of the system or even the person who maintains it. In many cases, the systems are leased, not owned, by the company, making the owner a party completely outside the organization. In understanding the infrastructure, it is important to get a picture of the people involved. The third set of questions addresses "where" issues. With the proliferation of networks, many IS are designed and built with components in multiple locations, often even crossing oceans. Learning about infrastructure means understanding where everything is located.

We can expand the use of this framework to also understand architecture. To illustrate the connections between strategy and systems, the table in Figure 6.3 has been populated with questions that typify those asked in addressing architecture and infrastructure issues associated with each component.

The questions shown in Figure 6.3 are only representative of those to be asked; the specific questions managers would ask about their organizations depend on the business strategy the organizations are following. However, this framework can help managers raise appropriate questions as they seek to translate business strategy into architecture and ultimately into infrastructure in their organizations. The answers derived with IT architects and implementers should provide a robust picture of the IT environment. That means that the IT architecture includes plans for the data and information, the technology (the standards to be followed and the infrastructure that provides the foundation), and the applications to be accessed via the company IT system.

Traditionally, there are three common configurations of IT architecture as shown in Figure 6.4. Enterprises liked the idea of a **centralized architecture** where everything is purchased, supported and managed centrally, usually in a **data center**, to eliminate the difficulties that come with managing a distributed infrastructure. In addition, since almost every enterprise had a large data center with mainframe at some point, there are a significant number of legacy mainframe environments still in operation today. However,

Component	What		Who		Where	
	Architecture	Infrastructure	Architecture	Infrastructure	Architecture	Infrastructure
Hardware	What type of personal device will our users use?	What size hard drives do we equip our laptops with?	Who knows the most about servers in our organization?	Who will operate the server?	Does our architecture require centralized or distributed servers?	What specific computers will we put in our Tokyo data center?
Software	Does fulfillment of our strategy require ERP software?	Shall we go with SAP or Oracle Applications?	Who is affected by a move to SAP?	Who will need SAP training?	Does our geographical organization require multiple database instances?	Can we use a cloud instance of Oracle for our database?
Network	How much bandwidth do we need to fulfill our strategy?	Will the Cisco switch provide what we need?	Who needs a connection to the network?	Who provides our wireless network?	Will we let each user's phone be a hotspot?	Shall we lease a cable or use satellite?
Data	What data do we need for our sales management system?	What format will we store our data in?	Who needs access to sensitive data?	How will authorized users identify themselves?	Will backups be stored on-site or off-site?	Will data be in the cloud or in our datacenter?

FIGURE 6.3 Infrastructure and architecture analysis framework with sample questions.

one large computer at the center of the IT architecture is not used as regularly today as it was in the recent past. Instead, many computers are linked together to form a centralized IT core that operates very much like the mainframe, providing the bulk of IT services necessary for the business.

A more common configuration is a **decentralized architecture**. The hardware, software, networking, and data are arranged in a way that distributes the processing and functionality between multiple small computers, servers, and devices and they rely heavily on a network to connect them together. Typically, a decentralized architecture uses numerous servers, often located in different physical locations, at the backbone of the infrastructure, called a **server-based architecture**.

Although some would debate this point, a third increasingly common configuration is **service-oriented architecture (SOA)**, the architecture that Valero decided to use. An example of a service might be an online employment form that, when completed, generates a file with the data for use in another service. Another example might be a ticket processing service that identifies available concert seats and allocates them. These relatively small chunks of functionality are available for many applications, or **reuse**. The type of software used in an SOA architecture is often referred to as

Architecture	Description	Other Terms	When to Use?
Centralized Architecture	Large central computer system handles all functionality of the system. Typically, the computer is housed in a data center and managed directly by the IT department. Data stored and Applications all run on the central computer. Networking allows users to access the mainframe from remote locations.	Mainframe architecture	When you want to make it easier to manage—all functionality is located in one place. When the business is highly centralized.
Decentralized Architecture	The computing power needed to run the business is spread out among a number of devices, including servers in different locations, PCs and laptops, smart phones and tablets. The devices (sometimes called the client) have enough processing capabilities to perform many of the services needed, and goes to the central servers as needed for data and specialized services.	Server-based architecture	When you are concerned about scalability—modularity helps here. When the business is primarily decentralized.
Service Oriented Architecture (SOA)	Larger software programs are broken down into services connected to each other, in a process called orchestration. Together they form an application for an entire business process. Usually, the services are available from a range of vendors on the Internet, and applications are combinations of these services linked together.	Web-based architecture	When you want to be agile—reusability and componentization useful for creating new apps. When the business is new and rapid app design is important.

FIGURE 6.4 Common architectures.

software-as-a-service or SaaS. Another term for these applications, when delivered over the Internet, is **Web services**.

A manager must be aware of the trade-offs when considering centralized versus decentralized architectural decisions. For example, decentralized architectures are more modular than the centralized architectures, allowing additional servers to be added with relative ease and provide greater flexibility for adding clients with specific functionality for specific users. Decentralized organizational governance, such as that associated with the networked organization structure (discussed in Chapter 3) is consistent with decentralized architectures. In contrast, a centralized architecture is easier to manage in some ways because all functionality is centralized in the main computer instead of distributed throughout all the devices and servers. A centralized architecture tends to be a better match in companies with highly centralized governance, for example, those with hierarchical organization structures. SOA is increasingly popular because the design enables large units of functionality to be built almost entirely from existing software service components. It is useful for building applications quickly because it offers managers a modular and componentized design, and therefore a more easily modifiable, approach to building applications.

An example of an organization making these trade-offs is the Veterans Health Administration (VHA), a part of the Department of Veterans Affairs of the U.S. federal government.[3] The organization included 14 different business units that served various administrative and organizational needs. The primary objective of the organization was to provide health care for veterans and their families. In addition, the VHA was a major contributor to medical research, allowing medical students to train at VHA hospitals. The medical centers operated independently and sometimes competed against each other. When the U.S. Congress passed an act that enabled the VHA to restructure itself from a system of hospitals to a single health-care system, the IT architecture was reconfigured from a very centralized design, which enabled the Office of Data Management and Telecommunications to retain control, to a decentralized hospital-based architecture that gave local physicians and administrators the opportunity to deploy applications addressing local needs, while ensuring that standards were developed across the different locations. The VA then introduced the "One-VA" architecture to unify the decentralized systems and "to provide an accessible source of consistent, reliable, accurate, useful, and secure information and knowledge to veterans and their families. . ." Efforts were made to encrypt, secure, and account for every piece of computer hardware in the system and a national and regional data warehouse initiative was launched to standardize business data storage and management.

Recent technological advances make designs possible such as peer-to-peer and wireless or mobile infrastructures. These designs do not necessarily need to be the firm's exclusive infrastructure. For example, a wireless infrastructure may operate separately or may be built on a mainframe or server-based backbone. **Peer-to-peer** allows networked computers to share resources without a central server playing a dominant role. ThePirateBay.org, the Web site for sharing music, movies, games, and more, and Skype, a site for teleconferencing, texting, and telephoning, are examples of businesses that use a peer-to-peer architecture. **Wireless (mobile) infrastructures** allow communication from remote locations using a variety of wireless technologies (e.g., fixed microwave links, wireless LANs, data over cellular networks, wireless WANs, satellite links, digital dispatch networks, one-way and two-way paging networks, diffuse infrared, laser-based communications, keyless car entry, and global positioning systems).

Web-based architectures are architectures in which significant hardware, software, and possibly even data elements reside on the Internet. Web-based architectures

---

[3] Adapted from V. Venkatesh, H. Bala, S. Venkatraman, and J. Bates, "Enterprise Architecture Maturity: The Story of the Veterans Health Administration," *MIS Quarterly Executive* (June 2007), 6(2), 79–90; and J. Walters, "Transforming Information Technology at the Department of Veteran Affairs: IBM Transformation Series, 2009".

offers greater flexibility when used as a source for **capacity-on-demand**, or the availability of additional processing capability for a fee. IT managers like the concept of capacity on demand to help manage peak processing periods when additional capacity is needed. It allows them to use the Web-available capacity as needed, rather than purchasing additional computers to handle the larger loads.

With the proliferation of smart phones and intelligent computing tablets like the iPad, enterprises are increasingly faced with employees who want to bring their own devices and connect to enterprise systems. Some call this **Bring Your Own Device**, or BYOD, and it raises some important managerial considerations. When employees connect their own devices to the corporate network, issues such as capacity, security, and compatibility arise. For example, many corporate applications are not designed to function on the small screen of a smart phone. Redesigning it for personal devices may require significant investment to accommodate the smartphone platform. And not all smartphone platforms are the same. Designing for an iPhone is different than for an Android phone. Even if a system were redesigned for these two platforms, the resources required to maintain the system increase since each platform evolves at a different rate and the applications need to appear similar on each device. In some circles, the drive to port applications to personal devices and the ensuing issues to make them work is referred to as the **consumerization of IT**.

Consumerization of IT is a growing phenomenon. Not only do employees want to use their own devices to access corporate systems, but customers increasingly expect to access company systems from their mobile devices. Making applications robust yet simple enough for customers to use from virtually any mobile device over the Web is a challenge for many information systems departments. Companies such as Good Technology have been created to provide services that allow enterprise employees to connect, communicate, and collaborate using their own devices, supplementing the IT organization's ability to meet this new demand.

▶ FROM STRATEGY TO ARCHITECTURE TO INFRASTRUCTURE: AN EXAMPLE[4]

This section considers a simple example to illustrate the process of converting strategy to architecture to infrastructure. The case discussed is TennisUp, a fictitious maker of tennis rackets.

Define the Strategic Goals

The managers at TennisUp recognize the increasing popularity of tennis; in fact, they can hardly keep up with demand for their rackets. At the same time, however, TennisUp's president, Love Addin, is concerned that tennis mania may end. Addin

---

[4] Only a few questions raised from the framework are provided; a comprehensive, detailed treatment of this situation would require more information than provided in this simple example.

wants to ensure that TennisUp can respond to sudden changes in demand for rackets. Along with the board of directors, Addin sets TennisUp's strategic goals:

- To lower costs by outsourcing racket manufacturing
- To lower costs by outsourcing racket distribution
- To improve market responsiveness by outsourcing racket manufacturing
- To improve market responsiveness by outsourcing racket distribution

Translate Strategic Goals to Business Requirements

To keep things simple, consider more closely only one of TennisUp's strategic goals: To lower costs by outsourcing racket manufacturing. How can TennisUp's architecture enable this goal? Its goal must be translated into business requirements. The business requirements reflect the following key interfaces to the new manufacturing partners:

- Sales to manufacturing partners: Send forecasts, confirm orders received.
- Manufacturing partner to sales: Send capacity, confirm orders shipped.
- Manufacturing partner to accounting: Confirm orders shipped, electronic invoices, various inventory levels, returns.
- Accounting to manufacturing partner: Transfer funds for orders fulfilled.

Translate Business Requirements into Architecture

To support the business requirements, architectural requirements are specified that dictate the architecture to be established. One major component of the architecture deals with how to obtain, store, and use data to support those business requirements.

The database can be designed to provide the sales data to support sales applications such as sending forecasts and confirming orders received. The database can also be designed to support manufacturing applications that confirm orders shipped, manage inventory, and estimate capacity. The database also needs to be designed to support accounting applications for invoicing, handling returns, and transferring funds.

Translate Architecture to Infrastructure

With the architecture goals in hand, the framework presented in Figure 6.2 outlines how to build the infrastructure. The architecture informs the architect of the functions needed by the infrastructure, and a functional specification is created. Those specs are then translated into hardware, software, data protocols, interface designs, and other components that will make up the infrastructure. For TennisUp's database, the functional specification would include details such as how big it should be, how fast data access should be, what the format of the data will be, and more. These functional specifications then help narrow down the technical specifications, which answer these questions. For example, TennisUp's database needs to accommodate up to 10,000 terabytes as determined by projecting the current database growth for the next five years. The programming language for the database will be SQL, to be compatible with the other applications in the enterprise. Additional technical specifications would be created until the entire infrastructure is designed. Then TennisUp's IT department is ready to pick specific hardware, software, network, data, etc., to put into its infrastructure.

Figure 6.5 lists questions raised when applying the framework to TennisUp's architecture goals and related infrastructure. Note that not all questions apply in a given situation. Figure 6.6 lists possible infrastructure components.

Component	What		Who		Where	
	Architecture	Infrastructure	Architecture	Infrastructure	Architecture	Infrastructure
Hardware	What kind of supplemental server capacity will the new supply chain (SCM) transactions require?	Will TennisUp's current dual-CPU NT servers handle the capacity, or will the company have to add additional CPUs and/or disks?	NA	Who is responsible for setting up necessary hardware at partner site?	Where does responsibility for owning and maintaining SCM hardware fall within TennisUp?	Which hardware components will need to be replaced or modified to connect to new SCM hardware?
Software	What parts of TennisUp's software architecture will the new architecture affect?	Will TennisUp's current Access database interface adequately with new SCM software?	Who knows the current software architecture well enough to manage the SCM enhancements?	Who will do any new SQL coding required to accommodate new software?	NA	Where will software patches be required to achieve compatibility with changes resulting from new software components?
Network	What is the anticipated volume of transactions between TennisUp and its manufacturing partners?	High volume may require leased lines to carry transaction data; dial-up connections may suffice for low volume.	Who is responsible for additional networking expense incurred by partners due to increased demands of SCM architecture?	NA	Where will security concerns arise in TennisUp's current network architecture?	Where will TennisUp house new networking hardware required for SCM?
Data	Will data formats supporting the new architecture be compatible with TennisUp's existing formats?	Which formats must TennisUp translate?	Who will be responsible for using sales data to project future volumes to report to manufacturing partner?	Who will be responsible for backing up additional data resulting from new architecture?	Where does the current architecture contain potential bottlenecks given changes anticipated in data flows?	Does the new architecture require TennisUp to switch from its current 100Base-TX Ethernet to 1000Base T?

FIGURE 6.5 Framework application to TennisUp.

Hardware	Software	Network	Data
3 servers: • manufacturing • sales • accounting Storage systems	ERP system with modules for: • manufacturing • sales • accounting • inventory Enterprise application integration (EAI) software	Cable modem to ISP Dial-up lines for backup Routers Hubs Switches Firewalls	Database: • manufacturing • sales • accounting

FIGURE 6.6 TennisUp's infrastructure components.

▶ ARCHITECTURAL PRINCIPLES

Any good architecture is based on a set of principles, or fundamental beliefs about how the architecture should function. Architectural principles must be consistent with both the values of the enterprise as well as with the technology used in the infrastructure. They are designed by considering the key objectives of the organization, and then translated into principles to apply to the design of the IT architecture. The number of principles vary widely, and there is no set list of what must be included in a set of architectural principles. However, a guideline for developing architectural principles is to make sure they are directly related to the operating model of the enterprise and IS organization. Principles should define the desirable behaviors of the IT systems and the role of the organization(s) that support it. A sample of architectural principles is shown in Figure 6.7.

▶ ENTERPRISE ARCHITECTURE

Many companies apply even more complex frameworks than those described earlier for developing an IT architecture and infrastructure, employing an **enterprise architecture (EA)**, or the "blueprint" for all IS and their interrelationships in the firm. Enterprise architecture is the term used for the organizing logic for the entire organization, often specifying how information technologies will support business processes. It differs from an IT architecture in its level of analysis, although it shares some design principles of the lower-level architectures. It identifies the core processes of the company and how they will work together, how the IT systems will support the processes, the standard technical capabilities and activities for all parts of the enterprise, and guidelines for making choices. As experts Jeanne Ross, Peter Weill, and David Robertson describe in their book, *Enterprise Architecture as Strategy*,

> "Top-performing companies define how they will do business (an operating model) and design the processes and infrastructure critical to their current and future operations (enterprise architecture). . . Then these smart companies exploit their foundation,

Principle	Description
Ease of use	The IT architecture will promote ease of use in building and supporting the architecture and solutions based on the architecture.
Single point of view	The IT architecture will enable a consistent, integrated view of the business, regardless of access point.
Buy over build	Business applications, system components, and enabling frameworks will be purchased unless there is a competitive reason to develop them internally.
Speed and quality	Architectural decisions will be made with an emphasis on accelerating time to market for solutions, while still maintaining required quality levels.
Flexibility and agility	The IT architecture will incorporate flexibility to support changing business needs and enable evolution of the architecture and the solutions built on it.
Innovative	The IT architecture will support incorporation of new technologies and facilitate innovation.
Data security	Data is protected from unauthorized use and disclosure.
Common data vocabulary	Data is defined consistently throughout the enterprise, and the definitions are understandable and available to all users.
Data quality	Each data element will have a trustee accountable for data quality.
Data asset	Data must be managed like other assets that have value to the enterprise.

FIGURE 6.7 Sample architectural principles.
Source: Adapted from examples of IT architecture from IBM, TOGAF, the U.S. Government, and the State of Wisconsin.

embedding new initiatives and using it as a competitive weapon to seize new business opportunities."[5]

The components of an enterprise architecture typically include four key elements:

- Core business processes—the key enterprise processes that create the capabilities the company uses to execute its operating model and create market opportunities
- Shared data—the data that drives the core processes
- Linking and automation technologies—the software, hardware, and networking technologies provide the links between applications (applications themselves are

[5] Jeanne W. Ross, Peter Weill, and David C. Robertson, *Enterprise Architecture as Strategy* (Boston, MA: Harvard Business School Press, 2006), viii–ix.

part of the IT architecture, but the way applications will link together is part of the bigger picture of the enterprise architecture)

- Customer groups—key customers to be served by the architecture[6]

One example of an enterprise architecture framework is the **TOGAF** (The Open Group Architecture Framework).[7] TOGAF includes a methodology and set of resources for developing an enterprise architecture. It is based on the idea of an open architecture, an architecture whose specifications are public (as compared to a proprietary architecture, where specifications are not made public). It is based on the U.S. Department of Defense frameworks and has been developing and continuously evolving since the mid-1990s. It provides a practical, standardized methodology (called Architecture Development Methodology) to successfully implement an enterprise architecture for an organization. The architect implements the enterprise architecture by setting up the foundation architecture, which is composed of services, functions, and standards. Subsets of the enterprise architecture are the business, data, application, and technology architectures. While there is no well-accepted standard for enterprise architecture, architects who understand and use TOGAF speak a common language and use the same basic framework and processes to build their company's IS architecture. TOGAF is designed to translate strategy into architecture and then into a detailed infrastructure; however, it supports a much higher level of architecture that includes more components of the enterprise.[8]

Another example of enterprise architecture frameworks is the Zachman Framework. The **Zachman Framework** determines architectural requirements by providing a broad view that helps guide the analysis of the detailed view. Its perspectives range from the company's scope to its critical models and, finally, to very detailed representations of the data, programs, networks, security, and so on. The models it uses are the conceptual business model, the logical system model, and the physical technical model.[9]

Because enterprise architecture is more about how the company operates than how the technology is designed, building an enterprise architecture is a joint exercise to be done with business leaders and IT leaders. IT leaders cannot and should not do this alone. Because virtually all business processes today involve some component of IT, the idea of trying to align IT with business processes is outdated. Instead, business processes are designed concurrently with IT systems.

Building an enterprise architecture is more than just linking the business processes to IT. It starts with organizational clarity of vision and strategy and places a high value on consistency in approach as a means of optimal effectiveness. The consistency manifests itself as some level of standardization—standardization of processes, deliverables,

---

[6] Ibid., 50–52.

[7] The Open Group at http://www.opengroup.org.

[8] For more information on the TOGAF framework, visit the Open Group's Web site at www.opengroup.org/togaf/.

[9] For more information on the Zachman framework, visit Zachman International's Web site at www.zachman.com.

and/or people Every enterprise architecture has elements of all these types of standard-ization; however, the degree and proportion of each vary with the organizational needs, making it dynamic. A good enterprise architect understands this and looks for the right blend for each activity the business undertakes. That means that because organizational groups and individuals are resources for business processes, the organi-zational design decisions should be part of the enterprise architecture. However, this is a sophisticated capability, and new enterprise architects often seek to put more rigid standards in place and do not attempt to tackle the more complex organizational design issues.

Barclay's Bank[10] servicing more than 48 million customers worldwide, had an IT architecture that included more than 2000 applications and spent in excess of £1 billion annually on IT. The resulting complexity was managed with an enterprise architecture that specified frameworks, tools, and processes that created a common language and format. The EA governance model dictated that both business and technology exec-utives sign off on projects to insure accountability and ownership. Roadmaps helped clarify the enterprise architecture design and direction, which informed planning and portfolio management and created a common vision and a repeatable mechanism for future investments. The EA insured appropriate linkages between IT investment and business needs.

▶ VIRTUALIZATION AND CLOUD COMPUTING

Physical corporate data centers are rapidly being replaced by virtual infrastructure, called **virtualization**. A virtual infrastructure originally meant one where software replaced hardware in a way that a "virtual machine" or a "virtual desktop system" was accessible to provide computing power. Typically, computing capabilities, storage, and networking are provided by a third party or group of vendors, usually over the Internet or through a private network. In most virtual architectures, the five core components available virtually are servers, storage, backup, network, and disaster recovery. Virtualizing the desktop is a common application of virtualization. In a virtualized desktop, the user's device locally accesses desktop software on a remote server, essentially separating the operating system from the applications. Virtualization is a useful way to design architec-ture because it enables resources to be shared and allocated as needed by the user, and makes maintenance easier since resources are centralized.

Cloud computing is another term used to describe an architecture based on services provided over the Internet. It is based on the concept of a virtual infrastructure. Entire computing infrastructures are available "in the cloud."

In addition to software as a service (Saas), PaaS (platform as a service), and IaaS (infrastructure as a service) are typical services found in cloud computing. These are described more fully in Chapter 9. Using the cloud to provide infrastructure means that the cloud is essentially a large cluster of virtual servers or storage devices. Using the

---

[10] Adapted from Phil LeClare and Eric Knorr, "The 2010 Enterprise Architecture Awards" (September 10, 2010), http://www.infoworld.com/d/architecture/the-2010-enterprise-architecture-awards-823?

cloud for a platform means that the manager will use an environment with the basic software available, such as Web software, applications, database, and collaboration tools. Using the cloud for an entire application generally means that the software is custom designed or custom configured for the business but resides in the cloud.

Consumers of cloud computing purchase capacity on demand and are not generally concerned with the underlying technologies. It's the next step in **utility computing** or purchasing entire capability on an as-needed basis. Much like the distribution of electricity, the vision of utility computing is that computing infrastructure would be available when needed in as much quantity as needed. When the lights and appliances are turned off in a home, the electricity is not consumed. Ultimately, the customer is billed only for what is used. In utility computing, a company uses a third-party infrastructure to do their processing or transactions and pay only for what they use. And as in the case of the electrical utility, the economies of scale enjoyed by the computing utility enable very attractive financial models for their customers. As the cost of connectivity falls, models of cloud computing emerge.

Salesforce.com, Facebook. Gmail, Windows Azure, Apple iTunes, and LinkedIn are examples of applications in the cloud. Users access LinkedIn through the Web, and build networks of business professionals on the LinkedIn Web site. But LinkedIn provides additional services, such as linking a user's blog to their profile, sharing and storing documents among group's members, access applications like GoodReads to see what network peers are reading and Tripit to learn about their travel plans.

Benefits of virtualization and cloud computing are many. Businesses who embrace a virtual infrastructure can consolidate physical servers, and possibly eliminate them, greatly reducing the physical costs of the data center. There is no upgrade and maintenance cost, no power and electricity cost, no physical space needed and no storage servers needed. Typically, the network is much simpler, too since the virtual infrastructure manages the network within all the applications.

But the biggest benefit of virtualization and cloud computing is the speed at which additional capacity, or provisioning, can be done. In a traditional data center, additional capacity is often a matter of purchasing additional hardware, waiting for its delivery, physically installing it, and insuring its compatibility with the existing systems. It can take weeks. In a virtual infrastructure, the nature of the architecture is dynamic by design, making it relatively easy and quick to add additional capacity.

For example, the *New York Times* decided to make all public domain articles from 1851 to 1922 available on the Internet. To do that they decided to create PDF files of all the articles from the original papers in their archives. This meant they had to scan each column of the story, create a series of graphic pictures of the scanned image, and then cobble them together to create the single PDF for each story. This was a lot of work and required significant computing power. Once this batch of articles was converted and added to their existing library, the *New York Times* would have 11 million stories from 1851 to 1989 available free on the Internet.

The manager of this project had an idea to try using the cloud. He selected a service offered by Amazon.com, Amazon EC2, wrote some code to do the project he envisioned, and tested it on the Amazon servers. He used his credit card to charge the $240 it cost him to do this conversion. He calculated it would have taken him at least a month to do the conversion if he used only the few servers available to him in the *New York Times* network. However, using the Amazon cloud services, he was able to use a virtual server cluster of 100 servers, and it took just under 24 hours to do the entire 11 million articles.[11]

But managers considering virtualization and cloud computing must also understand the risks. First is the dependence on the third-party supplier. Building applications that work in the cloud may mean retooling existing applications for the cloud's infrastructure. Although there are no standards for virtual infrastructures offered by the various vendors, one dominate vendor, as of the writing of this text, is VMware, a company that offers software for workstations, virtual desktop infrastructures, and servers. No standards for virtual infrastructure, however, means that applications running on one vendor's infrastructure may not port easily to another vendor's environment.

Architectures are increasingly including cloud computing and virtualization as alternatives to the in-house infrastructures. As coordination costs drop, and platforms in the cloud open up, cloud computing utilization will increase.

▶ OTHER MANAGERIAL CONSIDERATIONS

The framework guides the manager toward the design and implementation of an appropriate infrastructure. Defining an IT architecture that fulfills an organization's needs today is relatively simple; the problem is, by the time it is installed, those needs change. The primary reason to base an architecture on an organization's strategic goals is to allow for inevitable future changes—changes in the business environment, organization, IT requirements, and technology itself. Considering future impacts should include an analysis of the existing architecture, the strategic time frame, technological advances, and financial constraints.

Understanding Existing Architecture

At the beginning of any project, the first step is to assess the current situation. Understanding existing IT architecture allows the manager to evaluate the IT requirements of an evolving business strategy against current IT capacity. The architecture, rather than the infrastructure, is the basis for this evaluation because the specific technologies used to build the infrastructure are chosen based on the overall plan, or architecture. As previously discussed, it is these architectural plans that support the business strategy. Assuming some overlap is found, the manager can then evaluate the associated infrastructure and the degree to which it can be utilized going forward.

Relevant questions for managers to ask include the following:

- What IT architecture is already in place?
- Is the company developing the IT architecture from scratch?
- Is the company replacing an existing architecture?

[11] Galen Gruman, "Early Experiments in Cloud Computing," *InfoWorld*, www.infoworld.com (accessed on July 25, 2008); and Derek Gottfrid, "Self-Service, Prorated Super Computing Fun," Blog "Open All the Code that's Fit to Print" (November 1, 2007), open.nytimes.com (accessed on July 25, 2008).

- Does the company need to work within the confines of an existing architecture?
- Is the company expanding an existing architecture?

Starting from scratch allows the most flexibility in determining how architecture will enable a new business strategy, and a clean architectural slate generally translates into a clean infrastructure slate. However, it can be a challenge to plan effectively even when starting from scratch. For example, in a resource-starved start-up environment, it is far too easy to let effective IT planning fall by the wayside. Sometimes, the problem is less a shortcoming in IT management and more one of poorly devised business strategy. A strong business strategy is a prerequisite for IT architecture design, which is in turn a prerequisite for infrastructure design.

Of course, managers seldom enjoy the relative luxury of starting with a clean IT slate. More often, they must deal in some way with an existing architecture, infrastructure, and legacy systems already in place. In this case, they encounter both opportunity—to leverage the existing architecture and infrastructure and their attendant human resource experience pool—and the challenge of overcoming or working within the old system's shortcomings. By implementing the following steps, managers can derive the most value and suffer the least pain when working with legacy architectures and infrastructures.

1. **Objectively analyze the existing architecture and infrastructure.** Remember, architecture and infrastructure are separate entities; managers must assess the capability, capacity, reliability, and expandability of each.

2. **Objectively analyze the strategy served by the existing architecture.** What were the strategic goals it was designed to attain? To what extent do those goals align with current strategic goals?

3. **Objectively analyze the ability of the existing architecture and infrastructure to further the current strategic goals.** In what areas is alignment present? What parts of the existing architecture or infrastructure must be modified? Replaced?

Whether managers are facing a fresh start or an existing architecture, they must ensure that the architecture will satisfy their strategic requirements, and that the associated infrastructure is modern and efficient. The following sections describe evaluation criteria including strategic time frame, technical issues (adaptability, scalability, standardization, maintainability, security), and financial issues.

Assessing Strategic Timeframe

Understanding the life span of an IT infrastructure and architecture is critical. How far into the future does the strategy extend? How long can the architecture and its associated infrastructure fulfill strategic goals? What issues could arise and change these assumptions?

Answers to these questions vary widely from industry to industry. Strategic time frames depend on industry-wide factors such as level of commitment to fixed resources, maturity of the industry, cyclicality, and barriers to entry. The competitive environment has increased the pace of change to the point that requires any strategic decision be viewed as temporary.

Architectural longevity depends not only on the strategic planning horizon, but also on the nature of a manager's reliance on IT and on the specific rate of advances affecting the information technologies on which he or she depends. Today's architectures must be designed with maximum flexibility and scalability to ensure they can handle the imminent business changes. Imagine the planning horizon for a dot-com company in an industry in which Internet technologies and applications are changing daily, if not more often. Even oil giant Valero found that flexibility and agility were critical to their business and hence to their IT architecture.

Assessing Technical Issues: Adaptability

With the rapid pace of business, it is no longer possible to build a static information system to support businesses. Instead, adaptability is a core design principle of every IT architecture, and one reason why cloud computing and virtualization are increasingly popular. A manager may think of technological advances as primarily affecting IT infrastructure, but the architecture must be able to support any such advance. Can the architecture adapt to emerging technologies? Can a manager delay the implementation of certain components until he or she can evaluate the potential of new technologies?

At a minimum, the architecture should be able to handle expected technological advances, such as innovations in storage capacity and computing power. An exceptional architecture also has the capacity to absorb unexpected technological leaps. Both hardware and software should be considered when promoting adaptability. For example, new Web-based applications emerge daily that may benefit the corporation. The architecture must be able to integrate these new technologies without violating the architecture principles or significantly disrupting business operations.

The following are guidelines for planning adaptable IT architecture and infrastructure. At this point, these two terms are used together, because in most IT planning they are discussed together. These guidelines are derived from work by Meta Group.[12]

- **Plan for applications and systems that are independent and loosely coupled rather than monolithic.** This approach allows managers to modify or replace only those applications affected by a change in the state of technology.

- **Set clear boundaries between infrastructure components.** If one component changes, others are minimally affected, or if effects are unavoidable, the impact is easily identifiable and quantifiable.

- **When designing a network architecture, provide access to all users when it makes sense to do so (i.e., when security concerns allow it).** A robust and consistent network architecture simplifies training and knowledge sharing and provides some resource redundancy. An example is an architecture that allows employees to use a different server or printer if their local one goes down.

---

[12] Larry R. DeBoever and Richard D. Buchanan, "Three Architectural Sins," *CIO Magazine* (May 1, 1997).

Note that requirements concerning reliability may mitigate the need for technological adaptability under certain circumstances. If the architecture requires high reliability, a manager seldom is tempted by bleeding-edge technologies. The competitive advantage offered by bleeding-edge technologies is often eroded by downtime and problems resulting from pioneering efforts with the technology.

Assessing Technical Issues: Scalability

A large number of other technical issues should also be considered when selecting an architecture or infrastructure. A frequently used criterion is scalability. To be **scalable** refers to how well an infrastructure component can adapt to increased, or in some cases decreased, demands. A scalable network system, for instance, could start with just a few nodes but could easily be expanded to include thousands of nodes. Scalability is an important technical feature because it means that an investment can be made in an infrastructure or architecture with confidence that the firm will not outgrow it.

What is the company's projected growth? What must the architecture do to support it? How will it respond if the company greatly exceeds its growth goals? What if the projected growth never materializes? These questions help define scalability needs.

Consider a case in which capacity requirements were poorly anticipated. In early 2007, an ice storm on the East Coast of the United States forced JetBlue Airlines to scramble to take care of stranded customers, grounded planes, checked luggage, and cancelled flights. In the aftermath, executives told investors that the computers didn't fail. Indeed, they did not fail, but the system failed to scale as needed. The system was set up to accommodate 650 agents and was able to be increased to 950, but no more.[13] It's unlikely that JetBlue, or its software provider, would have had to do any serious systems redesign to respond to the increase in demand; it simply needed to increase its infrastructure capacity. Ultimately, this planning failure cost JetBlue millions to recover from the failure and even more in defending its image, which suffered severe negative word of mouth from the poor service that resulted. It subsequently contracted with Verizon to manage its infrastructure as a way of responding to the scalability issue. JetBlue's plight underscores the importance of analyzing the impact of strategic business decisions on IT architecture and infrastructure and at least ensuring a contingency plan exists for potential unexpected effects of a strategy change.

Assessing Technical Issues: Standardization

Another important feature deals with commonly used **standards**. Hardware and software that uses a common standard, as opposed to a proprietary approach, are easier to plug into an existing or future infrastructure or architecture because interfaces often accompany the standard. For example, many companies use Microsoft Office software, making it an almost de facto standard. Therefore, a number of additional packages come with translators to the systems in the Office suite to make it easy to move data between systems.

---

[13] Mel Duvall, "What Really Happened to JetBlue," www.cioinsight.com (July 2008).

Assessing Technical Issues: Maintainability

How easy is the infrastructure to maintain? Are replacement parts available? Is service available? Maintainability is a key technical consideration because the complexity of these systems increases the number of things that can go wrong, need fixing, or simply need replacing. In addition to availability of parts and service people, maintenance considerations include issues such as the length of time the system might be out of commission for maintenance, how expensive and how local the parts are, and obsolescence. Should a technology become obsolete, costs skyrocket for parts and expertise.

Assessing Technical Issues: Security

Security is a major concern for business managers and IT managers alike. Businesses feel vulnerable to attack. IT managers worry about protecting key data and process elements of the IT infrastructure. Security is a concern that extends outside the corporate boundaries; for example, customers wonder how safe their credit card numbers are when typed into a vendor's order form. Technologies have come a long way to provide security. Innovations encrypt or otherwise disguise sensitive information, financial information, and business information.

Architectures have different inherent security profiles. Securing assets in a highly centralized, mainframe architecture means building protection around the centralized core. Because data and software are stored and executed on the mainframe computer, methods of protecting these assets revolve around protecting the mainframe itself. Decentralized, server-based architecture are more difficult to secure due to the dispersion of servers. Security is a matter of protecting every server instead of one centralized system. A Web-based SOA architecture that utilizes SaaS and capacity on demand raises a whole new set of security issues. The data and applications not only reside on servers in the various vendor systems around the Web, but also the linking mechanism, the network that ties the Web together, introduces another level of security concerns.

What if, for example, someone was to steal a file of credit card numbers as they were relayed over the Internet? The risk of the interception of e-commerce data may be no greater than the risks of paper transactions: credit card receipts (and credit cards themselves) are stolen and the numbers used fraudulently. Checkbooks are stolen and signatures are fraudulently forged. Transactions with a paper trail are hardly foolproof and may indeed be riskier than e-commerce transactions. The difference is in the speed of the communication. A file with secure information can be sent anywhere in the world in a matter of seconds over the Internet, whereas the paper-based file takes longer to reach a destination. The good news is that the security of networks continues to improve. Innovations such as authentication, passwords, digital signatures, encryption, secure servers, and firewalls are already in place, and new schemes for security, such as securing specific assets instead of just securing the perimeter of a system, are being explored.

Managing security is often a matter of managing risk. It is virtually impossible to be totally secured regardless of the security model employed. Hackers and thieves will find a way around just about any security system. Therefore, managing risk often means assessing the likelihood of a breach and the cost of that breach in terms of loss and recovery. For example, one forward-thinking executive suggested that instead of trying to protect all his employees' Social Security numbers from theft, he preferred to purchase insurance to cover any losses that might result from the identity theft. He chose a service, LifeLock, that closely monitors its customers' identity, proactively takes steps to minimize identity theft, and offers a $1 million service guarantee to cover any losses that do occur.

Assessing Financial Issues

Like any business investment, IT infrastructure components should be evaluated based on their expected financial value. Unfortunately, payback from IT investments is often difficult to quantify; it can come in the form of increased productivity, increased interoperability with business partners, improved service for customers, or yet more abstract improvements. This suggests focusing on how IT investments enable business objectives rather than on their quantitative returns.

Still, some effort can and should be made to quantify the return on infrastructure investments. This effort can be simplified if a manager works through the following steps with the IT staff.

1. **Quantify costs.** The easy part is costing out the proposed infrastructure components and estimating the total investment necessary. Don't forget to include installation and training costs in the total.

2. **Determine the anticipated life cycles of system components.** Experienced IT staff or consultants can help establish life cycle trends both for a company and an industry to estimate the useful life of various systems.

3. **Quantify benefits.** The hard part is getting input from all affected user groups, as well as the IT group—which presumably knows most about the equipment's capabilities. If possible, form a team with representatives from each of these groups and work together to identify all potential areas in which the new IT system may bring value.

4. **Quantify risks.** Work with the IT staff to identify cost trends in the equipment the company proposes to acquire. Also, assess any risk that might be attributable to delaying acquisition, as opposed to paying more to get the latest technology now.

5. **Consider ongoing dollar costs and benefits.** Examine how the new equipment affects maintenance and upgrade costs associated with the current infrastructure.

Once this analysis is complete, the manager can calculate the company's preferred discounted cash flow (i.e., net present value or internal rate of return computation) and the payback period. Approaches to evaluating IT investments are discussed in greater detail in Chapter 7.

Applying these considerations to the fictitious TennisUp company, The last task is to weigh the managerial considerations against the same architectural goals outlined above. Figure 6.8 shows how these considerations apply to TennisUp's situation.

Again, note that not every issue in the evaluation criteria was addressed for TennisUp, but this example shows a broad sampling of the kinds of issues that will arise.

Criteria	Architecture	Infrastructure
Strategic time frame	Indefinite: Addin's strategic goal is to be able to respond to fluctuations in market demand.	NA
Technology advances	SCM technology is fairly stable, but transaction capacity needs to be assessed, and links with smaller suppliers and customers verified.	NA
Financial issues:		
NPV of investment	NA—In this limited case, NPV analysis applies only to infrastructure.	TennisUp will analyze NPV of various hardware and software solutions and ongoing costs before investing.
Payback analysis	TennisUp expects the new architecture to pay for itself within three years.	Various options will be evaluated using conservative sales growth projections to see how they match the three-year goal.
Incidental investments	The new architecture represents a radical shift in the way TennisUp does business and will require extensive training and work force adjustment.	Training costs for each option will be analyzed. Redeployment costs for employees displaced by the outsourcing must also be considered.
Growth requirements/ scalability	Outsourcing should provide more scalability than TennisUp's current model, which is constrained by assembly line capacity. Both primary and secondary vendors will be identified to provide scalability of volume.	The scalability required of various new hardware and software components is not significant, but options will be evaluated based on their ability to meet scalability requirements.
Standardization	NA	TennisUp will adopt the ANSI X12 EDI standard, and make it a requirement of all manufacturing partners.
Maintainability	The new architecture raises some maintenance issues, but also eliminates those associated with inhouse manufacturing.	Various options will be evaluated for their maintenance and repair costs.
Staff experience	The new model will displace some current employees. The cost and effect on morale needs to be analyzed.	Current staff is not familiar with EDI. Training and work force adjustment will be needed. Some new staff will be hired.

FIGURE 6.8 TennisUp's managerial considerations.

Social Business Lens: Building Social-Mobile Applications

As companies adopt social IT, they are finding that it's closely intertwined with mobile platforms. Employees want, and in some cases expect, to be able to access their social IT from their smart phones, tablets, and more. As companies look globally, in some countries the mobile screen is the only screen used. In 2011, more than one-third of the U.S. population used the mobile Internet. Social business requires that companies extend their architecture to include mobile, called *social mobile*.

Social mobile applications began to take off with the widespread adoption of the smartphones. The first devices combined features of a personal digital assistant with a mobile phone, giving developers the opportunity to link applications to the Web instantly. RIM's BlackBerry was one of the first to give users mobile access to communication tools such as their e-mail. More recent devices use a mobile operating system such as Apple's iOS, Google's Android, Microsoft's Windows Phone, Nokia's Symbian, and RIM's BlackBerry OS.

Initial social mobile apps were social networks, either ported to the mobile platform, like LinkedIn and Facebook, or designed just for the mobile platform, like Foursquare and Gowalla, social network sites linking community members who "check in" at physical locations and sometimes earn virtual rewards for doing so. Social mobile applications have extended to many other types of applications as software designers realize the large market available to them if their applications run on mobile platforms, and as device users demand increasing functionality for their mobile devices.

Source: Amy Gahran, "Survey: U.S. Mobile Web Access Growing Fast" (July 8, 2010), http://articles. cnn.com/2010-07-08/tech/mobile.internet.access.pew_1_cell-phone-users-feature-phones-mobile-internet.

▶ SUMMARY

- Strategy drives architecture, which drives infrastructure. Strategic business goals dictate IT architecture requirements. These requirements provide an extensible blueprint suggesting which infrastructure components will best facilitate the realization of the strategic goals.

- Enterprise architecture is the broad design that includes both the information systems architecture and the interrelationships in the enterprise. Often this plan specifies the logic for the entire organization. It identifies core processes, how they work together, how IT systems will support them, and the capabilities necessary to create, execute, and manage them.

- Three configurations for IT architecture are centralized, decentralized, and SOA (or Web-based) architectures. Applications are increasingly being offered as a service, reducing the cost and maintenance requirements for clients. Virtualization and cloud computing provide architectures for Web-based delivery of services.

- The manager's role is to understand how to plan IT to realize business goals. With this knowledge, he or she can facilitate the process of translating business goals to IT architecture and then modify the selection of infrastructure components as necessary.
- Frameworks guide the translation from business strategy to IS design. This translation can be simplified by categorizing components into broad classes (hardware, software, network, data), which make up both IT architecture and infrastructure
- Enterprise leaders are increasingly faced with new devices that employees want to connect to the corporate network. The consumerization of IT describes the trend to redesign corporate systems for smart phone, tablets and other consumer-oriented devices.
- While translating strategy into architecture and then infrastructure, it is important to know the state of any existing architecture and infrastructure, to weigh current against future architectural requirements, and strategic time frame, and to analyze the financial consequences of the various systems options under consideration. Systems performance should be monitored on an ongoing basis.

▶ KEY TERMS

architecture (p. 169)
bring-your-own-device (BYOD) (p. 177)
capacity-on-demand (p. 177)
centralized architecture (p. 173)
cloud computing (p. 183)
consumerization of IT (p. 177)
data center (p. 173)
decentralized architecture (p. 174)

enterprise architecture (p. 180)
infrastructure (p. 169)
peer-to-peer (p. 176)
platform (p. 172)
reuse (p. 174)
scalable (p. 188)
server-based architecture (p. 174)
service-oriented architecture (SOA) (p. 174)
software-as-a-service (p. 175)

standards (p. 188)
system software (p. 172)
TOGAF (p. 182)
utility computing (p. 184)
virtualization (p. 183)
Web-based architectures (p. 176)
Web services (p. 175)
wireless (mobile) infrastructures (p. 176)
Zachman Framework (p. 182)

▶ DISCUSSION QUESTIONS

1. Think about a company you know well. What would be an example of IT architecture at that company? An example of the IT infrastructure?

2. What, in your opinion, is the difference between a decentralized architecture and a centralized architecture? What is an example of a business decision that would be affected by the choice of the architecture?

3. From your personal experience, what is an example of software as a service? Of BYOD?

4. Saab Cars USA, with its network of 212 dealerships and 30 service centers, dedicated itself to providing its customers a level of service reflective of the high quality of its cars. To improve productivity and reduce costs, Saab wanted to facilitate dealer access to corporate information and applications through the Internet using Web browsers. Saab knew it needed to leverage both its legacy hardware and code to make it a cost-effective e-business initiative. It outsourced to IBM Global Services to build its Intranet Retailer Information System (IRIS). IRIS is written in Java,

using IBM DB2 Universal Database running on Saab's existing IBM AS/400 server. Lotus Domino is the middleware that leverages the existing infrastructure. Using a standard Web browser, any authorized employee at a Saab dealership or service center in the United States has access to enterprise applications stored on the AS/400 server at the Saab U.S. headquarters. The applications make use of a consolidated repository of vehicle, customer, warranty, sales, and service information stored in DB2 Universal Database. Says Director of IS, Jerry Rode, "DB2 Universal Database has demonstrated incredible scalability and reliability as the data management solution for our IRIS system." Lotus Domino, residing in another logical partition on the AS/400 server, is the middleware that mediates between the back-end applications and the front-end Web interface. For example, if a customer walks in and asks for a black model 9-3 Saab with a tan leather interior; a sales associate logs into the IRIS menu created by Domino and initiates a search. Domino queries DB2 by location, model, and color and puts the results of the query into an HTML form for the dealer. Upon locating the customer's vehicle, that dealer clicks to another vehicle distribution application and orders the car to be brought on site.[14]

    a. Use this case to describe how Saab went from vision to infrastructure.

    b. What criteria did Saab use in selecting its infrastructure?

CASE STUDY 6-1

ENTERPRISE ARCHITECTURE AT AMERICAN EXPRESS

Enterprise architecture (EA) at American Express was the framework the organization used to align IT and the business. It provided a common language for leaders to use to collaborate and transform the business. At American Express, enterprise architects were the change agents who streamlined processes and designed ways to more effectively do business using IT resources. In 2011, American Express was named an InfoWorld/Forrester Enterprise Architecture Award recipient for its EA practices. As American Express leaders considered new payment methods using mobile devices, the EA guided their progress.

Mobile payments were forcing the payments industry to review their practices and significantly transform the way business was done. The new business environment introduced additional complexity with the addition of new delivery channels and the need for shorter time-to-market of payment products and services. American Express's business strategy for its payments products focused on delivering a "consistent, global, integrated customer experience based on services running on a common application platform."

To achieve this goal, the EA team created reference architectures and road maps for standardized applications across the firm. They then worked with multiple business solution delivery teams to create and manage the common application architecture and create strategies that facilitated each business's objectives. Each strategy included a road map of initiatives. Initiatives included a set of actions, the metrics to evaluate the success of these actions, and the commitments IT and the businesses made to make it happen. The road map was American Express's way to standardize language, tools, lifecycle management of the applications, architecture and governance processes. They included technology, reference architecture and capabilities for the business.

---

[14] IBM, "Saab Rolls Out Dealer Intranet to Improve Customer Service," http://www3.ibm.com/software/success/cssdb.nsf/CS/NAVO-4LJQ8N?OpenDocument&Site=software (accessed on June 25, 2002).

The next steps for American Express were to extend the road maps to cover the maturing of SOA and to develop new reference architectures and a new taxonomy to increasingly align IT with the needs of the business. As new technologies emerged and new ways of doing business over social tools created opportunities for new payment products and services, American Express expected to continually evolve their EA.

Discussion Questions

1. What are the key components of the architecture American Express has created?
2. Why was it important to standardize so much of the architecture? What are the advantages and disadvantages of a standard EA for American Express?
3. Describe how the new architecture supports the goals and strategy of American Express.
4. What types of future payment products and services should be anticipated and prepared for by the EA group? What is your vision of how payments might work? If you were advising the CIO of American Express, what would you suggest his group prepare for?

Source: Adapted from Phil LeClare and Eric Knorr, "The 2011 Enterprise Architecture Awards" (September 19, 2011), http://www.infoworld.com/d/enterprise-architecture/the-2011-enterprise-architecture-awards-173372.

CASE STUDY 6-2

THE CASE OF EXTREME SCIENTISTS

Scientists doing research often need serious computing capability to run simulations and crunch data. Often that meant working for a large company who could provide the significant investment in information systems infrastructure. But cloud computing changed all that. Consider the case of biologist Dr. Eric Schadt, a researcher who claims that approaches to studying the complexity of living systems have failed. Studying one gene at a time doesn't explain what causes diseases, making it impossible to find the cures sought by the scientific and pharmacology communities. Dr. Schadt's vision is to manage this area of research, and the large amount of data generated, which appears to be too much for any one individual or company to manage, by creating a human social network. Dr. Schadt believes this organization reflects the complexity of the living systems he studies, and therefore it's necessary to understand it.

Dr. Schadt cofounded a nonprofit organization dedicated to biological research using an open-source sharing of data, called Sage Bionetworks. He deeply believes that sharing is the key to finding cures, and creating drugs, that will combat diseases. And his company has millions of dollars worth of data from some of the major pharmaceutical companies to use to begin their research. But by day, he's the Chief Scientific Officer of a start up, Pacific Biosciences, whose technology helps biologists look at individual molecules of DNA in real-time. His job is to work on how to use this technology for PacBio and to collaborate with others who want to use this technology for their research. So he travels a lot. But to do his research, he needs access to the capacity of a supercomputer since the amount of data he needs to use for his research is very large.

With the use of the Web, he's able to do his work anyplace. Planes are especially favored because he has significant uninterrupted time. According to one article about Dr. Schadt,

> "He has the same access to supercomputers that every other American with an Internet connection and a credit card has. He waits till the plane climbs to a cruising altitude, then when allowed to use electronic devices, he uses the plane's WiFi to get on Amazon."

Dr. Schadt is able to initiate a complex analysis of his data using Amazon's services, which crunch the data while Dr. Schadt flies across the country. When he lands, the analysis is done and he has the results. This world be equivalent to the computing power of a scientist working on his company's multimillion dollar supercomputer, but in this case, the cost is just a few hundred dollars.

Companies like Amazon.com have become vendors of extreme computing power. Some have compared the amount of computing power Dr. Schadt uses while flying on an airplane to the amount of computing power available to a scientist at major pharmaceutical companies, where they have multimillion dollar supercomputers. With services like the computing power available in the cloud, Dr. Schadt may even have more power available to him than the scientist.

Discussion Questions

1. How would you describe the architecture Dr. Schadt uses to do his research?
2. What are the risks Dr. Schadt faces by using Amazon for his supercomputing? What are the benefits?
3. If you were advising a company trying to make a decision about using cloud computing for key business applications, what would you advise and why?

Source: Adapted from Tom Junod, "Adventures in Extreme Science," *Esquire Magazine* (March 22, 2011), http://www.esquire.com/features/eric-schadt-profile-0411-4 (accessed on February 12, 2012).

CHAPTER 7

THE BUSINESS OF IT

This chapter explores the business of IT and the customers it serves. Beginning with the introduction of a maturity model to understand the balancing act between IS supply and business demand, key IT organization activities are described and related to one of the three maturity levels. The chapter continues with a discussion about what the IT organization does and does not do and how the leadership within the IT organization ensures that the IT organization's activities are conducted efficiently and effectively, both domestically and globally. We then look at business processes within the IT department such as building a business case, IT portfolio management, and valuing and monitoring IT investments. The remainder of the chapter focuses on funding models and total cost of ownership.

The CIO of Avon Products, Inc., in New York relies heavily on hard-dollar metrics such as net present value (NPV) and internal rate of return (IRR) to demonstrate the business value resulting from information technology (IT) investments. Although these are not the typical IT metrics, they are the language of business. Funding IT becomes a matter of speaking the language of business. "We apply all of the analytical rigor and financial ROI tools against each of our IT projects as well as other business projects," the CIO (Chief information officer) of Avon Products remarked. Avon uses payback, NPV, IRR, and risk analyses for every investment. Further, each IT project is monitored using a green/yellow/red-coded dashboard to convey the status as "on target," "warning," or "having serious problems." Monthly reports to the senior management team inform them about the status of major projects. Other business tools, such as investment-tracking databases and monitors on capital spending, assist the CIO's office in managing the funds allocated to the IT group.[1]

The business side of IT is similar to the business itself. The IS organization has to consider what services and products it needs to deliver to the other departments in the organization and how it can fund and effectively deliver those offerings. Projects are created and presented through a business case. They are funded through budget allocations or a multitude of other sources. And they are managed and monitored with prudent business practices. As Avon's CIO's comments indicate, the basic tools of finance and accounting are also the basic tools for the financial management of IT and, further, for determining and communicating the value received from IT investments.

---

[1] Adapted from Thomas Hoffman, "How Will You Prove IT Value?" *Computerworld* (January 6, 2003).

In this chapter, issues related to the business side of IT are explored. It begins by looking at key activities managers can expect of their IT organization, and probably just as importantly, what the IT organization does not provide. It continues with a discussion of key business processes within the IT organization, such as building a business case, IT portfolio management, and valuing and monitoring IT investments. This is followed with a discussion of ways of funding the IT department and an exploration of several ways to calculate the cost of IT investments, including total cost of ownership and activity-based costing. These topics are critical for the IT manager to understand, but a general manager must also understand how the business of IT works to successfully propose, plan, manage, and use information systems.

▶ ORGANIZING TO RESPOND TO BUSINESS DEMAND: A MATURITY MODEL

Responding to the demands of business requires that the IT department organize to supply the services and products that are needed. IT managers must be partners with their business colleagues in every sense of the word. It's not enough to call in the IT manager late in the project discussion to identify tools to support the project. Rather, IT managers are business people, and can do a better job of being a partner if they are consulted early in the project. Sometimes the misalignment between the demands on the business side and the IT offerings on the supply side is because IT and the business are at different levels of maturity in their growth and development. A **Business-IT Maturity Model** framework is a useful tool for understanding the differences in capabilities. Figure 7.1 is one such model.

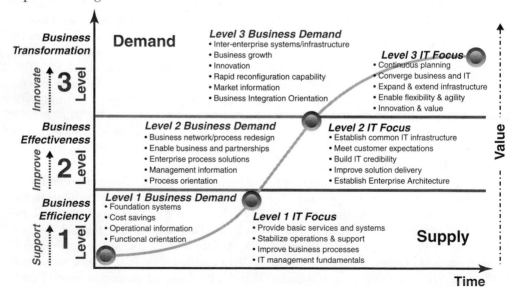

FIGURE 7.1 Business-IT maturity model.
Source: Vaughan Merlyn, http://vaughanmerlyn.com/2007/09/22/business-it-maturity-a-helpful-lens-for-the-future/ (accessed on February 14, 2012).

This model differentiates between the supply of IT (the capabilities) and the demand for IT (what the business wants). The time dimension highlights that over time, there is a difference in supply and demand. Yet, at each level they are mutually dependent. Further, since business capability is a function of IT capability, a low supply maturity constrains a higher level of business demand. Misalignment occurs when business demand is too far ahead of IT supply. Overspending occurs when IT supply is too far ahead of business demand. This model does not comment on the type of technology, but rather the way the business organization approaches its use of IT. For example, in Level 3, the business leaders think about IT's role in rapid reconfiguration of the business, as compared to Level 2, where the focus might be on creating effective business processes. That's different from Level 1, where the business demand for IT is primarily all about cost savings and foundation systems. When the capabilities of the IT organization are in balance with the demand of the business, both are at the same level.

This chapter applies the model to explain how the IT department can anticipate what it must do to meet the demands of business. Since running the business of IT requires funding, we explore how to fund IT projects to meet the demand and how to cover the operational costs.

▶ UNDERSTANDING THE IT ORGANIZATION

Consider an analogy of a ship to help explain the purpose of an IT organization and how it functions. A ship transports people and cargo to a particular destination in much the same way that an IT organization directs itself toward the strategic goals set by the larger enterprise. While all ships navigate waters, different ships have different structures, giving them unique capabilities such as transporting people versus cargo. Even among similar categories, ships have different features, such as transporting a cargo of products from China versus a cargo of oil and liquids. IT organizations all provide services to their businesses, but based on the skills and capabilities of their people and the organizational focus of their management, they, too, differ in what they can do and how they work with the businesses. Sometimes the IT organization must navigate perilous waters or storms to reach port. For both the IT organization and the ship, the key is to perform more capably than any competitors. It means doing the right things at the right time and in the right way to propel the enterprise through the rough waters of business.

But different firms need to do different things when it comes to IT. Because firms have different goals, they need to act in different ways and as a result, there are differences in the IT activities that are provided. But even if two firms have similar goals, the firms' size, organization structure and level of maturity might affect what the IT organization in each firm is expected to do.

▶ WHAT A MANAGER CAN EXPECT FROM THE IT ORGANIZATION

We look at the IT organization from the perspective of the customer of the IT organization, the general manager or "user" of the systems. What can a manager expect from the IT organization?

Managers must learn what to expect from the IT organization so they can plan and implement business strategy accordingly. While the nature of the activities may vary in each IT organization depending upon its overall goal, a manager typically can expect some level of support in 14 core activities: (1) developing and maintaining information systems, (2) managing supplier relationships, (3) managing data, information, and knowledge, (4) managing Internet and network services, (5) managing human resources, (6) operating the data center, (7) providing general support, (8) planning for business discontinuities, (9) innovating current processes, (10) establishing architecture platforms and standards, (11) promoting enterprise security, (12) anticipating new technologies, (13) participating in setting and implementing strategic goals, and (14) integrating social IT.[2] These activities are briefly described in Figure 7.2.

While the activities could be found at any maturity level, we indicate in Figure 7.2 the level where they are especially important. At Level 1, the IT organization is focused on the basic services needed to generate cost savings and provide operational information needed to make the business run efficiently. The functional view predominates. At Level 2, the IT organization adopts a process view to provide services of an integrated nature across the organization. Information delivered by IS supports managerial decision making and enables business partnerships. The goal is to make the business effective. At Level 3, innovation is the key focus. IS not only provide support for strategic initiatives, but also help spur innovation.

It appears that the scope of activities in the IT organization is expanding. For example, integrating the use social IT into the business has been added as a core activity in this edition of the text because it is an emerging function that increasingly offers companies the potential for business transformation if the resources are correctly managed and leveraged. Integrating social IT means more than just providing basic social IT such as wikis, forums, and social networks. It also means deriving benefit from the conversations that are generated, encouraging new forms of collaboration, and creating new processes to accomplish the firm's goals. Two examples are USAA's use of social IT to attract and retain Generation Y IT hires and IBM's use of social networks for newer and more senior managers to connect. Other examples are the use of social IT to generate, vet, and assess innovative ideas such as Starbucks' mystarbucks.com and Dell's Ideastorm.

The IT organization can be expected to be responsible for most, if not all, of the activities listed in Figure 7.2. However, instead of actually performing the activities, increasingly the IT organization identifies and then works with vendors who provide them. More traditional activities such as data center operations, network management, and system development and maintenance (including application design, development, and maintenance) have been outsourced to vendors for decades. More recently, enterprises are turning to outsourcing providers to perform more newly acquired IT activities such as process management (alternatively called business process outsourcing). In our increasingly flat world, many companies are successfully drawing from labor

---

[2] Eight activities are described by John F. Rockart, Michael J. Earl, and Jeanne W. Ross, "Eight Imperatives for the New IT Organization," *Sloan Management Review* (Fall 1996), 52–53. Six activities have been added to their eight imperatives.

Activity	Description	Maturity Level
Developing and Maintaining Systems	Work together with business users to analyze needs, design the software, write or code the software, and test it to make sure it works and meets the business objectives; identify, acquire, and install outside software packages to fill business needs; maintain systems; address post-implementation needs, such as correcting system errors or enhancing the system to respond to changing business environments and governmental regulations.	1
Managing Supplier Relationships	Maximize the benefit of supplier relationships to the enterprise and preempt problems that might occur.	1
Managing Data, Information, and Knowledge	Database administration: collect and store data created, developed, or discovered by the enterprise (Level 1); manage enterprise information and knowledge (Level 2).	1,2
Managing Internet and Network Systems	Develop and maintain Internet capabilities; manage private networks, telephone systems, access to the Internet, and new wireless technologies; design network architecture; build and maintain the network infrastructure.	1,2 (depending on nature of network)
Managing Human Resources	Provide sufficient business and technical training so that staff can perform effectively and retain their value to the enterprise; hire staff; work to retain staff; fire poor performers; track time; work with enterprise HR personnel, who may be familiar with interviewing approaches, personnel laws, regulations, and trends.	1
Operating the Data Center	Operate and maintain large mainframe computers, rows of servers, or other platforms on which the company's data and business applications reside, or other hardware.	1
Providing General Support	Varies but may include helpdesk activities: maintain the first client contact through a centralized helpdesk even for such diverse services as networking and telecommunications; collect pertinent information, record it, determine its priority, contact the appropriate support personnel, and follow up with the business contacts with updates or resolution information.	1
Planning for Business Discontinuities	Develop and implement business continuity plan to counter terrorist attacks, intentional fraud, hurricanes, tornadoes, floods, or other man-made and natural disasters that could cripple the enterprise.	1

FIGURE 7.2 IT organization activities and related level of maturity.

Innovating Current Processes	Work with managers to innovate processes that can benefit from technological solutions (i.e., Social IT, installing voice mail to networking personal computers, automating general ledger transactions, ERP implementations); design systems that facilitate new ways of doing business.	2
Establishing Architecture Platforms and Standards	Develop, maintain, and communicate standards; ensure consistent data so that the integrity of a data warehouse won't be undermined.	2
Promoting Enterprise Security	Maintain the integrity of the enterprise infrastructure; implement enterprise information security strategy; identify and prioritize threats to the enterprise's information assets; develop and implement security policies and technical controls and infrastructure to address each threat; work with the business units to make their operational practices more secure and to train employees about security risks and the importance of security to their work; implement an awareness program that keeps security on employees' minds as they deal with information on a daily basis; participate in discussions about security investments.	2
Anticipating New Technologies	Scout new technology trends and help the business integrate them into planning and operations; assess the costs and benefits of new technologies for the enterprise; work closely with business groups to determine which technologies can provide the greatest benefit, how the technologies might affect the organization, how they might advance the business strategy, and when they should be implemented; ensure that the enterprise does not invest heavily in new technologies that quickly become obsolete or incompatible with other enterprise standards.	3
Participating in Setting and Implementing Strategic Goals	Enable business managers to achieve strategic goals by acting as consultants or by teaching them about developing technologies; advise managers on best practices within IT and work with them to develop IT-enhanced solutions to business problems; educate managers about current technologies; serve as partners in moving the enterprise forward.	3
Integrating the Use of Social IT	Leverage the use of social IT to create a business transformation; transform social IT from personal to business use; provide customer-, supplier-, and employee-facing applications for engagement, collaboration, and innovation; and manage the data resulting from social IT to provide business insights.	3

FIGURE 7.2 (Continued)

Geographic Lens: What Should You Look Out For When Managing Global Supplier Relationships?

Many companies are finding that managing global supplier relationships is fraught with challenges. Following a fracas outside an Apple store in Beijing that erupted when potential customers couldn't get their hands on the latest iPhone, local police ordered the store closed citing safety concerns.

Under pressure from the Western and Asian activists who complained about conditions at Asian suppliers, Apple issued a twenty-seven-page report detailing working conditions throughout its supply chain, but particularly in China. The activists may have been pacified by the thorough study based on 229 audits of factories, but the Chinese authorities were concerned that the report surfaced too much information about Chinese business practices. In many cases Apple's suppliers acted in ways that did not meet the company's standards: 62% of the suppliers violated Apple's working hours standards of a maximum of 60 hours per week; 49% of the facilities weren't properly storing, moving, or handling hazardous chemicals; 32% did not abide by Apple's standards on wages and benefits; Five facilities employed underage workers.

Apple took steps to better monitor and improve education and working condition in Malaysia and Singapore. However, it met resistance in China. Apple found that standards for some suppliers are easier to implement than for others. Apple focused on bringing all of its suppliers up to standard, but it did not want to anger the government of a country with such a large potential market.

Source: J. E. Vascellaro and O. Fletcher, "Apple Navigates China Maze," *Wall Street Journal* (January 14–15, 2012), B1–B2.

---

supplies in other parts of the world to meet the business demand that they can't handle internally in their own IT organization. Managing the sourcing relationships and global labor supply is so important that a whole chapter (i.e., Chapter 9) is devoted to discussing these sourcing issues in greater depth.

▶ MANAGING IT ACTIVITIES GLOBALLY

How does the management of IT differ when the scope of the organization is global, rather than just within one country's borders? Typically, large global IT organizations perform many of the same activities listed above. Further, they typically face many of the same organizational issues as any other global department. Managers must figure out how to manage when employees are in different time zones, speak different languages, have different customs and holidays, and come from different cultures. In the case of information management, various issues arise that put the business at risk beyond the typical global considerations. Figure 7.3 summarizes how a global IT perspective affects six information management issues.

Issue	Global IT Perspective	Example
Political Stability	Investments in IT in a country with an unstable government should be carefully considered: How much do you invest? How risky is the investment?	Much offshoring is done with companies in India, a country that is facing an atomic war in its conflict with Pakistan.
Transparency	Domestically, an IT network can be end-to-end with little effort compared to global networks, which makes it difficult for these two types of systems to have the same look and feel, or, sometimes, to get to the data.	SAP-R3 is used to support production processes. When it is not installed in one country, managers cannot monitor the processes in that country the same way.
Business Continuity Planning	When crossing borders, it is important to make sure that contingency plans are in place and working.	After 9/11, many businesses are considering placing backup data centers in remote locations, but the concern when crossing borders is whether that data center will be available when/if needed.
Cultural Differences	Different countries have different cultures; some things are acceptable one place but not another. IT systems must not offend or insult those of a different culture	Using images or artifacts from one culture may be insulting to another culture. For example, DitchWitch could not use its logo globally because a witch is offensive in some countries.
Sourcing	Getting the IT hardware within every country of operation may be difficult. Some technologies cannot be exported from the United States, and other technologies cannot be imported into specific countries. Vendors do not always have the same technologies available in every country.	Some technology is considered a potential threat to national security, such as encryption technologies, so exporting it to some countries, especially those that are not political allies of the United States, is not possible.
Data Flow Across Borders	Data, especially private or personal data, are not allowed to cross some borders.	Brazil refused to let data come across its borders from other countries, making it difficult for businesses to integrate their Brazilian operations into the corporate operations.

FIGURE 7.3 Global considerations for the IT organization.

▶ WHAT THE IT ORGANIZATION DOES NOT DO

This chapter presents core activities for which the IT organization is typically responsible. Although most IT professionals are asked to perform a wide range of tasks for their organization, in reality the IT organization should not do certain tasks. Clearly, the IT organization does not directly do other core business functions such as selling, manufacturing, and accounting. Sometimes, however, managers of these functions inadvertently delegate key operational decisions to the IT organization. When general managers ask the IT professional to build an information system for their organization and do not become active partners in the design of that system, they are in effect turning over control of their business operations. Likewise, asking an IT professional to implement a software package or app without partnering with that professional to ensure the package meets both current and future needs is ceding control. The IT organization does not typically design business processes.

Partnerships between the general managers and IT professionals are also important for a number of other decisions. For instance, IT professionals should not have the sole responsibility for deciding which business processes receives IT dollars. Giving carte blanche to the IT professional would mean that it is the IT organization that decides what is important to the business units. If the IT professionals then try to do their best to respond to every request from their business counterparts, they are likely to face a backlog of delayed initiatives and be overwhelmed. Similarly, IT professional should not solely decide the acceptable level of IT services or security. These are examples of decisions that should be made jointly with business counterparts. Perfection comes at a price that many business leaders may be unwilling to pay. Not every system needs to have gold-plated functionality and not every system needs to be fortified from every conceivable danger. It is senior managers who run the business who must decide on the level of service and security that should be delivered by the IT organization.[3]

As discussed in Chapter 2, when using IT for strategic advantage, the general manager, not the IT professional, sets business strategy. However, in many organizations, the general manager delegates critical technology decisions to the Chief Information Officer (CIO). This may limit the strategic options available to the firm. The role for the IT professional in the discussion of strategy centers on suggesting technologies and applications that enable strategy, identifying limits to the technologies and applications under consideration, and consulting with all those involved with setting the strategic direction to make sure they properly consider the role and impact of IT on the decisions they make. The IT organization does not set business strategy. It does, however, partner with the business to insure that IT provides the infrastructure, applications, and support necessary to insure successful implementation of the business strategy. In that sense, IT leaders must be part of the business strategy discussions.

---

[3] J. W. Ross and P. Weill, "Six IT Decisions Your IT People Shouldn't Make," *Harvard Business Review* (2002), 1–8.

▶ CHIEF INFORMATION OFFICER

If an IT organization is like a ship, then the chief information officer is at the helm. The **Chief Information Officer (CIO)** is the senior-most executive in the enterprise responsible for technology vision and leadership for designing, developing, implementing, and managing IT initiatives for the enterprise to operate effectively in a constantly changing and intensely competitive marketplace. The CIO is an executive who manages IT resources to implement enterprise strategy and who works with the executive team in strategy formulation processes.

CIOs are a unique breed. They have a strong understanding of the business and of the technology. In many organizations they take on roles that span both of these areas. One recently coined term is the **business technology strategist**, or the strategic business leader who uses technology as the core tool in creating competitive advantage and aligning business and IT strategies.[4] The CIO, as the most senior IT professional in the corporate hierarchy, must champion the IT organization by promoting IT as a strategic tool for growth and innovation. The title *CIO* signals to both the organization and to outside observers that this executive is a strategic IT thinker and is responsible for linking IS strategy with the business strategy. In other words, CIOs must know the business vision and understand how the IT function contributes to making this vision happen. This means that CIOs must work effectively not only within the technical arena, but also in overall business management arena. They need the technical ability to plan, conceive, build, and implement multiple IT projects on time and within budget. However, their technical skills must be balanced against business skills such as the ability to realize the benefits and manage the costs and risks associated with IT, to articulate and advocate for a management vision of IT, and to mesh well with the existing management structure.

Just as the chief financial officer (CFO) is somewhat involved in operational management of the financial activities of the organization, the CIO is involved with operational issues related to IT. More often than not, CIOs are asked to perform strategic tasks at some part of their day and operational tasks at other times, rather than spending all their time on one or the other. Some of their operational activities include identifying and managing the introduction of new technologies into the firm, negotiating partnership relationships with key suppliers, setting purchasing and supplier policies, and managing the overall IT budget. Actual day-to-day management of the data center, IT infrastructure, applications development projects, the vendor portfolio, and other operational issues are typically not handled directly by the CIO, but by one of the managers in the IT organization. Ultimately, whether they directly function as operational managers, or as leaders with oversight of other operational managers, the CIO must assume responsibility for all the activities described in Figure 7.2 that the IT organization is charged to perform.

Where the CIO fits within an enterprise is often a source of controversy. In the early days of the CIO position, when the CIO was predominantly responsible for controlling costs, the CIO reported to the CFO. Because the CIO was rarely involved in enterprise governance or in discussions of business strategy, this reporting structure worked.

---

[4] M. Carter, V. Grover, and J. B. Thatcher, "The Emerging CIO Role of Business Technology Strategist," *MIS Quarterly Executive* (2011), 10(1), 19–29.

However, as IT became a source for competitive advantage in the marketplace, reporting to the CFO proved too limiting. Conflicts arose because the CFO misunderstood the vision for IT or saw only the costs of technology. They also arose because management still saw the CIO's primary responsibility as controlling costs. More recently, CIOs report directly to the CEO, president, or other executive manager. This elevated reporting relationship not only signals that the role of IT is critical to the enterprise, but it also makes it easier to implement strategic IT initiatives.

Some organizations choose not to have a CIO. These organizations do not believe that a CIO is necessary, in part because technology is highly integrated into virtually every aspect of the business and no single officer need provide oversight. Rather, the firms typically hire an individual to be responsible for running the computer systems and possibly to manage many of the activities described later in this chapter. But they signal that this person is not a strategist by giving him or her, the title of data processing manager or director of information systems or some other reference that clearly differentiates this person from other top officers in the company. Using the words *chief* and *officer* usually implies a strategic focus, and some organizations do not see the value of having an IT person on their executive team.

Although the CIO's role is to guide the enterprise toward the future, this responsibility is frequently too great to accomplish alone. Many organizations

Title	Responsibility
Chief technology officer (CTO)	Track emerging technologies; advise on technology adoption; design and manage IT architecture to ensure consistency and compliance
Chief knowledge officer (CKO)	Create knowledge management infrastructure; build a knowledge culture; make corporate knowledge pay off
Chief telecommunications officer (CTO)	Manage phones, networks, and other communications technology across entire enterprise
Chief network officer (CNO)	Build and maintain internal and external networks
Chief resource officer (CRO)	Manage outsourcing relationships
Chief information security officer (CISO)	Ensure information management practices are consistent with security requirements
Chief privacy officer (CPO)	Be responsible for processes and practices that ensure privacy concerns of customers, employees, and vendors are met
Chief mobility officer (CMO)	Oversee and ensure the viable use of the mobile platforms and apps
Chief social media officer (CSMO)	Maintain a social IT perspective that results in effectively implementing social media

FIGURE 7.4 The CIO's lieutenants.

Social Business Lens: Community Management

Social businesses make significant use of social tools as key components of their business foundation. Social networks, for example, provide a forum for businesses to engage their communities. But communities do not thrive without nurture and guidance (which is different than rules and demands). An emerging professional, the **community manager**, is the person in the position of helping build, grow and manage a community.

Community managers may take on a variety of roles, depending on the goals and nature of the community they manage. But their role is more than just moderating a discussion or validating the individuals in the community. Community managers are the advocate for the community, representing the members of the community to the business, listening to what the community is saying, and taking an active role in participating in the community activities. They might also engage community members by asking direct questions or responding when questions are asked. The community manager is also an evangelist, promoting events, services, and opportunities to the community, often on behalf of the community sponsors. The community manager is the communications expert in the community, understanding the tools available to the community members, and helping manage their use. In addition, should disputes arise within the community, it's the community manager who helps mediate. Companies who invest in a community manager find that this role is also a strategic role for their organizations, providing front-line input on the requirements, needs, and ideas from the community. Sometimes the community manager is the company's personification inside the community.

Emma Gannon is an example of a community manager for Dove brand's Facebook page (Dove is a brand owned by Procter and Gamble). In an interview about her role, Emma said, "I manage a global Facebook page, liaising with local markets across 31 different countries, working as one team to assist the brand in global social media engagement." She says, "behind every good online community is a good community manager. . . who is upbeat, creative and on the ball." She has a strong editorial calendar and posting schedule to keep her community active. She focuses on being friendly and helpful. She says that community managers are supposed to "support the community, not directly sell anything." By keeping posts short and engaging, and by using applications that engage the community in an interactive way, she keeps it interesting and keeps fans coming back.

Sources: Adapted from Jeremiah Owyang, "The Four Tenets of the Community Manager" (November 25, 2007), http://www.web-strategist.com/blog/2007/11/25/the-four-tenets-of-the-community-manager/ (accessed on April 12, 2012); and adapted from "Social Media Citizens Interview with Community Manager: Emma Gannon from Edelman" (September 6, 2011), http://www.smcitizens.com/2011/09/06/interview-with-community-manager-emma-gannon/ (accessed on January 19, 2012).

recognize that certain strategic areas of the IT organization require more focused guidance. This recognition led to the creation of new positions, such as the chief knowledge officer (CKO), chief technology officer (CTO), chief telecommunications officer (also CTO), chief network officer (CNO), chief information security officer (CISO), chief privacy officer (CPO), chief resource officer (CRO), chief mobility officer (CMO), and chief social business officer (CSBO). See Figure 7.4 for a list of their different responsibilities. Each of these positions typically subordinates to the CIO, with the occasional exception of the CTO. Together, they form a management team that leads the IT organization.

Many large corporations take the concept of CIO one step further and identify a business unit CIO. This is someone who has similar responsibilities to a corporate CIO, but the scope is the business unit and there is not as much concern about defining corporate standards and policies to ensure consistency across the business units. The business unit CIO is responsible for aligning the IT investment portfolio with the business unit's strategy. Typically, the business unit CIO has dual reporting responsibility to both the corporate CIO and the president of the business unit. At IBM, the CIO is a manager from a business unit who serves a two- to three-year term.[5]

▶ BUILDING A BUSINESS CASE

In order to meet demand, the IT organization is often charged with providing solutions. Businesses managers often turn to IT for good solutions, but their IT projects end up competing with those of other managers in tight economic times when there clearly isn't enough money to cover them all. Thus, they need to show that the solution they want would be a good IT investment.

To gain support and a "go-ahead" decision on an IT investment (or any business investment, for that matter), a manager must often create a business case. Similar to a legal case, a **business case** is a structured document that lays out all the relevant information needed to make a go/no-go decision. The business case for an IT project is also a way to establish priorities for investing in different projects, an opportunity to identify how IT and the business can deliver new benefits, gain commitment from business managers, and create a basis for monitoring the investment.[6]

The components of a business case vary from corporation to corporation, depending on the priorities and decision-making environment. However, there are several primary elements of any business case. They are listed in Figure 7.5. Critical to the business case is the identification of both costs and benefits, both in financial and nonfinancial terms.

In building the business case it is particularly important to describe the benefits to be gained with the acceptance of the project being sold in the business case. Ward,

[5] Ann Majchrzak, Luba Cherbakov, and Blake Ives, "Harnessing the Power of the Crowds with Corporate Social Networking Tools: How IBM Does it?" *MIS Quarterly Executive* (2009), 8(2), 103–108.

[6] John Ward, Elizabeth Daniel, and Joe Peppard, "Building Better Business Cases for IT Investments," *MISQE* (March 2008), 7(1), 1–15.

Section or Component	Description
Executive Summary	Describes in one- or two-pages the overall business case document.
Overview and Introduction	Includes a brief business background, the current business situation, a clear statement of the business problem or opportunity, and a recommended solution at a high level.
Assumptions and Rationale	Includes issues driving the proposal (could be operational, human resource, environmental, competitive, industry or market trends, financial or otherwise).
Program Summary	Includes high-level and then detailed description of the project, well-defined scope, objectives, contacts, resource plan, key metrics (financial and otherwise), implementation plan (high-level discussion and potential impacts) and key components to make this a success.
Financial Discussion and Analysis	Starts with financial summary. Then includes details such as projected costs/revenues/benefits, financial metrics, financial model, cash flow statement, and assumptions that went into creating financial statements. Total Cost of Ownership (TCO) calculations analysis would go in this section.
Benefits and Business Impacts	Starts with business impacts summary. Then includes details on all nonfinancial outcomes such as new business, transformation, innovations, competitive responses, organizational, supply chain, and human resource impacts.
Schedule and Milestones	Outlines the entire schedule for the project, highlights milestones and details of expected metrics at each stage (what makes the go/no-go decision at each stage). If appropriate, this section can also include a marketing plan and schedule (sometimes this is a separate section).
Risk and Contingency Analysis	Includes details on risks, risk analysis, and contingencies to manage those risks. Includes sensitivity analysis on the scenario(s) proposed and contingencies to manage anticipated consequences. Includes interdependencies and impact they will have on potential outcomes.
Conclusion and Recommendation	Reiterates primary recommendation and draws any necessary conclusions
Appendices	Includes any backup materials that were not directly provided in the body of the document such as detailed financial investment analysis, marketing materials, and competitors' literature.

FIGURE 7.5 Components of a business case.

		Type of Business Change		
		Innovation (Do new things)	Improvement (Do things better)	Cessation (Stop doing things)
High	Financial Benefits	Financial value can be calculated by applying a cost/price or other valid financial formula to a quantifiable benefit.		
	Quantifiable Benefits	There is sufficient evidence to forecast how much improvement/benefit should result from the changes.		
degree of explicitness	Measurable Benefits	Although this aspect of performance is currently measured, or an approximate measure could be implemented, it is not possible to estimate how much performance will improve when changes are implemented.		
Low	Observable Benefits	By using agreed criteria, specific individuals or groups will use their experience or judgment to decide the extent the benefit will be realized.		

FIGURE 7.6 Classification framework for benefits in a business case.
Source: Adapted from John Ward, Elizabeth Daniel, and Joe Peppard, "Building Better Business Cases for IT Investments," *MISQE* (March 2008), 7(1), 1–15.

Daniel, and Peppard[7] have suggested framework for identifying and describing both financial and nonfinancial benefits, shown in Figure 7.6. The first step in this framework is to identify each benefit as innovation, or allowing the organization to do new things; improvement, or allowing the organization to do things better; or cessation, stopping things. Then the benefits can be classified by degree of explicitness or the ability to assign a value to the benefit. As shown in Figure 7.6, benefits fall into one of these categories:

- Observable—They can only be measured by opinion or judgment. These are the subjective, intangible, soft, or qualitative benefits.
- Measurable—There is already a well-accepted way to measure the benefit (but it may not be a quantifiable measure). Using existing measures to ensure alignment with the business strategy.
- Quantifiable—There is a way to measure the size or magnitude of the benefit. Most business cases revolve around quantifiable benefits, so ensuring that as many benefits as possible have a quantifiable metric is important.
- Financial—There is a way to express the benefit in financial terms. These are the metrics that are most easily used to judge the go/no-go decision because financial terms are universal across all business decisions.

Consider this example of a U.K.-based mobile telephone company. The company's strategy was to differentiate itself with excellent customer service, and it identified a project to upgrade the call centers as a potential opportunity. Figure 7.7 contains a sample of the cost-risk-benefit analysis for this business case. Note that in this example, costs were described in terms of six categories: purchases, implementation technical

[7] Ibid.

Objective Type	Doing New Things	Doing Things Better	Stop Doing Things
Financial		**Benefit:** Increased customer retention due to improved service provision **Measure:** Reduction in customer defections. Avoided defections due to service failure = 1,750 pa. Cost per defection = £500—savings of £875,000 pa **Benefit Owner:** Customer accounts manager **Benefit:** 20% reduction in call servicing costs **Measure:** Cost per service call. Number of calls pa = 5.6 million, total servicing costs = £1.2 million—savings of £240,000 pa **Benefit Owner:** Telechannel sales manager	**Benefit:** Stop call-backs to customers after failed service calls **Measure:** Number of call-backs. Number in previous years = 1.5 million. Cost per call-back = £0.46—savings of £690,000 pa **Benefit Owner:** Call center operations manager
Quantifiable			**Benefit:** Eliminate call waiting times over 2 minutes for customers **Measure:** Number of calls currently waiting over 2 minutes = 1.1 million **Benefit Owner:** Call center operations manager
Measurable	**Benefit:** Call center staff able to undertake sales calls/promote new services **Measure:** Number of sales calls per staff member or sales per staff member. Current value = 0 (call center currently purely inbound) **Benefit Owner:** Telechannel sales manager	**Benefit:** Customers not switching to competitors' products and services **Measure:** Number of defections to competitors. Current number of customers switching = 5,500 pa **Benefit Owner:** Customer accounts manager	
Observable	**Benefit:** Call center staff motivated by being trained about newer services **Measure:** Increased call center motivation **Benefit Owner:** Call center staff manager	**Benefit:** Ability to develop future services based on customer data **Measure:** Quantity and quality of customer profile data **Benefit Owner:** New service development manager	**Benefit:** Stop customers becoming frustrated/rude because of service failure **Measure:** Call center staff opinion **Benefit Owner:** Call center staff manager

Investment Costs	
Purchase of new call center hardware and software:	£250,000
Cost of implementation technical consultants:	£120,000
Internal systems development costs (for configuration):	£150,000
Infrastructure upgrade costs:	£75,000
Business change costs:	£270,000
Training costs:	£80,000
Total:	**£945,000**
Net increase in annual systems support and license costs:	£80,000

FIGURE 7.7 Cost-risk-benefit analysis for a business case.
Source: Adapted from John Ward, Elizabeth Daniel, and Joe Peppard, "Building Better Business Cases for IT Investments," *MISQE* (March 2008), 7(1), 1–15.

Risk Analysis	
Technical Risks:	Complexity of the systems functionality
	Number of system interfaces and systems being replaced
Financial Risks:	Confidence in some investment costs—especially business change
	Confidence in the evidence for some of the benefits
	Business criticality of areas affected by the system
Organizational Risks:	The extent of changes to call center processes and practice
	Limited existing change management capability
	Call center staff capability to promote more technical services
	Customer willingness to share information for profiling purposes

FIGURE 7.7 (Continued)

consultants, development, infrastructure, business change, and training costs. Risks were categorized as financial risks, technical risks, and organizational risks.[8]

▶ IT PORTFOLIO MANAGEMENT

Managing the set of systems and programs in an IT organization is similar to managing resources in a financial organization. There are different types of IT investments, and together they form the business's IT portfolio. **IT portfolio management** refers to "evaluating new and existing applications collectively on an ongoing basis to determine which applications provide value to the business in order to support decisions to replace, retire, or further invest in applications across the enterprise."[9] This requires thinking about IT systems as a cohesive set of core assets, and not as a discontinuous stream of one-off, targeted investments as often has been the case in the past. IT portfolio management involves continually deciding on the right mix of investments from funding, management, and staffing perspectives. The overall goal of IT portfolio management is for the company to fund and invest in the most valuable initiatives that, taken together as a whole, generate maximum benefits to the business.

Professor Peter Weill and colleagues at MIT's Center for Information Systems Research (CISR) describe four asset classes of IT investments that typically make up the company's IT portfolio:

- Transactional Systems—systems that streamline or cut costs on the way business is done (equivalent to Level 1 in Business Maturity Model)
- Infrastructure Systems—the base foundation of shared IT services used for multiple applications such as servers, networks, databases, or laptops (equivalent to Level 2 in Business Maturity Model)

---

[8] Ibid.

[9] James D. McKeen and Heather A. Smith, "Developments in Practice XXXIV. Application Portfolio Management," *Communications of the Association for Information Systems* (2010), 26(9), http://aisel.aisnet.org/cais/vol26/iss1/9.

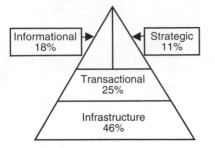

FIGURE 7.8 Average company's IT portfolio profile.
Source: Peter Weill and Marianne Broadbent, *Leveraging The New Infrastructure: How Market Leaders Capitalize on Information Technology* (Cambridge, MA: Harvard Business School Press, June 1998). © MIT Sloan Center for Information Systems Research 2005–12. Used with permission. For more information, see http://cisr.mit.edu.

- Informational Systems—systems that provide information used to control, manage, communicate, analyze, or collaborate (equivalent to Level 2 in Business Maturity Model)
- Strategic Systems—systems used to gain competitive advantage in the market-place (equivalent to Level 3 in Business Maturity Model)

From the portfolio management perspective, new systems are evaluated on their own merits as well as their overall impact on the portfolio. Often the systems can't standalone. Rather, their ability to meet business demand is based on an integrated web of applications. In analyzing the composition of any single company's IT portfolio, one can come up with a profile of the relative investment made in each IT asset class. Weill's study found that the average firm allocates 46% of its total IT investment each year to infrastructure and only 25% of its total IT investment in transactional systems. Figure 7.8 summarizes a typical IT portfolio. At a more detailed level, different industries allocate their IT resources differently.

Managers use a portfolio view of IT investments to manage IT resources. This view makes visible where money is being spent for IT. Decision makers use the portfolio to analyze risk, assess fit with business strategy, and identify opportunities for reducing IT spending. Portfolio management helps prioritize IT investments across multiple decision criteria, including value to the business, urgency, and financial return. Just like an individual or company's investment portfolio is aligned with the individual or company's objectives, the IT portfolio must be aligned with the business strategy.

Weill's work suggests that a different balance between IT investments is needed for a cost-focused strategy compared to an agility-focused strategy. A company with a cost-focused strategy would seek an IT portfolio that helps lower costs as the primary business objective. In that case, Weill's work suggests that on average 27% of the IT investments are made in transactional investments, suggesting higher use of applications that automate processes which and typically lower operational costs. On the other hand, a company with an agility focus would be more likely to invest a higher percent of their IT portfolio in infrastructure (e.g., 51% on average), and less in transactional systems

	Transactional Investments	Infrastructure Investments	Informational Investments	Strategic Investments
Average Firm	25%	46%	18%	11%
Cost Focus	27%	44%	18%	11%
Agility Focus	24%	51%	15%	10%

FIGURE 7.9 Comparative IT portfolios for different business strategies.

Source: Peter Weill and Marianne Broadbent, *Leveraging The New Infrastructure: How Market Leaders Capitalize on Information Technology* (Cambridge, MA: Harvard Business School Press, June 1998). © MIT Sloan Center for Information Systems Research 2005–12. Used with permission. For more information, see http://cisr.mit.edu.

(e.g., 24% on average). The infrastructure investment would create a platform that would likely be used to more quickly and nimbly create solutions needed by the business, whereas the transactional systems might lock in the current processes and take more effort and time to change. Figure 7.9 summarizes the differences.

▶ VALUING IT INVESTMENTS

New IT investments are often justified by the business managers proposing them in terms of monetary costs and benefits. Monetary costs and benefits are important but not the only considerations in making IT investments. Soft benefits, such as the ability to make future decisions, are often part of the business case for IT investments, making it difficult to measure the payback of the investment.

Several unique factors of the IT organization make it difficult to determine the value from IT investments. First, the systems are complex, and calculating the costs is an art, not a science. Second, because many IT investments are for infrastructure, calculating a payback period may be more complex than other types of capital investments. Third, many times the payback cannot be calculated because the investment is a necessity rather than a choice, without any tangible payback. For example, upgrading to a newer version of software or buying a new design of hardware may be required because the older models are broken or simply not supported any longer. Many managers do not want to be placed in the position of having to upgrade simply because the vendor thinks an upgrade is necessary. Instead, managers may resist IT spending on the grounds that the investment adds no incremental value. These factors and more fuel a long-running debate about the value of IT investments. IT managers need to learn to express benefits in a business-like manner such as ROI or increased customer satisfaction.

IT managers, like the business managers who propose IT projects, are expected understand, and even try to calculate, the true return on these projects. Measuring this return is difficult, however. To illustrate, consider the relative ease with which a manager might analyze whether the enterprise should build a new plant. The first step would be to estimate the costs of construction. The plant capacity dictates project production levels. Demand varies, and construction costs frequently overrun, but the manager can find sufficient information to make a decision about whether to build. Most of the time, the benefits of investing in IT are less tangible than those of building a plant because the IT cannot be felt and touched like a physical building can be. Such benefits might include tighter systems integration, faster response time, more accurate data, and more leverage to adopt future technologies, among others. How can a manager quantify these intangibles? He or she should also consider many indirect, or downstream, benefits and costs, such as changes in how people behave, where staff report, and how tasks are assigned. In fact, it may be impossible to pinpoint who will benefit from an IT investment when making the decision.[10]

Despite the difficulty, the task of evaluating IT investments is necessary. Knowing which approaches to use and when to use them are important first steps. A number of approaches are summarized in Figure 7.10. Managers should choose based on the attributes of the project. For example, **return on investment (ROI)** or payback analysis can be used when detailed analysis is not required, such as when a project is short-lived and its costs and benefits are clear. When the project lasts long enough that the time value of money becomes a factor, **net present value (NPV)** and **economic value added (EVA)** are better approaches. EVA is particularly appropriate for capital-intensive projects.

Both IT and business managers may encounter a number of pitfalls when analyzing return on investment. First, not every situation calls for in-depth analysis. Some decisions—such as whether to invest in a new operating system to become compatible with a client operating system—are easy to make. The costs are unlikely to be prohibitively high, and the benefits are clear.

Second, not every evaluation method works in every case. Depending on the assets employed, the duration of the project, and any uncertainty about implementation, one method may work better than another.

Third, circumstances may alter the way a particular valuation method is best used. For instance, in a software implementation, estimates of labor hours required often fall short of actual hours spent. Accordingly, some managers use an "adjusting" factor in their estimates.

Fourth, managers can fall into "analysis paralysis." Reaching a precise valuation may take longer than is reasonable to make an investment decision. Because a single right valuation may not exist, "close enough" usually suffices. Experience and an eye to the risks of an incorrect valuation help decide when to stop analyzing.

Finally, even when the numbers say a project is not worthwhile, the investment may be necessary to remain competitive. For example, UPS faced little choice but to invest heavily in IT. At the time, FedEx made IT a competitive advantage and was winning the overnight delivery war. More recently, companies are finding that they must reinvest in their applications in order to make them work on mobile devices.

---

[10] John C. Ford, "Evaluating Investment in IT," *Australian Accountant* (December 1994), 3.

Valuation Method	Description
Return on investment (ROI)	Percentage rate that measures the relationship between the amount the business gets back from an investment and the amount invested using the formula: ROI = (Revenue – Investment)/Investment. Although popular and easy to use and understand, ROI lacks sophistication in assessing intangible benefits and costs.
Net present value (NPV)	Finance departments typically use NPV because it accounts for the time value of money. After discounting and then adding the dollar inflows and outflows, a positive NPV indicates a project should be undertaken, as long as other IT investments do not have higher values. It is calculated by discounting the costs and benefits for each year of the system's lifetime using the present value factor calculated each year as $1/(1+ \text{discount rate})^{\text{year}}$.
Economic value added (EVA)	EVA accounts for opportunity costs of capital to measure true economic profit and revalues historical costs to give an accurate picture of the true market value of assets.[a] EVA is sufficiently complex that consultants typically are required to implement it. It provides no hard and fast rules for intangibles. Calculating EVA is simple: EVA = Net operating profit after taxes – [(Capital)(Cost of capital)].[a]
Payback analysis	Simple, popular method that determines the payback period, or how much time will lapse before accrued benefits overtake accrued and continuing costs.
Internal rate of return (IRR)	Calculation is made to determine the return that the IT investment would have, and then it is compared to the corporate policy on rate of return. If IT investment's rate of return is higher than the corporate policy, the project is considered a good investment.
Weighted scoring methods	Costs and revenues/savings are weighted based on their strategic importance, level of accuracy or confidence, and comparable investment opportunities.
Prototyping	A scaled-down version of a system is tested for its costs and benefits. This approach is useful when the impact of the IT investment seems unclear.
Game theory or role-playing	These approaches may reveal behavioral changes or new tasks attributable to a new system. They are less expensive than prototyping.
Simulation	A model is used to test the impact of a new system or series of tasks. This low-cost method surfaces problems and allows system sensitivities to be analyzed.

[a] http://www.sternstewart.com.

FIGURE 7.10 Valuation methods.

▶ MONITORING IT INVESTMENTS

An old adage says: "If you can't measure it, you can't manage it." Management's role is to ensure that the money spent on IT results in benefits for the organization. Therefore, common, accepted set of metrics must be created, and those metrics must be monitored and communicated to senior management and customers of the IT department. These metrics are often financial in nature (i.e., ROI, NPV). But financial measures are only one category of measures used to manage IT investments. Other IT metrics include logs of errors encountered by users, end-user surveys, user turnaround time, logs of computer and communication up-/downtime, system response time, and percentage of projects completed on time and/or within budget. Additional, business-focused metrics might include measures such as the number of contacts with external customers, sales revenue accrued from Web channels, and new business leads generated.

The Balanced Scorecard

Deciding on appropriate measures is half of the equation for effective IT organizations. The other half of the equation is ensuring that those measures are accurately communicated to the business. Two methods for communicating these metrics are scorecards and dashboards.

Financial measures may be the language of stockholders, but managers understand that they can be misleading if used as the sole means of making management decisions. One methodology used to solve this problem, created by Robert Kaplan and David Norton, and first described in the *Harvard Business Review* in 1992, is the **balanced scorecard**, which focuses attention on the organization's value drivers (which include, but are not limited to, financial performance).[11] Companies use it to assess the full impact of their corporate strategies on their customers and workforce, as well as their financial performance.

This methodology allows managers to look at the business from four perspectives: customer, internal business, innovation/learning, and financial. For each perspective, the goals and measures are designed to answer these basic questions:

- How do customers see us? (Customer perspective)
- At what must we excel? (Internal business perspective)
- Can we continue to improve and create value? (Innovation and learning perspective)
- How do we look to shareholders? (Financial perspective)

Figure 7.11 graphically shows the relationship of these perspectives.

Since the introduction of the Balanced Scorecard, many have modified it or adapted it to apply to their particular organization. Managers of information technology found

---

[11] For more detail, see R. Kaplan and D. Norton, "The Balanced Scorecard—Measures That Drive Performance," *Harvard Business Review* (January–February 1992).

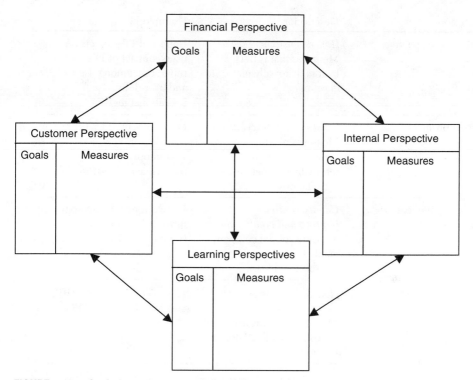

FIGURE 7.11 The balanced scorecard perspectives.
Source: Based on R. Kaplan and D. Norton, "The Balanced Scorecard—Measures That Drive Performance," *Harvard Business Review* (January–February 1992), 72.

the concept of a scorecard useful in managing and communicating the value of the IT department.

Applying the categories of the balanced scorecard to IT might mean interpreting them more broadly than originally conceived by Kaplan and Norton. For example, the original scorecard speaks of the customer perspective, but for the IT scorecard, the customer might be a user within the company, not the external customer of the company. The questions asked when using this methodology within the IT department are summarized in Figure 7.12.

David Norton commented, "[D]on't start with an emphasis on metrics—start with your strategy and use metrics to make it understandable and measurable (that is, to communicate it to those expected to make it happen and to manage it)."[12] He found the balanced scorecard to be the most effective management framework for achieving organizational alignment and strategic success.

FirstEnergy, a multibillion-dollar utility company, provides a good example of how the IS scorecard can be used. The company set a strategic goal of creating "raving fans" among its customers. In addition, they identified three other business value drivers:

[12] "Ask the Source: Interview with David Norton," *CIO Magazine* (July 25, 2002), www.cio.com (accessed on February 22, 2003).

Dimension	Description	Example IT Measures
Customer perspective	*How do customers see us?* Measures that reflect factors that really matter to customers	Impact of IT projects on users, impact of IT's reputation among users, and user-defined operational metrics
Internal business perspective	*What must we excel at?* Measures of what the company must do internally to meet customer expectations	IT process metrics, project completion rates, and system operational performance metrics
Innovating and learning perspective	*Can we continue to improve and create value?* Measures of the company's ability to innovate, improve, and learn	IT R&D, new technology introduction success rate, training metrics
Financial perspective	*How do we look to shareholders?* Measures to indicate contribution of activities to the bottom line	IT project ROI, NPV, IRR, cost/benefit, TCO, ABC

FIGURE 7.12 Balanced scorecard applied to IT departments.
Source: Adapted from R. Kaplan and D. Norton, "The Balanced Scorecard—Measures That Drive Performance," *Harvard Business Review* (January–February 1992), 72.

reliability, finance, and winning culture. The MIS group interpreted "raving fans" to mean satisfied internal customers. They used three metrics to measure their performance along this dimension:[13]

- Percentage of projects completed on time and on budget
- Percentage of projects released to the customer by agreed-on delivery date
- Client satisfaction recorded on customer surveys done at the end of a project

A scorecard used within the IT organization helps senior IT managers understand their organization's performance and measure it in a way that supports its business strategy. The IT scorecard is linked to the corporate scorecard and ensures that the measures used by IT are those that support the corporate goals. At DuPont Engineering, the balanced scorecard methodology forces every action to be linked to a corporate goal, which helps promote alignment and eliminate projects with little potential impact. The conversations between IT and the business focus on strategic goals, the merits of the project at hand, and impact rather than on technology and capabilities.[14]

[13] Adapted from Eric Berkman, "How to Use the Balanced Scorecard," *CIO Magazine* (May 15, 2002).
[14] Ibid., also Hall of Fame Organizations: Dupont, http://www.thepalladiumgroup.com/about/hof/Pages/HofViewer.aspx?MID=27 (accessed on February 19, 2012).

IT Dashboards

Scorecards provide summary information gathered over a period of time. Another common IT management monitoring tool is the IT **dashboard**, which provides a snapshot of metrics at any given point in time. Much like the dashboard of an automobile or airplane, the IT dashboard summarizes key metrics for senior managers in a manner that provides quick identification of the status of the organization. Like scorecards, dashboards are useful outside the IT department and are often found in executive offices as a tool for keeping current on critical measures of the organization. This section focuses on the use of these tools within the IT department.

Dashboards provide frequently updated information on areas of interest within the IT department. Depending on who is actually using the dashboard, the data tend to focus on project status or operational systems status. For example, a dashboard used by GM North America's IT leadership team contains a metric designed to monitor project status.[15] Because senior managers question the overall health of a project rather than the details, the dashboard they designed provides red, yellow, or green highlights for rapid comprehension. A green highlight means that the project is progressing as planned and performance is within acceptable limits. A yellow highlight means at least one key target has been missed. A red highlight means the project is significantly behind and needs some attention or resources to get back on track.

At GM, each project is tracked and rated monthly. GM uses four dashboard criteria: (1) performance to budget, (2) performance to schedule, (3) delivery of business results, and (4) risk. At the beginning of a project, these metrics are defined and acceptable levels set. The project manager assigns a color status monthly, based on the defined criteria, and the results are reported in a spreadsheet. When managers look at the dashboard, they can immediately tell whether projects are on schedule based on the amount of green, yellow, or red on the dashboard. They can then drill down into yellow or red metrics to get the projects back on track. The dashboard provides an easy way to identify where their attention should be focused. The director of IT operations explains, "Red means I need more money, people or better business buy-in. . . The dashboard provides an early warning system that allows IT managers to identify and correct problems before they become big enough to derail a project."[16]

There are really four types of IT dashboards.[17] *Portfolio dashboards* like GM's help senior IT leaders manage the IT projects. These dashboards show senior IT leaders the status, problems, milestones, progress, expenses, and other metrics related to specific projects. *Business-IT dashboards* show relevant business metrics and link them to the IT systems that support them. The metrics on the balanced scorecard provide a sample of the type of metrics followed by this dashboard. A *service dashboard* is geared towards the internal IS department, showing important metrics about the IS such as up-time, through-put, service tickets, progress on bug fixes, helpdesk satisfaction, etc. The fourth type is an *improvement dashboard*, which monitors the three to five key improvement

---

[15] Adapted from Tracy Mayor, "Red Light, Green Light," *CIO Magazine* (October 1, 2001).

[16] Ibid.

[17] Adapted from Chris Curran, "The 4 types of CIO dasboards," *CIO.com* (June 15, 2009), http://www.ciodashboard.com/metrics-and-measurement/the-4-types-of-cio-dashboards/ (accessed on April 9, 2012).

goals for the IT group. Like the portfolio dashboard, the metrics to be monitored are based on the projects undertaken, but unlike the other dashboards, this one is geared toward monitoring progress toward important goals of the IT organization itself.

In order to increase its transparency, the U.S. federal government created an IT dashboard Web site in 2009. This Web site, which was built in six weeks, displays the status of each IT investment currently under development within the U.S. government. It provides status information by investment and agency and offers the ability to drill down for details. For each investment, it provides color-coded (i.e., green, yellow and red) performance metrics (cost, schedule, and CIO evaluation), along with a project history. For each agency, it provides an agency rating and count of investment projects/programs in each color grouping. For example, the Department of Homeland Security has a rating of 6.1 out of 10. Of its 87 current projects, it has a green count of 41 projects, a yellow count of 38, and a red count of eight. Drilling down to the investment entitled National Flood Insurance Program with the extremely low rating of 0.0 and a current cumulative cost of $19.7 million, one can see the assessment of the CIO of the Federal Emergency Management Agency that the program "suffered from a lack of proper adherence to IT program management disciplines and oversight, which has resulted in the development of a system that does not meet the needs of the users." Of course, with the increased transparency comes increased accountability for managing the investments.[18]

Dashboards are built on the information contained in the other applications, databases, and analytical systems of the organization (see Chapter 11 for a more complete discussion of business intelligence and business analytics). Figure 7.13 contains the architecture of a sample dashboard for Western Digital, a $3 billion global designer and manufacturer of high-performance hard drives for PCs, networks, storage devices, and entertainment systems.[19]

▶ FUNDING IT RESOURCES

Who pays for IT? The users? The IT organization? Headquarters? Certain costs are associated with designing, developing, delivering, and maintaining the IT systems. How are these costs recovered? The three main funding methods are chargeback, allocation, and corporate budget. Both chargeback and allocation methods distribute the costs back to the businesses, departments, or individuals within the company. This distribution of costs is used for management reasons, so that managers can understand the costs associated with running their organization, or for tax reasons, where the costs associated with each business must be paid for by the appropriate business unit. Corporate budgeting, on the other hand, is a completely different funding method in which IT costs are not linked directly with any specific user or business unit; costs are recovered using corporate coffers.

---

[18] U.S. Federal Government IT Dashboards, http://www.itdashboard.gov/portfolios (accessed on February 18, 2012).

[19] Robert Houghton, O. A. El Sawy, P. Gray, C. Donegan, and A. Joshi, "Vigilant Information Systems for Managing Enterprises in Dynamic Supply Chains: Real-Time Dashboards at Western Digital," *MISQE* (March 2004), 3(1), 19–35.

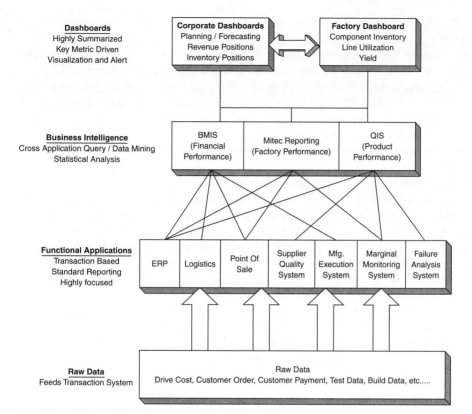

FIGURE 7.13 Example architecture of a dashboard.
Source: Robert Houghton, O. A. El Sawy, P. Gray, C. Donegan, and A. Joshi, "Vigilant Information Systems for Managing Enterprises in Dynamic Supply Chains: Real-Time Dashboards at Western Digital," *MISQE* (March 2004), 3(1).

Chargeback

With a **chargeback funding method**, IT costs are recovered by charging individuals, departments, or business units based on actual usage and cost. The IT organization collects usage data on each system it runs. Rates for usage are calculated based on the actual cost to the IT group to run the system and billed out on a regular basis. For example, a desktop PC might be billed out at $100/month, which includes the cost of maintaining the system, any software license fees for the standard desktop configuration, e-mail, network access, a usage fee for the helpdesk, and other related services. Each department receives a bill showing the number of desktop computers they have and the charge per desktop, the number of printers they have and the charge per printer, the number of servers they have and the charge per server, the amount of mainframe time they have used and the cost per second of that time, and so on. When the IT organization wants to recover administrative and overhead costs using a chargeback system, these costs are built into rates charged for each of the services.

Chargeback systems are popular because they are viewed as the most equitable way to recover IT costs. Costs are distributed based on usage or consumption of resources, ensuring that the largest portion of the costs is paid for by the group or individual who consumes the most. Chargeback systems can also provide managers with the most options for managing and controlling their IT costs. For example, a manager may decide to use desktop systems rather than laptop systems because the unit charge is less expensive. The chargeback system gives managers the details they need to understand both what IT resources they use and how to account for IT consumption in the cost of their products and services. Because the departments get a regular bill, they know exactly what their costs are.

Creating and managing a chargeback system, however, is a costly endeavor itself. IT organizations must build systems to collect details that might not be needed for anything other than the bills they generate. For example, if PCs are the basis for charging for network time, then the network connect time per PC must be collected, stored, and analyzed each billing cycle. The data collection quickly becomes large and complex, which often results in complicated, difficult-to-understand bills. In addition, picking the charging criteria is challenging. For example, it is relatively easy to count the number of PCs located in a particular business unit, but is that number a good measure of the network resources used? It might be more accurate to charge based on units of network time used, but how would that be captured and calculated? Chargeback methods are most appropriate when there is a wide variation in usage among users or when actual costs need to be accounted for by the business units.

Allocation

To simplify the cost recovery process compared to the chargeback method, an allocation system can be used. An **allocation funding method** recovers costs based on something other than usage, such as revenues, login accounts, or number of employees. For example, suppose the total spending for IT for a year is $1 million for a company with 10,000 employees. A business unit with 1,000 employees might be responsible for 10%, or $100,000, of the total IT costs. Of course, with this type of allocation system, it does not matter whether these employees even use the IT; the department is still charged the same amount.

The allocation mechanism is simpler to implement and apply each month compared to the chargeback mechanism. Actual usage does not need to be captured. The rate charged is often fixed at the beginning of the year. Allocation offers two main advantages. First, the level of detail required to calculate the allocations is much less, and for many companies that aspect saves expense. Second, the charges from the IT organization are predictable. Unlike the chargeback mechanism, where each bill opens up an opportunity for discussion about the charges incurred, the allocation mechanism seems to generate far less frequent arguments from the business units. Often, quite a bit of discussion takes place at the beginning of the year, when rates and allocation bases are set, but less discussion occurs each month because the managers understand and expect the bill.

Two major complaints are made about allocation systems. First is the free-rider problem: A large user of IT services pays the same amount as a small user when the charges are not based on usage. Second, deciding the basis for allocating the costs is an issue. Choosing the number of employees over the number of desktops or other basis is a management decision, and whichever basis is chosen, someone will pay more than their actual usage would imply. Allocation mechanisms work well when a corporate directive requires use of this method and when the units agree on the basis for dividing up the costs.

Often when an allocation process is used, a follow-up process is needed at the end of the fiscal year, in which total IT expenses are compared to total IT funds recovered from the business units, and any extra funds are given back to the business. Sometimes this process is called a "true-up" process because true expenses are balanced against payments made. In some cases, additional funds are needed; however, IT managers try to avoid asking for funds to make up for shortfalls in their budget. The true-up process is needed because the actual cost of the information system is difficult to predict at the beginning of the year. Cost changes over the year because hardware, software, or support costs fluctuate in the marketplace and because IT managers, like all managers, work constantly on improving efficiency and productivity, resulting in lower costs. In an allocation process, where the rate charged for each service is fixed for the year, a true-up process allows IT managers to pass along any additional savings to their business counterparts. Business managers often prefer the predictability of their monthly IT bills along with a true-up process over the relative unpredictability of being charged actual costs each month.

Corporate Budget

An entirely different way to pay for IT costs is to simply consider them all to be corporate overhead and pay for them directly out of the corporate budget. With the **corporate budget funding method**, the costs fall to the corporate bottom line, rather than levying charges on specific users or business units.

Corporate budgeting is a relatively simple method for funding IT costs. It requires no calculation of prices of the IT systems. And because bills are not generated on a regular cycle to the businesses, concerns are raised less often by the business managers. IT managers control the entire budget, giving them control of the use of those funds and, ultimately, more input into what systems are created, how they are managed, and when they are retired. This funding method also encourages the use of new technologies because learners are not charged for exploration and inefficient system use.

As with the other methods, certain drawbacks come with using the corporate budget. First, all IT expenditures are subjected to the same process as all other corporate expenditures, namely, the budgeting process. In many companies, this process is one of the most stressful events of the year: Everyone has projects to be done, and everyone is competing for scarce funds. If the business units do not get billed in some way for their usage, many companies find that they do not control their usage. Getting a bill for services motivates the individual business manager to reconsider his or her usage of those services. Finally, if the business units are not footing the bill, the IT group may feel less accountable to them, which may result in an IT organization that is less end-user or customer oriented.

Figure 7.14 summarizes the advantages and disadvantages of these methods.

Funding Method	Description	Why Do It?	Why Not Do It?
Chargeback	Charges are calculated based on actual usage.	Fairest method for recovering costs because it is based on actual usage. IT users can see exactly what their usage costs are.	IT department must collect details on usage, which can be expensive and difficult. IT must be prepared to defend the charges, which takes time and resources.
Allocation	Total expected IT expenditures are divided by nonusage basis such as number of login IDs, employees, or desktops.	Less bookkeeping for IT because rate is set once per fiscal year, and basis is well understood. Predictable monthly costs.	IT department must defend allocation rates; may charge low-usage department more than their usage would indicate is fair.
Corporate Budget	Corporate allocates funds to IT at annual budget session.	No billing to the businesses. IT exercises more control over what projects are done. Good for encouraging use of new technologies.	Competes with all other budgeted items for funds.

FIGURE 7.14 Comparison of IT funding methods.

▶ HOW MUCH DOES IT COST?

The three major IT funding approaches in the preceding discussion are designed to recover the costs of building and maintaining the information systems in an enterprise. The goal is to simply cover the costs, not to generate a profit (although some IT organizations are actually profit centers for their corporation). The most basic method for calculating the costs of a system is to add the costs of all the components, including hardware, software, network, and the people involved. IT organizations calculate the initial costs and ongoing maintenance costs in just this way.

Activity-Based Costing

Another method for calculating costs is known as activity-based costing (ABC). Traditional accounting methods account for direct and indirect costs. Direct costs are those costs that can be clearly linked to a particular process or product, such as the components used to manufacture the product and the assembler's wages for time spent building the product. Indirect costs are the overhead costs, which include everything from the electric bill, the salary of administrative managers, and the expenses of administrative function, to the wages of the supervisor overseeing the assembler, the cost of running the factory, and the maintenance of machinery used for multiple products. Further, depending on the funding method used by the enterprise, indirect costs arc allocatcd or absorbed elsewhere in the pricing model. The allocation process can be cumbersome and complex and often is a source of trouble for many organizations. The alternative is ABC.

Activity-based costing calculates costs by counting the actual activities that go into making a specific product or delivering a specific service. *Activities* are processes, functions, or tasks that occur over time and produce recognized results. They consume assigned resources to produce products and services. Activities are useful in costing because they are the common denominator between business process improvement and information improvement across departments.

Rather than allocate the total indirect cost of a system across a range of services according to an allocation formula, ABC calculates the amount of time that system was spent supporting a particular activity and allocates only that cost to that activity. For example, an accountant would look at the ERP (enterprise resource planning system) and divide its cost over the activities it supports by calculating how much of the system is used by each activity. Product A might take up one-twelfth of an ERP system's capacity to control the manufacturing activities needed to make it, so it would be allocated one-twelfth of the system's costs. The helpdesk might take up a whole server, so the entire server's cost would be allocated to that activity. In the end, the costs are put in buckets that reflect the products and services of the business, rather than the organization structure or the processes of any given department. In effect, ABC is the process of charging all costs to "profit centers" instead of to "cost centers."

Jonathan Bush, CEO of management services company Athenahealth, did activity-based costing for Children's Hospital in Boston. When he found that it cost the hospital about $120 to admit a patient, he recommended a solution of using the information received from the primary-care doctor. He argues: "Your primary-care doctor has already created 90% of that information to see you for your regular visit. Why wouldn't the hospital give the doctor $100 if it was costing them $120 to do it themselves?" The ABC approach allowed the hospital to realize the cost of running the hospital systems to perform the activity and to compare it with the cost of an alternative source that turned out to be cheaper. But until the thorny issues of electronic medical records are sorted out, the doctors and the hospitals will likely continue to create their own records.[20]

Total Cost of Ownership

When a system is proposed and a business case is created to justify the investment, summing up the initial outlay and the maintenance cost does not provide an entirely accurate total system cost. In fact, if only the initial and maintenance cost are considered, the decision is often made on incomplete information. Other costs are involved, and a

[20] David Lidsky, "#43 Athenahealth," fastcompany.com (February 17, 2010), http://www.fastcompany.com/mic/2010/profile/athenahealth (accessed on January 30, 2012).

time value of money affects the total cost. One technique used to calculate a more accurate cost that includes all associated costs is **total cost of ownership (TCO)**. It is fast becoming the industry standard. Gartner Group introduced TCO in the late 1980s when PC-based IT infrastructures began gaining popularity.[21] Other IT experts have since modified the concept, and this section synthesizes the latest and best thinking about TCO.

TCO looks beyond initial capital investments to include costs associated with technical support, administration, training, and system retirement. Often, the initial cost is an inadequate predictor of the additional costs necessary to successfully implement the system. TCO techniques estimate annual costs per user for each potential infrastructure choice; these costs are then totaled. Careful estimates of TCO provide the best investment numbers to compare with financial return numbers when analyzing the net returns on various IT options. The alternative, an analysis without TCO, can result in an "apples and oranges" comparison. Consider a decision about printers. The initial cost of one printer may be much less than a second choice. However, the cost and longevity of the ink cartridges necessary to run each printer may vary significantly. Likewise, a laser printer may be more expensive initially, but when considering the expected lifetime of the printer, compared to an inexpensive alternative, the total cost of ownership may be much less. A similar analysis of a larger IT system clarifies similar alternatives and comparisons.

A major IT investment is for infrastructure. Figure 7.15 uses the hardware, software, network, and data categories to organize the TCO components the manager needs to evaluate for each infrastructure option. This table allows the manager to assess infrastructure components at a medium level of detail and categorically to allocate "softer" costs like administration and support. More or less detail can be used as needed by the business environment. The manager can adapt this framework for use with varying IT infrastructures.

TCO Component Breakdown

To clarify how the TCO framework is used, this section examines the hardware category in greater detail. As used in Figure 7.15, hardware means computing platforms and peripherals. The components listed are somewhat arbitrary, and an organization in which every user possesses every component would be highly unusual. For shared components, such as servers and printers, TCO estimates should be computed per component and then divided among all users who access them.

For more complex situations, such as when only certain groups of users possess certain components, it is wise to segment the hardware analysis by platform. For example, in an organization in which every employee possesses a desktop that accesses a server and half the employees also possess stand-alone laptops that do not access a server, one TCO table could be built for desktop and server hardware and another for

---

[21] M. Gartenberg, "Beyond the Numbers: Common TCO Myths Revealed," GartnerGroup Research Note: Technology (March 2, 1998).

	Infrastructure	Cost per end user of	Cost per end user of
Category	Component	Option 1	Option 2
Hardware	Desktops Servers Mobile platforms Printers Archival storage Technical support Administration Training Informal support Retirement Total Hardware Cost		
Software	OS Office Suite Database Proprietary Technical support Administration Training Informal support Total Software Cost		
Network	LAN WAN Dial-in lines/modems Technical support Administration Total Network Cost		
Data	Removable media On-site backup storage Off-site backup storage Total Data Cost		

FIGURE 7.15 TCO component evaluation.

Soft Cost Areas	Components of Cost	User	Annual Costs	Cost/ Hour	Total Cost
Technical support	Hardware phone support	Call center			
	In-person hardware troubleshooting	IT operations			
	Hardware hot swaps	IT operations			
	Physical hardware repair	IT operations			
	Total cost of technical support				
Administration	Hardware setup	System administrator			
	Hardware upgrades/ modifications	System administrator			
	New hardware evaluation	IT operations			
	Total cost of administration				
Training	New employee training	IT operations			
	Ongoing administrator training	Hardware vendor			
	Total cost of training				
	Total soft costs for hardware				

FIGURE 7.16 Soft costs considerations.

laptop hardware. Each table would include software, network, and data costs associated only with its specific platforms.

Soft costs, such as technical support, administration, and training, are easier to estimate than they may first appear. To simplify, these calculations can be broken down further using a table such as Figure 7.16.

The final soft cost, informal support, may be harder to pin down, but it is important nonetheless. Informal support comprises the sometimes highly complex networks that develop among co-workers through which many problems are fixed and much training takes place without the involvement of any official support staff. In many circumstances, these activities can prove more efficient and effective than working through official channels. Still, managers want to analyze the costs of informal support for two reasons:

1. The costs—both in salary and in opportunity—of a nonsupport employee providing informal support may prove significantly higher than analogous costs for a formal support employee. For example, it costs much more in both dollars

per hour and foregone management activity for a mid-level manager to help a line employee troubleshoot an e-mail problem than it would for a formal support employee to provide the same service.

2. The quantity of informal support activity in an organization provides an indirect measure of the efficiency of its IT support organization. The formal support organization should respond with sufficient promptness and thoroughness to discourage all but the briefest informal support transactions.

Various IT infrastructure options affect informal support activities differently. For example, a more user-friendly systems interface may alleviate the need for much informal support, justifying a slightly higher software expenditure. Similarly, an investment in support management software may be justified if it reduces the need for informal support. Web-based applications change the equation even further. Those companies who use a vendor-supplied Web-based application may find support activities are provided by the vendor, or the applications are written in such a way as to minimize or eliminate support entirely.

Although putting dollar values on informal support may be a challenge, managers want to gauge the relative potential of each component option to affect the need for informal support. Further, even if managers can't get a completely accurate figure of costs, they can be more aware of areas where costs can be cut.

TCO as a Management Tool

This discussion focused on TCO as a tool for evaluating which infrastructure components to choose, but TCO also can help managers understand how infrastructure costs break down. Research has consistently shown that the labor costs associated with an IT infrastructure far outweigh the actual capital investment costs. TCO provides the fullest picture of where managers spend their IT dollars. Like other benchmarks, TCO results can be evaluated over time against industry standards (much TCO target data for various IT infrastructure choices are available from industry research firms). Even without comparison data, the numbers that emerge from TCO studies assist in decisions about budgeting, resource allocation, and organizational structure.

However, like the ABC approach, the cost of implementing TCO can be a detriment to the program's overall success. Both ABC and TCO are complex approaches that may require significant effort to determine the costs to use in the calculations. Managers must weigh the benefits of using these approaches with the costs of obtaining reliable data necessary to make their use successful.

▶ SUMMARY

- IT organizations can be expected to anticipate new technologies, participate in setting and implementing strategic goals, innovate current processes, develop and maintain information systems, manage supplier relationships, establish architecture platforms and standards, promote enterprise security, plan for business discontinuities, manage data/information/knowledge, manage Internet and network services, manage human resources, operate the data center, provide general support and integrate social IT.

These activities display different levels of maturity. The IT organization does not perform core business functions, independently make all decisions about selecting IT projects, or independently develop business strategy.

- Global IT organizations face a host of issues that domestic departments avoid. Geopolitical risk, language and cultural barriers, business continuity planning, and transborder data flow issues must be reexamined in a global organization, and each country's laws and policies considered in the architectural design.

- The chief information officer (CIO) is a high-level IS officer who oversees many important organizational activities. The CIO must display both technical and business skills. The role requires both a strategist and an operational manager.

- Because each organization differs depending on the nature of the enterprise, business managers must know the particular needs of their own organization—just as the IS manager must educate them on the IT available. If neither seeks the other out, then a schism can develop between business and IS. The enterprise will suffer due to missed opportunities and expensive mistakes.

- A business case is a tool used to support a decision or a proposal of a new investment. It is a document containing a project description, financial analysis, marketing analysis, and all other relevant documentation to assist managers in making a go/no-go decision.

- Benefits articulated in a business case can be categorized as observable, measurable, quantifiable, and financial. These benefits are often for innovations, improvements, or cessation.

- The portfolio of IT investments must be carefully evaluated and managed.

- ROI is difficult, at best, to calculate for IT investments because the benefits are often not tangible. The benefits might be difficult to quantify, difficult to observe, or long range in scope.

- Popular metrics for IT investments measure quality of information outputs, IT contributions to a firm's financial performance, operational efficiency, management/user attitudes, and the adequacy of systems development practices.

- Monitoring and communicating the status and benefits of IT is often done through the use of balanced scorecards and IT dashboards.

- IT is funded using one of three methods: chargeback, allocation, or corporate budget.

- Chargeback systems are viewed as the most equitable method of IT cost recovery because costs are distributed based on usage. Creating an accounting system to record the information necessary to do a chargeback system can be expensive and time consuming and usually has no other useful application.

- Allocation systems provide a simpler method to recover costs, because they do not involve recording system usage to allocate costs. However, allocation systems can sometimes penalize groups with low usage.

- The corporate budget method does not allocate costs at all. Instead, the CIO seeks and receives a budget from the corporate overhead account. This method of funding IT does not require any usage recordkeeping, but is also most likely to be abused if the users perceive "it is free."

- Activity-based costing is another technique to group costs into a meaningful bucket. Costs are accounted for based on the activity, or product or service, they support. ABC is useful for allocating large overhead expenses.

- Total cost of ownership is a technique to understand all the costs, beyond the initial investment costs, associated with owning and operating an information system. It is most useful as a tool to help evaluate which infrastructure components to choose and to help understand how infrastructure costs occur.

▶ KEY TERMS

activity-based costing (ABC) (p. 227)

allocation funding method (p. 224)

balanced scorecard (p. 218)

business case (p. 209)

business-IT maturity model (p. 198)

business technology strategist (p. 206)

chargeback funding method (p. 223)

Chief Information Officer (CIO) (p. 206)

community manager (p. 208)

corporate budget funding method (p. 225)

dashboard (p. 221)

economic value added (EVA) (p. 216)

IT portfolio management (p. 213)

net present value (NPV) (p. 216)

return on investment (ROI) (p. 216)

total cost of ownership (TCO) (p. 228)

▶ DISCUSSION QUESTIONS

1. Using an organization with which you are familiar, describe the role of the most senior IS professional. Is that person a strategist or an operational manager?

2. What advantages does a CIO bring to a business? What might be the disadvantages of having a CIO?

3. Under what conditions would you recommend using each of these funding methods to pay for information systems expenses: allocation, chargeback, and corporate budget?

4. Describe the conditions under which ROI, payback period, NPV, and EVA are most appropriately applied to information systems investments.

5. A new inventory management system for ABC Company could be developed at a cost of $260,000. The estimated net operating costs and estimated net benefits over six years of operation would be:

Year	Estimated Net Operating Costs	Estimated Net Benefits
0	$260,000	$0
1	7,000	42,000
2	9,400	78,000
3	11,000	82,000
4	14,000	115,000
5	15,000	120,000
6	25,000	140,000

a. What would the payback period be for this investment? Would it be a good or bad investment? Why?

    b. What is the ROI for this investment?

    c. Assuming a 15% discount rate, what is this investment's NPV?

6. Compare and contrast the IT scorecard and dashboard approaches. Which, if any, would be most useful to you, as a general manager? Please explain.

7. TCO is one way to account for costs associated with a specific infrastructure. This method does not include additional costs such as disposal costs—the cost to get rid of the system when it is no longer of use. What other additional costs might be of importance in making total cost calculations?

8. Check out the U.S. Federal government IT dashboard site at http://www.itdashboard.gov/portfolios. Based upon the site:

    a. Describe the portfolio for the Department of Justice.

    b. Which investments, if any, appear to be in trouble in the Department of Justice. Based on the information that is provided can you estimate the status of those projects. Is there any additional information that you think a manager would like to see about the status of the project?

CASE STUDY 7-1

TROON GOLF

Troon Golf, headquartered in Scottsdale, Arizona, is one of the world's leading luxury-brand golf management and marketing firm with 197 golf courses worldwide in its portfolio. When it saw its IT expenses spiraling out of control, Cary Westmark, its vice president for technology decided to introduce the concept of total cost of ownership.

Like most companies, managers had viewed hardware as one-time expense and had failed to recognize the hidden cost of operating and maintaining the hardware. Often support costs increased over the projected life of IT, contributing to unexpected rise in IT expenses. For better planning of IT costs and to develop a funding mechanism for IT projects throughout their planned lives, managers created a strategic replacement program.

Under the program, managers calculated total cost by including cost of technical support, user productivity loss, downtime loss, and any associated data quality loss. This allowed Troon management to refresh its aging hardware at the optimal cost level. As a result, its support costs reduced from $800 per month to $300, saving roughly over $50,000.

Discussion Questions

1. Why does the TCO approach allow Troon management to refresh its hardware at the optimal cost level?

2. Why, in your opinion, were IT expenses spiraling out of control before the TCO system? What are examples of the hidden costs of operating and maintaining the hardware?

3. If you were the head of marketing for Troon, what benefit would you receive from Mr. Westmark's decision to implement TCO?

Source: Adapted from "Slicing Through IT Costs," *Baseline Magazine* (March 31, 2008).

BALANCED SCORECARDS AT BIOCO

BIOCO is a profitable and growing medium-sized bio-pharmaceutical company located in the southeast United States. It develops, produces and markets vaccines and antibody-based pharmaceutical products. As part of the company's strategic transformation, BIOCO's CEO introduced a top-down, strategy-driven management process called the "BIOCO Way." The CEO has a strong conviction that the success of a company starts with a clear vision of what the company wants to be and a corporate strategy that reflects that vision. In the BIOCO Way, the corporate vision and strategy are translated into a long-term corporate strategic plan, which in turn is used to generate the corporate strategy map. To measure progress against the strategy map a cascade of balanced scorecards (corporate, division/department) are developed and used. As a result of the full integration of the levels of balanced scorecards into the planning process, the BIOCO Way emphasizes how the strategies and related tactics should be carried out and measured at all levels. The CEO is a strong champion of the balanced scorecards and is considered an in-house guru for the method.

Each year, BIOCO managers at the corporate and department levels review performance and assess the appropriateness of their respective balanced scorecards for the prior year. Based on the results of the performance reviews and a short-term execution plan for the upcoming year, strategic initiatives are added, modified or removed and the metrics in the scorecards are adjusted accordingly. The CIO thinks that the balanced scorecards help the departments look beyond their own operations and the Vice President thinks they mobilize everyone in the company by setting up tangible goals that are clearly linked to the overall goals of the company. The CIO thinks it enhances communications because it "provides a focal point and common language around the key value drivers of the organization" and it helps IT understand other business areas.

Discussion Questions

1. What benefits has BIOCO realized from its use of balanced scorecards?
2. Do you think the BIOCO way was useful in helping the IT department align its goals with that of the company? Why or why not?
3. Do you think that the BIOCO approach could be implemented successfully in large companies? Why or why not? If so, what, if any, adjustments need to be made?
4. BIOCO recently was sold and now has a new CEO. Do you think the BIOCO way will be as successful under the new CEO? Why or why not?

Source: Q. Hu and C. D. Huang, "Using the Balanced Scorecard to Achieve Sustained IT-Business Alignment: A Case Study," *Communications of the Association for Information Systems* (2006), 17(1), Article 8.

CHAPTER 8

GOVERNANCE OF THE INFORMATION SYSTEMS ORGANIZATION

Governance structures define the way decisions are made in an organization. This chapter explores three models of governance based on organization structure (centralized, decentralized and federal), decision rights, and control (i.e., COSO, COBIT, ITIL). Examples and strategies for implementation are discussed.

In April 2011, Sony was hit by one of the biggest data breaches in history when a hacker to its PlayStation Network service compromised the personal information of potentially 100 million users. Sony took the on-line platform, which lets people play games with others and access multimedia content, offline for weeks. To woo back its customers it offered them a "welcome back package," which included free games and movies, as well as $1 million identity theft insurance policy per customer in the event that their personal information was used for illegal purposes. The estimated cost of the breach is a whopping 104 million British pounds, not counting reputational damage. A U.S. Congressional Committee, the U.K. Minister of Culture, and the city of Taipei were among those demanding more information about the breach.

Sony appears to have placed little value on its security prior to the breach. Just two weeks before the breach it had laid off 205 employees, a substantial percentage of the unit responsible for network security. That is all changed now. In September 2011, Sony posted its new security policy and standards on its Web site and appointed a former official at the U.S. Department of Homeland Security, Philip Reitinger, as its first Chief Information Security Officer. "Certainly the network issue was a catalyst for the appointment," a Sony spokesman said. "We are looking to bolster our network security even further."[1]

---

[1] For more information about the breach see Nicole Henderson, "Sony Names Philip R. Reitinger SVP and Chief Information Security Officer" (September 6, 2011), http://www.thewhir.com/web-hosting-news/ (accessed on September 22, 2011); and Chris Pereira, "Sony Fired Network Security Employees Prior to PSN Breach, Lawsuit Claims" (June 24, 2011), http://www.1up.com/news/sony-fired-network-security-employees-prior-psn-breach-lawsuit (accessed on September 22, 2011).

Mr. Reitinger reports to the Sony Executive President and General Counsel, who is also a Corporate Executive. He is responsible for assuring the security of Sony's information assets and services, overseeing corporate information security, privacy and Internet safety, and coordinating closely with key headquarters groups on security issues.[2]

When Sony belatedly learned the full importance of security, it recognized that it would need to place the decision rights for security decisions in the hands of a capable individual who had the ear of executives at the top level of the corporation. In place now is a governance structure to help Sony's security professionals, its IS organization, and the business units work toward achieving corporate goals, which now include information security.

Although each IS organization is unique in many ways, all have elements in common. The focus of this chapter is to introduce managers to issues related to the way decisions about IT are made in the organization. These issues should reflect the typical activities of an IS organization that were discussed in the previous chapter (Chapter 7). This chapter examines governance of the IS organization as it relates to decisions about IT issues.

▶ IT GOVERNANCE

Expectations (or more specifically, what managers should and should not expect from the IS organization) are at the heart of IT governance. **Governance** in the context of business enterprises is all about making decisions that define expectations, grant authority, or ensure performance. In other words, governance is about aligning behavior with business goals through empowerment and monitoring. Empowerment comes from granting the right to make decisions, and monitoring comes from evaluating performance. As noted in Chapter 3, a decision right is an important organizational design variable since it indicates who in the organization has the responsibility to initiate, supply information for, approve, implement, and control various types of decisions. A traditional perspective of IT governance focuses on how decision rights can be distributed differently to facilitate centralized, decentralized, or hybrid modes of decision making. In this view of governance, the organization structure plays a major role.

Centralized versus Decentralized Organizational Structures

Organizational structures for IS evolved in a cyclic manner. At one end of the spectrum, **centralized IS organizations** bring together all staff, hardware, software, data, and processing into a single location. **Decentralized IS organizations** scatter these components in different locations to address local business needs. Companies' organizational strategies exist along a continuum from centralization to decentralization, with

---

[2] Warwick Ashford, "Sony Appoints Philip Reitinger as CISO after data breach hits 100m," ComputerWeekly. com (September 6, 2011), http://www.computerweekly.com/Articles/2011/09/06/247806/Sony-appoints-Philip-Reitinger-as-CISO-after-data-breach-hits-100m.htm (accessed on September 22, 2011).

Geographic Lens: Looking at Governance Globally

IT governance is an important issue to business around the globe. A large study of 834 IT and business managers in 21 countries revealed that governance of enterprise IT (GEIT) is a priority with 95% of the enterprises participating in the survey. Two-thirds of respondent enterprises have some GEIT. They indicated that the main driver for GEIT activities is to ensure that IT functionality aligns with business needs, and the most commonly experienced outcomes are improvements in management of IT-related risk and communication and relationships between business and IT. The study concluded that good governance can increase the transparency of IT supply and demand and help in assigning priorities for IT projects and services.

Source: IT Governance Institute, "Global Status Report on the Governance of Enterprise IT (GEIT)" (2011), 7, http://www.isaca.org/Knowledge-Center/Research/Documents/Global-Status-Report-GEIT-10Jan2011-Research.pdf (accessed on February 27, 2011).

---

a combination of the two, called federalism, found in the middle (see Figure 8.1). Enterprises of all shapes and sizes can be found at any point along the continuum. Over time, however, each enterprise may gravitate toward one end of the continuum or the other, and often reorganization is in reality a change from one end to the other.

To illustrate these tendencies, consider the different approaches taken to organize IS in the five eras of information usage (see Chapter 2, Figure 2.1). In the 1960s, mainframes dictated a centralized approach to IS because the mainframe resided in one physical location. Centralized decision making, purchasing, maintenance, and staff kept these early computing behemoths running. The 1970s remained centralized due in part to the constraints of mainframe computing, although the minicomputer began to create a rationale to decentralize. The 1980s saw the advent of the personal computer (PC). PCs allowed computing power to spread beyond the raised-floor, super-cooled rooms of mainframes. This phenomenon gave rise to decentralization, a trend that exploded with the advent of LANs and client/server technology. The users especially liked the shift to decentralization because it put them more in control and it increased their agility. However, the pressures for secure networks and massive corporate databases shifted some organizations back to a more centralized approach. However, the increasingly global nature of many businesses makes complete centralization impossible. A recent global survey found that 70.6% of the participating

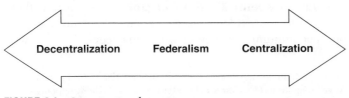

FIGURE 8.1 Organizational continuum.

Approach	Advantages	Disadvantages	Companies Adopting
Centralized	• Global standards and common data • "One voice" when negotiating supplier contracts • Greater leverage in deploying strategic IT initiatives • Economies of scale and a shared cost structure • Access to large capacity • Better recruitment and training of IT professionals • Better control of security and databases • Consistent with centralized enterprise structure	• Technology may not meet local needs • Slow support for strategic initiatives • Schism between business and IT organization • Us versus them mentality when technology problems occur • Lack of business unit control over overhead costs	Zara UPS[3]
Decentralized	• Technology customized to local business needs • Closer partnership between IT and business units • Greater flexibility • Reduced telecommunication costs • Consistency with decentralized enterprise structure • Business unit control over overhead costs	• Difficulty maintaining global standards and consistent data • Higher infrastructure costs • Difficulty negotiating preferential supplier agreements • Loss of control • Duplication of staff and data	VeriFone FedEx[4]

FIGURE 8.2 Advantages and disadvantages of organizational approaches.

organizations are centralized in terms of IT, 13.5% are decentralized, and 12.7% are federated.[5] While the high percentage of centralized companies in the sample may seem surprising, the study suggested that with the increasing appreciation for governance found in companies with higher levels of governance maturity comes the need for control that is made possible in the centralized structure. What are the most important considerations in deciding how much to centralize or decentralize? Figure 8.2 shows some advantages and disadvantages of each approach.

[3] J. W. Ross and P. Weill, "Six IT Decisions Your IT People Shouldn't Make," *Harvard Business Review* (2002), 1–8.

[4] Ibid.

[5] IT Governance Institute, "Global Status Report on the Governance of Enterprise IT (GEIT)" (2011), 49, http://www.isaca.org/Knowledge-Center/Research/Documents/Global-Status-Report-GEIT-10Jan2011-Research.pdf (accessed on February 27, 2011).

Consider two competing parcel delivery companies, UPS and FedEx, in the year that they both reported spending about $1 billion on IT. UPS's IT strategy focused on delivering efficiencies to meet the business demands of consistency and reliability. UPS's centralized, standardized IT environment supported dependable customer service at a relatively low price. In contrast, FedEx chose a decentralized IT strategy that allowed it to focus on flexibility in meeting business demands generated from targeting various customer segments. The higher costs of the decentralized approach to IT management were offset by the benefits of localized innovation and customer responsiveness.[6]

In earlier chapters, two companies that have adopted different centralization/decentralization IS strategies are discussed. Zara used a centralized approach. The head of IS, who was not a CIO, reported directly to the deputy general manager, who was two levels below the CEO.[7]

This way of structuring the IS department was consistent with the organization's predominately centralized structure. It was also well suited to organizational processing where most administrative decisions were made in the headquarters at LaCoruña, Spain. The users did not require a lot of hand-holding with regard to the POS systems in the stores. For these reasons, a centralized approach was a good fit for Zara. The store managers, however, did retain decision rights about which products to order. Thus, Zara was not totally at the end of the centralization continuum. Verifone, which we discussed in Chapter 4, needs a decentralized structure for its globally distributed employees.

The centralized and decentralized approaches amalgamated in the 1990s. Companies began to adopt a strategy based on lessons learned from earlier years of centralization and decentralization. Most companies want to achieve the advantages derived from both organizational paradigms. This desire leads to federalism.[8] **Federalism** is a structuring approach that distributes power, hardware, software, data, and personnel between a central IS group and IS in business units. Many companies adopt a form of federal IT, yet still count themselves as either decentralized or centralized, depending on their position on the continuum. Organizations, such as Home Depot and the U.S. Department of Veteran Affairs, recognize the advantages of a more hybrid approach and actively seek to benefit from adopting a federal structure. Figure 8.3 shows how these approaches interrelate.

Another Perspective on IT Governance

Sometimes the centralized/decentralized/federal approaches to governance are not fine-tuned enough to help managers deal with the many contingencies facing today's organizations. This issue is addressed by a framework developed by Peter Weill and

---

[6] J. W. Ross and P. Weill, "Six IT Decisions Your IT People Shouldn't Make," *Harvard Business Review* (2002), 1–8.

[7] Andrew McAfee, Vincent Dessain, and Anders Sjman, "Zara: IT for Fast Fashion," Harvard Business School Case 9-604-081 (September 6, 2007).

[8] John F. Rockart, Michael J. Earl, and Jeanne W. Ross, "Eight Imperatives for the New IT Organization," *Sloan Management Review* (Fall 1996), 52–53.

The federal IT attempts to capture the benefits of centralized and decentralized organizations while eliminating the drawbacks of each.

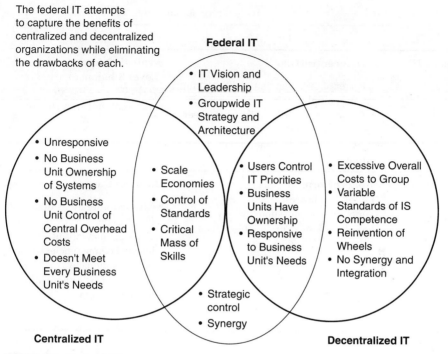

Federal IT

- IT Vision and Leadership
- Groupwide IT Strategy and Architecture

Centralized IT

- Unresponsive
- No Business Unit Ownership of Systems
- No Business Unit Control of Central Overhead Costs
- Doesn't Meet Every Business Unit's Needs

- Scale Economies
- Control of Standards
- Critical Mass of Skills

- Users Control IT Priorities
- Business Units Have Ownership
- Responsive to Business Unit's Needs

- Strategic control
- Synergy

Decentralized IT

- Excessive Overall Costs to Group
- Variable Standards of IS Competence
- Reinvention of Wheels
- No Synergy and Integration

FIGURE 8.3   Federal IT.

Source: Michael J. Earl, "Information Management: The Organizational Dimension," in *The Role of the Corporate IT Function in the Federal IT Organization*, S. L. Hodgkinson (ed.) (New York: Oxford University Press, 1996), Figure 12.1. By permission of Oxford University Press, Inc.

Jeanne Ross. They define **IT governance** as "specifying the decision rights and accountability framework to encourage desirable behavior in using IT."[9] IT governance is not about what decisions are actually made but rather about who is making the decisions (i.e., who holds the decision rights) and how the decision makers are held accountable for them.

It is important to match the manager's decision rights with his or her accountability for a decision. Figure 8.4 indicates what happens when there is a mismatch. Where the CIO has a high level of decision rights and accountability, the firm is likely to be at maturity Level 3 (which was introduced in Chapter 7). Where both the decision rights and accountability are low, the company is likely to be at Level 1. Mismatches result in either an oversupply of IT resources or the inability of IT to meet business demand.

Good IT governance provides a structure to make good decisions. It can also limit the negative impact of organizational politics in IT-related decisions. IT governance has

---

[9] Peter Weill and Jeanne W. Ross, *IT Governance: How Top Performers Manage IT Decision Rights for Superior Results* (Cambridge, MA: Harvard Business School Press, 2004). Also, Peter Weill, "Don't Just Lead, Govern: How Top-Performing Firms Govern IT," *MIS Quarterly Executive* (2004), 3(1), 1–17. The quote is on page 3.

		Accountability	
		Low	High
Decision Rights	High	**Technocentric Gap** • Danger of overspending on IT creating an oversupply • IT assets may not be utilized to meet business demand • Business group frustration with IT group	**Strategic Norm (Level 3 balance)** Works where IT is viewed as competent and strategic to business
	Low	**Support Norm (Level 1 balance)** Works for organizations where IT is viewed as a support function; focus is on business efficiency	**Business Gap** • Cost considerations dominate IT decision • IT assets may not utilize internal competencies to meet business demand • IT group frustration with business group

FIGURE 8.4 IS Decision rights-accountability gap.
Source: Adapted from V. Grover, R. M. Henry, and J. B. Thatcher, "Fix IT-Business Relationships through Better Decision Rights," *Communications of the ACM* (December 2007), 50(12), 82, Figure 1.

two major components: (1) the assignment of decision-making authority and responsibility, and (2) the decision-making mechanisms (e.g., steering committees, review boards, policies). When it comes specifically to IT governance, Weill and his colleagues proposed five generally applicable categories of IT decisions: IT principles, IT architecture, IT infrastructure strategies, business application needs, and IT investment and prioritization. A description of these decision categories with an example of major IS activities affected by them is provided in Figure 8.5.

Weill and Ross's study of 256 enterprises shows that a defining trait of high-performing companies is the use of proper decision right allocation patterns for each of the five major categories of IT decisions. They use six political archetypes (business monarchy, IT monarchy, feudal, federal, IT duopoly, and anarchy) to label the combinations of people who either input information or have decision rights for the key IT decisions. An **archetype** is a pattern from decision rights allocation. Decisions can be made at several levels in the organization: enterprise-wide, by business unit, and by region or group within a business unit. Figure 8.6 summarizes the level and function for the allocation of decision rights in each archetype.

For each decision category, the organization adopts an archetype as the means to obtain inputs for decisions and to assign responsibility for them. Although there is little

Category	Description	Examples of Affected IS Activities
IT Principles	High-level statements about how IT is used in the business	Participating in setting strategic direction
IT Architecture	An integrated set of technical choices to guide the organization in satisfying business needs. The architecture is a set of policies and rules for the use of IT and outlines a migration path for doing business.	Establishing architecture and standards
IT Infrastructure Strategies	Strategies for the foundation of budgeted-for IT capability (both technical and human) shared throughout the firm as centrally coordinated and reliable services	Managing Internet and network services; providing general support; managing data; managing human resources; accommodating mobile computing needs
Business Application Needs	Specifications of the business need for purchased or internally developed IT applications	Developing and maintaining information systems
IT Investment and Prioritization	Decisions about how much and where to invest in IT including project approvals and justification techniques	Anticipating new technologies

FIGURE 8.5 Five major categories of IT decisions.
Source: Adapted from P. Weill, "Don't Just Lead, Govern: How Top-Performing Firms Govern IT," *MIS Quarterly Executive* (2004), 3(1), 4, Figure 2.

variation in the selection of archetypes regarding who provides information for decision making, there is significant variation across organizations in terms of archetypes selected for decision right allocation. For instance, the duopoly is used by the largest portion (36%) of organizations for IT principles decisions, whereas the IT monarchy is the most popular for IT architecture and infrastructure decisions (i.e., 73% and 59%, respectively).[10]

There is no one best arrangement for the allocation of decision rights. Rather, the most appropriate arrangement depends on a number of factors, including the type of performance indicator. Some common performance indicators are asset utilization, profit, or growth.

---

[10] Peter Weill and Jeanne W. Ross, *IT Governance: How Top Performers Manage IT Decision Rights for Superior Results* (Cambridge, MA: Harvard Business School Press, 2004).

Decision rights or inputs rights for a particular IT decision are held by:		CxO Level Execs	Corp. IT and/or Business Unit IT	Business Unit Leaders or Process Owners
Business Monarchy	A group of, or individual, business executives (i.e., CxOs). Includes committees comprised of senior business executives (may include CIO). Excludes IT executives acting independently.	✓		
IT Monarchy	Individuals or groups of IT executives.		✓	
Feudal	Business unit leaders, key process owners or their delegates.			✓
Federal	C level executives and at least one other business group (e.g., CxO and BU leaders)—IT executives may be an additional participant. Equivalent to a country and its states working together.	✓	✓	✓
		✓		✓
IT Duopoly	IT executives and one other group (e.g., CxO or BU leaders).	✓	✓	
			✓	✓
Anarchy	Each individual user.			

© MIT Sloan Center for Information Systems Research 2003 - Weill

FIGURE 8.6 IT governance archetypes.
Source: P. Weill, "Don't Just Lead, Govern: How Top-Performing Firms Govern IT," *MIS Quarterly Executive* (2004), 3(1), 5, Figure 3.

▶ IT GOVERNANCE AND SECURITY

The framework for decision rights allocation can be used to understand governance of a variety of organizational decisions. For example, it offers IT security professionals a new perspective for assigning responsibility for key information security decisions. We use it to illustrate appropriate roles of business managers and IT managers in making a company's security decisions. Below we apply the framework to five critical decisions about information security that are frequently discussed in the security literature. A governance pattern that is appropriate for each decision is discussed next and displayed in Figure 8.7.[11]

1. **Information Security Strategy.** A company's information security strategy is based on such IT principles as protecting the confidentiality of customer information, strict compliance with regulations, and maintaining a security

[11] Andy Wu, "What Color is Your Archetype? Governance Patterns for Information Security," Ph.D. Dissertation, University of Central Florida (2007).

Information Security Decision	Recommended Archetype	Rationale	Major Symptoms of Improper Decision Rights Allocation
Information Security Strategy	Business monarchy	Business leaders have the knowledge of the company's strategies, on which security strategy should be based. No detailed technical knowledge is required.	Security is an afterthought and patched on to processes and products.
Information Security Policies	IT duopoly	Technical and security implications of behaviors and processes need to be analyzed and trade-offs between security and productivity need to be made. Need to know the particularities of company's IT infrastructure.	Security policies are written based on theory and generic templates. They are unenforceable due to a misfit with the company's specific IT and users.
Information Security Infrastructure	IT monarchy	In-depth technical knowledge and expertise is needed.	There is a mis-specification of security and network typologies or a misconfiguration of infrastructure. Technical security control is ineffective.
Information Security Education/ Training/ Awareness	IT duopoly	Business buy-in and understanding are needed. Technical expertise and knowledge of critical security issues is needed in building programs.	Users are insufficiently trained, bypass security measures, or do not know how to react properly when security breaches occur.
Information Security Investments	IT duopoly	Requires financial (quantitative) and qualitative evaluation of business impacts of security investments. Business case has to be presented for rivaling projects.	Under- or over-investment in information security occurs. The human or technical security resources are insufficient or wasted.

FIGURE 8.7 Matching information security decisions and archetypes.

Sources: Adapted from Andy Wu, "What Color Is Your Archetype? Governance Patterns for Information Security," Ph.D. Dissertation, University of Central Florida (2007); and Wu, Y. and Saunders, C., "Governing Information Security: Governance Domains and Decision Rights Allocation Patterns," *Information Resources Management Journal* (January–March 2011), 24(1), 28–45.

baseline that is above the industry benchmark. Security strategy is not a technical decision. Rather, it should reflect the company's mission, overall strategy, business model, and business environment. Deciding on the security strategy requires decision makers who are knowledgeable about the company's strategy and management systems. Thus, a business monarchy is a good match for such situations in which the top business executives, including the CIO or CISO, set the tone for the company's security. The IS organization likely needs to provide the required technical input for supporting the decision.

2. **Information Security Policies.** Security policies encourage standardization and integration. Following best practices, they broadly define the scope of and overall expectations for the company's information security program. From these security policies, lower-level policies are developed to control specific security areas (e.g., Internet use, access control) and/or individual applications (e.g., payroll systems, telecom systems). Policies must reflect the delicate balance between the enhanced information security gained from following them versus productivity losses and user inconvenience. As security attacks become more sophisticated, obeying security measures to deflect those attacks places greater cognitive demands on users. For example, they may need a different password for every account and these passwords must often be longer and less easy to remember because they must have special characters. The user productivity is often sacrificed when they have to come up with new passwords every month or when they have to scan e-mails to spot phishing attempts each day. Not surprisingly, both IT and business perspectives are important in setting policies. Business users must be able to say what they want from the information security program and how they expect the security function to support their business activities. On the other hand, IT leaders should be consulted for two reasons: (1) their judgment prevents unrealistic goals for standardization and integration, and (2) policy decisions require the ability to analyze the technical and security implications of user behaviors and business processes. If either users or IT leaders are not consulted, unenforceable policies will probably result. Thus, for high-level security architecture decisions, the IT duopoly is a good fit.

3. **Information Security Infrastructure.** The information security infrastructure provides protection by aligning security mechanisms to the IS architecture specifications. Firewalls, intrusion detection systems (IDSs), and encryption devices are the most popular examples of information security infrastructure, but other security and control tools are listed in Figure 12.3. Infrastructure decisions deal with technology selection and configuration. Common objectives are to achieve consistency in protection, economies of scale, and synergy among the components. Top executives typically lack the experience or expertise to make these decisions. For these reasons, corporate IT typically is responsible for managing the dedicated security mechanisms and general IT infrastructure, such as enterprise network devices. Thus, a fitting governance for these decisions is the IT monarchy, where corporate IT takes the lead and makes sure that the technology components in the infrastructure are correctly specified and configured.

4. **Information Security Education/Training/Awareness.** It is very important to make business users aware of security policies and practices. Training and awareness programs build a security-conscious culture. To promote effectiveness and post-training retention, training and awareness programs must be linked to the unique requirements of individual business processes. Business user participation in planning and implementing training and awareness programs helps gain acceptance of security initiatives. However, IT security personnel are in the best position to know critical issues. Thus, an IT duopoly is effective for combining the business and technical perspectives.

5. **Information Security Investments.** The "FUD factor" (fear, uncertainty, and doubt) used to be all that was needed to get top management to invest in information security. As information security becomes a routine concern in daily operations, security managers increasingly must justify their budget requests financially. But, it is hard to show how important security is until there has been a breach—and even then it is hard to put a dollar amount on the value of security. As when determining business needs, different units within the company may have rival or conflicting "wish lists" for information security-related purchases that benefit their unique needs. The IS organization also should have a significant say in these decisions, as it is in the best position to assess whether and how the investments may fit with the company's current IT infrastructure and application portfolio. Thus, an appropriate governance pattern for investment and prioritization decisions is IT duopoly. The most typical governance mechanism for this archetype is executive committees/councils composed of business and IT executives, such as the IT steering committee and budget committee, with the CIO having overlapping memberships in both. These committees are where IT and business leaders make business cases for their proposed investments and debate the merit and priorities of the investments. These decisions about the appropriate level of investment are made with the company's best interest in mind.

The critical decision-archetype matches described are by no means etched in stone. Organizational and environmental factors may suggest other governance patterns. For instance, it is easy to imagine that business monarchy governs security investments decisions if a company emphasizes stringent budget review and control from a pure business/financial perspective. In enterprises with many relatively independent business units, a federal archetype that involves the corporate center, business unit leaders, and IT leaders may be the proper archetype for business requirement decisions.

The archetypes clearly define the responsibilities of the major players in the company—business executives, business unit leaders, corporate IT, business unit IT, and so forth. By matching appropriate archetypes to the key security decisions, the board of directors in effect puts the decisions in the hands of those who are in the most appropriate positions for making quality decisions. In addition, decision makers are truly empowered when they hold the authority to make decisions that (1) are suitable for their positions, (2) make the best use of their expertise and knowledge, and (3) cater to the needs and specialization of the organization units to which they belong. Good matches of archetypes with key security decisions help avoid some of the symptoms of poor decision making described in Figure 8.7.

Social Business Lens: The Consumerization of Technology

Consumerization of technology is a term used to describe the increasingly powerful tools available in the consumer space that are impacting the corporate space. One arena where the impact is particularly significant is in mobility, as described in Chapter 6. More broadly, however, the increasing use of smart phones, tablets, and smaller/more powerful laptops, coupled with Web-based applications that offer everything from free business productivity tools such as Google Docs to sharing applications like YouTube and SlideShare, to social tools such as Twitter and LinkedIn created a new IT environment. Consumerization covers cloud services, desktop applications, social networking, devices, and the management policies surrounding them. It's changing the business of IT, too. Sometimes referred to as "BYOD" or "Bring Your Own Device," the consumerization of IT forced IT leaders to reevaluate how IT services are offered. Traditional IT organizations operated with a command and control mentality—IT leaders made decisions about which technologies would be used. Standardized desktops were the vehicle to cost control and security. But the consumerization of technology trend changed the management approach from "How do we stop it?" to "How do we work with this?"

The U.S. Army is one example of an organization embracing this approach. In order to support global communications and provide all soldiers with the information tools they need, the U.S. Army launched a project called "Connecting Soldiers to Digital Apps" aimed at insuring every soldier has a smartphone loaded with applications for military purposes.

High schools are experimenting, too. One high school in Austin, Texas issued iPads to every eleventh- and twelfth-grade student, supported by an apps store modeled after the Apple apps store, loaded with applications students need to do their classwork and homework. A help desk, fashioned after the Apple Genius Bar, is available physically during school hours and virtually after hours should tech support be needed (but in reality the students just support each other over social tools). Teachers are rewarded for creating and using teaching tools that take advantage of this technology, and the school rebuilt its networks to support the storage and transfer of files for the 2,000 students issued the iPads. The vision is for all of the high school students to have iPads or similar tablets as a standard component of their high school experience.

Source: Ellen Messmer, "U.S. Army wants soldiers to have advanced smartphones, wireless technology," *Infoworld* (July 8, 2011), http://www.infoworld.com/d/mobile-technology/us-army-wants-soldiers-have-advanced-smartphones-wireless-technology-282 (accessed on January 19, 2012).

▶ DECISION-MAKING MECHANISMS

Many different types of mechanisms can be created to ensure good IT governance. Policies are useful for defining the process of making a decision under certain situations. However, often the environment is so complex that policies are too rigid. In a recent worldwide study of IT governance almost 60% of the respondents relied on policies and standards for governance, making it the most popular mechanism for governance.[12] A **review board**, or committee that is formally designated to approve, monitor, and review specific topic, can be an effective governance mechanism. For example, Twila Day, CIO of Sysco, established an architecture review board to look at new technologies and processes.[13]

A third mechanism that is used very frequently for IT decisions is the IT **steering committee**, or an advisory committee of key stakeholders or experts that provides guidance on important IT issues. Steering committees work especially well with the federal archetypes, which calls for joint participation of IT and business leaders in the decision-making process. Steering committees can be geared toward different levels of decision making. At the highest level, the steering committee, also called an IT Governance Council, might report to the board of the directors or the CEO. The steering committee at this level is composed of top-level executives and the CIO. It provides strategic direction and funding authority for major IT projects. It ensures that adequate resources be allocated to the IS organization for achieving strategic goals. Committees with lower-level players typically are involved with allocating scarce resources effectively and efficiently. Lower-level steering committees provide a forum for business leaders to present their IT needs and to offer input and direction about the support they receive from IT operations. Either level may have working groups to help the steering committee to be effective. Further, either level is concerned with measuring the performance of the IS organization, although the assessment of performance is more detailed for the lower-level committee. For example, the lower-level committee would focus on the progress of the various projects and adherence to the budget. The higher-level committee would focus on the performance of the CIO and the ability of the IS organization to contribute to the company's achievement of its strategic goals.

Although an organization may have both levels of steering committees, it is more likely to have one or the other. If the IS organization is viewed as being critical for the organization to achieve its strategic goals, the C-level executives are likely to be on the committee. Otherwise, the steering committee tends to be larger to have widespread representation from the various business units. In this case, the steering committee is an excellent mechanism for helping the business units realize the competing benefits of proposed IT projects and develop an approach for allocating among the project requests.

For example, when Hilton Worldwide CIO started working on a project to create a new loyalty program, he and the business sponsor of the project convened a lower-level steering committee made up of people from IT, marketing, HR, finance, and other departments. They discussed change management and business issues that arose as they designed the system to be used in 85 countries over ten brands in the Hilton portfolio. The project went very smoothly. But earlier another project, one to outsource the hotel help desk, didn't go as well. The CIO learned from the second experience that there is no such thing as too much communication, and created weekly steering committee

---

[12] IT Governance Institute, "Global Status Report on the Governance of Enterprise IT (GEIT)" (2011), 49, http://www.isaca.org/Knowledge-Center/Research/Documents/Global-Status-Report-GEIT-10Jan2011-Research.pdf (accessed on February 27, 2011).

[13] Martha Heller, *"How to Make Time for Strategy,"* CIO.com (April 22, 2010), http://www.cio.com/article/591719/How_to_Make_Time_for_Strategy (accessed on January 16, 2012).

Business Process Continuity

One of the most important goals of security is business continuity. The Japanese earthquake and tsunami in 2011, Hurricane Katrina in 2005, and the events of September 11, 2001 presented disaster impacts that few organizations ever face. *Disaster* is broadly defined here as a sudden, unplanned calamitous event that makes it difficult for the firm to provide critical business functions for some period of time and results in great damage or loss. To counter terrorist attacks, hurricanes, tornadoes, floods, or countless other disasters, firms are realizing more than ever the importance of business continuity planning (BCP) to help them survive such disasters.

A **business continuity plan (BCP)** is an approved set of preparations and sufficient procedures for responding to a variety of disaster events. It requires careful and thoughtful preparation. The Disaster Recovery Institute International (DRII) defines three major stages of BCP: preplanning, planning, and postplanning. In the *preplanning stage*, management's responsibility is defined, possible risks are evaluated, and a business impact analysis is performed.

In the *planning stage*, alternative business recovery operating strategies are determined. Business recovery operating strategies deal with how to recover business and IT within the recovery time objective while still maintaining the company's critical functions. The IT organization must be involved in preparing off-site storage and alternate recovery sites or in selecting business continuity vendors. An important part of the BCP planning stage is to develop emergency response procedures designed to prevent or limit injury to personnel on site, damage to structures and equipment, and the degradation of vital business functions. These procedures must be kept up-to-date. The final activity in the planning stage is to implement the plan by publishing it and gaining top-management approval for the plan.

The *postplanning stage* of BCP familiarizes employees with the plan through awareness and training programs. Regular exercises to test and evaluate the plan should be conducted. Companies are increasingly using virtual worlds such to conduct simulations, often under the aegis of the IT organization. With the simulations, the companies can quickly assess the plan, make any adjustments needed, and perform a second simulation with almost no additional costs. Also in this third stage, the BCP should be discussed with public authorities, and public relations and crisis communications should be mapped out.

BCP is designed to respond to threats. In preparing a BCP, it is important to remember that the biggest threat may come not from terrorist attacks or natural disasters, but from disgruntled or dishonest employees. Companies need to screen their employees carefully, create a culture of loyalty to inhibit the internal threats, and develop systems that help promote security. The tremendous loss of human capital in the collapse of the World Trade Center in New York City on 9/11 highlighted the problem of keeping all of a company's talent in one location. Decentralizing operations, flextime, and telecommuting are ways of dispersing a company's human assets. Similarly, critical technology systems, proprietary computer codes, and other core business assets may need to be distributed.

Because the information resources are so integral to business operations, the IS organization is typically in charge of planning for possible scenarios leading to business discontinuity and taking steps to avoid them or alleviate their impact. Clearly firms do not have enough resources to develop a response for every conceivable risky scenario. Thus, each firm needs to determine which detrimental scenarios are likely to occur and/or which are more like to have the greatest impact. These are the risky scenarios that the firm has to devote the most attention to avoiding or mitigating.

Source: "Business Continuity Planning Review," DRI International Professional Development Program DRP 501.

---

meetings for each project. He is quoted as saying, "E-mail is great for scheduling meetings, but it's the steering committees where we are working through really difficult issues together, and making promises and keeping promises, where the foundations of trust are established."[14]

▶ GOVERNANCE FRAMEWORKS FOR CONTROL DECISIONS

The framework described above focuses on which department is responsible for decisions. More recently governance frameworks have been employed specifically to define responsibility for control decisions. They are being implemented to help ward off future accounting fiascos. These frameworks focus on processes and risks associated with them.

Sarbanes–Oxley Act of 2002

In response to rogue accounting activity by major global corporations such as Enron, Worldcom, and their accounting firms, such as Arthur Andersen, the **Sarbanes–Oxley Act (SoX)** was enacted in the United States in 2002 to increase regulatory visibility and accountability of public companies and their financial health. The U.S. federal government wanted to assure the investing public that financial markets could be relied on to deliver valid performance data and accurate stock valuation. All corporations that fall under the jurisdiction of the U.S. Securities and Exchange Commissions are subject to SoX requirements. This includes not only U.S. and foreign companies that are traded on U.S. exchanges, but also those that make up a significant part of a U.S. company's financial reporting. All told, 15,000 U.S. companies, 1,200

---

[14] Adapted from "Candid Talk Trumps the Blame Game," CIO.com (November 2011), http://www.cio.com/article/693018/Candid_Talk_Trumps_the_Blame_Game, and "How CIOs Build Bridges with Other C-Level Execs," CIO.com (November 2011), http://www.cio.com/article/693026/How_CIOs_Build_Bridges_With_Other_C_Level_Execs?page=2&taxonomyId=3127.

non-U.S.-based companies and over 1,400 accounting firms in 76 countries have been affected by SoX.[15]

According to SoX, CFOs and CEOs must personally certify and be accountable for their firms' financial records and accounting (Section 302), auditors must certify the underlying controls and processes that are used to compile the financial results of a company (Section 404), and companies must provide real-time disclosures of any events that may affect a firm's stock price or financial performance within a 48-hour period (Section 409). Penalties for failing to comply range from fines to a 20-year jail term.

Although SoX was not originally aimed at IT departments, it soon became clear that IT played a major role in ensuring the accuracy of financial data. Consequently, in 2004 and 2005, there was a flurry of activity as IT managers identified controls, determined design effectiveness, and validated operation of controls through testing. Five IT control weaknesses repeatedly were uncovered by auditors:[16]

1. Failure to segregate duties within applications, and failure to set up new accounts and terminate old ones in a timely manner.

2. Lack of proper oversight for making application changes, including appointing a person to make a change and another to perform quality assurance on it.

3. Inadequate review of audit logs to ensure that not only were systems running smoothly but also that there was an audit log of the audit log.

4. Failure to identify abnormal transactions in a timely manner.

5. Lack of understanding of key system configurations.

Although SoX's focus is on financial controls, many auditors encouraged (forced) IT managers to extend their focus to organizational controls and risks in business processes. This means that IT managers must assess the level of controls needed to mitigate potential risks in organizational business processes. As companies move beyond SoX certification into compliance, IT managers must be involved in ongoing and consistent risk identification, actively recognize and monitor changes to the IS organization and environment that may affect SoX compliance, and continuously improve IS process maturity. It is likely that they will turn to software to automate many of the needed controls.

Frameworks for Implementing SoX

COSO

The recent Enron and Worldcom major financial scandals were not the first. In the wake of financial scandals in the mid 1980s, the Treadway Commission (or National

---

[15] These figures were derived from the Public Company Accounting Oversight Board (PCAOB) as were reported in Ashley Braganza and Arnoud Franken's "SoX, Compliance, and Power Relationships," *Communications of the ACM* (September 2007), 50(9), 97–102.

[16] Ben Worthen, "The Top Five IT Control Weaknesses," (July 1, 2005), http://www.cio.com/archive/070105/sox_sidebar_two.html.

Commission on Fraudulent Financial Reporting) was created. Its head, James Treadway, had previously served as commissioner of the SEC. The members of the Treadway Commission came from five highly esteemed accounting organizations: Financial Executives International (FEI), American Accounting Association (AAA), American Institute of Certified Public Accountants (AICPA), Institute of Internal Auditors (IIA), and Institute of Management Accountants (IMA). These organizations became known as the Committee of Sponsoring Organizations of the Treadway Commission (COSO). Together they created three control objectives for management and auditors that focused on dealing with risks to internal control. These control objectives deal with:

- Operations—to help the company maintain and improve its operating effectiveness and protect the assets of shareholders.

- Compliance—to ensure that the company is in compliance with relevant laws and regulations.

- Financial reporting—to ensure that the company's financial statements are produced in accordance with Generally Accepted Accounting Principles (GAAP). *SoX is focused on this control objective.*

To make sure a company is meeting its control objectives, COSO established five essential control components for managers and auditors. These control components are (1) control environment, which addresses the overall culture of the company; (2) risk assessment of the most critical risks to internal controls; (3) control processes that outline important processes and guidelines; (4) information and communication of the procedures; and (5) monitoring by management of the internal controls. The Sabanes–Oxley Act requires public companies to define their control framework, and it specifically recommends COSO as that business framework for general accounting controls. It is not IT specific.

COBIT

COBIT (Control Objectives for Information and Related Technology) is an IT governance framework that is consistent with COSO controls. It is a governance tool that focuses on making sure that IT provides the systematic rigor needed for the strong internal controls and Sarbanes–Oxley compliance. It provides a framework for linking IT processes, IT resources, and IT information to a company's strategies and objectives. As a governance framework, it provides guidelines about who in the organization should be making decisions about the IT processes, resources, and information.

Information Systems Audit & Control Association (ISACA) issued COBIT in 1996. COBIT consists of several overlapping sets of guidance with multiple components, which almost form a cascade of process goals, metrics, and practices. At the highest level, key areas of risks are defined in four major domains (planning and organization, acquisition and implementation, delivery and support, and monitoring). When implementing a COBIT framework, the company determines the processes that are the most susceptible to the risks that it judiciously chooses to manage. There are far too many risks for a company to try to manage all of them.

Once the company identifies processes that it is going to manage, it sets up a control objective and then more specific key goal indicators. As with any control system, metrics

Component	Description	Example
Domain	One of four major areas of risk (plan and organize, acquire and implement, deliver and support, and monitor and evaluate); each domain consists of multiple processes	Delivery and support
Control Objective	Focuses on control of a process associated with risk; there are 34 processes	DS (delivery and support) 11—Manage data: ensures delivery of complete, accurate, and valid data to the business
Key Goal Indicator	Specific measures of the extent to which the goals of the system in regard to a control objective have been met	"A measured reduction in the data preparation process and tasks"
Key Performance Indicator	Actual, highly specific measures for measuring accomplishment of a goal	"Percent of data input errors" (Note: the percentage should decrease over specified periods of time)
Critical Success Factor	Describes the steps that a company must take to accomplish a control objective; there are 318 critical success factors	"Data entry requirements are clearly stated, enforced, and supported by automated techniques at all levels, including database and file interfaces"
Maturity Model	A uniquely defined six-point ranking of a company's readiness for each control objective made in comparison with other companies in the industry	"0—Data is not recognized as a corporate resource and asset. There is no assigned data ownership or individual accountability for data integrity and reliability; data quality and security is poor or non-existent"

FIGURE 8.8 Components of COBIT and their examples.
Source: Adapted from Hugh Taylor, *The Joy of SoX* (Indianapolis, IN: Wiley Publishing Inc., 2006).

need to be established to ensure that the goals are being met. These specific metrics are called key performance indicators. Then, activities to achieve the key goal indicators are selected. These activities, or critical success factors, are the steps that need to be followed to successfully provide controls for a selected process. When a company wants to compare itself with other organizations, it uses a well-defined maturity model. The components of COBIT and examples of each component are provided in Figure 8.8.

One advantage of COBIT is that it is well-suited to organizations focused on risk management and mitigation. Another advantage is that it is very detailed. Unfortunately, this high level of detail can serve as a disadvantage in the sense that it makes COBIT very costly and time consuming to implement. Yet, despite the costs, companies are starting to realize benefits from implementing COBIT. As a governance framework, it designates clear ownership and responsibility for key organizational processes in such a way that is understood by all organizational stakeholders. Consistent with the Information Systems Strategy Triangle discussed in Chapter 1, COBIT provides a formal framework for aligning IS strategy with the business strategy. It does so by recognizing who is responsible for important control decisions using a governance framework and focusing on risks of internal control and associated processes. Finally, it makes possible the fulfillment of the COSO requirements for the IT control environment that is encouraged by the Sarbanes–Oxley Act.

Other Control Frameworks

Although COBIT is the most common set of IT control guidelines for SoX, it is by no means the only control framework. Others include those provided by the International Standards Organization (ISO), as well as **Information Technology Infrastructure Library (ITIL)**. ITIL is a set of concepts and techniques for managing information technology infrastructure, development, and operations that was developed in the United Kingdom. ITIL offers eight sets of management procedures in eight books: service delivery, service support, service management, ICT infrastructure management, software asset management, business perspective, security management, and application management. ITIL is a widely recognized framework for IT service management and operations management that has been adopted around the globe.

IS and the Implementation of Sarbanes–Oxley Act Compliance

Because of the level of detail, the involvement of the IS department and the CIO in implementing SoX, most notably Section 404, which deals with management's assessment of internal controls, is considerable. Although the IS department typically plays a major role in SoX compliance, it often is without any formal authority. Thus, the CIO needs to tread carefully when working with auditors, the CFO, the CEO, and business leaders. Braganza and Franken provide six tactics that CIOs can use in working effectively in these relationships.[17] These strategies include knowledge building, knowledge deployment, innovation directive mobilization, standardization, and subsidy. A definition for each of these tactics, along with examples of activities to enact these tactics, is provided in Figure 8.9.

The extent to which a CIO could use these various tactics depends on the power that he or she holds relating to the SoX implementation. Those few CIOs who are given a carte blanche by their CEOs to implement SoX compliance can employ more directive activities. That is, they can use subsidy, standardization, and innovative directives tactics. For example, they can establish standards and enforce their compliance. They can create an overarching corporate compliance architecture and use mandate compliance to various controls. They can direct the SoX implementation from top down and put 404 implementation drivers in place. If, on the other hand, the CEO does not vest the CIO with the considerable power to employ such tactics, the CIO may need to take more of a

[17] Braganza and Franken, "SoX, Compliance, and Power Relationships."

Tactic	Definition	Examples of Activities
Knowledge Building	Establishing a knowledge base to implement SoX	Acquiring technical knowledge about SoX and 404
Knowledge Deployment	Disseminating knowledge about SoX and developing an understanding of this knowledge among management and other organizational members	Moving IT staff with knowledge of 404 to parts of the organization that are less knowledgeable; creating a central repository of 404 knowledge; absorbing 404 requirements from external bodies; conducting training programs to spread an understanding of SoX
Innovation Directive	Organizing for implementing SoX and announcing the approach	Issuing instructions that encourage the adoption of 404 compliance practices; publishing progress reports of each subsidiary's progress toward 404 implementation; putting drivers for 404 implementation in place; directing 404 implementation from top down and/or bottom up
Mobilization	Persuading decentralized players and subsidiaries to participate in SoX implementation	Creating a positive impression of SoX (and 404) implementation; conducting promotional and awareness campaigns
Standardization	Negotiating agreements between organizational members to facilitate the SoX implementation	Using mandatory controls, often embedded within the technology, to which users must comply; indicating formal levels of compliance or variance from prescribed controls; establishing standards of control throughout the organization; creating an overarching corporate compliance architecture
Subsidy	Funding implementers' costs during the SoX implementation and users' costs during its deployment and use	Centralizing template development; developing Web-based resources; investing in developing the skills of IT staff to implementing 404; funding short-term skill gaps; investing in tracking implementation; managing funds during implementation to achieve specific IT-related 404 goals

FIGURE 8.9 CIO Tactics for implementing SoX compliance.

persuasive stance and be more involved in training programs and building an electronic knowledge database of SoX documents. In this case, it is especially important to sell the CIO and CFO on the importance of complying with prescribed procedures and methods. In either situation, the CIO needs to acquire and manage the considerable IT resources to make SoX compliance a reality.

▶ SUMMARY

- Alternative governance approaches are possible. One approach is based on structure. Centralized IS organizations place IT staff, hardware, software, and data in one location to promote control and efficiency. At the other end of the continuum, decentralized IS organizations with distributed resources can best meet the needs of local users. Federalism is in the middle of the centralized/decentralized continuum.

- A second governance approach involves decision rights. In this approach IT governance specifies how to allocate decision rights in such a way as to encourage desirable behavior in the use of IT. The allocation of decision rights can be broken down into six archetypes (business monarchy, IT monarchy, feudal, federal, IT duopoly, and anarchy). High-performing companies use the proper decision rights allocation patterns for each of the five major categories of IT decisions.

- Security may best be enacted using a framework that assigns responsibility for security-related decision making based on governance archetypes.

- A third governance approach is based on controls. The Sarbanes–Oxley Act (2002) was enacted to improve internal controls. COBIT is an IT governance framework based on control that can be used to promote IT-related internal controls and Sarbanes–Oxley compliance.

▶ KEY TERMS

archetype (p. 242)
business continuity plan (BCP) (p. 250)
centralized IS organizations (p. 237)
COBIT (Control Objectives for Information and

Related Technology) (p. 253)
decentralized IS organizations (p. 237)
federalism (p. 240)
governance (p. 237)
IT governance (p. 241)

ITIL (Information Technology Infrastructure Library) (p. 255)
review board (p. 249)
Sarbanes–Oxley Act (SoX) (p. 251)
steering committee (p. 249)

▶ DISCUSSION QUESTIONS

1. The debate about centralization and decentralization is heating up again with the advent of B.Y.O.D. and the increasing use of the Web. Why does the Internet make this debate topical?

2. Why is the discussion of decision rights among managers in a firm important?

3. Why can an IT governance archetype be good for one type of IS decision but not for another?

IT GOVERNANCE AT UNIVERSITY OF THE SOUTHEAST

University of the Southeast was one of the largest universities in the United States. It has been growing rapidly and that growth was spurred, in part, by information technology. The University embraced lecture capture technologies that allowed lectures to be streamed to students in a classroom, in dorm rooms, on the grass near the main campus' central fountain, and at a variety of other places of the students' choosing whenever they chose to watch. This made it possible to have sections of classes with over 1,000 students without having to build physical classrooms with enough seats to accommodate each person enrolled. It also made it possible to offer classes that were streamed to students at remote campuses. Each student was charged a technology fee (i.e., $5.16 for undergraduates and $13.85 for graduates per credit hour each semester) which was administered by the Information Technologies and Resources (IT&R) Office to help fund the costs of providing IT to students and faculty.

IT&R was responsible for providing computer services, technologies and telecommunications across the campus (Computer Services and Technology), helping faculty with their instructional delivery and multimedia support (Office of Instructional Resources), helping faculty develop and deliver Web-based and lecture capture courses (Center for Distributed Learning) and the library. The IT&R Office developed IT-related policies with very little input from the faculty and was responsible for deciding and implementing decisions concerning IT architecture and infrastructure. IT&R worked with the President and other top administrators in making IT investment decisions. IT&R staff also worked with the various colleges and administrative offices and an advisory board in making decisions about applications that need to be developed. However, faculty was not consulted at all when the lecture capture system was selected.

As was often the case at large universities, many decision rights on a wide range of issues had been allocated to the colleges. The College of Business Administration had its own server and Technology Support Department (TSD). A recent survey of faculty and staff in the College indicated a high level of satisfaction with the college TSD, but far less satisfaction with the services provided by the university-level IT&R. Some College respondents indicated their displeasure about IT&R's support of the technology for the lecture capture courses, help desk and classroom technologies.

The problems with the technology support for lecture capture software were particularly troublesome. The software would not authenticate students who had paid to enroll in some lecture capture courses, making it impossible for them to download the lectures even though they were registered in the course. Further, some university-affiliated housing did not have adequate network bandwidth to allow students to download the lectures. When problems occurred—which they did on a daily basis—the IT&R Help Desk often referred the students to instructors who could not resolve their problems. One faculty who was teaching a lecture class with 1,400 students exclaimed, "It is utter chaos for me when something goes wrong with the system and hundreds of my students are trying to call, see or email me in panic to get me to fix something that I can't fix."

Recently, the CIO argued that all email accounts should be placed on one central server. This would allow the IT&R greater control and make maintenance easier and more efficient. It also would considerably improve security. But it was not ideal for the faculty. A faculty meeting about email revealed some concerns with this move. First, faculty wanted emails sent to the central university server forwarded to their accounts on their other university-based servers (i.e., the college, department, or institute servers), but found it was impossible to do so. Second, faculty wanted to retain their control over archiving emails. Third, faculty wanted to have control over their preferred e-mail address. In some cases, the faculty email addresses that they had used for a decade had been changed in the printed university directory to the email address on the central university server without their knowledge. This meant that they did not receive (or even know about) messages sent to them via the address on the university server. They could not change the printed email address in the university directory to the address on the College server that they had been using, nor forward the mail sent to the central server to a different account.

The IT&R spokesman said that having a centralized server for email accounts was more secure, reliable and efficient. He said that faculty shouldn't have control over their preferred email address, even if it were on a campus server, because of the identity management problems that it would create. A frustrated faculty member at the meeting asked the IT&R spokesman to describe one time when issues about ease of use and functionality of the system by the user were weighted more highly than security in decisions about email. The IT&R spokesman could not think of an example.

Discussion Questions

1. Describe the IT governance system currently in place at the University of the Southeast using both decision rights and structure as the bases of governance.
2. The CIO wants to implement a centralized IT governance system. As demonstrated by the case above what are the advantages of a centralized IT governance system? What are the disadvantages?
3. In your opinion, what assignment of decision rights would be best for University of the Southeast? Please explain.

CASE STUDY 8-2

THE BIG FIX AT TOYOTA MOTOR SALES (TMS)

"I would describe it as almost 1970s-like," said Barbra Cooper of the basic and somewhat insular IS organization she inherited when she joined Toyota Motor Sales as CIO in late 1996. She found PC and network management, and such basic IS disciplines as business relationship and financial management, lacking, with the result that "No one understood the cost of delivering IS." Far from being business partners, IS personnel, when they were consulted at all, were little more than "order takers." More often, business units that perceived in-house IS as unable to deliver were buying their own IS with no thought to architecture standards, systems integration, or business benefits.

When a downturn in the global economy prompted Toyota executives to look more closely at the American division's spending, Cooper, already coping with local complaints about IS's bureaucratic unresponsiveness, found herself under pressure to explain costs as well. She subsequently formulated, over the course of many weeks, a strategy that would focus the energy of a decentralized, highly transparent IS organization on the company's major business segments. A team of eight staffers assembled by Cooper to make her vision reality generated a list of 18 initiatives, each of which was provided with a project owner, a team, and a mechanism for evaluating the team's success.

Improved alignment with the business side was at the top of the list of initiatives. Cooper identified and embedded in all the business units top-performing senior personnel, whom she called divisional information officers (DIOs). Accountable for IS strategy, development, and services, the DIOs were charged with forging relationships with, and gaining the respect of, the high-level business executives who headed the management committees on which the DIOs sat. "I still believe in managing IS centrally," insisted Cooper, "but it was incumbent on us to physically distribute IT into the businesses. They could provide more local attention while keeping the enterprise vision alive."

DIOs' accountability and responsibility was for the vertical area they served. Corporate Manager of Business Systems Ken Goltara, for example, headed up a small group of internal customers all of the associated vehicle-ordering systems, logistics, and dealer portals. For Ken's customers, it's a one-stop shop as he handles all the systems for the Toyota, Lexus and Scion organizations.

Situating approval for all major IT projects in an executive steering committee (ESC) chartered by Cooper served to further strengthen the IS-business bond, and fundamentally altered accountability for projects. The committee included, Cooper, her boss, Senior Vice President and Planning and Administrative Officer Dave Illingworth; Senior Vice President and Treasurer Mikihiro Mori; and Senior Vice President and Coordinating Officer Masanao Tomozoe. The goal for the ESC was to shift responsibility for IS project vetting and monitoring away from IS towards the business by exposing IS's inner workings to Toyota Motor Sales' business side.

Project funds were to be maintained by the ESC as a single pool of cash, distributed on a project-by-project basis as each phase of a project's goals was achieved. This window into what was spent (and not) would enable other projects to identify and go after unexpended funds, and the administrators to reallocate those funds accordingly. The more regular pacing of projects throughout the year, moreover, eliminated spending swings.

Many business executives initially balked at the new approval process. Instead of following the prescribed channel for seeking funding through the ESC, they allied themselves with lower-level business sponsors engaged with IS in business case development and implementation. After about half a year of dealing with senior-level business execs' unwillingness to take responsibility for IS projects, Cooper dictated that the ESC would not approve any project not backed by a higher-level business executive, a corporate manager at the VP-level or above. With business executives, not the IS executive, held accountable for achieving the business benefits of IS projects, both departments had the same stake in the outcome.

Discussion Questions

1. Describe the advantages of TMS's new decentralized IS structure. What are its disadvantages?
2. How did the new structure change decision rights? How did it change accountability for IS project success?
3. Why, in your opinion, would business executives shy away from the new approval process? In your opinion, will Cooper's demand that each project be backed by an executive solve the problem? Explain.

Sources: Adapted from Thomas Wailgum, "The Big Fix," *CIO Magazine* (April 15, 2005), http://www.cio.com/archive/041505/toyota.html (accessed on August 15, 2005); and Michael Fitzgerald, "How to Develop the Next Generation of IT Leaders," *CIO Magazine* (May 2, 2008), http://www.cio.com/article/print/341067 (accessed on July 23, 2008).

CHAPTER 9

INFORMATION SYSTEMS SOURCING

This chapter is organized around decisions in the Sourcing Decision Cycle. The first question in the cycle starts with the decision to *Make* (insource) or *Buy* (outsource). This chapter's focus is on issues related to outsourcing, whereas issues related to insourcing are discussed in the other chapters of this book. Discussed are the critical decisions in the Sourcing Decision Cycle: *How?* and *Where?* (cloud computing, onshoring, offshoring). When the choice is offshoring and the next decision is: *Where abroad?* (farshoring, nearshoring, captive centers). Explored next in this chapter is the final decision in the cycle, *Status Quo or Change?*, in which case the current arrangements are assessed and modifications are made to the outsourcing arrangement, a new outsourcing provider is selected, or the operations and services are backsourced, or brought back in-house. Risks and strategies to mitigate risks are discussed at each stage of the cycle.

After 13 years, Kellwood, an American apparel maker, ended its soups-to-nuts IS outsourcing arrangement with EDS. The primary focus of the original outsourcing contract was to integrate 12 individual acquired units with different systems into one system. Kellwood had been satisfied enough with EDS' performance to renegotiate the contract in 2002 and 2008, even though at each renegotiation point it had considered bringing the IS operations back in-house, or backsourcing. The 2008 contract iteration resulted in a more flexible $105 million contract that EDS estimated would save Kellwood $2 million in the first year and $9 million over the remaining contract years. But the situation at Kellwood had changed drastically. In 2008, Kellwood had been purchased by Sun Capital Partners and taken private. The Chief Operating Officer, who was facing a mountain of debt and possibly bankruptcy, wanted to consolidate and bring the operations back in-house in 2012 to give some order to the current situation and reduce costs. Kellwood suffered from a lack of IS standardization as a result of its many acquisitions. The Chief Information Officer (CIO) recognized the importance of IS standardization and costs, but she was concerned that the transition from outsourcing to insourcing would cause serious disruption to IS service levels and project deadlines if it went poorly. Kellwod hired a third-party consultant to help it explore the issues and decided that backsourcing would help it save money and respond to changes caused by both the market and internal forces. Kellwood decided to backsource and started the process in late 2009. It carefully planned for the transition and the implementation went smoothly. By performing streamlined operations in-house it was able to report an impressive $3.6 million savings, or about 17% of annual IS expenses after the first year.[1]

The Kellwood case demonstrates a series of decisions made in relation to sourcing. Both the decision to outsource, and then the decision to bring IS operations back in-house, were based on a series of factors. These factors are similar to those used by many companies in the sourcing decisions. The global outsourcing market has been growing steadily. Companies of all sizes pursue outsourcing arrangements, and many multi-million deals have been widely publicized. As more companies adopt outsourcing as a means of controlling IS costs and acquiring "best of breed" capabilities, managing these supplier relationships becomes increasingly important. IS departments must maximize the benefit of these relationships to the enterprise and preempt problems that might occur. Failure in this regard could result in deteriorating quality of service, loss of competitive advantage, costly contract disputes, low morale, and loss of key personnel.

How IS services are provided to a firm has become an important strategic and tactical discussion. As briefly mentioned in Chapter 6, there are numerous alternatives to sourcing computing power, applications, and infrastructure. This chapter looks at the sourcing cycle to consider the full range of decisions related to who should perform the information systems work of an organization. The cycle begins with a decision to make or buy information services and products. If the decision is to buy, a series of questions must be answered about where and how these services should be delivered or products developed. The discussion in this chapter is built around the Sourcing Decision Cycle Framework discussed in the next section. Considering the answers to sourcing decisions can help explain a number of terms associated with sourcing: insourcing, outsourcing, cloud computing, full outsourcing, selective outsourcing, onshoring, offshoring, nearshoring, farshoring, captive center, and back-sourcing. For each type of sourcing decision the risks, or likelihood of something negative occurring as a result of the decision, are discussed and some steps that can be taken to manage the risks are proposed.

▶ SOURCING DECISION CYCLE FRAMEWORK

Sourcing doesn't really just involve one decision. It involves many decisions. The rest of this chapter is built around critical sourcing decision making as shown in Figure 9.1. The chapter headings are tied to key decisions in Figure 9.1. Though it is a cycle, and we could start anywhere, we choose to start with the original make-or-buy decision. In cases where the "buy" option is selected and the company outsources, the client company must decide on "how" and "where." The answers to the "how" question focus on the scope of the outsourcing and the steps that should be taken to ensure success. The answers to the "where"

---

[1] For more information see Stephanie Overby, "Company Saves Millions by Ending Outsourcing Deal," CIO.com, http://www.cio.com/article/549463/Company_Saves_Millions_By_Ending_IT_Outsourcing_Deal?page=1&taxonomyId=3195 (accessed on January 31, 2012); and B. Bacheldor, "Kellwood Stayed on Top of Its Outsourcing All the Way to the End," CIO.com, http://blogs.cio.com/beth_bacheldor/kellwood_stayed_on_top_of_its_outsourcing_all_the_way_to_the_end?page=0 (accessed on February 10, 2012).

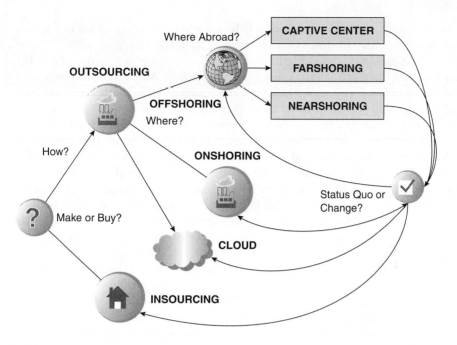

FIGURE 9.1 Sourcing Decision Cycle Framework.

question focus on whether to work with an outsourcing provider in its own country, offshore, or in the cloud. If the company decides to go offshore because labor is cheaper or needed skills are more readily available, the client company is faced with another decision: It must decide if it wants the work done in a country that is relatively nearby or in a country that is quite distant. It may even decide to have one of its own companies, a captive center, perform the work. Finally, the client company settles in on an outsourcing provider (or decides to do its own IS work). After a while, it faces another decision. It periodically must evaluate the arrangement and see whether a change is in order. If the in-house work is unsatisfactory or if other opportunities have become available that are preferable to the current arrangement, then the company may turn to outsourcing. If, on the other hand, the outsourcing arrangement is unsatisfactory, the client company has several options to consider: correct any existing problems and continue outsourcing with its current provider, outsource with another provider, or backsource. If the company decides to make a change in its sourcing arrangements at this point, the sourcing decision cycle starts over again.

Starting the Cycle: Make or Buy Decision

Managers decide whether to make or buy information services. A simple "make" decision often involves insourcing some or all of their infrastructure, and a simple "buy" decision is mostly involves outsourcing. In its simplest form, the make-or-buy decision hinges on whether to insource ("make") or outsource ("buy").

Insourcing

The most traditional approach to sourcing is **insourcing**, or the situation in which a firm provides IS services or develops IS in its own in-house IS organization. Several "Yes" answers to the questions in Figure 9.2 favor the decision to insource. Probably the most common is to keep core competencies in house. Managers are concerned that if they outsource a core competency, they risk losing control over that competency or losing contact with suppliers who can help them remain innovative in relation to that competency. Failing to control the competency or stay innovative is a sure way to forfeit the company's competitive advantage. On the other hand, by outsourcing commodity work, a firm can concentrate on its core competencies. Other factors that weigh in favor of insourcing are having an IS service or product that requires considerable security or confidentiality, or that requires resources that are adequately available in house (i.e., qualified personnel or IS professionals with the needed skills).

In some companies, the IS function is underappreciated by top management. As long as everything is running smoothly, top managers may not appreciate the services and products provided by the IS organization. Often, IS departments that insource have found they have to compete for resources differently than if they outsource. It is necessary for them to have the respect and support from top management needed to acquire resources and get the department's job done. A major risk of insourcing is that the complexities of running IS in-house requires management attention and resources that might better serve the company if focused on other value-added activities.

Outsourcing

Outsourcing means the purchase of a good or service that was previously provided internally or that could be provided internally, but is now provided by outside vendors. In the early days of outsourcing, providers often took over entire IS departments, including people, equipment, and management responsibility. The primary motivation for outsourcing then was on reducing costs. This classic approach prevailed through most of the 1970s and 1980s, but then experienced a decline in popularity. In 1989, Eastman Kodak Company's multivendor approach to meeting its IS needs created the "Kodak effect." Kodak outsourced its data center operations to IBM, its network to Digital Equipment Company, and its desktop supply and support operations to Businessland.[2] Kodak managed these relationships through strategic alliances.[3] Kodak retained a skeleton IS staff to act on behalf of its business personnel with outsource providers. Its approach to supplier management became a model emulated by Continental Bank, General Dynamics, Continental Airlines, and National Car Rental and many more.[4]

---

[2] L. Applegate and R. Montealegre, "Eastman Kodak Co.: Managing Information Systems Through Strategic Alliances," Harvard Business School case 192030 (September 1995).

[3] Anthony DiRomualdo and Vijay Gurbaxani, "Strategic Intent for IT Outsourcing," *Sloan Management Review* (June 22, 1998).

[4] Mary C. Lacity, Leslie P. Willcocks, and David F. Feeny, "The Value of Selective IT Sourcing," *Sloan Management Review* (March 22, 1996).

"Make" or "Buy"	Suggests Insourcing	Suggests Outsourcing	Examples of Associated Risk in Worse Case Scenarios
Questions			
Does it involve a core competency?	Yes	No	*If outsourced:* Loss of control over strategic initiatives, loss of strategic focus
Does it involve confidential or sensitive IS services or software development?	Yes	No	*If outsourced:* Competitive secrets may be leaked
Is there enough time available to complete software development projects in-house?	Yes	No	*If insourced:* Project not completed on time
Do the in-house IS professionals have adequate training, experience, or skills to provide the service or develop the software?	Yes	No	*If outsourced:* Technological innovations limited to what provider offers; overreliance on provider's skills
Are there reliable outsourcing providers who are likely to stay in business for the duration of the contract?	No	Yes	*If outsourced:* Project not completed, or, if completed, project is over budget and late when another provider takes it over
Is there an outsourcing provider that has a culture and practices that are compatible with the client?	No	Yes	*If outsourced:* Conflict between client and provider personnel
Are there economies of scale that make it cheaper to provide the service or develop the software in-house?	Most Likely No	Most Likely Yes	*If outsourced:* Costs of project or operations becomes excessive because of the way the contract is written
Does it offer a better ability to handle peaks?	Most Likely No	Most Likely Yes	*If insourced:* Loss of business
Does it involve consolidating data centers?	Most Likely No	Most Likely Yes	*If insourced:* Inefficient operations

FIGURE 9.2 Make or buy? Questions and risks.

Kodak's watershed outsourcing arrangement ushered in changes to outsourcing practices in the 1990s that put all IS activities up for grabs, including aspects that provide competitive advantage. As relationships with outsourcing providers become more sophisticated, companies realize that even such essential functions as customer service are sometimes better managed by experts on the outside. Over the years, motives for outsourcing broadened beyond cost control. The next section examines factors and risks to be considered in making the outsourcing decision. The sourcing strategy suggested by the answers to key "Make/Buy" questions and associated risks are listed in Figure 9.2.

Factors in the Outsourcing Decision

Under what conditions is the answer to the "Insource/Outsource" question "Outsource"? That is, what factors drive companies to decide to outsource? There are three factors that are likely to lead to the decision to outsource: cheaper costs due to economies of scale, ability to handle peaks in processing, and the client company's need to consolidate data centers.

One of the most common reasons given for outsourcing is the desire to reduce costs. Outsourcing providers derive savings from economies of scale that client companies often can't realize. Providers achieve these economies through centralized (often "greener") data centers, preferential contracts with suppliers, and large pools of technical expertise. Most often, enterprises lack such resources on a sufficient scale within their own IS departments. A single company may need only 5,000 PCs, but an outsourcing provider can negotiate a contract for 50,000 and achieve a much lower unit cost.

Second, as long as contract terms effectively address contingencies, the larger resources of an outsourcing provider make available greater capacity on demand. For instance, at year-end, outsourcing providers potentially can allocate additional mainframe capacity to ensure timely completion of nightly processing in a manner that would be impossible for an enterprise running its own bare-bones data center.

Third, an outsourcing provider may help a client company overcome inertia to consolidate data centers that could not be consolidated by an internal group or following a merger or acquisition. Outsourcing may also offer an infusion of cash as a company sells its equipment to the outsourcing vendor.

Above it was noted that if the service or product under consideration involved a core competency, then the company should strongly consider insourcing. However, if the product or service is considered to be a commodity instead of a core competency then there are some distinct advantages to outsourcing. By bringing in outside expertise, client company management often can focus less attention on IS operations and more on core activities. Although they must still manage the relationships with outsourcing providers, using outsourcing providers frees up their time so that they can devote their energies, and that of their employees, to areas that reflect core competencies for the business. It is important to remember, however, that client company managers are ultimately still responsible for IS services provided to their firm.

It was noted in discussing insourcing that if a client company does not have employees with the training, experience, or skills in-house to successfully implement the new technologies it should consider outsourcing. Outsourcing can be employed to help a company transition to new technologies. This is because outsourcing providers generally offer access to larger pools of talent with more current knowledge of advancing technologies. For example, many outsourcing providers gain vast experience solving business intelligence problems, whereas IS staff within a single company only have limited experience, if any. The provider's experienced consultants are more readily available to the marketplace advances and best practices than any comparably trained and experienced in-house IT professionals. Client companies turn to outsourcing providers to help them implement such technologies as Enterprise 2.0, Web 2.0 tools, and ERP systems.

Outsourcing providers also have an added advantage when it comes to having employees with the necessary skills, training, and experience because they can specialize in IS services. Outsourcing providers' extensive experience in dealing with IS professions likely helps them to understand how to hire, manage, and retain IS staff effectively. Outsourcing providers often can offer IS personnel a professional environment that a typical company cannot afford to build. For example, a Web designer would have responsibility for one Web site within a company, but for multiple sites when working for an outsourcing provider. It becomes the outsourcing provider's responsibility to find, train, and retain highly marketable IS talent. An outsourcing provider often opens greater opportunity for training and advancement in IT than can a single IS organization. Outsourcing relieves a client of costly investments in continuous training so that IS staff can keep current with marketplace technologies and the headaches of hiring and retaining a staff that easily can change jobs with more pay or other lures. These factors are listed in Figure 9.2.

Outsourcing Risks

Opponents of outsourcing cite a considerable number of risks (see Figure 9.2). A manager should consider each of these before making a decision about outsourcing. Each can be mitigated with effective planning and ongoing management.

First, outsourcing requires that a client company surrender a degree of control over critical aspects of the enterprise. The potential loss of control could extend to several areas: control of the project, scope creep, the technologies, the costs, financial controls, accuracy and clarity of financial reports, and the company's IS direction. By turning over data center operations, for example, a company puts itself at the mercy of an outsourcing provider's ability to manage this function effectively. A manager must choose an outsourcing provider carefully and negotiate terms that encourage an effective working relationship.

Second, outsourcing clients may not adequately anticipate new technological capabilities when negotiating outsourcing contracts. Outsourcing providers may not recommend so-called bleeding-edge technologies for fear of losing money in the process of implementation and support, even if implementation would best serve the client. Thus, poorly planned outsourcing can result in a loss in IS flexibility. For example, some outsourcing providers were slow to adopt social technologies for their clients because they feared the benefits would not be as tangible as the costs of entering the market.

This reluctance impinged on clients' ability to realize social business strategies. To avoid this problem, outsourcing clients should have a chief technology officer (CTO) or technology group that is charged with learning about and assessing emerging technologies for their ability to support their company's business strategy.

Third, by surrendering IS functions, a company gives up any real potential to develop them for competitive advantage—unless, of course, the outsourcing agreement is sophisticated enough to comprehend developing such advantage in tandem with the outsourcing company. However, even these partnerships potentially compromise the advantage when ownership is shared with the outsourcing provider, and the advantage may become available to the outsourcing provider's other clients. Under many circumstances, the outsourcing provider becomes the primary owner of any technological solutions developed, which allows the outsourcing provider to leverage the knowledge to benefit other clients, possibly even competitors of the initial client.

Fourth, contract terms may leave clients highly dependent on their outsourcing provider, with little recourse in terms of terminating troublesome provider relationships. That is, the clients may be locked-in to an arrangement that they no longer want. The more reliant the client company is on the provider the harder and more expensive it is to switch to another outsourcing provider when the contract sours. Despite doing due diligence and background checks, the outsourcing provider may be unreliable or go out of business before the end of the contract. The risk of over-reliance for any number of reasons typically increases as the size of the outsourcing contract increases. DHL Worldwide Express entrusted 90% of its IT development and maintenance projects to a large Indian-based company, Infosys. "There's a lot of money wrapped up in a contract this size, so it's not something you take lightly or hurry with," said Ron Kifer, DHL's Vice President of Program Solutions and Management.[5] Clearly DHL faced considerable risk in offshoring with Infosys because of its reliance on them.

Fifth, when a company turns to an outsourcing provider, it must realize that its competitive secrets might be harder to keep. Its databases are no longer kept in house, and the outsourcing provider's other customers may have easier access to sensitive information. Although all outsourcing agreements contain clauses to keep customer data and system secure, managers still voice concern about data security and process skills when it's managed by a third party. This risk is mitigated by thinking through the security issues carefully and implementing controls where possible. Often, the outsourcing provider has more secure processes and practices in place simply because their business depends on it—it's a competitive necessity and often a core competency of the outsourcing provider.

Sixth, the outsourcing provider's culture or operations may be incompatible with that of the client company, making it difficult to deliver the contracted service or system. Conflicts between the client's staff and the staff of the outsourcing provider may delay progress or hurt the quality of the service or product delivered by the outsourcing provider.

---

[5] Stephanie Overby, "The Hidden Costs of Offshore Outsourcing," *CIO Magazine* (September 1, 2003), 7, http://www.cio.com/article/29654/The_Hidden_Costs_of_Offshore_Outsourcing (accessed on June 4, 2012).

Seventh, although many companies turn to outsourcing because of perceived cost savings, these savings may never be realized. Typically, the cost savings are premised on activities that were performed by the company. However, implementation of new technologies may fail to generate any savings because the old processes on which they were premised are no longer performed. Further, the outsourcing client is, to some extent, at the mercy of the outsourcing provider. Increased volumes due to unspecified growth, software upgrades, or new technologies not anticipated in the contract may end up costing a firm considerably more than it anticipated when it signed the contract. Also, some savings, although real, may be hard to measure.

Finally, there may be challenges that come from working with multiple vendors. While multiple vendors allow client companies to distribute work to the "best of breed," it comes with its downsides. Having more vendors requires more coordination than with working with a single outsourcing provider. Further, when a major problem occurs, there may be a tendency to "finger-point." That is, each vendor may claim that the problem is caused by, or can only be corrected by, another vendor. And as vendors expand their service offerings, an unexpected competition among vendors can result.

Decisions about How to Outsource Successfully

Clearly the decision about whether or not to outsource must be made with adequate care and deliberation. It must be followed with numerous other decisions about how to mitigate outsourcing risks and make the outsourcing arrangement work. Three major decision areas are selection, contracting, and scope.

Selection-related decisions focus on finding compatible outsourcing providers whose capabilities, managers, internal operations, and culture complement those of the client company. This means that compatibility and cultural fit might trump price, especially when long-term partnerships are envisioned.

Many "how" decisions center around the outsourcing contract. In particular, client companies must ensure that contract terms allow them the flexibility they require to manage and, if necessary, sever supplier relationships. The ten-year contracts that were so popular in the early 1990s are being replaced with shorter-duration contracts lasting three to five years and full life-cycle service contracts that are broken up into stages. In fact, the average contract for outsourcing today, is nearly a third of the 2000 average of $360 million.[6] Often, outsourcing arrangements have formal service contracts between clients and outsourcing providers, called **Service Level Agreements (SLAs)**, where the level of service is defined. SLAs often describe the contracted delivery time and expected performance of the service. Contracts are tightened by adding clauses describing actions to be taken in the event of a deterioration in quality of service or non-compliance to service-level agreements. Service levels, baseline period measurements, growth rates, and service volume fluctuations

---

[6] Stephanie Overby, "IT Outsourcing: Multi-Billion-Dollar Mega Deals End in Break Up," CIO.com (March 31, 2010), http://www.cio.com/article/588960/IT_Outsourcing_Multi_Billion_Dollar_Mega_Deals_End_in_Break_Up (accessed on February 11, 2012).

are specified to reduce opportunistic behavior on the part of the outsourcing vendor. Research demonstrates that tighter contracts tend to lead to more successful outsourcing arrangements.[7] Unfortunately, a tight contract does not provide much solace to an outsourcing client when an outsourcing provider goes out of business. It also does not replace having a good relationship with the outsourcing provider that allows the client to work out problems when something unanticipated occurs.

Most enterprises outsource at least some IS functions. This is where scope questions come into play. Defining on the scope of outsourcing means that the client must decide on whether to pursue outsourcing fully or selectively.

Full outsourcing implies that an enterprise outsources all its IS functions from desktop services to software development. An enterprise would outsource everything if it does not view IT as a strategic advantage that it needs to cultivate internally. Full outsourcing can free resources to be employed in areas that add greater value. It can also reduce overall cost per transaction due to size and economies of scale.[8] Many companies outsource IS simply to allow their managers to focus attention on other business issues. Others outsource to accommodate growth and respond to their business environment. Kellwood, the case discussed at the beginning of the chapter, appeared to have used full outsourcing to improve operations.

With **selective outsourcing**, an enterprise chooses which IT capabilities to retain in house and which to give to an outsider. A "best-of-breed" approach is taken in which suppliers are chosen for their expertise in specific technology areas. Possible areas for selective sourcing include Web site hosting, Web 2.0 applications, business process application development, help desk support, networking and communications, social IT services, and data center operations. Although an enterprise can acquire top-level skills and experience through such relationships, the effort required to manage them grows tremendously with each new provider. Still, selective outsourcing, sometimes called "strategic sourcing," reduces the reliance of the client company being locked-in to outsourcing with only one provider. It also provides greater flexibility and often better service due to the competitive market.[9] To illustrate, an enterprise might retain a specialist firm to develop social business applications and at the same time select a large outsourcing provider, such as EDS, to assume mainframe maintenance.

Consider JetBlue, an airline that recently turned to Verizon to manage its IT infrastructure—its network, data center, and help desk. The six-year contract with Verizon will allow the data centers to scale as JetBlue grows and it will also help JetBlue "reduce the cycle time for delivery of those capabilities and allow the rest of IT to focus on other capabilities," said JetBlue CIO, Joe Eng. Eng asserts that JetBlue will still have control over IT: "We own the decision paths, the service-level agreements and what direction we want to take, but Verizon will be key in the implementation." Verizon was

---

[7] See, for example, C. Saunders, M. Gebelt, and Q. Hu, "Achieving Success in Information Systems Outsourcing," *California Management Review* (1997), 39(2), 63–79; and M. Lacity and R. Hirschheim, *Information Systems Outsourcing: Myths, Metaphors and Realities* (Hoboken, NJ: John Wiley & Sons, 1995).

[8] Tom Field, "An Outsourcing Buyer's Guide: Caveat Emptor," *CIO Magazine* (April 1, 1997).

[9] Ibid.

chosen over other providers for a number of reason, but especially because the operation of networks is its core business.[10]

Deciding Where—Onshore, Offshore or in the Cloud?

Until recently, outsourcing options were either to use services onshore (worked performed in the same country as the client) or offshore (work performed in a distant country). More recently a new sourcing option has become more available and more accepted by managers: cloud computing. Below we describe each of the three sourcing options. We also describe some answers to the "how" to make the arrangement successful. Many best practices were discussed in the previous subsection because they are common to all three outsourcing options. Some are unique to the various options, as indicated in Figure 9.3.

"How" area	Cloud Computing	Onshoring	Offshoring
SELECTION			
Do not negotiate solely on price	x	x	x
Carefully evaluate your own company's capabilities	x	x	x
Thoroughly evaluate provider's capabilities	x	x	x
Choose provider with complementary capabilities	x	x	x
Be sure there is a technical fit	x	x	x
Be sure there is a cultural fit		x	x—especially critical based on national cultures
Be sure relationship produces net benefit	x	x	x
Select location to mitigate risk, reduce time zone differences and match culture			x

FIGURE 9.3 Trade-offs between outsourcing options.
Source: Partially adapted from J. Rottman and M. C. Lacity, "Twenty Practices for Offshore Sourcing," *MIS Quarterly Executive* (2004), 3(3), 119, Table 1.

---

[10] M. Hamblen, "Verizon to Manage JetBlue's Network, Data Centers and Help Desk," CIO.com (October 6, 2009), http://www.computerworld.com/s/article/9138965/
Verizon_to_manage_JetBlue_s_network_data_centers_and_help_desk (accessed on January 31, 2012).

"How" area	Cloud Computing	Onshoring	Offshoring
RELATIONSHIP/CONTRACTING			
Establish short-term contracts	x	x	x—fixed price if possible
Establish life cycle contracts that are broken into stages		x	x
Make contracts as tight as possible	x	x	x
Carefully define contracts when using multiple, "best of breed"	x	x	x
Develop skills in contract management	x	x	x
Hire legal experts (area noted)		x (outsourcing)	x (outsourcing, offshore laws)
Openly communicate sourcing strategy to all stakeholders to mitigate political risks			x
Elevate client organization's CMMI certification to close the process gap between client and provider			x
Negotiate CMMI processes that will not be paid for to save money			x
Manage bottlenecks to relieve substantial time zone differences			x
SCOPE			
Decide on full or selective outsourcing models	Usually Selective	Selective or Full	Usually Selective

FIGURE 9.3 (Continued)

Cloud Computing

As discussed in Chapter 6, **cloud computing** is the dynamic provisioning of third-party-provided IT services over the Internet. Companies offering cloud computing make an entire data center's worth of servers, networking devices, systems management, security, storage, and other infrastructure available to their clients. In that way their clients can buy the exact amount of storage, computing power, security, or other IT functions that they need, when they need it, and pay only for what they use. Thus, the client can realize cost savings by sharing the provider's resources with other clients. They also provide 24/7 access from multiple mobile devices, high availability for large backup data storage, and ease of use.

Netflix realized the advantages of cloud computing to support its strategic initiative to stream movies to its customers instead of mailing them DVDs. To do so it needed so much more infrastructure that the cloud appeared to be their only option. "Netflix.com is nearly 100% in the cloud. . . We really couldn't build data centers fast enough," says Jason Chan, Netflix's cloud security architect. The introduction of a Netflix application for iPhones will place even greater spikes in demand, at least temporarily. But Chan isn't concerned: "That's what cloud is really intended for."[11]

Cloud computing comes in many different forms. Options include on-premise or private clouds, community clouds, public clouds, and hybrid clouds that are combinations of two or more other clouds. In private clouds the data is managed by the company and remains within the company's existing infrastructure, or it is managed offsite by a third party for the company. In community clouds, the cloud infrastructure is shared by several organizational and supports the shared concerns of a specific community. In public clouds data is stored outside of the corporate data centers in the cloud provider's environment. Public clouds include:

- Infrastructure as a Service (IaaS)—provides infrastructure through grids or clusters or virtualized servers, networks, storage, and systems software designed to augment or replace the functions of an entire data center; the customer may have full control of the actual server configuration allowing more risk management control over the data and environment.

- Platform as a Service (PaaS)—provides services using virtualized servers on which clients can run existing applications or develop new ones without having to worry about maintaining the operating systems, server hardware, load balancing, or computing capacity; the cloud provider manages the hardware and underlying operating system, which limits their enterprise risk management capabilities.

- Software as a Service (SaaS)—provides software application functionality through a Web browser. Both the platform and the infrastructure are fully managed by the cloud provider with means that if the operating system or underlying service isn't configured correctly, the data at the higher application layer may be at risk. This is the most widely known and used form of cloud computing. SaaS is sometimes calls an ASP, or Application Service Provider.[12]

Despite its advantages, some managers shy away from cloud computing. They are concerned about security, specifically about external threats from remote hackers and security breaches as the data travels to and from the cloud. Tied to the concerns about security are concerns about data privacy. The standards, monitoring, and maintenance tools for cloud computing are still not mature. This makes security, interoperability, and data mobility difficult. Finally, the ability to tailor service-level requirements, such as uptime, response time, availability, performance, and network latency, to the specific

[11] Tim Greene, "Netflix Deals with Cloud Security Concerns," CIO.com (September 21, 2011), http://www.cio.com/article/print/690236 (accessed on September 22, 2011).

[12] Diana Kelley, "How Data-Centric Protection Increases Security in Cloud Computing and Virtualization," *Security Curve* (2011), http://www.securitycurve.com (accessed on September 22, 2011).

Social Business Lens: iCloud

A key component of social business is the use of the cloud as a sourcing platform for applications. One implementation of the cloud that has drawn significant attention is Apples' iCloud. Like all cloud applications, it uses a seemingly endless supply of technology accessed over the Internet. iCloud is an app for backup and synchronizing across all the user's devices, including the laptop, iPod, iPhone, iPad, and future Apple devices. It's interesting because it provides sourcing for individual users, rather than for entire organizations.

A key feature of most social business applications is their ease of use. What has captured the attention of many who like the iCloud is the way it works automatically to synchronize sharing data, photos, video, music, and documents across all the individual's devices over a wireless network with no interaction from the user. Apple is known for creating systems that are intuitive and simple to use, but built on systems of great complexity and technical creativity. iCloud is such an innovation. Built into the Apple operating system, iCloud is turned on as an option when the user's system is set up. It then automatically and securely stores all the content on the device on the cloud computers. It's a game-changing sourcing option, since it takes all the decisions about sourcing out of the hands of the user and makes them automatically when the application is used. Users are pleased because their information is automatically synched with all their devices and everything is backed up without any additional effort on the part of the user.

---

needs of a client is far less than with insourcing, or even with many other outsourcing options. To manage this risk, an SLA needs to spell out these requirements.

Onshoring

Outsourcing does not necessarily mean that the IT services and software development is shipped abroad. **Onshoring**, also called inshoring, is performing outsourcing work domestically. Onshoring may be considered the "opposite" of offshoring. A growing trend in onshoring in the United States is rural sourcing, which is hiring outsourcing providers with operations in rural parts of America. Rural sourcing firms can be competitive because they take advantage of lower salaries and living costs when compared to firms in metropolitan areas. Dealing with a rural company can have advantages in terms of closer time zones, similar culture, and fewer hassles that crop up when dealing with foreign outsourcing providers. However, the rural sourcing firms are usually too small to handle large-scale projects and may not have the most technologically advanced employees. Rural sourcing is often viewed as more politically correct.[13] See Figure 9.4 for a discussion of related political issues.

---

[13] Bob Violino, "Rural outsourcing on the rise in the U.S.," *Computerworld* (March 7, 2011), http://www.computerworld.com/s/article/353556/Lure_of_the_Countryside?taxonomyId=14&pageNumber=1 (accessed on September 22, 2011).

Government actions to support offshoring	Government actions to protect against offshoring
Politicians in countries around the world are trying to create an environment so that their country can become "the next India." But India invested in a substantial infrastructure in human capital, telecommunications, and technology parks. Countries emulating India must lay a foundation in science and technology education, especially IT education. Offshoring is only possible if its key resource, the country's potential job pool, consists of highly skilled workers. Other actions that governments can take to make their countries more appealing to outsourcing clients are to give marketing assistance to offshore vendors, assist firms in attaining recognized standards of quality in the global marketplace, and promote collaborative efforts between the government, software companies, financial institutions, and universities. Governments can also offer specific incentives to companies that are considering their country as an offshoring destination. They can, for example reduce/eliminate various taxes or ease the bureaucratic process required for the company.	Politicians in countries such as the United States and United Kingdom where there have been large numbers of job losses attributed to jobs being moved offshore are turning to defensive legislative strategies. Government funding for education and training, health care insurance and pension portability, and unemployment-compensation programs for the displaced workers are being considered. To stem the outflow of lost jobs, the U.S. Congress proposed numerous federal laws ("bills") to restrict offshoring and to protect U.S. jobs by restricting the number of visas for people entering the country. It can do so according to the Commerce Clause of the U.S. Constitution. In addition, state legislatures including those of Arizona, California, Colorado, Florida, Illinois, Maryland, New Jersey, North Carolina, North Dakota, and Utah passed laws to restrain offshoring by more heavily regulating the "privatization" of state services. Because the number of contracts offered by state governments is limited, these "privatization" bills, if constitutional, may have little impact on offshoring. Nonetheless, lobbying efforts and public pressure to legislate against offshoring and for making the business dealings of publicly owned firms that engage in offshoring more transparent are likely to continue.

FIGURE 9.4 Government involvement with offshoring.

Source: Erran Carmel and Paul Tjia, *Offshoring Information Technology* (Cambridge, UK: University Press, 2005).

Offshoring

Offshoring (which is short for outsourcing offshore) is when the IS organization uses contractor services, or even builds its own data center in a distant land. The functions sent offshore range from routine IT transactions to increasingly higher-end, knowledge-based business processes.

Programmer salaries can be a fraction of those in the home country in part because the cost of living and the standard of living in the distant country are much lower, maybe as much as 70% when only considering direct labor costs. However, these savings come at a price because other costs increase. Additional technology, telecommunications, travel, process changes, and management overhead are required to relocate and supervise operations overseas. For example, during the transition period, which can be rather lengthy, offshore workers must often be brought to the U.S. headquarters for extended periods to become familiar with the company's operations and technology. Because of the long transition period, it may often take several years for offshoring's labor savings to be fully realized. And even if they are realized, they may never reflect the true cost to a country. Many argue, especially those who have lost their jobs to offshore workers, that offshoring cuts into the very fiber of the society in the origin country where companies are laying off workers. Yet it helps the economies of the countries where offshoring is performed. For example, in December 2011, the IT services industry in India was a $76 billion industry, the largest source for IT services and offshoring, primarily from foreign companies offshoring.[14]

Even though the labor savings are often very attractive, companies sometimes turn to offshoring for other reasons. The employees in many offshore companies are typically well educated (often holding master's degrees) and proud to work for an international company. The offshore service providers are often "profit centers" that have established Six Sigma, ISO 9001, or another certification program. They usually are more willing to "throw more brainpower at a problem" to meet their performance goals than many companies in the United States or Western Europe. In offshore economies, technology know-how is a relatively cheap commodity in ample supply.[15]

Offshoring raises the fundamental question of what you send offshore, and what you keep within your enterprise IS organization when implementing the selective outsourcing model. Because communications are made difficult by differences in culture, time zones, and possibly language, outsourced tasks are usually those that can be well specified. They typically, but not always, are basic non-core transactional systems that require little in-depth knowledge of the users or customers. In contrast, early stage prototypes and pilot development are often kept in-house because this work is very dynamic and needs familiarity with business processes. Keeping the work at home allows CIOs to offer learning opportunities to in-house staff. In summary, the costs savings that lure many companies to turn to offshoring need to be assessed in relation to the increased risks and communication problems in working with offshore workers and relying on them to handle major projects.

---

[14] "Offshoring: U.S., Europe opening opportunities for Indian entrepreneurs and start-ups," *India Times* (December 13, 2011), http://articles.economictimes.indiatimes.com/2011-12-14/news/30516031_1_virtual-assistant-small-businesses-offshoring (accessed on February 21, 2012).

[15] Aditya Bhasin, Vinay Couto, Chris Disher, and Gil Irwin, "Business Process Offshoring: Making the Right Decision," *CIO Magazine* (January 29, 2004), http://www2.cio.com/consultant/report2161.html (accessed on August 14, 2005).

Geographic Lens: Corporate Social Responsibility

Many outsourcing clients are increasing their corporate social responsibility (CSR) expectations for themselves and for their global IS outsourcing providers. Pessimists of global IS outsourcing are concerned that it maximizes profit for the rich but offers little or no benefits for other groups, especially the poor in developing countries. They are concerned that global IS outsourcing will deepen income inequalities and have disruptive effects on society around the globe. Optimists of global IS outsourcing see it as a way of sharing wealth on a global basis. It is ethically justified because it can improve efficiency, help developing countries by providing jobs where unemployment is very high, lead to transfers of knowledge and information technology, and encourage better educational systems in less developed countries so that people can do the outsourcing work. Ironically, global IS outsourcing may benefit both the more developed origin country (frequently the United States, Western Europe, and Australia) as well as the destination country through free trade and reduced the prices of computers and communications equipment. It also may fuel the creation of high-level jobs for workers in more developed countries.

For companies that want to promote corporate social responsibility, the following guidelines should be implemented by both clients and outsourcing providers: understand relevant CSR regulatory requirements to ensure compliance, establish measures and report CSR performance and compliance to stakeholders, respond to inquiries about CSR compliance, embed CSR in ongoing operations, and develop a CSR culture through hiring and education.

Sources: R. Babin and B. Nicholson, "Corporate Social and Environmental Responsibility and Global IT Outsourcing," *MIS Quarterly Executive* (2009), 8(4), 203–212; and Laura D'Andrea Tyson, "Outsourcing: Who's Safe Anymore?" *Executive Viewpoint* (February 23, 2004).

Deciding Where Abroad—Nearshoring, Farshoring, or Captive Center?

As the outsourcing phenomenon has matured, the marketplace has differentiated across ways of offshoring. Offshoring can be either relatively proximate (nearshoring) or in a distant land (farshoring). An alternative to offshoring is a captive center. Each of these is described in more detail below.

Farshoring

Farshoring is a form of offshoring that involves sourcing service work to a foreign, lower-wage country that is relatively far away in distance or time zone (or both). For big outsourcing countries such as the United States and United Kingdom, India and China are the most popular farshoring destinations. Ironically, companies in India and China are now farshoring themselves to countries with lower labor costs.

Nearshoring

Nearshoring on the other hand, is when work is sourced to a foreign, lower-wage country that is relatively close in distance or time zones. With nearshoring, the client company hopes to benefit from one or more ways of being close: geographically, temporally, culturally, linguistically, economically, politically, or from historical linkages. Nearshoring basically challenges the assumption on which offshoring is premised: Distance doesn't matter. The advocates of nearshoring argue that distance does matter, and being closer on one or more of these dimensions, the client company faces less challenges in terms of communication, control, supervision, coordination, or bonding socially.

A recent analysis of the nearshoring literature found three major global clusters of countries focused on building a reputation as a home for nearshoring: a cluster of 20 nations around the United States and Canada, a cluster of 27 countries around Western Europe, and a smaller cluster of three countries in East Asia. This smaller cluster contains China, Malaysia, and Korea.[16]

The ways, or dimensions, of being close clearly extend beyond distance and time zone. For example, language makes a difference in nearshoring. That is why Latin American nearshoring destinations are appealing to Texas or Florida, where there is a large Spanish-speaking population and why French-speaking North African nations are appealing to France. These dimensions likely play a key role when companies are trying to decide between a nearshore or a farshore destination (particularly India). Ironically, India, which exports roughly five times the software of the strictly nearshoring nations, is responding to the competitive threat that these nations pose by offering clients nearshoring options. For example, India-based Tata Consulting Services (TCS) offers its British clients services that are nearshore (Budapest, Hungary), farshore (India), or onshore (London, United Kingdom). It is likely that the differentiation based on "distance" is likely to continue to be important in the outsourcing arena.

Captive Centers

With the cost advantages firms have found in less expensive economies, and to manage the risks associated with outsourcing vendors managing such an important resource as the information systems, a new type of sourcing arose: captive centers. A **captive center** is an overseas subsidiary that is set up to serve the parent company. Firms have set up these subsidiaries to operate like an outsourcing provider, but they are owned by the firm. Two common types of captive centers are hybrid and shared.[17] The hybrid captive center typically performs the more expensive, higher-profile or mission-critical work for the parent company and outsources the more commoditized work that is more cheaply provided by an offshore provider. The shared captive center performs work for both a parent company and external customers. Captive centers can be nearshore or farshore. Their distinguishing characteristics are that they are in less expensive

---

[16] Erran Carmel and Pamela Abbott, "Why 'Nearshore' Means that Distance Matters," *Communications of the ACM* (October 2007), 50(10), 40–46.

[17] I. Oshri, J. Kotalarsky, and C.-M. Liew, "What to Do with Your Captive Center: Four Strategic Options," *Wall Street Journal* (May 12, 2008).

locations, usually away from the company's headquarters or major operating units, and that they are owned by the parent company rather than by an outsourcing provider.

Selecting an Offshore Destination: Answering the "Where Abroad?" Question

A difficult decision that many companies face is selecting an offshoring destination. To answer the *Where Abroad?* question client companies must consider attractiveness, level of development, and cultural differences.

Attractiveness

Approximately 100 countries are now exporting software services and products. For various reasons, some countries are more attractive than others as hosts of offshoring business because of the firm's geographic orientation. With English as the predominant language of outsourcing countries (i.e., United States and United Kingdom), countries with a high English proficiency are more attractive than those where different languages are spoken. Geopolitical risk is another factor that affects the use of offshore firms in a country. Countries on the verge of war, countries with high rates of crime, and countries without friendly relationships with the home country are typically not suitable candidates for this business. Regulatory restrictions, trade issues, data security, and intellectual property also affect the attractiveness of a country for an offshoring arrangement. Hiring legal experts who know the laws of the provider's company can mitigate legal risks. Nonetheless, some countries are more attractive than others because of their legal systems. The level of technical infrastructure available in some countries also can add to or detract from the attractiveness of a country. Although a company may decide that a certain country is attractive overall for offshoring, it still must assess city differences when selecting an offshore outsourcing provider or creating wholly owned subsidiaries ("captives"). For example, Chennai is a better location in India for finance and accounting, but Delhi has better call-center capabilities.[18]

Some countries created an entire industry of providing IT services through offshoring. India, for example, took an early mover advantage in the industry. With a large, low-cost English-speaking labor pool, many entrepreneurs set up programming factories that produce high-quality software to meet even the toughest standards. One measure of the level of proficiency of the development process within an IS organization is the Software Engineering Institute's Capability Maturity Model (CMM)[19] Level 1 means that the software development processes are immature, bordering on chaotic. Few processes are formally defined, and output is highly inconsistent. At the other end of the model is level 5, where processes are predictable, repeatable, highly refined, and consistently innovating, growing, and incorporating feedback. The software factories in many Indian enterprises are well known for their CMM level 5 software development processes, making them extremely reliable, and, thus, desirable as vendors. However, if the client company is not at the same CMM

---

[18] Ben Worthen and Stephanie Overby, "USAA IT Chief Exits," *CIO Magazine* (June 15, 2004), http://www.cio.com/archive/061504/tl_management.html (accessed on August 14, 2005).

[19] Capability Maturity Model Integration (CMMI) has superseded CMM for many.

level as the provider, it may want to specify which CMM processes it will pay for to avoid wasting money. Further, it may seek to elevate its own CMM certification to close the process gap between what it can do and what the outsourcing provider can do.

Development Tiers

A very important factor in selecting an offshore destination is the level of development of the country, which often subsume a variety of other factors. For example in the highest tier, the countries have an advanced technological foundation and a broad base of institutions of higher learning. Carmel and Tjia suggest that there are three tiers of software exporting nations:[20]

- **Tier 1:** Mature Software Exporting Nations—These include such highly industrialized nations as United Kingdom, United States, Japan, Germany, France, Canada, the Netherlands, Sweden, and Finland. It also includes the three "I's" (i.e., India, Ireland, and Israel) that became very prominent software exporters in the 1990s, as well as China and Russia, which entered the tier in the 2000s.

- **Tier 2:** Emerging Software Exporting Nations—These nations are the up-and-comers. They tend to have small population bases or unfavorable conditions such as political instability or an immature state of economic development. Countries in this tier include Brazil, Costa Rica, South Korea, and many Eastern European countries.

- **Tier 3:** Infant Stage Software Exporting Nations—These nations have not significantly affected the global software market, and their software industry is mostly a "cottage industry" with smaller, isolated firms. Some Tier 3 countries are Cuba, Vietnam, Jordan, and 15 to 25 others.

The tiers were determined on the basis of industrial maturity, the extent of clustering of some critical mass of software enterprises, and export revenues. The higher tiered countries tend to offer higher levels of skills, but also higher costs.

Cultural Differences

Often misunderstandings arise because of differences in culture and, sometimes, language. For example, GE Real Estate's CIO quickly learned that American programmers have a greater tendency to speak up and offer suggestions, whereas Indian programmers might think something does not make sense, but they go ahead and do what they were asked, assuming that this is what the client wants.[21] Thus, a project that is common sense for an American worker—like creating an automation system for consumer credit cards—may be harder to understand and take longer when undertaken by an offshore worker. The end result may be a more expensive system that responds poorly to situations unanticipated by its offshore developers. It is important to be aware of and to manage the risks due to cultural differences.

[20] Erran Carmel and Paul Tjia, *Offshoring Information Technology* (Cambridge, UK: Cambridge University Press, 2005).

[21] Stephanie Overby, "The Hidden Costs of Offshore Outsourcing," *CIO Magazine* (September 1, 2003), 7, http://www.cio.com/article/29654/The_Hidden_Costs_of_Offshore_Outsourcing (accessed on June 4, 2012).

Sometimes cultural and other differences are so great that companies take back in-house operations that were previously outsourced offshore. Carmel and Tjia outlined some examples of communication failures with Indian developers due to differences in language, culture, and perceptions about time:[22]

- Indians are less likely than Westerners, especially the British, to engage in small talk.

- Indians often are not concerned with deadlines. When they are, they are likely to be overly optimistic about their ability to meet the deadlines of a project. One cultural trainer was heard to say, "When an Indian programmer says the work will be finished tomorrow, it only means it will not be ready today."[23]

- Indians, like Malaysians and other cultures, are hesitant about saying "no." Questions where one option for response is "no" are extremely difficult to interpret.

- What is funny in one culture is not necessarily funny in another culture.

Reevaluation—Status Quo or Change?

The final decision in the Sourcing Decision Cycle requires an assessment as to whether the sourcing arrangement is working as it should be. If everything is satisfactory then the arrangement can continue. If everything is not totally satisfactory, adjustments may need to be made to the arrangement. If the arrangement is unsatisfactory, another outsourcing provider may be selected or backsourcing may occur. Kellwood, the company described at the start of this chapter, frequently re-evaluated its outsourcing arrangements. Eventually it backsourced.

Backsourcing is a business practice in which a company takes back in-house assets, activities, and skills that are part of its information systems operations and were previously outsourced to one or more outside IS providers.[24] It may be partial or complete reversal of an outsourcing contract. A growing number of companies around the globe have brought their outsourced IS functions back in-house after terminating, renegotiating, or letting their contracts expire. Some companies, such as Continental Airlines, Cable and Wireless, Halifax Bank of Scotland, Sears, Bank One, and Xerox, have backsourced contracts worth over a billion dollars or more.

The biggest backsourcing of a contract to date was the one that JP Morgan Chase had signed with IBM for a whopping $5 billion dollars. JP Morgan Chase terminated its contract and brought information systems (IS) operations back in house only 21 months into a seven-year mega-contract. The CIO of JP Morgan Chase, Austin Adams, stated at that time, "We believe managing our own technology infrastructure is

---

[22] Erran Carmel and Paul Tjia, *Offshoring Information Technology* (Cambridge, UK: Cambridge University Press, 2005).

[23] Ibid., 181.

[24] Rudy Hirschheim, "Backsourcing: An Emerging Trend," *Outsourcing Journal* (1998); Mary C. Lacity and Leslie P. Willcocks, "Relationships in IT Outsourcing: A Stakeholder's Perspective," in *Framing the Domains of IT Management. Projecting the Future. . . Through the Past*, Robert W. Zmud (ed.) (Cincinnati, OH: Pinnaflex Education Resources, Inc., 2000), 355–384.

best for the long-term growth and success of our company, as well as our shareholders. Our new capabilities will give us competitive advantages, accelerate innovation, and enable us to become more streamlined and efficient."[25] A number of factors appear to have played a role in the decision to bring the IS operations back in house. As stated in the press release, outsourcing appeared to stagnate IT at JP Morgan Chase under the outsourcing arrangement. Another factor that it did not mention in its press releases is that it had undergone a major change with its July 2004 merger with Bank One, which had gained a reputation for consolidating datacenters and eliminating thousands of computer applications. And the man who had played a big role in the consolidation was Bank One's CIO Austin Adams. Adams, in his new role at JP Morgan Chase, managed the switch from IBM to self-sufficiency by taking advantage of the cost-cutting know-how he had gained at Bank One. The underperforming JP Morgan Chase learned much from the efficient Bank One.[26]

It isn't only large companies that are backsourcing. Many outsourcing clients report having negative experiences with outsourcing and a number of these have backsourced or are considering backsourcing. Given the size and number of the current outsourcing contracts and the difficulties of delivering high-quality information services and products, backsourcing is likely to remain an important option to be considered by many client companies.

Ironically, the reasons given for backsourcing often mirror the reasons for outsourcing in the first place. That is, companies often claim that they backsource to reduce costs and become more efficient. Based on reports in the popular press, the most common reasons given for backsourcing are a change in the way the IS is perceived by the organization, the need to regain control over critical activities that had been outsourced, a change in the executive team (where the new executives favored backsourcing), higher than expected costs, and poor service. The study found that backsourcing wasn't always due to problems. Sometime companies saw opportunities, such as mergers, acquisition, or new roles for IS, that required backsourcing to be realized.[27]

Outsourcing decisions can be difficult and expensive to reverse because outsourcing requires the enterprise to acquire the necessary infrastructure and staff. Unless

[25] Stephanie Overby, "Outsourcing—and Backsourcing—at JP Morgan Chase," *CIO* (2005), http://www.cio.com/article/print/10524 (accessed on July 23, 2008).

[26] Paul Strassmann, "Why JP Morgan Chase Really Dropped IBM," *Baseline Magazine* (January 13, 2005), http://www.baselinemag.com/c/a/Projects-Management/Why-JP-Morgan-Chase-Really-Dropped-IBM/.

[27] N. Veltri, C. Saunders, and C. B. Kavan, "Information Systems Backsourcing: Correcting Problems and Responding to Opportunities," *California Management Review* (2008). These economic and relationship issues are similar to the three empirical studies to date that have performed backsourcing research: Bandula Jayatilaka, "IS Sourcing a Dynamic Phenomena: Forming an Institutional Theory Perspective," in *Information Systems Outsourcing: Enduring Themes, New Perspectives and Global Challenges*, Rudy Hirschheim, Armin Heinzl, and Jens Dibbern (eds.) (Berlin: Springer-Verlag, 2006), 103–134; R. Hirschheim and M. C. Lacity, "Four stories of information systems sourcing," in *Information Systems Outsourcing: Enduring Themes, New Perspectives and Global Challenges*, R. Hirschheim, Armin Heinzl, and J. Dibbern (eds.), (Berlin: Springer-Verlag, 2006), 303–346; and Dwayne Whitten and Dorothy Leidner, "Bringing IT Back: An Analysis of the Decision to Backsource or Switch Vendors," *Decision Sciences* (2006), 37(4), 605–621.

experienced IT staff can contribute elsewhere in the firm, outsourcing major IT functions means staff will be lost either to the outsourcing provider or to other companies. When IT staff gets news that their company is considering outsourcing, they often seek work elsewhere. Even when staff are hired by the outsourcing provider to handle the account, they may be transferred to other accounts, taking with them critical knowledge. Though backsourcing represents the final decision in one sourcing decision cycle, it is invariably followed by another cycle of decisions as the company seeks to respond to its dynamic environment.

▶ OUTSOURCING AND STRATEGIC NETWORKS

Typically outsourcing relationships are couched in terms of an outsourcing provider and a client—just as we have done in this chapter. A different approach to viewing outsourcing arrangements: the strategic network.[28] A **strategic network** is a long-term, purposeful "arrangement by which companies set up a web of close relationships that form a veritable system geared to providing product or services in a coordinated way."[29] The client firm becomes a hub and its suppliers, including its outsourcing providers, are part of its network. The advantage of the strategic network is that it lowers the costs of working with others in its network. In doing so, the company can become more efficient than its competitors, as well as flexible enough to respond to its rapidly changing environment. Perhaps the strategic network is the best way to think about outsourcing arrangements in today's world. An example of a strategic network is the keiretsu. Japanese *keiretsu* is similar to a strategic network in that it has a hub company, a policy that encourages specialization within the network, and investments (financial and otherwise) in long-term relationships.[30] The Japanese companies manage their outsourcing activities based on the types of inputs from different types of suppliers.[31] The strategic suppliers (kankei kaisa) fall into the keiretsu category, whereas independent suppliers (dokuritsu kaisha) do not. Japanese companies work very closely with companies in the keiretsu. Another type of strategic network that increasingly affects outsourcing arrangements is a network with a parent organization or multinational and a number of their subsidiaries. Often one subsidiary performs outsourcing services for another subsidiary in the network. Given the increasingly complex structure of today's multinationals, the role of strategic networks in outsourcing arrangements is likely to grow.

[28] J. C. Jarillo, *Strategic Networks: Creating the Borderless Organization* (Oxford, UK: Butterworth-Heinemann, 1993).

[29] Ibid., 7

[30] Ibid., 122.

[31] Masaaki Kotabe and Janet Y. Murray, "Global Sourcing Strategy and Sustainable Competitive Advantage," *Industrial Marketing Management* (2004), 33, 7–14.

▶ SUMMARY

- Firms typically face a range of sourcing decisions. The Sourcing Decision Cycle Framework highlights decisions about where the work will be performed. Decisions include insourcing versus outsourcing, onshoring versus cloud computing versus offshoring, and selecting among offshoring options (nearshoring versus farshoring). Captive centers are an offshoring option with a subsidiary of the client firm. The relationships are shown below in Figure 9.5. The cycle involves an assessment of the adequacy of the IS service/product delivery. The assessment can trigger a new cycle.

- Cost savings or filling the gaps in the organization's IT skills are powerful reasons for outsourcing. Other reasons include the ability for the company to adopt a more strategic focus, manage IS staff better, better handle peaks, or consolidate data centers. The numerous risks involved in outsourcing arrangements must be carefully assessed by IS and general managers alike.

- Full or selective outsourcing offers organizations an alternative to keeping top-performing IS services in-house. Firms can meet their outsourcing needs by using a single-vendor or multiple-vendor models.

- Cloud computing allows client firms to buy the exact amount of storage, computing power, security or other IT functions that they need. . . when they need it. It includes Infrastructure as a Service (IaaS), Platforms as a Service (PaaS), and Software as a Service (SaaS).

- Offshoring may be performed in a country that is proximate along one or a number of dimensions (nearshoring) or that is distant (farshoring). Offshoring must be managed carefully and take into consideration functional differences.

Insourcing (Firm provides IS services from internal group, developing and deploying products in-house)	Outsourcing (products or services provide by outside vendors)			
	Cloud Computing (third party provides services over the Internet)	Onshoring (outsourcing work performed domestically)	Offshoring (outsourcing work performed in distant country)	
			Nearshoring (at a country nearby)	Farshoring (at a country further away, usually India, China or Eastern block countries)
Captive Center (a subsidiary of the firm, but located offshore to take advantage of economic and resource benefits of foreign country)				

FIGURE 9.5 Sourcing options.

► KEY TERMS

backsourcing (p. 281)
captive center (p. 278)
cloud computing (p. 272)
farshoring (p. 277)
full outsourcing (p. 270)

insourcing (p. 264)
nearshoring (p. 278)
offshoring (p. 275)
onshoring (p. 274)
outsourcing (p. 264)

selective outsourcing
(p. 270)
service level agreement
(SLA) (p. 269)
strategic network (p. 283)

► DISCUSSION QUESTIONS

1. The make-versus-buy decision is important every time a new application is requested of the IS group. What, in your opinion, are the key reasons an IS organization should make its own systems? What are the key reasons it should buy an application?

2. Is offshoring a problem to your country? To the global economy? Please explain.

3. When does cloud computing make sense for a large corporation that already has an IS organization? Give an example of when cloud computing might make sense for a start-up company?

4. Does a captive center resolve the concerns managers have about outsourcing to a third party vendor? Why or why not?

CASE STUDY 9-1

CROWDSOURCING AT AOL

Where would you go if you needed to find hundreds of people each willing to take on a tiny portion of a large task for minimal pay? Projects like these include filling out surveys, verifying or entering data, writing articles, and transcribing audio files. They are increasingly common in the digital age, so you might turn to an online marketplace such as Crowdsourcing.com, CrowdFlower, or Amazon's Mechanical Turk where people around the globe go to find work.

Daniel Maloney, an AOL executive, recently turned to crowdsourcing for help inventorying AOL's vast video library. (*Note: This definition of crowdsourcing differs from the one used in Chapter 5 to describe crowdsourcing as a way to spur innovation*). He broke the large job into micro-tasks and described the tasks that he needed to be done on Mechanical Turk. In particular, each worker was asked to find Web pages containing a video and identify the video's source and location on those pages. The over half a million workers that were registered at Mechanical Turk could read about the tasks and decide if they wanted to perform them.

Using the crowdsourcing service, the AOL project took less than a week to get up and running, and only a couple of months to reach completion. The total cost was about as much as it would have been to hire two temp workers for the same period.

Mr. Maloney was pleased with the cost savings and added: "We had a very high number of pages we needed to process. Being able to tap into a scaled work force was massively helpful."[32] However, he really didn't know very much about the workers who did the work for AOL and he likely had to make sure that their work was done correctly.

---

[32] R. E. Silverman, "Big Firms Try Crowdsourcing," *Wall Street Journal* (January 17, 2012), http://online.wsj.com/article/SB10001424052970204409004577157493201863200.html?mod=djem_jiewr_IT_domainid (accessed on November 2, 2011).

Critics of crowdsourcing feel it can lead to "digital sweatshops," where workers, many of whom may be underage, put in long hours to generate very little pay and no benefits. Some also feel crowdsourcing will eliminate full-time jobs. The crowdsourcing marketplace services counter that they are trying to register stay-at-home parents or college students with spare time.

Discussion Questions

1. Is crowdsourcing as used by AOL a form of outsourcing? Why or why not?
2. What steps do you think Maloney might have taken to ensure that the crowdsourcing would be a success for the inventory project?
3. What factors should be considered when deciding whether or not to crowdsource a particular part of a business?
4. Describe the advantages and disadvantages of crowdsourcing.

Sources: Amazon Web Services Web site, http://aws.amazon.com/mturk (accessed on April 17, 2012); Haydn Shaughnessy, "How to Cut Consulting Costs by 90% and Keep Your Talent Happy!" *Forbes* (April 16, 2012), www.forbes.com; Scott Kirsner, "My Life as a Micro-Laborer," *The Boston Globe* (April 1, 2012), www.boston.com; and R. E. Silverman, "Big Firms Try Crowdsourcing," *Wall Street Journal* (January 17, 2012), http://online.wsj.com/article/SB10001424052970204409004577157493201863200.html?mod=djem_jiewr_IT_domainid (accessed on November 2, 2011).

CASE STUDY 9-2

ALTIA BUSINESS PARK

The road to Altia Business Park in San Pedro Sula, Honduras is quite memorable. On one side of the road are gated communities with small, but neatly maintained stucco houses. On the other side of the road is a small river with clear running water. One bank of the river is covered with tightly-cramped shanties. Further down the road towers a thirteen story monolith in black glass. This is the home of Altia Business Park, a technological park developed by Grupo Karims, a multinational corporation with core businesses in textiles and real estate and operations in Asia, North America, Central America and the Caribbean. The building is anti-seismic and Leed Certified, which means that it follows green building practices. It is energy self-sufficient and connected to North and South America through three fiber optic submarine cables. The building is the first of two that will comprise the Business Park.

On a recent visit, the Corporate Marketing Director, Barbara Rivera, guided an American student group through the marbled halls of the building. She introduced Marcus, who was a manager in the call center in the building. Marcus explained that call center business, especially to North America, was picking up. He was born and raised in the U.S. and graduated from the University of Maryland. Since he couldn't find work in the U.S. upon graduation, he moved to Honduras where he has family. Barbara also introduced Lena, a 20-something professional, who spoke to the visiting group in perfect English, complete with current idioms. Lena had recently graduated from a university in Honduras with a Masters degree in graphical design. She said this degree was very helpful in managing the room full of graphic designers working for the company that maintains the Web site for Sandal's Resorts. Barbara told the visitors that the average salary of the workers in the companies in the Business Park was $4,800 a year[33] and people were eager to get the jobs because of the excellent pay in a country where 65% of the population lives below the poverty line. The country has a literacy rate of 84.3% and 47% of the employable workforce between the ages of 20 and 34, so the competition for good jobs can be fierce. Honduras actually has more English speakers as a proportion of population than the average Central American economy.

Discussion Questions

1. Discuss offshoring from the perspective of potential workers in your country. Discuss offshoring from the perspective of potential workers in Honduras.

2. Barbara Rivera is marketing Altia Business Park as a nearshoring site to companies in North America. What characteristics make it a desirable nearshoring site to companies in North America?

3. Is this a good idea to market Altia Business Park as a nearshoring site to people in North America? Why or why not?

---

[33] The CDP is $4,300 according to CIA World Fact Book Honduras, https://www.cia.gov/library/publications/the-world-factbook/geos/ho.html (accessed on February 13, 2012); see also http://hondurasoutsourcing.nearshoreamericas.com/.

CHAPTER 10

MANAGING IT PROJECTS

A major function of the IS organization always has been to build and implement systems. This chapter describes that process using a project framework. It begins by defining what a project is and who the key players are. It then describes how IT projects are conducted. Various system development methodologies and approaches are introduced and compared. The chapter concludes with a discussion of two critical management areas for project success: risk management and change management.

The Rural Payments Agency (RPA), an agency responsible for administering agricultural subsidies to U.K. farmers, blamed poor planning and lack of testing of their IT system for delays in paying out £1.5bn of EU subsidies. The UK government developed a complex system for administering the Single Payment Scheme, which maps farmers' land to a database. By the end of 2006, only 15% of the subsidies had been paid to farmers and, as a result a large number of farmers faced bankruptcy after not receiving due subsidies. Problems still plagued the system in early 2012 when the RPA CEO stated that the agency had deep-rooted problems that won't be corrected until 2014. His litany of the problems included inaccurate data sources of past, present and future schemes claims, a lack of standard processes and controls, ageing systems, unsuitable technology, and an organizational structure and associated corporate services that do not offer a good fit with the RPA purpose. The CEO concluded: "Our systems and tools are insufficient to allow us to deliver the level of customer service we expect and, across the agency, we don't have the necessary the commitment to our customer development. That is a long list."[1]

An independent watchdog group investigated the situation and learned that the implementation of the system began before final specifications and regulations were agreed on by the European Commission. The RPA then had to make many substantial changes in the system after implementation. Further, the investigation found that testing did not take into account the real environment, leading to unanticipated work to populate the database with what has now been realized to be often inaccurate data. Four separate governmental reviews have all been deeply critical of the system and its implementers. The July 2010 report commented, "the review process was made unnecessarily difficult by the RPA leadership resisting its commencement."[2]

---

[1] Warmwell, (February 26, 2012), http://www.warmwell.com/rpa.html (accessed on April 10, 2012).

[2] Warmwell, (July 20, 2010), http://www.warmwell.com/rpa.html (accessed on April 10, 2012).

Where was the project manager for the project? Despite receiving three "red" warnings from the Office of Government Commerce during reviews, the implementation continued. Time was not built into the schedule for testing the whole system as well as the individual components. The components were not compatible with the business processes they were supposed to support.[3] The system itself has cost £350m, which is considerably more than the original estimated cost of £75.5m. An additional £304m has been spent on staff costs to respond to the early payment fiascos. Further, £280m has been set aside to pay expected EU fines and £38m was lost in overpayments. Unfortunately, according to the June 2010 review of the system, it remains an expensive and inflexible resource.

This example highlights the possible financial and social consequences of a failed information systems (IS) project. Such failures occur at an astonishing rate. The Standish Group, a technology research firm, found that 67% of all software projects are challenged—that is, delivered late or over budget or simply fail to meet their performance criteria.[4] Business projects increasingly rely on IS to attain their objectives, especially with the increased focus to do business on the Internet. Thus, managing a business project means managing, often to a large degree, an information systems project. To succeed, a general manager must be a project manager and must learn how to manage this type of risk.

In the current business environment, the quality that differentiates firms in the marketplace—and destines them for success or failure—is often the ability to adapt existing business processes and systems to innovative ideas faster than the competition. The process of continual adaptation to the changing marketplace drives the need for business change and thus for successful project management. Typical adaptation projects include the following elements:

- Rightsizing the organization
- Reengineering business processes
- Adopting more comprehensive, integrative processes
- Incorporating new information technologies

Projects are made up of a set of one-time activities that can transform the current situation into the desired new one. Firms seek to compete through new products and processes, but the work of initially building or radically changing them falls outside the scope of normal business operations. That is where projects come in. When work can only be accomplished through methods that fundamentally differ from those employed to run daily operations, the skilled project manager plays a crucial role.

---

[3] Adapted from http://www.silicon.com/publicsector/0,3800010403,39168359,00.htm (accessed on July 28, 2008); and "Review calls for rationalisation of Rural Payments Agency IT systems," Computing.co.UK (July 21, 2010), http://www.computing.co.uk/ctg/news/1842966/review-calls-rationalisation-rural-payments-agency-it-systems (accessed on January 22, 2012).

[4] The information from the Standish Group CHAOS Report for 2006 was quoted in C. Sauer, A. Gemino, and B. H. Reich, "The Impact of Size and Volatility on IT Project Performance," *Communications of the ACM* (November 2007), 50(11), 79–84.

Successful business strategy requires executive management to decide which objectives can be met through normal daily operations and which require specialized project management. Virtually all projects involve both information technology (IT) and information flow components Many projects involve the Internet, using Web applications in the systems design. Rapidly changing business situations make it difficult to keep the IT projects aligned with dynamic business strategy. Furthermore, the complexity of IT-intensive projects has increased over the years, magnifying the risk that the finished product or process will no longer satisfy the needs of the business originally targeted to benefit from the project in the first place. Thus, learning to manage projects successfully, especially the IT component of the projects, is a crucial competency for every manager. Executives acknowledge skilled IT project management as fundamental to business success.

This chapter provides an overview of what a project is and how to manage one. It begins with a general discussion of project management, and then continues with aspects of IT-intensive projects that make them uniquely challenging. It identifies the issues that shape the role of the general manager in such projects and help them to manage risk. Finally, it considers what it means to successfully complete IT projects.

▶ WHAT DEFINES A PROJECT?

In varying degrees, organizations combine two types of work—projects and operations—to transform resources into profits. Both types are performed by people and require a flow of limited resources. Both are planned, executed, and controlled. The flight of an airplane from its point of departure to its destination is an operation that requires a pilot and crew, the use of an airplane, and fuel. The operation is repetitive: After the plane is refueled and maintained, it takes new passengers to another destination. The continuous operation the plane creates is a transportation service. However, developing the design for such a plane is a project that may require years of work by many people. When the design is completed, the work ends. Figure 10.1 compares characteristics of both project and operational work. The last two characteristics are distinctive and form the basis for the following formal definition:

> [A] **project** is a temporary endeavor undertaken to create a unique product, service or result. Temporary means that every project has a definite beginning and a definite end.[5]

All projects have stakeholders. **Project stakeholders** are the individuals and organizations that either involved in the project, or whose interests may be affected as a result of project.[6] Project stakeholders include the project manager and project team. They also include the project sponsor who typically is a general manager who provides the resources for the project and who often expects to use the project deliverables. The customer is an important stakeholder group that shouldn't be

---

[5] Project Management Institute, *A Guide to the Project Management Body of Knowledge*, 3rd ed., (Newton Square, PA: Project Management Institute: Newton Square, PA, 2004), 5.

[6] Ibid., 24.

Characteristics	Operations	Projects
Purpose	To sustain the enterprise	To reach a specific goal or accomplish a task
When it is time to change	When the operation no longer allows enterprise to meet its objectives	When a project goal is reached or the task is completed
Quality control	Formal	Informal
Product or service	Repetitive	Unique
Duration	On-going	Temporary

FIGURE 10.1 Characteristics of operational and project work.

forgotten. Customers are individuals or organizations who use the project product. Multiple layers of customers may be involved. For example, the customers for a new pharmaceutical product may include the doctors who prescribe it, the patients who take it; and the insurers who pay for it. Finally, employees in the organization undertaking the project are stakeholders with varying degrees of involvement. The relationships among the project stakeholders are displayed in Figure 10.2.

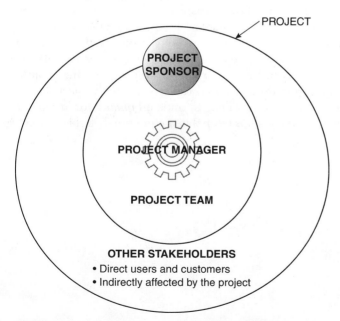

FIGURE 10.2 Relationships among project stakeholders.
Source: Adapted from Project Management Institute, *A Guide to the Project Management Body of Knowledge*, 3rd ed., (Newton Square, PA: Project Management Institute, 2004), p. 25, Figure 2-5.

To organize the work facing a project team, the project manager may break a project into subprojects. He or she then organizes these subprojects around distinct activities, such as quality control testing. This organizing method allows the project manager to contract certain kinds of work externally to limit costs or other drains on crucial project resources. At the macro level, a general manager may choose to organize various projects as elements of a larger program, if doing so creates efficiencies. Such programs then provide a framework from which to manage competing resource requirements and shifting priorities among a set of projects.

▶ WHAT IS PROJECT MANAGEMENT?

Project management is the "application of knowledge, skills, tools, and techniques to project activities in order to meet project requirements."[7] Project management always involves continual trade-offs, and it is the manager's job to manage them. Even the tragic sinking of the *Titanic* has been attributed, in part, to project trade-offs. The company that built the *Titanic*, Harland and Wolff of Belfast, Northern Ireland, had difficulty finding the millions of rivets it needed for the three ships it was building at the same time. Under time and cost pressures to build these ships, the company managers decided to sacrifice quality by purchasing low-grade rivets that were used on some parts of the *Titanic*. When making the trade-offs, it was unlikely that the company's management knew that they were purchasing something so substandard that their ship would sink if it hit an iceberg. Nonetheless, the trade-off proved disastrous.[8]

Trade-offs can be subsumed in the project triangle (see Figure 10.3), which highlights the importance of balancing scope, time, and cost. *Scope* may be divided into product scope (the detailed description of the product's quality, features, and functions), and project scope (the work required to deliver a product or service with the intended product scope). *Time* refers to the time required to complete the project, whereas *cost* encompasses all the resources required to carry out the project. In the tragic case of the *Titanic*, the managers were willing to trade off *quality* for lower-*cost* rivets that allowed them to build all three ships (*scope*) in a more timely fashion (*time*).

FIGURE 10.3 Project triangle.

---

[7] Ibid., 8.

[8] This research was described in J. H. McCarty and T. Foecke, *What Really Sank the Titanic* (2007) and is based on J. H. McCarty's dissertation.

In contrast, a successful balance of scope, time, and cost yields a high-quality project—one in which the needs and expectations of the users are met.

The tricky part of project management is successfully juggling these three elements while on a high wire, which amounts to shifting the triangle's base to keep it in balance. Changes in any one of the sides of the triangle affect one or both of the other sides. For example, if the project scope increases, more time and/or more resources (cost) are needed to do the additional work. This increase in scope after a project has begun is aptly called *scope creep*.

In most projects only two of these elements can be optimized, and the third must be adjusted to maintain balance. For example, a project with a fixed budget and fixed deadline may need to restrict scope. Likewise, a project that must be completed in a short period of time, with a large scope, may need flexibility in budget to obtain the resources necessary to meet the goal. It is important that the project stakeholders decide on the overriding "key success factor" (i.e., time, cost, or scope), though the project manager has the important responsibility of demonstrating to the stakeholders the impact on the project of selecting any of these. In the RPA case at the beginning of this chapter, scope was a key success factor that was managed inappropriately, ultimately resulting in a much longer time and much higher cost.

But the key success factor is only one metric to use when managing a project. Stakeholders are concerned about all facets of the project. Measuring and tracking progress is often done by tracking time (How are we doing compared to the schedule?), cost (How are we doing compared to the budget?), scope (Does the scope continue to be reasonable?), as well as resources (How much of our resources have we consumed so far?), quality (Is the quality of the output/deliverables at the level required for success?), and risks (How are we doing managing the risk associated with this project?).

A successful business project often begins with a well-written business case that spells out the components of the project. The business case clearly articulates the details of the project and argues for resources for the project, For example, UPS prioritizes projects on the strength of their business cases and financial metrics. They also make non-financial considerations such as weighing international projects more heavily to spur the company's growth.[9] The components of a business case and the financial metrics are discussed in Chapter 7.

The process used to develop the business case sets the foundation for the project itself. Therefore detailed planning, along with contingency planning, is an important part of project management. It is often in the planning phase that implementation issues, areas of concern, and gaps are first identified. Further, a strong business plan gives all members of the project team a reference document to help guide decisions and activities.

Project management software is often used to manage projects and keep track of key metrics. Programs such as Microsoft Project, Intuit Quickbase, Basecamp, and many others keep track of team members, deliverables, schedules, budgets, priorities, tasks, and other resources. Many of these programs provide a dashboard of key metrics to

[9] UPS, "IT Governance: The Key to Aligning Technology Initiatives with Business Direction," http://www.pressroom.ups.com (accessed on July 22, 2008).

help project managers quickly identify areas of concern or potentially critical issues that need attention.

The PMO

Although managing projects is not a new set of activities for management, it is a struggle for many to bring a project in on time, on budget, and within scope. Some organizations create a **Project Management Office (PMO)**, which is a department responsible for boosting efficiency, gathering expertise, and improving project delivery. A PMO is created to bring discipline to the project management activities within the enterprise. The Sarbanes–Oxley Act is also a driver because it forces companies to pay closer attention to project expenses and progress. Although companies may not immediately realize cost savings, the increased efficiencies and project discipline may eventually lead to cost savings.

PMOs can be expected to function in the following seven areas, according to *CIO Magazine*:

- Project support
- Project management process and methodology
- Training
- Project manager home base
- Internal consulting and mentoring
- Project management software tools and support
- Portfolio management (managing multiple projects)

The responsibilities of a PMO range widely, based on the preferences of the CIO under which the PMO typically falls. Sometimes the PMO is simply a clearinghouse for best practices in project management, and other times it is the organization that more formally manages all major projects. At risk management company Assurant Group, for example, a number of project managers work in the PMO under the direction of the COO. Using well-defined software development and project management methodologies, these PMO managers work with business managers to refine their project management efforts—from requirements definition to post-implementation audits. Within four years of the installation of its PMO, 97% of Assurant's projects were delivered on schedule and within budget.[10]

The structure of the PMO may vary, but usually mirrors the organization, culture, and bureaucracy of the CIO's organization. If the culture is rigid and strictly controlled, then the PMO likely has first-hand and significant oversight of projects.

Likewise, if the culture is collaborative and open, then the PMO likely plays a more coordinating role.

---

[10] M. Santosus, "Why You Need a Project Management Office (PMO)," *CIO Magazine*, http://www.cio.com/article/29887/Why_You_Need_a_Project_Management_Office_PMO_/1 (accessed on July 15, 2008).

► PROJECT ELEMENTS

Project work requires in-depth situational analyses and the organization of complex activities into often coincident sequences of discrete tasks. The outcomes of each activity must be tested and integrated into the larger process to produce the desired result. The number of variables affecting the performance of such work is potentially enormous.

Four elements essential for any project include (1) project management, (2) a project team, (3) a project cycle plan, and (4) a common project vocabulary. Project management includes the project sponsor who initiates the project and a **project manager** who makes sure that the entire project is executed appropriately and coordinated properly. A good project manager defines the project scope realistically, and then manages the project so that it can be completed on time and within budget.

The project team has members who work together to ensure that all parts of the project come together correctly and efficiently. The plan represents the methodology and schedule to be used by the team to execute the project. Finally, a common project vocabulary allows all those involved with the project to understand the project and communicate effectively.

It is essential to understand the interrelationships among these elements and with the project itself. Both a commitment to working together as a team and a common project vocabulary must permeate the management of a project throughout its life. The project plan consists of the sequential steps of organizing and tracking the work of the team. Finally, the project manager ensures the completion of work by team members at each step of the project cycle plan and as situational elements evolve throughout the project cycle.

Project Management

Two key players in project management are the sponsor and the manager. The project sponsor liaises between the project team and the other stakeholders. The sponsor is the project champion and works with the project manager in providing the leadership to accomplish project objectives. Often the sponsor is a very senior level executive in the firm and is someone who has influence with the key stakeholders and C-level team. It is the project sponsor that provides the financial resources for the project.

The project manager is central to the project. The project manager role is not an easy one since it requires a range of management skills to make the project successful. The challenge facing a project manager is to learn and apply these skills properly in the situations that require them. The skills include (1) identifying requirements of the systems to be delivered, (2) providing organizational integration by defining the team's structure, (3) assigning team members to work on the project, (4) managing risks and leveraging opportunities, (5) measuring the project's status, outcomes and exception to provide project control, (6) making the project visible to general management and other stakeholders, (7) measuring project status against plan, often using project management software, (8) taking corrective action when necessary to get the project back on track, and (9) project leadership. The first three of these skills are formulative; they require considerable planning and designing ability. The remaining skills are all about taking

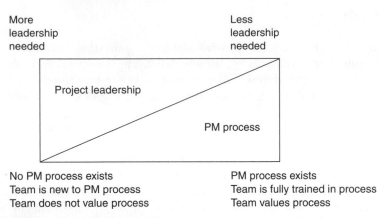

More
leadership
needed

Less
leadership
needed

Project leadership

PM process

No PM process exists
Team is new to PM process
Team does not value process

PM process exists
Team is fully trained in process
Team values process

FIGURE 10.4 Project leadership vs. project management (PM) process.

action and reacting. When a project deviates from its desired path, corrective action is needed to get the project back on track.[11]

Project leadership guides the other eight skills. Lack of leadership can result in unmotivated or confused people doing the wrong things and ultimately derailing the project. Strong project leaders skillfully manage team composition, reward systems, and other techniques to focus, align, and motivate team members. Figure 10.4 reflects the inverse relationship between the magnitude of the project leader's role and the experience and commitment of the team. In organizations with strong processes for project management and professionals trained for this activity, the need for aggressive project leadership is reduced.

A number of factors influence project managers and, ultimately their team's performance. These include organizational culture and socioeconomic influences. *Organizational culture influences* the leadership style of the project manager and the communication between team members. For example, a culture that rewards individual achievement over team participation may hinder a project team. Members might hoard information instead of sharing it. A leader who sets a good example for the team and who encourages teamwork has the opportunity to eliminate these barriers. *Socioeconomic influences* on projects include government and industry standards, globalization, and cultural issues. Trends external to the organization, such as changes in industry standards and regulations, usually affect all projects in varying degrees. Globalization trends create the need for projects that span time zones, oceans, and national boundaries, adding to already complex conditions. Cultural influences, such as economic, ethical, and religious factors, affect the relationships between people and between organizations. The project manager watches for these influences and makes decisions to minimize any negative impacts.

[11] Adapted from K. Forsberg, H. Mooz, and H. Cotterman, *Visualizing Project Management* (Hoboken, NJ: John Wiley & Sons, 1996).

Project Team

The project team consists of those people who work together to complete the project. Business teams often fail because members don't understand the nature of the work required to make their team effective. Teamwork begins by clearly defining the team's objectives and each member's role in achieving these objectives. Teams need to have norms about conduct, shared rewards, a shared understanding of roles, and team spirit. Project managers should leverage team member skills, knowledge, experiences, and capabilities when assigning the team members to complete specific activities on an as-needed basis. In addition to their completing team activities, team members also represent their departments and transmit information about their department to other team members. Such information sharing constitutes the first step toward building consensus on critical project issues that affect the entire organization. Thus, effective project managers use teamwork both to organize and apply human resources, to motivate an acceptance of change, and to collect and share information throughout the organization.

Project Cycle Plan

The project cycle plan organizes discrete project activities and sequences them in steps along a timeline so that the project delivers according to the requirements of customers and stakeholders. It identifies critical beginning and end dates and breaks the work spanning these dates into phases. Using the plan, the time and resources needed to complete the work based on the project's scope are identified, and tasks are assigned to team members. The general manager tracks the phases to coordinate the eventual transition from project to operational status, a process that culminates on the "go live" date. The project manager uses the phases to control the progress of work. He or she may establish control gates at various points along the way to verify that project work to date has met key requirements regarding cost, quality, and features. If it has not met these requirements, he or she can make corrections to the project plan and adjust the cycle as necessary.

The project cycle plan can be developed using various approaches and software tools. The three most common approaches are the project evaluation and review technique (PERT), critical path method (CPM), and Gantt chart. PERT identifies the tasks within the project, orders the tasks in a time sequence, identifies their interdependencies, and estimates the time required to complete the task. Tasks that must be performed individually and that, together, account for the total elapsed time of the project are considered to be critical tasks. Non-critical tasks are those for which some slack time can be built into the schedules without affecting the duration of the entire project. A PERT chart is shown in Figure 10.5.

CPM is a project planning and scheduling tool that is similar to PERT. Unlike PERT, CPM incorporates a capability for identifying relationships between costs and the completion date of a project, as well as the amount and value of resources that must be applied in alternative situations. The two approaches differ in terms of time estimates. PERT builds on broad estimates about the time needed to complete project tasks. It calculates the optimistic, most probable, and pessimistic time estimates for each task. In contrast, CPM assumes that all time requirements for completion of individual tasks are

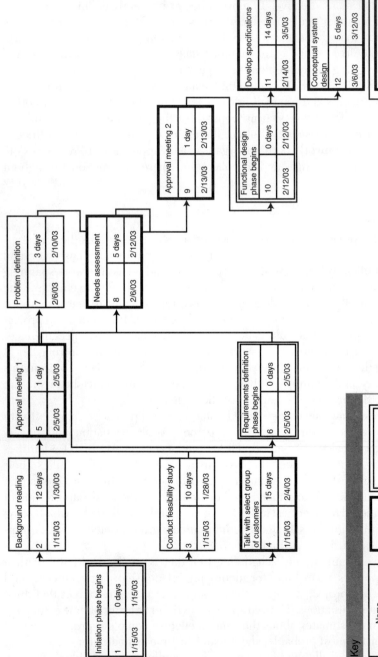

FIGURE 10.5 PERT chart.

relatively predictable. Because of these differences, CPM tends to be used on projects for which direct relationships can be established between time and resources (costs).

Gantt charts are a commonly used visual tool for displaying time relationships of project tasks and for monitoring the progress toward project completion. Gantt charts list project tasks. For each task, a bar indicates the relative amount of time expected to complete the task. Milestones (i.e., due dates) are noted with diamonds. At the start of the project, Gantt charts are useful for planning purposes. As the project progresses, the chart is modified to reflect the extent to which each task is completed at the time the project is monitored. A Gantt chart is displayed in Figure 10.6.

Figure 10.7 compares both a generic project cycle plan and the Project Management Institute's project life cycle with one for a typical high-tech commercial business and with one for an investigative task force. Notice that although each of these life cycles has unique phases, all can loosely be described by three major periods (shown at the top of the diagram): requirements period, development period, and production/distribution period.

Projects are all about change. They bring new products, services, or systems into organizations or make them available for the organizations' customers. These project deliverables need to be integrated into the organization's (or their customers') operations. Not surprisingly, the three major periods in the project life cycle correspond to Lewin's classic change model: unfreezing, changing, and refreezing. (This model was introduced in Chapter 4.) First, according to Lewin, people need to be given a motivation for change in the unfreezing stage. People don't want to change unless they see some reason for doing so. This is what happens in the requirements definition period when it is determined what needs to be changed and why. The project sponsor is often a key mover in providing answers to these questions. Then in the changing stage, people in the organization are made aware of what the change is and they receive training about how to take advantage of the new service, project, or system. In the project life cycle it is not possible for people to fully understand the change until the service, product, or system is designed or built in the development phase and they are then trained to use it. Those on the project team can better understand what the project deliverable is and why it was designed the way it was. Finally, the refreezing stage occurs when the organization helps the employees integrate the change into their normal way of working. This occurs in the deployment/dissemination period.

Common Project Vocabulary

The typical project teams include a variety of members from different backgrounds and parts of the organization. Often the team is made up of consultants who are new to the organization, a growing number of technical specialists, and business members. Each area of expertise represented by team members uses a different technical vocabulary. When used together in the team context, these different vocabularies make it difficult to carry on conversations, meetings, and correspondence. For example, a market research analyst and software analyst may use words unique to their specialty or attach different meanings to the same words.

To avoid misunderstandings, project team members need to commit to a consistent meaning for terms used on their project. After agreeing on definitions and common

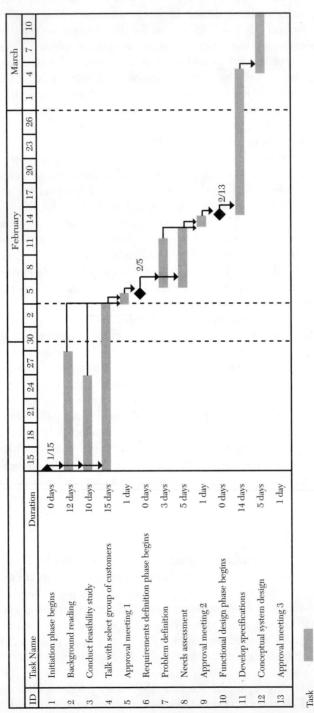

FIGURE 10.6 Gantt chart.

Requirements Definition Period			Production Period					Deployment/ Dissemination Period		

Investigation Task Force

User requirement definition	Research concept definition	Information use specification	Collection planning phase	Collection and analysis phase			Draft report phase	Publication phase		Distribution phase

Typical High-Tech Commercial Business

Product requirements phase	Product definition phase	Product proposal phase	Product development phase	Engineer model phase	Internal test phase	External test phase	Production phase	Manufacturing sales & support phase

Generic Project Cycle Template

User requirement definition phase	Concept definition phase	System specification phase	Acqui-sition planning phase	Source selection phase	Development phase	Verification phase	Deploy-ment or produc-tion phase	Operations/ maintenance or sales/ support phase	Deacti-vate phase

Project Management Institute Process Groups in a Project Life Cycle

Initiating	Planning	Executing	Monitoring and Controlling	Closing

FIGURE 10.7 Project cycle template.
Source: Adapted from K. Forsberg, H. Mooz, and H. Cotterman, *Visualizing Project Management* (Hoboken, NJ: John Wiley & Sons, 1996). Used with permission.

meanings, the project team should record and explain the terms in its own common project vocabulary. The common project vocabulary includes many terms and meanings that are unfamiliar to the general manager and the team's other business members. To improve their communications with general managers, users, and other non-technical people, technical people should limit their use of acronyms and cryptic words and should strive to place only the most critical ones in the common project vocabulary. Good management of the common project vocabulary, along with the project management, project team, and project life cycle are all essential to project success.

▶ IT PROJECTS

IT projects are a specific type of business project. Much research has been done to observe, understand, and help managers increase chances of IT project success. One industry saying is that there is no such thing as an IT project; all projects are really business projects involving varying degrees of IT. Sometimes, managing the IT compo-nent of a project is referred to separately as an IT project, not only for simplicity, but also because the business world perceives that managing an IT project is somehow different from managing any other type of project. However, projects done by the IT department

---

Geographic Lens: Allocating Software Development Projects to Available Sites Around the Globe

Increasingly software development is being conducted around the globe to take advantage of distributed talent, cheaper labor costs, and "follow the sun" development strategies. Multinational companies and outsourcing providers increasingly are faced with the problem of how to allocate the software development projects to development teams in different parts of the globe. Steffan Zimmermann, Arne Katzmarzik, and Dennis Kundisch have proposed an approach that relies on Modern Portfolio Theory. Their approach is based on the premise that companies should look at the expected costs, risks, and interdependencies among projects and sites when making software development site decisions. Transaction costs and productivity differences based on location affect the expected costs at the different sites. Variations in risks among the sites can be attributed to geographical, legal, and cultural differences. Interdependencies arise when a number of projects are under way at the same time in the same enterprise or outsourcing provider. The coauthors developed a software development site selection model using Modern Portfolio Theory and tested the model on an actual business case. They believe that use of the model can reduce project costs and risk across the portfolio.

Source: S. Zimmermann, A. Katzmarzik, and D. Kundisch, "IT Sourcing Portfolio Management for IT Services Providers—An Approach for Using Modern Portfolio Theory to Allocate Software Development Projects to Available Sites," *The DATA BASE for Advances in Information Systems* (2012), 43(10), 2445.

---

typically include an associated business case; and even though the project owner may be an IT person, mounting evidence indicates that IT projects are just business projects involving significant amounts of technology. The more complex the IT aspect of the project is, the higher is the risk of failure of the project.

IT projects are difficult to estimate, despite the increasing amount of attention given to mastering this task. Like the case of the RPA's Single Payment Scheme most software projects fail to meet their schedules and budgets. Managers attribute that failure to poor estimating techniques, poorly monitored progress protocols, and the idea that schedule slippage can be solved by simply adding additional people.[12] Not only does this assume that people and months are interchangeable, but also if the project is off schedule, it may be that the project was incorrectly designed in the first place, and putting additional people on the project just hastens the process to an inappropriate end.

Many projects are measured in terms of function points, or the functional requirements of the software product, which can be estimated earlier than total lines of code. Others are measured in "man-months," the most common unit for discussing the size of a project. For example, a project that takes 100 man-months means that it will take one person 100 months to do the work, or 100 people can do it in a month.

---

[12] Frederick Brooks, *The Mythical Man-Month: Essays on Software Engineering* (Reading, MA: Addison-Wesley, 1982).

A recent study found that managing projects using the man-months metric was linked to more underperforming projects than managing projects using any other metric of size (i.e., budget, duration, team size).[13] Man-months may be a poor metric for project management because some projects cannot be sped up with additional people. An analogy is that of pregnancy. It takes one woman nine months to carry a baby, and putting nine people on the job for one month cannot speed up that process. Software systems often involve highly interactive, complex sets of tasks that rely on each other to make a completed system. Further, adding people means that more communication is needed to coordinate all the team members' activities. In sum, additional people can speed up the process in some cases, but most projects cannot be made more efficient simply by adding labor. Often, adding people to a late project only makes the project later.[14]

▶ IT PROJECT DEVELOPMENT METHODOLOGIES AND APPROACHES

The choice of development methodologies and managerial influences also distinguish IT projects from other projects. The general manager needs to understand the issues specific to the IT aspects of projects to select the right management tools for the particular challenges presented in such projects. The **systems development life cycle (SDLC)** is a traditional tool for developing information systems, or for implementing software developed by an outsourcing provider or software developer. Many steps in the SDLC are used by other methodologies, although not to the extent found in the SDLC. For example most other methodologies, to some extent, try to determine user needs and test the new system, even though these other methodologies don't perform all of the other steps in the SDLC. Thus, this chapter provides greater detail on SDLC than on the other methodologies. The SDLC discussion is followed by a short description of two key iterative approaches—agile programming and prototyping.

Systems Development Life Cycle

Systems development is the set of activities used to create an IS. The SDLC typically refers to the process of designing and delivering the entire system. Although the system includes the hardware, software, networking, and data (as discussed in Chapter 6), the SDLC generally is used in one of two distinct ways. On the one hand, SDLC is the general project plan of all the activities that must take place for the entire system to be put into operation, including the analysis and feasibility study, the development or acquisition of components, the implementation activities, the maintenance activities, and the retirement activities. In the context of an information system, however, SDLC can refer to a highly structured, disciplined, and formal process for design and development of system software. In either view, the SDLC is grounded on the systems approach and allows the developer to focus on system goals and trade-offs.

---

[13] Sauer et al., "The Impact of Size and Volatility on IT Project Performance."

[14] Brooks, *The Mythical Man-Month*.

SDLC refers to a process in which the phases of the project are well documented, milestones are clearly identified, and all individuals involved in the project fully understand what exactly the project consists of and when deliverables are to be made. This approach is much more structured than other development approaches, such as agile programming or prototyping. However, despite being a highly structured approach, no single well-accepted SDLC process exists.

For any specific organization, and for a specific project, the actual tasks under each phase may vary. In addition, the checkpoints, metrics, and documentation may vary somewhat. SDLC typically consists of seven phases (see Figure 10.8). Each phase is carefully planned and documented. The first phase, project initiation, is where it is first considered, scoped, and carefully planned. Approval is acquired before proceeding to the second phase, after it is determined that the project is technically, operationally, and financially feasible. The second phase is the requirements definition phase, where the problem is defined and needs and prerequisites are assessed and documented. Often the requirements are determined by studying the existing systems. Again, approval is obtained before proceeding. The third phase involves the functional design, at which point the specifications are discussed and documented. The system is designed in conceptual terms. Approval is obtained on the functional specifications before technical design is begun.

At phase four, functional specifications are translated into a technical design, and construction takes place. Here the system is actually built. If the system is acquired, it is at this point that it is customized as needed for the business environment. Following construction is the verification phase, where multiple levels of testing are performed to ensure system usability, security, and operability. The tests verify that the system meets the specifications for which it is designed.

After acceptance testing, project sign-off and approval signal that the system is acceptable to the users, and implementation, the sixth phase, begins. This phase is the "cutover" where the new system is put in operation and all links are established. Cutover may be performed in several ways: The old system may run alongside the new system (**parallel conversion**), the old system may stop running as soon as the new system is installed (**direct cutover**), or the new system may be installed in stages across locations, or in phases. The safest way to convert from an old system to a new system is parallel conversion because if the new system fails, users easily can revert to the old system. The riskiest approach is direct cutover because there is no backup system to turn to in the event of problems with the new system. Usually direct cutover is reserved from smaller, less-critical systems or for systems that were not previously available. Another instance when direct cutover was a good idea was Dagen H (*Högertrafik* day) on September 3, 1967, when Swedish drivers were to change from driving on the left-hand to the right-hand side of the road. On Dagen H, all vehicles on the road had to come to a complete stop at 04:50, then carefully change to the right-hand side of the road and stop again before being allowed to proceed at 05:00.[15]

Finally, the system enters the maintenance and review phase, where the system goes into operation and an evaluation is conducted to ensure it continues to meet the needs

[15] H. Dagen, Wikipedia, http://en.wikipedia.org/wiki/Dagen_H.

Phase	Description	Sample Activities
Initiation and feasibility	Project is begun with a formal initiation and overall project is understood by IS and user/customers.	Document project objectives, scope, benefits, assumptions, constraints, estimated costs and schedule, and user commitment mechanisms; plan for human resources, communication, risk management, and quality.
Requirements definition	The system specifications are identified and documented.	Define business functionality; review existing systems; identify current problems and issues; identify and prioritize user requirements; identify potential solutions; develop user acceptance plan, user documentation needs, and user training strategy.
Functional design	The system is designed.	Complete a detailed analysis of new system including entity-relationship diagrams, data-flow diagrams, and functional design diagrams; define security needs; revise system architecture; identify standards, define systems acceptance criteria; define test scenarios; revise implementation strategy; freeze design.
Technical design and construction	The system is built or a purchased system is customized and implemented.	Finalize architecture, technical issues, standards and data needs; complete technical definition of data access, programming flows, interfaces, special needs, inter-system processing, conversion strategy, and test plans; construct system; monitor and control the development process; revise schedule, plan, and costs, as necessary.
Verification	The system is reviewed to make sure it meets specifications and requirements.	Finalize verification testing, user testing, security testing, error handling procedures designed, end-user training, documentation, and support.
Implementation	The system is brought up for use.	Put system into production environment; establish security procedures; deliver user documentation; execute training and complete monitoring of system.
Maintenance and review	The system is maintained and repaired as needed throughout its lifetime.	Run system; conduct user review and evaluation, and internal review and evaluation; check metrics to ensure usability, reliability, utility, cost, satisfaction, business value, etc.; ensure contract closure.

FIGURE 10.8 Systems development life cycle (SDLC) phases.

for which it was designed. The system development project is evaluated using post-project feedback (sometimes called post-implementation audit) from all involved in the project. Post-project feedback brings closure to the project by identifying what went right and what could be done better next time. Maintenance and enhancements are conducted on the system until it is decided that a new system should be developed and the SDLC begins anew. The maintenance and review phase is typically the longest phase of the life cycle.

Agile Development

Several problems arise with using traditional SDLC methodology for current IT projects. First, many systems projects fail to meet objectives, even with the structure of SDLC. The primary reason is often because the skills needed to estimate costs and schedules are difficult to obtain, and each project is often so unique that previous experience may not provide the skills needed for the current project. Second, even though objectives that were specified for the system were met, those objectives may reflect a scope that is too broad or too narrow. Thus, the problem the system was designed to solve may still exist, or the opportunity that it was to capitalize on may not be appropriately leveraged. Third, organizations need to respond quickly because of the dynamic nature of the business environment. Not enough time is available to adequately do each step of the SDLC for each IT project. Newer methodologies designed to address these concerns use an iterative approach, as shown in Figure 10.9.

One of the dangers developers face is expecting a predictable development process when in reality it's not predictable at all. In response to this challenge, **agile development** methodologies are being championed. These include XP (Extreme Programming), Crystal, Scrum, Feature-Driven Development, and Dynamic System Development Method (DSDM). To deal with unpredictability, agile methodologies tend to be people- rather than process-oriented. They adapt to changing requirements by iteratively developing systems in small stages and then testing the new code extensively. The mantra for agile programming is "Code a little; test a little." Some agile methodologies build on existing methodologies. For example, DSDM is an extension of Rapid Application Development (RAD) used in the United Kingdom that draws on the underlying principles of active user interaction, frequent deliveries, and empowered teams. It incorporates a project planning technique that divides the

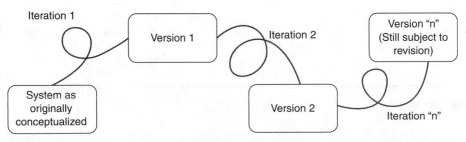

FIGURE 10.9 Iterative approach to systems development.

schedule into a number of separate time periods (timeboxes), with each part having its own deliverables, deadline, and budget. DSDM is based on four types of iterations: study (business and feasibility), functional model, design and build, and implementation. These iterations occur (and reoccur) in cycles of between two and six weeks. In contrast is XP, a more prescriptive agile methodology that revolves around 12 practices, including pair programming, test-driven development, simple design, and small releases.[16]

While it allows speedy development and creates happy customers, there are some downsides to agile development. For large projects, it is difficult to estimate the effort that will be required. Further in the rush to get the project completed, designing and documentation might be underemphasized. Further, an agile development project can easily get off track if the customer representatives are not clear about what final outcome that they want.

Prototyping

Another iterative approach is prototyping. **Prototyping** is a type of evolutionary development, the method of building systems where developers get the general idea of what is needed by the users, and then build a fast, high-level version of the system at the beginning of the project. The idea of prototyping is to quickly get a version of the software in the hands of the users and to jointly evolve the system through a series of iterative cycles of design. In this way, the system is done either when the users are happy with the design or when the system is proven impossible, too costly, or too complex. Some IS groups use prototyping as a methodology by itself because users are involved in the development much more closely than is possible with the traditional SDLC process. Users see the day-to-day growth of the system and contribute frequently to the development process. In other cases prototyping is used as a phase in the SDLC to capture project requirements. Through this iterative process, the system requirements usually are made clear.

There are several drawbacks to prototyping. First, documentation may be more difficult to write as the system evolves. Second, users often do not understand that a final prototype may not be scalable to an operational version of the system without additional costs and organizational commitments. Once users see a working model, they typically assume the work is also almost done, which is not usually the case. An operational version of the system needs to be developed. However, an operational version may be difficult to complete because the user is unwilling to give up a system that is up and running, and they often have unrealistic expectations about the amount of work involved in creating an operational version. This reluctance leads to the fourth drawback. Because it may be nearly impossible to definitively say when the prototype is done, the prototyping development process may be difficult to manage. Fifth, since it is difficult to integrate across a broad range of requirements, this approach is really only suited for "quick-and-dirty" types of systems. Developers should rely on a more structured approach such as the SDLC for extremely large and complex systems. Finally, because of the speed of development, system design flaws may be more prevalent in this approach, and the

---

[16] Kent Beck, *Extreme Programming Explained: Embrace Change* (Reading, MA: Addison-Wesley Longman, Inc., 1999).

Methodology	Advantages	Disadvantages
SDLC	• Structured approach with mile-stones and approvals for each phase • Uses system approach • Focuses on goals and trade-offs • Emphasizes documentation • Requires user sign-offs	• Systems often fail to meet objectives • Needed skills are often difficult to obtain • Scope may be defined too broadly or too narrowly • Very time consuming
Agile Development	• Good for adapting to changing requirements • Good for understanding and responding to changing user requirements • Allows face-to-face communication and continuous inputs from users • Speeds up development process • Users like it	• Hard to estimate system deliverables at start of project • Under-emphasis of designing and documentation • Easy to get project off-track if user not clear about what the final outcome should be
Prototyping	• Improved user communications • Users like it • Speeds up development process • Good for eliciting system requirements • Provides a tangible model to serve as basis for production version	• Often under-documented • Not designed to be an operational version • Often creates unrealistic expectations • Difficult-to-manage development process • Integration often difficult • Design flaws more prevalent than in SDLC • Often hard to maintain

FIGURE 10.10 Comparison of IT development methodologies.

system may be harder to maintain than when the system is developed using the SDLC. The advantages and disadvantages of the SDLC, agile development, and prototyping are summarized in Figure 10.10.

Other Development Methodologies and Approaches

A variety of other methodologies and approaches exist. These include rapid applications development (RAD), joint applications development (JAD), Object-Oriented analysis, design, and development, and the open sourcing approach.

Rapid Applications Development and Joint Applications Development

Rapid applications development (RAD) is similar to prototyping in that it is an interactive process, in which tools are used to drastically speed up the development process. RAD systems typically have tools for developing the user interface—called the graphical user interface (GUI)—reusable code, code generation, and programming language testing and debugging. These tools make it easy for the developer to build a library of standard sets of code (sometimes called objects) that can easily be used (and reused) in multiple applications. Similarly, RAD systems typically have the ability to allow the developer to simply "drag and drop" objects into the design, and the RAD system automatically writes the code necessary to include that functionality. Finally, the system includes a set of tools to create, test, and debug the programs written in the pure programming language. However, one must remember that "A fool with a tool is still a fool." RAD is more than just using advance systems development tools. Rather, it is about making systems developers work more effectively.

RAD is commonly used for developing user interfaces and rewriting legacy applications. It may incorporate prototyping to involve users early and actively in the design process. Although RAD is an approach that works well in the increasingly dynamic environment of systems developers, it does have some drawbacks. Sometimes basic principles of software development (e.g., programming standards, documentation, data-naming standards, backup and recovery) are overlooked in the race to finish the project. Also, the process may be so speedy that requirements are frozen too early.[17] As a result, systems developed using RAD may lack quality.

Joint applications development (JAD) is a version of RAD or prototyping in which users are more integrally involved, as a group, with the entire development process up to and, in some cases, including coding. JAD uses a group approach to elicit requirements in a complete manner. Interviewing groups of users saves interviewing and data collection time, but it can be expensive in terms of the travel and living expenses needed to get the participants together.

Object-Oriented Development

Object-oriented development is becoming increasingly popular as a way to avoid the pitfalls of procedural methodologies. Object-oriented development, unlike more traditional development using the SDLC, builds on the concept of objects. An **object** encapsulates both the data stored about an entity and the operations that manipulate that data. A program developed using an object orientation is basically a collection of objects. The object orientation makes it easier for developers to think in terms of reusable components. Using existing components can save programming time. Such component-based development, however, assumes that the components have been saved in a repository and can be retrieved when needed. It also assumes that the components in the programs in newly developed information systems can communicate with one another.

Open Sourcing Approach

Linux, the brainchild of Linus Torvalds, is a world-class operating system created from part-time hacking by several thousand developers scattered all over the planet and

[17] Joey F. George, "The Origins of Software: Acquiring Systems at the End of the Century," in *Framing the Domains of IT Management*, R. Zmud (ed.) (Cincinnati, OH: Pinnaflex Education Resources, 2000).

connected only by the Internet. This system was built using a development approach called **open sourcing**, or the process of building and improving "free" software by an Internet community. The brilliance of Linux was that Torvalds took a very powerful, but proprietary operating system, Unix, and rewrote it to make it available as open source. In fact, the kernel of Linux contains the statement, "Linux is a Unix clone written from scratch by Linus Torvalds with assistance from a loosely-knit team of hackers across the Net." Torvalds managed the development process by releasing early and often, delegating as much as possible, being open to new ideas, and archiving and managing the various versions of the software.

Eric Raymond, the author of *The Cathedral and the Bazaar*, suggests that the Linux community resembles a great bazaar of differing agendas and approaches (with submissions from *anyone*) out of which a coherent and stable system emerged. This development approach is in contrast to cathedrals, in which software is carefully crafted by company employees working in isolation. The most frequently cited example of a cathedral is Microsoft, a company known, if not ridiculed, for espousing a proprietary approach to software development.[18]

Software is **open source software (OSS)** if it is released under a license approved by the Open Source Initiative (OSI). The most widely used OSI license is the GNU general public license (GPL), which is premised on the concept of free software. *Free software* offers the following freedoms for the software users:[19]

- The freedom to run the program, for any purpose.
- The freedom to study how the program works, and adapt it to your needs. Access to the source code is a precondition for this.
- The freedom to distribute copies so that you can help your neighbor.
- The freedom to improve and release your improvements to the public, so that the whole community benefits. Access to source code is a precondition for this.

A user who modifies the software must observe the rule of *copyleft*, which stipulates that the user cannot add restrictions to deny other people their central freedoms regarding the free software.

Open sourcing is a movement that offers a speedy way to develop software. Further, because it is made available to a whole community, testing is widespread. Finally, its price is always right—it is free. However, a number of managerial issues are associated with its use in a business organization.

- *Preservation of intellectual property.* The software is open to the whole community. It cannot be sold, and its use cannot be restricted. So the community is the "owner" of the code. Yet, how are the contributions of individuals recognized?

---

[18] Eric S. Raymond, "The Cathedral and the Bazaar," http://www.catb.org/~esr/writings/cathedral-bazaar/cathedral-bazaar/ (accessed on June 4, 2012).

[19] GNU Project—Free Software Foundation, "The Free Software Definition," http://www.gnu.org/philosophy/free-sw.html (accessed on February 27, 2002).

Social Business Lens: Mashups

Social IT applications are often designed with an open architecture to make them easy to adapt. One way organizations take advantage of this feature and create new applications is called *mashups*. **Mashups** are Web apps that combine other apps to create a new app, data, functionality, and even interfaces. The goal of a mashup is to be able to create new applications quickly using existing applications, data, and infrastructure. Some mashups are used internally within a firm, but others are set up on the Web and become a new app.

An example of a mashup is Zillow.com, the real-estate Web site. It has relationship with numerous data providers across the country and accesses public records, which they use in their service. But in addition, Zillow uses Google's street-views, and shows the Google logo in that window. It also uses home data from walkscore.com, and again gives credit to that site for that data. In 2012, Zillow launched a social home-shopping site, called Neighborhood Advice that links the users' search for a home with information about their community of friends on Facebook. Zillow then displays circles on a map to indicate where the user's friends live or have checked in, enabling the user to locate areas where they have many, or few, friends.

- *Updating and maintaining open source code.* A strength of the open source movement is that it is open to the manipulation of members of an entire community. That very strength makes it difficult to channel the updating and maintenance of code.

- *Competitive advantage.* Because the code is available to all, a company would not want to open-source a system that it hopes can give it a competitive advantage.

- *Tech support.* The code may be free, but technical support usually isn't. Users of a system that was open-sourced must still be trained and supported.

- *Standards.* Standards are open. Yet in a technical world that is filled with incompatible standards, open sourcing may be unable to charter a viable strategy for selecting and using standards.

Applications written following the open source standards were initially rejected by corporate IT organizations. Executives wondered how code that was free, open, and available to all could be counted on to support critical business applications. However, a number of case studies recorded by OSI highlight the benefits of open source code. In addition to Linux, *Mozilla* (a popular Web browser core), *Apache* (Web server), *PERL* (Web scripting language) *OpenOffice* (a Sun Microsystems-originated set of office applications that support the Microsoft Office suite formats), and *PNG* (graphics file format) are all examples of very popular software that is based on open source. Advances in the applications available on the Internet, particularly many of the Web 2.0 applications that are making their way slowly into the corporate infrastructure, are open sourced. Corporations are learning to manage the open-source process by more clearly stating their requirements and interfacing with developers on what are typically their non-core systems.

Many good references are available for systems development, but further detail is beyond the scope of this text. The interested general manager is referred to a more detailed systems development text for a deeper understanding of this critical IS process.

▶ MANAGING IT PROJECT RISK

IT projects are often distinguished from many non-IT projects on the basis of their high levels of risk. Although every manager has an innate understanding of what risk is, there is little consensus as to the definition of risk. Risk is perceived as the possibility of additional cost or loss due to the choice of alternative. Some alternatives have a lower associated risk than others. Risk can be quantified by assigning a probability of occurrence and a financial consequence to each alternative. We consider project risk to be a function of complexity, clarity, and size.[20]

Complexity

The first determinant of risk on an IT project is the complexity level, or the extent of difficulty and interdependent components, of the project. Several factors contribute to greater complexity in IT projects. The first is the sheer pace of technological change. The increasing numbers of products and technologies affecting the marketplace cause rapidly changing views of any firm's future business situation. For example, introducing a new development approach such as open sourcing creates significantly different ideas in people's minds about the future direction of IT development in the firm. Such uncertainty can make it difficult for project team members to identify and agree on common goals. This fast rate of change also creates new vocabularies to learn as technologies are implemented, which can undermine effective communication.

The development of more complex technologies accelerates the trend toward increased specialization among members of a project team and multiplies the number of interdependencies that must be tracked in project management. Team members must be trained to work on the new technologies. More subprojects must be managed, which, in turn, means developing a corresponding number of interfaces to integrate the pieces (i.e., subprojects) back into a whole.

High complexity played a part in the 2008 failure at Heathrow's Terminal 5.[21] The terminal project involved 180 IT suppliers and over 160 IT systems. There are more than 9,000 devices connected to it along with another 2,100 PCs. The system includes 175 lifts (elevators), 131 escalators, and 18 km of conveyor belts for baggage handling. According to the British Airports Authority (BAA), "It has taken 400,000 man-hours of software engineering just to develop the complex system, and coding is set to continue even after

---

[20] The ideas were derived from this source, but we used different names and expanded the application: L. Applegate, F. W. McFarlan, and J. L. McKenney, *Corporate Information Systems Management: Text and Cases*, 5th ed. (Boston, MA: Irwin/McGraw-Hill, 1999).

[21] Adapted from Michael Krigsman, blogs.zdnet.com/projectfailures/?p=681 (accessed on July 28, 2008).

installation begins." The British Airways CIO was quoted as saying that "even the construction of T5 involved creating a small town with a full telecommunications network for the construction workers, merely to enable the terminal to be built."[22] But the failure in 2008 resulted in cancelled flights, lost baggage, substantial delays and frustrated customers and employees. According to blogger Michael Krigsman, "the systems incorporated in T5 severely taxed BA's planning, testing and deployment capabilities."[23]

Complexity can be determined once the context of the project has been established. Consider the hypothetical case of a manager given six months and $500,000 to build a corporate Web site to sell products directly to customers. Questions that might be used to build context for this case include the following:

- How many products will this Web site sell?
- Will this site support global, national, regional, or local sales?
- How will this sales process interface with the existing customer fulfillment process?
- Does the company possess the technical expertise in-house to build the site?
- What other corporate systems and processes will this project affect?
- How and when will these other systems be coordinated?

Clarity

A project is more risky if it is hard to define. Clarity is concerned with the ability to define the requirements of the system. A project has low clarity if the users cannot easily state their needs or define what they want from the system. The project also has low clarity if user demands for the system or regulations that guide the structure of the system change considerably over the life of a project. A project with high clarity is one in which the systems requirements do not change and can be easily documented. Purchasing a scheduling software package that applies scheduling rules across a broad range of organizations would be an example of a high-clarity project for most firms.

Size

Size also plays a big role in project risk. All other things being equal, big projects are riskier than smaller ones. A project can be considered big if it has the following characteristics:

- Large budget relative to other budgets in the organization
- Large number of team members (and hence reflecting a large number of man-months)

---

[22] CIO UK, www.cio.co.uk/concern/change/news/index.cfm?articleid=2487&pn=2. (accessed on April 11, 2012).

[23] Michael Krigsman, "IT failure at Heathrow T5: What really happened" (April 7, 2008), blogs.zdnet.com/projectfailures/?p=681 (accessed on August 1, 2008).

- Large number of organizational units involved in the project
- Large number of programs/components
- Large number of function points
- Large number of source lines of code (i.e., the number of lines of code in the source file of the software product)

It is important to consider the relative size. At a small company with an average project budget of $30,000, $90,000 would be a large project. However, to a major corporation that just spent $2 million implementing an ERP, a $90,000 budget would be peanuts.

Managing Project Risk Level

The IS project management literature usually views risk management as a two-stage process: first the risk is assessed and then actions are taken to control it.[24] The project's complexity, clarity, and size determine its risk. Varying levels of these three determinants differentially affect the amount of project risk. At one extreme, large, highly complex projects that are low in clarity are extremely risky. In contrast, small projects that are low in complexity and high in clarity are low risk. Everything else is somewhere in between.

The level of risk determines how formal the project management system and detailed the planning should be. When it is difficult to estimate how long or how much a project will cost because it is so complex or what should be done because its clarity is so low, using formal management practices or planning is inappropriate. A high level of planning is not only almost impossible in these circumstances because of the uncertainty surrounding the project, but it also makes it difficult to adapt to external changes that are bound to occur. On the other hand, formal planning tools may be useful in low-risk projects because they can help structure the sequence of tasks as well as provide realistic cost and time targets.[25]

Managing the Complexity Aspects of Project Risk

The more complex the project, the greater is the risk. The increasing dependence on IT in all aspects of business means that managing the risk level of an IT project is critical to a general manager's job. Organizations increasingly embed IT deeper into their business processes, raising efficiency but also increasing risk. Many companies now rely entirely on IT for their revenue-generating processes, whether the process uses the Internet or not. For example, airlines are dependent on IT for generating reservations and ultimately sales. If the reservation system goes down, that is, if it fails, agents simply cannot sell tickets. In addition, even though the airplanes technically can fly if the reservation system fails, the airline cannot manage seat assignments, baggage, or passenger loads without the reservation system. In short, the airline would have to stop doing business should its reservation system fail. That type of dependence on IT

[24] R. Schmidt, K. Lyytinen, M. Keil, and P. Cule, "Identifying Software Project Risks: An International Delphi Study," *Journal of Management Information Systems* (Spring 2001), 17(4), 5–36.

[25] H. Barki, S. Rivard, and J. Talbot, "An Integrative Contingency Model of Software Project Risk Management," *Journal of Management Information Systems* (Spring 2001), 17(4), 37–69.

raises the risk levels associated with adding or changing the system. The manager may adopt several strategies in dealing with complexity, including leveraging the technical skills of the team, relying on consultants to help deal with project complexity, and other internal integration strategies.

Leveraging the Technical Skills of the Team

When a project is complex, it is helpful to have a project manager with experience in similar situations, or who can translate experiences in many different situations to this new complex one. For projects high in complexity, it also helps to have team members with significant work experience, especially if it is related.

Relying on Consultants and Vendors

Few organizations develop or maintain the in-house capabilities they need to complete complex IT projects. Risk-averse managers want people who possess crucial IT knowledge and skills. Often that skill set can be attained only from previous experience on similar IT projects. Such people are easier to find at consulting firms because consultants' work is primarily project based. Consulting firms rely on processes that develop the knowledge and experience of their professionals. Thus, managers often choose to "lease" effective IT team skills rather than try to build them within their own people. However, the project manager must balance the benefits achieved from bringing in outsiders with the costs of not developing that skill set in house. When the project is over and the consultants leave, will the organization be able to manage without them? Having too many outsiders on a team also makes alignment more difficult. Outsiders may have different objectives, such as selling more business, or learning new skills, which might conflict with the project manager's goal of completing the project.

Integrating Within the Organization

Highly complex projects require good communication among the team members, which helps them to operate as an integrated unit. Ways of increasing internal integration include holding frequent team meetings, documenting critical project decisions, and conducting regular technical status reviews.[26] These approaches ensure that all team members are "on the same page" and are aware of project requirements and milestones.

Managing Clarity Aspects of Project Risk

When a project has low clarity, project managers need to rely more heavily on the users to define system requirements. It means managing project stakeholders and sustaining commitment to projects.

Managing Project Stakeholders

A project's low clarity may be the result of its multiple stakeholders' conflicting needs and expectations for the system. The project manager must balance the goals of the various project stakeholders to achieve desired project outcomes. The project manager

---

[26] Barki et al., "An Integrative Contingency Model of Software Project Risk Management"; and Applegate et al., *Corporate Information Systems Management*.

may also need to specifically manage stakeholders. It is not always a simple task to identify project stakeholders. They may be employees, managers, users, other departments, or even customers. However, failure to manage these stakeholders can lead to costly mistakes later in the project if a particular group is not supportive of the project.

Managing the expectations and needs of stakeholders often involves both the project manager and the general manager. Project sponsors are especially critical for IT projects with organizational change components. Sponsors use their power and influence to remove project barriers by gathering support from various social and political groups both inside and outside the organization. They often prove to be valuable when participating in communication efforts to build the visibility of the project.

Pulling the Plug

These various risk management strategies are designed to turn potentially troubled projects into successful ones. Often projects in trouble persist long after they should be abandoned. Research shows that the amount of money already spent on a project biases managers toward continuing to fund the project, even if its prospects for success are questionable.[27]

Other factors can also enter in the decision to keep projects too long. For example, when the penalties for failure within an organization are high, project teams are often willing to go to great lengths to ensure that their project persists, even if it means extending resources. Also, a propensity for taking risks or an emotional attachment to the project by powerful individuals within the organization can contribute to a troubled project continuing well beyond reasonable time limits. A recent global survey found that ultimately the plug is pulled on approximately one project out of five.[28]

Sustaining Commitment to Projects

An important way to increase the likelihood of project success is to gain commitment from stakeholders and to sustain that commitment throughout the life of the project. Research indicates four primary types of determinants of commitment to projects (see Figure 10.11).[29] They include project determinants, psychological determinants, social determinants, and organizational determinants. Project teams often focus on only the project factors, ignoring the other three types because of their complexity.

---

[27] M. Keil, et al., "A Cross-Cultural Study on Escalation of Commitment Behavior in Software Projects," *MIS Quarterly* (2000), 24(2), 299–325.

[28] Governance Institute, Global Status Report on the Governance of Enterprise IT (GEIT) (2011), 7, http://www.isaca.org/Knowledge-Center/Research/Documents/Global-Status-Report-GEIT-10Jan2011-Research.pdf (accessed on February 27, 2011).

[29] See, for example, Mark Keil, "Pulling the Plug: Software Project Management and the Problem of Project Escalation," *MIS Quarterly* (December 1995), 19(4), 421–447; and Michael Newman and Rajiv Sabherwal, "Determinants of Commitment to Information Systems Development: A Longitudinal Investigation," *MIS Quarterly* (March 1996), 20(1), 23–54.

Determinant	Description	Example
Project	Objective attributes of the project such as cost, benefits, expected difficulty, and duration.	Projects are more likely to have higher commitment if they involve a large potential payoff.
Psychological	Factors managers use to convince themselves things are not so bad, such as previous experience, personal responsibility for outcome, and biases.	Projects are more likely to have higher commitment when there is a previous history of success.
Social	Elements of the various groups involved in the process, such as rivalry, norms for consistency, and need for external validation.	Projects are more likely to have higher commitment when external stakeholders have been publicly led to believe the project will be successful.
Organizational	Structural attributes of the organization, such as political support, and alignment with values and goals.	Projects are more likely to have higher commitment when there is strong political support from executive levels.

FIGURE 10.11 Determinants of commitment for IT projects.
Sources: Adapted from Mark Keil, "Pulling the Plug: Software Project Management and the Problem of Project Escalation," *MIS Quarterly* (December 1995); and Michael Newman and Rajiv Sabherwal, "Determinants of Commitment to Information Systems Development: A Longitudinal Investigation," *MIS Quarterly* (March 1996).

By identifying how these factors are manifested in an organizational project, managers can use tactics to ensure a sustained commitment. For example, to maintain commitment, a project team might continually remind stakeholders of the benefits to be gained from completion of this project. Likewise, assigning the right project champion the task of selling the project to all levels of the organization can maintain commitment. Other strategies to encourage stakeholder, especially user, buy-in so that they can help clarify project requirements are making a user or the project sponsor the project team leader; encouraging the project sponsor to provide public support for the project; placing key stakeholders on the project team; placing key stakeholders in charge of the change process, training, or installing the system; and formally involving stakeholders in the specification approval process. Being involved in the project makes stakeholders more aware of the trade-offs that inevitably occur during a system implementation. They may be more willing to accept the consequences of the trade-offs. In addition, being involved in the project allows users to better understand how the system works, and thus may make it easier for them to use the system.

Gauging Success

How does a manager know when a project has been a success? At the start of the project, the general manager who built the business case would have considered several aspects based on achieving the business goals. It is important that the goals be measurable so

Success Dimension	Low Tech	Medium Tech	High Tech
	Existing technologies with new features	*Most technologies are new but available before the project*	*New, untested technologies*
Resource Constraint	Important	Overruns acceptable	Overruns most likely
Impact on Customers	Added value	Significantly improved capabilities	Quantum leap in effectiveness
Business Success	Profit; return on investment	High profits; market share	High, but may come much later; market leader
Prepare the Future	Gain additional capabilities	New market; new service	Leadership-core and future technologies

FIGURE 10.12 Success dimensions for various project types.
Source: Adapted from Aaron Shenhar, Dov Dvir, and Ofer Levy, "Project Success: A Multidimensional Strategic Approach," Technology and Innovation Management Division (1998).

that they can be used throughout the project to provide the project manager with real-time feedback. The general manager probably also wants to know if the system meets the specifications and project requirements laid out in the project scope. But measuring this is complex. Metrics may be derived specifically from the requirements and business needs that generated the project to determine whether or not the system meets expectations. Such metrics need to be based on the specific system, such as automating the order entry process or building a knowledge management system for product design.

Four dimensions that are useful in determining if a project is successful or not are shown in Figure 10.12 . The dimensions are defined as follows:

- *Resource constraints:* Does the project meet the established time and budget criteria? Was there *schedule slip* (i.e., the current scheduled time divided by the original scheduled time.) Most projects set some measure of success along this dimension, which is a short-term success metric that is easy to measure.

- *Impact on customers:* How much benefit does the customer receive from this project? Although some IT projects are transparent to the organization's end customer, every project can be measured on the benefit to the immediate customer of the IS. This dimension includes performance and technical specification measurements.

- *Business success:* How high are the profits and how long do they last? Did the project meet its return on investment goals? This dimension must be aligned with the business strategy of the organization.

- *Prepare the future:* Has the project altered the infrastructure of the organization so that in the future business success and customer impact are more likely?

Today many companies are building Internet infrastructures in anticipation of future business and customer benefits. Overall success of this strategy will only be measurable in the future, although projects underway now can be evaluated on how well they prepare the business for future opportunities.

What other considerations should be made when defining success? Is it enough just to complete a project? Is it necessary to finish on time and on budget? What other dimensions are important? The type of project can greatly influence how critical each of these dimensions is in determining the overall success of the project. It is the responsibility of the general manager to coordinate the overall business strategy of the company with the project type and the project success measurements. In this way, the necessary organizational changes can be coordinated to support the new information system. After the project is completed, a post-project feedback (post-implementation audit) should be completed to ensure that the system met its requirements and the system development process was a good one.

► SUMMARY

- A general manager fulfills an important role in project management. As a project sponsor, the general manager may be called on to select the project manager, to provide resources to the project manager, and to provide direction to and support for the project.

- The business case provides foundation for a well-managed project by specifying the objectives of the project, the required resources, the critical elements, and the stakeholders.

- Project management involves continual trade-offs. The project triangle highlights the need to delicately balance cost, time, and scope to achieve quality in a project.

- Four important project elements are project management, project team, project cycle plan, and common project vocabulary.

- Understanding the complexity of the project, the environment in which it is developed, and the dimensions used to measure project success allows the general manager to balance the trade-offs necessary for using resources effectively and to keep the project's direction aligned with the company's business strategy.

- Three popular information technology project development methodologies are the SDLC, agile programming and prototyping. Each of these methodologies offers both advantages and drawbacks. Other methodologies and approaches are emerging.

- In increasingly dynamic environments, it is important to manage project risk. Project risk is a function of project size, clarity, and level of complexity. For low-clarity projects, it is important to interface with users and gain their commitment in the project. Projects that are highly complex require leveraging the technical skills of the team members, bringing in consultants when necessary, and using other strategies to promote internal integration.

- The PMO, Project Management Office, brings focus and efficiency to project management activities. Often the PMO is a formal organization under the CIO.

- Projects are here to stay, and every general manager must be a project manager at some point in his or her career. As a project manager, the general manager is expected to lead the daily activities of the project. This chapter offers insight into the necessary skills, processes, and roles that project management requires.

• Mashups are new applications derived from combining existing applications on the Web.

▶ KEY TERMS

agile development (p. 306)
direct cutover (p. 304)
joint applications
 development (JAD)
 (p. 309)
mashups (p. 311)
object (p. 309)
open source software (OSS)
 (p. 310)

open sourcing (p. 310)
parallel conversion (p. 304)
project (p. 290)
project management (p. 292)
project management office
 (PMO) (p. 294)
project manager (p. 295)
project stakeholders (p. 290)
prototyping (p. 307)

rapid applications
 development (RAD)
 (p. 308)
systems development life
 cycle (SDLC) (p. 303)

▶ DISCUSSION QUESTIONS

1. What are the trade-offs between cost, quality, and time when designing a project plan? What criteria should managers use to manage this trade-off?

2. Why does it often take a long time before troubled projects are abandoned or brought under control?

3. What are the critical success factors for a project manager? What skills should managers look for when hiring someone who would be successful in this job?

4. What determines the level of technical risk associated with a project? What determines the level of organizational risk? How can a general manager assist in minimizing these risk components?

5. Lego's Mindstorms Robotics Invention System was designed for 12-year-olds. But after more than a decade of development at the MIT Media Lab using the latest advances in artificial intelligence, the toy created an enormous buzz among grown-up hackers. Despite its stiff $199 price tag, Mindstorms sold so quickly that store shelves were emptied two weeks before its first Christmas in 1998. In its first year, a staggering 100,000 kits were sold, far beyond the 12,000 units the company had projected. Seventy percent of Mindstorms' early customers were old enough to vote. These customers bought the software with the intention of hacking it. They wanted to make the software more flexible and powerful. They deciphered Mindstorms' proprietary code, posted it on the Internet, began writing new advanced software, and even wrote a new operating system for their robots. To date Lego has done nothing to stop this open source movement, even though thousands of Lego's customers now operate their robots with software the company didn't produce or endorse and can't support. The software may end up damaging the robot's expensive infrared sensors and motors.[30]

 a. What are the advantages of Lego's approach to open sourcing?
 b. What are the disadvantages of Lego's approach to open sourcing?
 c. How should Lego manage the open source movement?

---

[30] Adapted from Paul Keegan, "Lego: Intellectual Property Is Not a Toy," *Business 2.0* (October 2001), http://www.business2.com/articles/mag/0,1640,16981,FF.html (accessed on June 27, 2002).

IMPLEMENTING ENTERPRISE CHANGE MANAGEMENT AT SOUTHERN COMPANY

Atlanta-based Southern Company, a leading utility provider in the southeast United States, is valued by its 4.4 electricity customers for its excellent service, and it ranks as *Fortune* magazine's "most admired" company in its industry. That means quality is important in everything the company does. When David Traynor, business excellence manager at the company, was charged with implementing a new enterprise change management (ECM) site, he knew its key users, employees in the IT department, would scrutinize the new system and be very critical if anything didn't work exactly as it should.

The projected investment for the ECM was in the seven figures range, but the business case was straightforward. The justification was based on the savings in time and costs from reduced meetings and the ability to devote more attention to risky projects. The IT department was handling over seven thousand change requests a year, each of which required a time-consuming approval process no matter how small or routine the change was. Each change request needed to be approved at one of the three hour-long review committee meetings that were held each week. Some frustrated employees were even starting to circumvent the approval process. Clearly something had to be done. But even though the ECM had clear benefits, the IT department was not eager to work on a system that didn't promise to be very exciting. Further, installing the ECM promised to markedly change the way the IT folks performed their work. "They had to log all their changes, gain approval, take all these steps that they weren't being tasked with before," said Traynor.

The department selected BMC's Remedy software suite after spending six months designing the new process. Next came ten months to customize the systems and seven months to build them. The first ECM phase was rolled out in August 2010. Surprisingly, the new system produced even more change requests than before—almost 3,000 additional ones each year. Traynor reasoned that, before the ECM was switched on, a lot of changes must have been processed without any review. That was problematic given that about eight of ten requested projects have at least some level of risk and 100 percent require resources to complete. Now the change advisory board meets monthly (rather than three times weekly) and deals only with emergency changes and high-risk changes that could affect critical sites or many users. Routine change requests are pre-approved using standard formats.

Traynor hadn't spent much time getting buy-in from the IT department during the first phase of the ECM project. He now believes he should have started the ECM communication and training effort much sooner in the first phase. The second phase of the implementation, the incident and problem management system, was done differently. Traynor appointed "ambassadors" from each IT unit as before, but this time they participated from the very first day of the second phase of the project. Traynor encouraged them to talk with the IT employees in their unit, so they were not playing catch-up as they had been in the first phase. Rather, the ambassadors were actively involved in designing system changes. "They've put their fingerprints on it. . . We get a lot of mileage from [the ambassadors]." Traynor wants them to learn the ECM and play a major role in training and testing the system. He adds, "The hope is that [they]. . . become the go-to person after we go live."

Discussion Questions

1. What type of development methodology appears to have been employed at Southern Company for the ECM project? Was this a good approach? Provide a rationale for your response.

2. Describe how Traynor could have applied Lewin's three stage model of change in implementing the ECM? What would have been the advantages of applying Lewin's three-stage model?

3. Assess Southern's ECM system on the four dimensions of project success? How successful do you think this project is?

Sources: Southern Company Web site, www.southerncompany.com (accessed on April 18, 2012); and S. Overby, "How Southern Company Revamped IT Change Management," CIO.com (October 18, 2010), http://www.cio.com/article/print/626323.

CASE STUDY 10-2

DEALING WITH TRAFFIC JAMS IN LONDON

As London entered the 21st century, it was confronted with a major issue that plagues many cities throughout the world—excessive automobile traffic. Many Londoners—and particularly the business community—rated traffic congestion as the city's most serious problem. At peak periods, the average speed was less than 10 miles per hour, a slower speed than the horse-drawn carriages of previous centuries. Drivers spent about half their time waiting in traffic. Not only was this congestion nightmare a major source of driver frustration, but it contributed to both environmental and economic problems as well. By one estimate, traffic-related problems cost London businesses roughly £2 million—more than $3 million—every week. Clearly, the city needed an aggressive policy to address this issue. The solution, proposed by a government study titled *Road Charging Options for London* (ROCOL), authorized by the 1999 Greater London Authority Act, and endorsed by incoming Mayor Ken Livingstone, was *congestion charging*. As the name suggests, the city would assess a fee, or charge, to every automobile that entered high-traffic sections of London during peak hours.

Rather than attempt a broad citywide implementation, the government focused specifically on the highly congested section of central London, where roughly 1 million people entered every day, about 150,000 of them by private automobile. Beginning in February 2003, drivers who entered this area between 7 AM and 6:30 PM had to pay a fee of £5 ($8) by midnight. (Certain types of vehicles, such as ambulances, buses, and taxis, were exempt.) Drivers have the option of paying the charge by mail (prepay), text messaging, telephone, or in person at various pay points. Failure to pay the fee results in a fine of £80 (roughly $130). Significantly, this solution makes extensive use of current technologies. The city installed almost 700 cameras at more than 200 sites in the designated high-traffic area. These cameras photograph the license plates of every vehicle that enters the area. They then transmit these photos to a data center that translates the photographic images into license plate numbers utilizing automatic number plate recognition technology. Drivers who fail to pay the fee receive a notice of the fine in the mail.

To create and implement the congestion charge plan, the government had to face a number of project risks:

- Tight Schedule: The project needed to be completed under tight deadlines in order to meet multiple statutory requirements and minimize disruptions to commuters.
- Technology: The cameras had to be strategically placed in order to accurately photograph tens of thousands of license plates every day.
- Lack of Pre-existing Models: There were no pre-existing models in the world to follow.
- Limited Experience and Expertise: Mayor Livingstone was newly elected, and the supervising governmental agency—Transport for London—had only recently been created. Thus, neither were experienced in building such a system.
- Political Fallout: The political risk of a system failure to the new mayor was so huge that it would be extremely damaging to his career.

Transport for London adopted a series of management strategies to navigate these waters and limit the risks resulting from their limited experience, IT ability, and management time. Perhaps the most significant decision was to outsource the basic management activities to firms that specialized in these areas. For example, to manage the competitive bidding process they contracted first with PricewaterhouseCoopers and then with Deloitte & Touche.

Early in the project, project managers identified the critical technical elements and divided the project into five "packages" that could, if required, be bought and managed separately. These included (1) the camera component; (2) the image store component that collected images, converted them into license numbers, and condensed the images (duplicates would occur when one vehicle was photographed by several cameras); (3) the telecommunications links between the cameras and the image store component; (4) the customer services infrastructure, including the ability to pay by phone, Web, and mail; and (5) an extensive network of retail outlet kiosks and gas stations where people could pay the toll.

The retail side was seen as a big enough risk that it was bought and managed separately. To further reduce the risks, it was decided to select the best available technologies for each of the five packages. Another risk-aversive move was to utilize only established technologies for the actual process of identifying the vehicles in the designated zone. For example, Transport for London rejected proposals to employ electronic tags because this technology had not been proved effective in scenarios such as this one. Finally, the city added roughly 200 buses to its fleet to accommodate increased ridership.

Transport for London requested bids on the project early in 2001. The estimated $116.2 million project was large enough to require listing in the European Union's public-sector register. Companies throughout Europe were allowed to bid on the project. Separate bids could be tendered for the camera and communications packages, whereas the remaining three could receive bids on a combined basis or individually. Deloitte & Touche reviewed more than 40 bids before deciding on a single contractor to manage the entire program. Their choice was The Capita Group, England's largest business process outsourcing firm. Significantly, before accepting Capita's bid, Deloitte required both that firm and the other final candidate to submit technical design studies. In addition, Capita's contract included penalties if the company failed to meet the established deadlines.

After awarding the contract to Capita, Deloitte closely monitored every step of the process, and it kept additions to the original plan to a minimum. As a result, scope creep—the process whereby a project increases in both size and costs as new features are added—was never a serious issue. One of the few changes added to the requirements was an option for motorists to pay fees through the popular SMS text messaging format.

Throughout the implementation of the new system, the city continually sought feedback from key stakeholders. In addition, it regularly updated the public concerning the project's status. Consequently, few drivers were caught unawares when the new policy went into effect on February 17, 2003. The mayor also wisely decided to begin operations during a school holiday period, when traffic volumes are significantly lower. Thus, by the time traffic returned to normal, drivers generally had adapted to the new procedures.

What were the results of these concerted efforts? Unlike so many systems projects, London's congestion charging plan was completed on time and within budget. Significantly, however, the demanding schedule did not compromise the quality of the work. Instead, the new program appears to have achieved its basic goals. A follow-up study indicated that traffic in central London had diminished by as much as 20%, and average driving speeds had improved. The fines and fees resulted in a project payback period of about one and a half years. It was estimated that total revenues would amount to $2.2 billion over a ten-year period. Moreover, vehicular emissions of toxic substances such as nitrogen dioxide were also reduced. One potential problem that did *not* emerge was "rat runs" in which traffic jams would appear in areas outside the zone as drivers altered their routes to avoid the charges. After reviewing the outcomes of the London program, many observers predicted that congestion charging would become a standard practice in cities throughout the world.

Discussion Questions

1. Assess the risks of this project. Given your assessment of the project complexity, clarity, and size, what management strategies would you recommend? What, if any, of these strategies were adopted in this project?

2. Describe the development methodology that was applied to this project. Was this the most appropriate approach? Provide a rationale for your response.

3. When a project is outsourced, who should manage the project—the internal group or the outsourcer? Why?

Sources: Ken Livingstone (Mayor of London), "The Challenge of Driving through Change: Introducing Congestion Charging in Central London" (December 2004), *Planning Theory and Practice* 5(4), 490–498, http://web.ebscohost.com.jerome.stjohns.edu:81/ehost/pdfviewer/pdfviewer?vid=23&hid=21&sid=9daf2014-9a51-45ea-8187-9f6bc0075556%40sessionmgr15; Bradford Wernie, "The World Watches As London Tries to End Congestion," (January 27, 2003), *Automotive News Europe* 8(2), 3–4, http://web.ebscohost.com/ehost/detail?sid=dd39c013-cbdf-4628-a244-c556c0fad40e%40sessionmgr15&vid=22&hid=9&bdata=JnNpdGU9 ZWhvc3QtbGl2ZZQ%3d%3d#db=bsh&AN=9127667; and Malcolm Wheatley, "How IT Fixed London's Traffic Woes" (July 15, 2003), *CIO* 16(19), http://search.proquest.com.jerome.stjohns.edu:81/docview/205943050/fulltext/13626A661B39C302E/3?accountid=14068.

CHAPTER 11

KNOWLEDGE MANAGEMENT, BUSINESS INTELLIGENCE, AND ANALYTICS

Business intelligence and analytics are quickly becoming a source of strategic advantage for those firms who understand and develop skills to manage big data. This chapter provides an overview of the ways businesses make decisions. Making better decisions begins by differentiation between knowledge management, business intelligence and analytics, including a discussion of intellectual property. Data, information, and knowledge (both tacit and explicit) are then defined and discussed, as they are the foundation of making better decisions. Managing knowledge is done through four main processes, which are outlined next. Competing with analytics, and the capabilities that enable it, follows. The chapter then takes a more technical turn, addressing the components of business analytics and big data amassed in data warehouses. The chapter concludes with a discussion of social analytics and caveats that managers must anticipate.

Caesars Entertainment Corporation, the largest gaming company in the world by some measures, found a way to more than double revenues by collecting and then analyzing customer data. According to CEO Gary Loveman, "We've come out top in the casino wars by mining our customer data deeply, running marketing experiments, and using the results to implement finely tuned marketing and service delivery strategies that keep our customers coming back."[1] This is more than just implementing loyalty cards to track customer activity and reward "frequent buyers." In 2000, the Harrah's brand was valued at close to $3 billion. When it was sold 7 years later to a private equity group, it was valued at $17 billion. Much of that increase was credited to the innovative and widespread use of business analytics to turn around the gaming company. In 2010, the company changed its name from Harrah's to Caesars Entertainment Corporation.

Analytics at Caesars begins when a customer is issued a loyalty card in the Total Rewards (TR) program. Similar to the ubiquitous cards used by airlines, grocery stores,

---

[1] Gary Loveman, "Diamonds in the Data Mine," *Harvard Business Review* (May 2003), 110.

and even coffeehouses, the TR card tracks customer usage of the various games offered in their casinos. What differentiates the TR card is what Caesars does with the information they collect when customers use the card. Management uses sophisticated analytical tools to understand as much as possible about their customers. For example, they thought their best customers were high rollers. In fact, they found that 82% of revenues came from 26% of customers, and they were not the stereotypical gold cuff-link-wearing, limousine-riding high rollers, but retirees who have time to spend their nest egg. The management wanted to know what motivated these customers. They conducted experiments and focus groups, using well-structured experiments designed to gather data and test hypotheses. They found that these customers were motivated by reduced rates on hotel rooms, or if they lived in the area, free chips. Special gifts and expensive rooms were not as effective as incentive.

They studied the customer's value over time and identified ways to increase spending on repeat visits. For example, when they looked at the data about their best customers, they learned that these customers wanted service quickly. So Caesars management found ways to reduce the wait at the valet parking lot and at the restaurants. Diamond customers, those that were the very best customers, rarely waited in line at all, providing a very visible "reward" for their business and motivating others to seek Diamond-level status (something they could earn through the TR program). They studied individual behaviors and created a program that was custom tailored to each customer offering specific incentives based on the results of their analytical models. As Loveman described, "If we discovered that a customer who spends $1,000 per month with us hadn't visited us in three months, a letter or telephone call would invite him back. If we learned that he lost money during his last visit, we invited him back for a special event."[2] They found ways to keep the small-level gamblers in the casino longer and to lure them back again at very low costs. By understanding the limit a customer normally spends in a casino, management was able to identify when a customer was about to leave the casino, and intervene, offering him a complimentary dinner or other incentive to stay in the casino. Analytics drives their business, and the results have turned the company into a model for successfully integrating technical algorithms with marketing techniques.

As baby-boomers age, the Caesar's management team began studying the next generation of potential gamblers. By 2015, Caesars estimates that 52% of spending in Las Vegas will come from twenty- to forty-somethings.[3] This means revisiting the way these gamblers spend money when they gamble, and what their preferences are. Their first experiment is Linq, an entertainment district with shops, nightclubs, bars, restaurants, and comfortable spaces to meet up scheduled to open in 2013. The prototypical Linq customer, executives say, isn't a graying slot player but rather, a thirty-something, middle-class man or woman who wants to meet up with friends for cocktails or beers. Linq is another example of Caesar's Entertainment's business intelligence at work, this time to create an experience aimed at the changing demographic of their customer base.

---

[2] Ibid., 112.

[3] Liz Benston, "Why Caesars Entertainment is shooting for 30-something customers for Linq" (August 18, 2011), http://www.vegasinc.com/news/2011/aug/18/why-caesars-entertainment-shooting-30-something-cu/ (accessed on February 27, 2012).

This chapter provides an overview of some of the ways business make decisions. Enterprises have long sought a way to harness the value locked inside the extensive data they collect and store about customers, markets, competitors, products, people, and processes. This chapter will review some of the basic concepts of knowledge management, business intelligence, analytics, and the concept of big data.

► KNOWLEDGE MANAGEMENT, BUSINESS INTELLIGENCE, AND BUSINESS ANALYTICS

It's all about making better decisions. Managing knowledge is not a new concept,[4] but it has been invigorated and enabled by new technologies for collaborative systems, the emergence of the Internet and intranets, which in themselves act as a large, geographically distributed knowledge repository, and the well-publicized successes of companies using business analytics, like Caesars. The discipline draws from many established sources, including anthropology, cognitive psychology, management, sociology, artificial intelligence, IT, and library science. Knowledge management remains, however, an emerging discipline, with few generally accepted standards or definitions of key concepts.

Knowledge management includes the processes necessary to generate, capture, codify, and transfer knowledge across the organization to achieve competitive advantage. Individuals are the ultimate source of organizational knowledge. The organization gains only limited benefit from knowledge isolated within individuals or among workgroups; to obtain the full value of knowledge, it must be captured and transferred across the organization.

Business intelligence (BI) is the term used to describe the set of technologies and processes that use data to understand and analyze business performance.[5] It is the management strategy used to create a more structured approach to decision making based on facts that are discovered by analyzing information collected in company databases. Although some may argue with this relationship, business intelligence can be considered a component of knowledge management. Knowledge management deals with the processes necessary to capture, codify, and make sense of all types of knowledge as described earlier. Business intelligence is more specifically about extracting knowledge from data. Davenport and Harris suggest that **business analytics** is the term used to refer to the use of quantitative and predictive models and fact-based management to drive decisions. By this definition, business analytics is a subset of BI. Some, however, use the terms BI and analytics interchangeably.

The most profound aspect of knowledge management and business intelligence is that, ultimately, an organization's only sustainable competitive advantage lies in what its employees know and how they apply that knowledge to business problems. Exaggerated promises and heightened expectations, couched in the hyperbole of technology vendors and consultants, may create unrealistic expectations. Knowledge management is not a

---

[4] The cuneiform texts found at the ancient city Ebla (Tall Mardikh) in Syria are, at more than 4,000 years old, some of the earliest known attempts to record and organize information.

[5] Thomas Davenport and Jeanne Harris, *Competing on Analytics* (Boston, MA: Harvard Business School Press, 2007), 7.

magic bullet, that is, an appropriate solution for all business problems. While reading this chapter, managers should consider the implications of managing knowledge, but should not believe that knowledge management by itself is the sole answer for managerial success. Knowledge must serve the broader goals of the organization, and analytics alone do not create competitive advantage. How the information is used and how the knowledge is linked back to business processes are important components of knowledge management.

Intellectual Property

Two other terms frequently encountered in discussions of knowledge are *intellectual capital* and *intellectual property*. **Intellectual capital** is defined as knowledge that has been identified, captured, and leveraged to produce higher-value goods or services or some other competitive advantage for the firm. Both knowledge management and intellectual capital are often used imprecisely and interchangeably to describe similar concepts. Information technology (IT) provides an infrastructure for capturing and transferring knowledge, but does not create knowledge and cannot guarantee its sharing or use.

Intellectual property allows individuals to own their creativity and innovation in the same way that they can own physical property. However, when the intellectual property is information-based, it differs from physical property in two important ways. First, information-based property is non-exclusive to the extent that when one person uses it, it can be used again by another person. Consider an MP3 file of music, which can be easily copied and shared with another without loss of the original property. Second, unlike the cost structure of physical property, the marginal cost of producing additional copies of information-based property is negligible compared with the cost of original production. These differences create differences in the ethical treatment of physical and information-based intellectual property. The economics of information versus the economics of physical property is further explored in the introduction of this text.

The concept of intellectual property makes it possible for owners to be rewarded for the use of their ideas and it allows them to have a say in how their ideas are used. To protect their ideas, owners typically apply for and are granted intellectual property rights, although some protection such as copyright arises automatically, without any registration, as soon as a record is made in some form of what has been created.

The four main types of intellectual property are patents for inventions, trademarks for brand identity, designs for product appearance, and copyrights for literary and artistic material, music, films, sound recordings, broadcasts, and software.[6] In 2002, the music sharing Web site Napster raised controversial issues long surrounding the practice of copyright. The Audio Home Recording Act (1992) was passed in the United States to prevent serial copying, but this didn't seem to apply to Napster, who only facilitated sharing. Although the act protected intellectual property, it also confirmed the freedom to copy music for personal use.

[6] "What Is Intellectual Property or IP?" http://www.intellectual-property.gov.uk/std/faq/question1.htm (accessed on June 25, 2002).

Geographic Lens: When Two National Views of Intellectual Property Collide

U.S. and Chinese government officials have been at odds over the issue of intellectual property for decades. For years, Chinese officials have promised to improve their protection of intellectual property. In December 2010, at a Joint Commission on Commerce and Trade in Washington, China's top economic policy maker promised better protection for foreign software, better tracking of the management of software in state-owned enterprises, no discrimination against foreign intellectual property in government procurement and improvements in the Chinese patent process.

These promises will be hard to keep since stringent protection of foreigners' intellectual property is at odds with China's development strategy and even its history and traditions. The concept of intellectual property protection did not exist into China until it was introduced by Westerners in the early 20th century. The emperors who ruled China prior to the 20th century were concerned about unauthorized publication because they wanted to control what was disseminated, and not because they wanted to encourage private, individual expression. Unfortunately, when Western ideas of intellectual property were introduced to China, it was done so in a threatening manner to protect Western economic interests. As a result, many Chinese viewed the concept of intellectual property as a foreign imposition. Furthermore, the impact of Marxist theories of collective ownership that marked China's communist period meant it was not until the 1980s that of modern notions of intellectual property were brought to China—notions that remain novel and alien ideas to many Chinese.

Further, many foreign companies operating in China complain that Beijing views the appropriation of foreign innovations as a viable approach developing domestic technology. They claim that the Chinese government tacitly supports forcing foreigners to disclose their technology and transfer patents to gain contracts. In fact, China's new antimonopoly laws allow compulsory licensing of foreign technologies in some cases and require foreign companies that wanted to merge with or buy a Chinese company to transfer technology to China. While such policies can ratchet Chinese firms up the tech ladder more rapidly, they are considered by many to reflect the misappropriation of intellectual property. While the United States has made some progress at the World Trade Organization against the theft of intellectual property in China and China has enacted some intellectual property laws, the battle over intellectual property is still raging.

Sources: Editorial, China and Intellectual Property, *The New York Times* (December 23, 2010), http://www.nytimes.com/2010/12/24/opinion/24fri1.html?pagewanted=print (accessed on February 22, 2012); and William Alford, "Understanding Chinese Attitudes Toward Intellectual Property (IP) Rights," *Cio.com* (September 15, 2006), http://www.cio.com/article/print/24969 (accessed on February 22, 2012).

In 1998, the more stringent Digital Millennium Copyright Act (DCMA) passed by a unanimous vote in the U.S. Senate with the active support of the entertainment industry.[7] The DCMA makes it a crime to circumvent copy protection, even if that copy protection impairs rights established by the Audio Home Recording Act. Furthermore, the Digital Tech Corps Act of 2002, passed in the U.S. House of Representatives, seeks to protect intellectual property by placing a lifetime ban on employees from revealing trade secrets, and imposing a criminal penalty of up to five years in prison and a $50,000 fine.[8] A senior-level position, Coordinator for International Intellectual Property Enforcement in the U.S. Department of Commerce, was created to coordinate the battle against global piracy of intellectual property.

The U.S. Congress continues to propose and discuss ways to protect intellectual property, particularly from piracy of online materials by sites and companies outside of U.S. jurisdiction. For example, though it was soundly rejected by the public and by Web sites around the world, the Stop Online Piracy Act (SOPA) and the Protect IP Act (PIPA) were introduced to the U.S. Congress in 2011 at the behest of the entertainment industry to protect intellectual property. House Judiciary Committee Chairman Lamar Smith (R-TX) postponed plans to draft a compromise bill, the Online Protection and Enforcement of Digital Trade Act (OPEN). He commented that "The committee remains committed to finding a solution to the problem of online piracy that protects American intellectual property and innovation. . . The House Judiciary Committee will postpone consideration of the legislation until there is wider agreement on a solution."[9]

▶ DATA, INFORMATION, AND KNOWLEDGE

The terms *data*, *information*, and *knowledge* are often used interchangeably, but have significant and discrete meanings within the knowledge management domain. As was first presented in the introduction of this textbook, the differences are shown in Figure 11.1. **Data** are specific, objective facts or observations, such as "inventory contains 45 units." Standing alone, such facts have no intrinsic meaning, but can be easily captured, transmitted, and stored electronically.

Information is defined by Peter Drucker as "data endowed with relevance and purpose."[10] People turn data into information by organizing them into some unit of analysis (e.g., dollars, dates, or customers). Deciding on the appropriate unit of analysis involves interpreting the context of the data and summarizing them into a more condensed form. Consensus must be reached on the unit of analysis.

---

[7] On March 10, 2004, the European Union passed the EU Copyright Directive, which is similar in many ways to DCMA.

[8] Jason Miller, "House Passes IT Employee Exchange Program," *Government Computer News*, http://www.gcn.com/vol1_no1/regulation/18347-1.html (accessed on June 25, 2002).

[9] Wikipedia, http://en.wikipedia.org/wiki/Stop_Online_Piracy_Act (accessed on February 1, 2012). Further, on a related matter, the Supreme Court ruled in 2012 that Congress was acting within it powers to grant copyright protection in compliance with the international Berne Convention of 1886.

[10] Peter F. Drucker, "The Coming of the New Organization," *Harvard Business Review* (January–February 1988), 45–53.

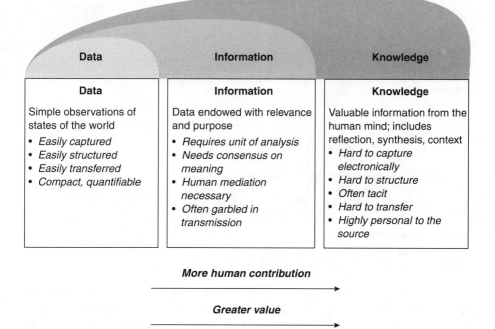

Data	Information	Knowledge
Data	**Information**	**Knowledge**
Simple observations of states of the world	Data endowed with relevance and purpose	Valuable information from the human mind; includes reflection, synthesis, context
• *Easily captured* • *Easily structured* • *Easily transferred* • *Compact, quantifiable*	• *Requires unit of analysis* • *Needs consensus on meaning* • *Human mediation necessary* • *Often garbled in transmission*	• *Hard to capture electronically* • *Hard to structure* • *Often tacit* • *Hard to transfer* • *Highly personal to the source*

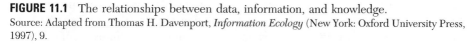

More human contribution

Greater value

FIGURE 11.1   The relationships between data, information, and knowledge.
Source: Adapted from Thomas H. Davenport, *Information Ecology* (New York: Oxford University Press, 1997), 9.

Knowledge is a mix of contextual information, experiences, rules, and values. It is richer and deeper than information and more valuable because someone has thought deeply about that information and added his or her own unique experience, judgment, and wisdom. One way of thinking about knowledge is to consider the different types of knowing.[11] *Knowing what* often is based on assembling information and eventually applying it. It requires the ability to recognize, describe, and classify concepts and things. The process of applying knowledge helps generate *knowing how* to do something. This kind of knowing requires an understanding of an appropriate sequence of events or the ability to perform a particular set of actions. Sometimes the first inkling of knowing how to do something stems from an understanding of procedures, routines, and rules. Knowing how to do something often begins with following procedures and is fully learned by actually experiencing a situation. Finally knowing how and knowing what can be synthesized through a reasoning process that results in *knowing why*. Knowing why is the causal knowledge of why something occurs. Often reasoning applied to knowing-how can lead to the understanding of knowing-why. These types of knowing are modeled in Figure 11.2.

---

[11] M. H. Zack, "Managing Codified Knowledge," *Sloan Management Review* (1999), 40(4), 45–58.

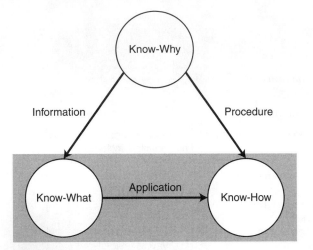

FIGURE 11.2 Taxonomy of knowledge.
Source: Adapted from H-W. Kim and S. M. Kwak, "Linkage of Knowledge Management to Decision Support: A System Dynamics Approach," presented at the National University of Singapore (July 2002).

Values and beliefs are also a component of knowledge; they determine the interpretation and the organization of knowledge. Tom Davenport and Larry Prusak, experts who have written about this relationship, say, "The power of knowledge to organize, select, learn, and judge comes from values and beliefs as much as and probably more than, from information and logic."[12] Knowledge also involves the synthesis of multiple sources of information over time.[13] The amount of human contribution increases along the continuum from data to information to knowledge. Computers work well for managing data, but are less efficient at managing information. The more complex and ill-defined elements of knowledge (for example, "tacit" knowledge, described later in this chapter) are difficult if not impossible to capture electronically.

Although knowledge has always been important to the success of an organization, it was presumed that the natural, informal flow of knowledge was sufficient to meet organizational needs. But managing knowledge has become far more complex, the amount of knowledge to manage far greater than every, and the tools to manage knowledge far more powerful. Managing knowledge provides value to organizations in several ways, as summarized in Figure 11.3.

Tacit versus Explicit Knowledge

Knowledge can be further classified into two types: tacit and explicit. **Tacit knowledge** was first described by philosopher Michael Polyani in his book, *The Tacit Dimension*, with the classic assertion that "We can know more than we can tell."[14] For example, try

[12] Thomas H. Davenport and Laurence Prusak, *Working Knowledge* (Boston, MA: Harvard Business School Press, 1998), 12.

[13] Thomas H. Davenport, *Information Ecology* (New York: Oxford University Press, 1997), 9–10.

[14] Michael Polanyi, *The Tacit Dimension*, 1966 ed. (Magnolia, MA: Peter Smith, 1983), 4.

Value	Sources of Value
Sharing Best Practices	• Avoid reinventing the wheel • Build on valuable work and expertise
Sustainable Competitive Advantage	• Shorten the life cycle of innovation • Promote view of an "infinite resource" that isn't used up • Impact bottom-line returns
Managing Overload	• Filter data to assimilate relevant knowledge into the company • Provide organization and storage for easier data retrieval
Rapid Change	• Build on previous work to make company more agile • Streamline processes/build dynamic processes • Sense and respond to changes more quickly • Customize preexisting solutions for unique customer needs
Embedded Knowledge from Products	• Use smart products to gather product information automatically for use in refining product, maintenance, upgrades, and customer usage. • Blur distinction between manufacturing and service firms when information system embedded in products • Add value through intangibles such as fixing systems before customer knows it's broken
Globalization	• Decrease cycle times for global processes since information moves faster than physical process components • Manage global competitive pressures • Provide global access to knowledge • Adapt to local conditions
Insurance for Downsizing	• Protect from loss of knowledge when workers leave • Provide portability for workers who move between roles • Reduce time for knowledge acquisition

FIGURE 11.3 The value of managing knowledge.

writing a memorandum, or even explaining verbally, how to swim or ride a bicycle. Tacit knowledge is personal, context-specific, and hard to formalize and communicate. It consists of experiences, beliefs, and skills. Tacit knowledge is entirely subjective and is often acquired through physically practicing a skill or activity.

In 2011, quarterback Drew Brees broke the NFL single-season record for the most passing yards with 5,476 yards passed. It would be nearly impossible to verbally describe all the factors that Brees had to consider when making those passes, yet he knew who to throw the ball to, where to put the ball, and why to make that throw, all in a matter of seconds. Brees' ability to pass the football incorporates so much of his own personal experience and kinesthetic memory that it is impossible to separate that knowledge from the player himself. His bone structure, muscular development, and the nerves between his arm and his brain all make it possible for him to throw the types of passes he does.

Tacit Knowledge	Explicit Knowledge
• Knowing how to identify the key issues necessary to solve a problem • Applying similar experiences from past situations • Estimating work required based on intuition and experience • Deciding on an appropriate course of action	• Procedures listed in a manual • Books and articles • News reports and financial statements • Information left over from past projects

FIGURE 11.4 Examples of explicit and tacit knowledge.

IT has traditionally focused on **explicit knowledge**, that is, knowledge that can be easily collected, organized, and transferred through digital means, such as a memorandum or financial report. Individuals, however, possess both tacit and explicit knowledge. Explicit knowledge, such as the knowledge gained from reading this textbook, is objective, theoretical, and codified for transmission in a formal, systematic method using grammar, syntax, and the printed word. Figure 11.4 summarizes these differences.

Knowledge conversion strategies are often of interest in the business environment. Companies often want to take an expert's tacit knowledge and make it explicit, or to take explicit, book-learning in their new hires and make it tacit. In their book *The Knowledge-Creating Company*, Ikujiro Nonaka and Hirotaka Takeuchi describe four different modes of *knowledge conversion* (see Figure 11.5). The modes are (1) from tacit knowledge to tacit knowledge, called socialization, (2) from tacit knowledge to explicit knowledge, called **externalization**, (3) from explicit knowledge to explicit knowledge,

		TO	
		Tacit Knowledge	Explicit Knowledge
FROM	Tacit Knowledge	SOCIALIZATION Transferring tacit knowledge through shared experiences, apprenticeships, mentoring relationships, on-the-job training, "talking at the water cooler"	EXTERNALIZATION Articulating and thereby capturing tacit knowledge through use of metaphors, analogies, and models
	Explicit Knowledge	INTERNALIZATION Converting explicit knowledge into tacit knowledge; learning by doing; studying previously captured explicit knowledge (manuals, documentation) to gain technical know-how	COMBINATION Combining existing explicit knowledge through exchange and synthesis into new explicit knowledge

FIGURE 11.5 The four modes of knowledge conversion.

Source: Ikujiro Nonaka and Hirotaka Takeuchi, *The Knowledge-Creating Company: How Japanese Companies Create the Dynamics of Innovation* (New York: Oxford University Press, 1995), 62. By permission of Oxford University Press, Inc.

called combination, and (4) from explicit knowledge to tacit knowledge, called internalization.[15] **Socialization** is the process of sharing experiences; it occurs through observation, imitation, and practice. Common examples of socialization are sharing war stories, apprenticeships, conferences, and casual, unstructured discussions in the office or "at the water cooler."

► KNOWLEDGE MANAGEMENT PROCESSES

Knowledge management involves four main processes: the generation, capture, codification, and transfer of knowledge. **Knowledge generation** includes all activities that discover "new" knowledge, whether such knowledge is new to the individual, the firm, or the entire discipline. **Knowledge capture** involves continuous processes of scanning, organizing, and packaging knowledge after it has been generated. **Knowledge codification** is the representation of knowledge in a manner that can be easily accessed and transferred. **Knowledge transfer** involves transmitting knowledge from one person or group to another, and the absorption of that knowledge. Nonaka's knowledge framework above in Figure 11.5 displays a form of knowledge transfer. Without absorption, a transfer of knowledge does not occur. Generation, codification, and transfer generally take place constantly without management intervention. Knowledge management systems seek to enhance the efficiency and effectiveness of these activities and leverage their value for the firm as well as the individual. But with the increasing introduction of new and more robust systems for managing and using knowledge, knowledge management processes are a dynamic and continuously evolving.

Knowledge management processes are different in the age of Web 2.0 and robust search tools such as Google. Whereas traditional knowledge management systems had well defined processes for generation, capture, codification and transfer, technologies such as large data warehouses, ubiquitous Web sites, search tools, and tagging made it possible to capture and find information without the formal processes. **Tagging**, where users themselves list key words that codify the information or document at hand, creates an ad-hoc codification system, sometimes referred to as a **folksonomy**. Search engines have changed the way information is accessed, making it possible to quickly find virtually anything on any system connected to the Internet. These technologies have replaced traditional knowledge management systems and given individuals the ability to find information that traditionally was locked within structures that had to be designed, managed, and then taught to users.

► BUSINESS INTELLIGENCE

Traditional business intelligence (BI) has been associated with providing dashboards and reports to assist managers in monitoring key performance metrics. Common elements of BI systems include reporting, querying, dashboards, and scorecards.

---

[15] Ikujiro Nonaka and Hirotaka Takeuchi, *The Knowledge-Creating Company* (New York: Oxford University Press, 1995), 62–70.

Dashboards tend to be a simple, online display of key metrics, often graphically displayed in pie charts, bar charts, red-yellow-green coded data, and other images that easily convey both the value of the metric and, with the color coding, if the metric is within acceptable parameters or not. In one example, a map of the United States was used to indicate sales performance by geography, and each state was color coded to indicate if targets were being met. Managers could drill down into each region by clicking on the state, and see the next level of detail, which provided information by region. Further drilling down indicated sales by city and ultimately by sales person. At each level, the data was presented and color coded to give a visual, and therefore quick indication of who was making targets, and who was missing them. Traditional BI is useful for strategic, tactical and operational decisions. Chapter 7 describes how dashboards and scoreboards are used for running the business of IT. The BI dashboards are similar in that they summarize information in similar ways, but the use of the BI dashboard is very different than the IT dashboard.

At the SAS Global Forum in 2010,[16] a discussion ensued about what has become known as BI 2.0, or collaborative BI, the next generation of business intelligence. BI 2.0 incorporates a more proactive perspective, and provides for querying of real-time data. It incorporates a number of characteristic that are seen in Web 2.0 applications such as providing BI as a service in the cloud, rather than as a software package purchased from a vendor and installed on the organization's computer; event-driven, instant access to real-time information rather than batch, after the fact report generation; mobile and ubiquitous access rather than access just from desktop computers; and mashup capability rather than static, stand-alone systems. Newer technologies have enabled BI to move to a new level with more robust user interfaces that provide visualization and analytics tools. Crowdsourcing allows the data structures and report designs to be created by the community, rather than a single designer. Data and reports are infused with narratives from the users to provide richer context. Dynamic capabilities in the BI system provide exceptions, alerts, and notifications that change based on what the system learns from the data itself. When a manager sees something in the data that requires an intervention, he will not only be able to do the intervention, but to tag it and link it with the data so that the collective knowledge grows over time.

▶ COMPETING WITH BUSINESS ANALYTICS

In recent years, many companies have found success competing through better use of analytics. Companies such as Caesars Entertainment, as described at the beginning of this chapter, have turned around an otherwise lackluster business to become a leader in their industry. Capital One has also emerged from a crowded field of financial services firms, to become one of the industry leaders through use of extensive business analytics to continuously create and invent new products and services to reach out to new customers and reinvigorate relationships with existing customers. In their case, the company was founded on the idea that by mining data about individual customers they

---

[16] Gregory Nelson, *Business Intelligence 2.0: Are we there yet?* Paper 040-2012, SAS Global Forum.

could create financial service products that addressed what the big players would consider "'niche markets," unattractive to the larger players because of the smaller number of potential customers, but profitable nonetheless. Using the customer database of a small bank, and running numerous analytical tests, they identified characteristics that would create a profitable service. They learned, for example, that the most profitable customers were ones who charged a large amount, but paid their credit cards off slowly. At the time, most credit cards companies didn't differentiate between these and other customers. The innovative idea was to create a product that catered to these customers. Today, Capital One runs hundreds of experiments, identifying new products that target individual customers. Using analytics to simulate and test is a very low-cost way to design and develop these products.[17]

Sports teams have propelled themselves to league success through business analytics. The systematic use of factual data in proprietary models is credited with helping the Oakland As and the Boston Red Sox. As seen in the movie *Moneyball*, Billy Beane was one of the first general managers in Major League Baseball to build his organization, the Oakland As, around analytics. Although this industry collected data extensively, it was mostly used to manage the game in process. The Oakland As managed by using data on things that they could measure such as the on-base percentage (the number of times a player gets on-base), instead of softer criteria such as determination or effort the player is willing to put in. They used analytics in their recruiting efforts to predict which young players had the best chances of becoming major league players. Their strategy paid off, consistently carrying them to the playoffs despite a budget for player's salaries that was a fraction of what some of their competitors had.

One reason for the rise in companies competing on analytics is that many companies in many industries offer similar products and use comparable technologies. Therefore, business processes are among the last remaining points of differentiation, and analytic competitors are wringing every last drop of value from those processes.[18] Business analytics fuel fact-based decision making. For example, a company may use inventory reports to figure out what products are selling quickly and which are moving slowly, but a company that uses analytics will also know who is buying them, what price each customer pays, how many items the customer will purchase in a lifetime, what motivates each customer to purchase, and which incentives to offer to increase the revenue from each sale.

Davenport and Harris suggest that companies who successfully compete using their business analytics skills have these five capabilities:

- *Hard to duplicate*: Because successfully using analytics to compete means having a strong culture and organizational support system, as well as business processes that utilize the results of the analytical analyses, copying the capability is difficult, if not impossible. A competitor may have the same tools, but success comes from how they are used.

---

[17] Davenport and Harris, *Competing on Analytics*, 41–42.
[18] Ibid.

- *Uniqueness*: There are many ways to use business analytics to compete. A specific business will choose a path based on their business, their strategy, their market, their competitors, and their industry.

- *Adaptability*: Successful companies use analytics across boundaries and in creative ways. Workers are not held back from using analytics, and in fact are encouraged to find new and innovative ways to apply their tools. By creating a culture of analytics, virtually everyone in the organization seeks applications for analytics to enhance their business operations.

- *Better than competition*: Some organizations are better at applying analytics than others. For example, the Oakland As and the Boston Red Sox are well known for their use of analytics in an industry, Major League Baseball, well known for its data collection and statistical analysis.

- *Renewability*: Agility is an important characteristic of sustainable competitive advantage. Companies who use analytics for competitive advantage are exceptionally adaptable, continuously reinvest, and constantly renew their capabilities.

▶ COMPONENTS OF BUSINESS ANALYTICS

To successfully build business analytics capabilities in the enterprise, companies make a significant investment in their technologies, their people, and their strategic decision-making processes. Four components are needed (these four components are summarized in Figure 11.6).

Data Repositories

Data used in the analytical processes must be gathered, cleaned up, common, integrated and stored for easy access. **Data warehouses**, or collections of data designed to support

Component	Definition	Example
Data Repository	Servers and software used to store data	Data warehouses
Software Tools	Applications and processes for statistical analysis, forecasting, predictive modeling, and optimization	Data mining process; forecasting software package
Analytics Environment	Organizational environment that creates and sustains the use of analytics tools	Reward system that encourages the use of the analytics tools; willingness to test or experiment
Skilled Workforce	Workforce that has the training, experience, and capability to use the analytics tools	Caesars and Capital One have such workforces

FIGURE 11.6 Components of business analytics.

management decision making, sometimes serve as repositories of organizational knowledge. They contain a wide variety of data used to create a coherent picture of business conditions at a single point in time. In fact, the data contained in data warehouses may represent a large part of a company's knowledge, for example, the business's knowledge about its clients and their demographics.

Software Tools

At the core of business analytics are the tools. An approach that simulates business intelligence is **data mining**, which is the process of analyzing data warehouses for "gems" that can be used in management decision making. It identifies previously unknown relationships among data. Typically, data mining refers to the process of combing through massive amounts of customer data to understand buying habits and to identify new products, features, and enhancements. The analysis may help a business better understand its customers by answering such questions as: Which customers prefer to contact us via the Web instead through a call center? How are customers in Location X likely to react to the new product that we will introduce next month? How would a proposed change in our sales commission policy likely affect the sales of Product Y? Using data mining to answer such questions helps a business reinforce its successful practices and anticipate future customer preferences. For example, the *New York Times* reported that using data mining, Walmart found the unlikely fact that its Florida customers stocked up on beer and strawberry pop tarts when a hurricane was threatening. It now supplies its stores with plenty of these two items when hurricanes are on the horizon in an area.[19]

There are four categories of tools that are typically included under the business analytics umbrella. They include:[20]

- Statistical Analysis—answers questions like, "Why is this happening?"
- Forecasting/Extrapolation—answers questions like, "What if these trends continue?"
- Predictive Modeling—answers questions like, "What will happen next?"
- Optimization—answers questions like, "What is the best that can happen?"

These tools are used with the data in the data warehouse to gain insights and support decision making.

Analytics Environment

Building an environment that supports and encourages analytics is a critical component. It requires aligning IS strategy and organizational strategy with the business strategy. This includes alignment of the corporate culture, the incentive systems, the metrics used to measure success of initiatives, and the processes for using analytics with the objective

---

[19] Constance Hays, "What Walmart Knows About Customer's Habits," *The New York Times* (November 14, 2004), http://www.nytimes.com/2004/11/14/business/yourmoney/14wal.html.
[20] Ibid.

of building competitive advantage through analytics. For example, one financial services firm encouraged the use of analytics by changing its appraisal system so that demonstration of skills associated applying analytics was made a significant factor in compensation decisions. This is an example of aligning organizational strategy with a business strategy promoting the use of analytics to gain competitive advantage.

Although many companies have some sort of analytical tools in place, most are not used for mainstream decision making, and they certainly do not drive the strategy formulation discussions of the company. Those who gain competitive advantage from analytics use analytics as an integral component of their business.

Leadership plays a big role in creating a strong analytics environment. Leaders must move the company's culture toward an **evidence-based management** approach in which evidence and facts are analyzed as the first step in decision making. Those in this type of culture are encouraged to challenge others by asking for the data, and where no data is available, to experiment and learn to generate facts. Use of evidence-based management encourages decisions based on data and analysis rather than on experience and intuition.

Skilled Workforce

It's clear that to be successful with analytics, data and technology must be used. But experts point out that even with the best data and the most sophisticated analytics, people must be involved. Managers must have enough knowledge of analytics to use them in their decision making. Leaders must set examples for the organization by using analytics and requiring that decisions made by others use analytics. Perhaps the most important role is sponsorship. Davenport and Harris point out that it was the CEO-level sponsorship and the corresponding passion for analytics that enabled firms such as Caesars and Capital One to achieve the success they did.

Levels of Analytical Capabilities

All businesses have data. Some do a better job at it than others, and that can be a source of competitive advantage. Companies tend to fall into one of 5 levels of maturity with analytical capabilities. Understanding the different levels can help organization envision how to improve their capabilities to gain additional advantages. Figure 11.7 summarizes these levels.

▶ BIG DATA

One of the impacts of our knowledge and information based economies today is the very large amount of data amassing in databases both inside companies and in the environment. Consider, for a moment, the vast amount of data Google must process every time a query is made. By some estimates there are Google tells the inquirer how many results they found, and how fast the found them. A recent query of "big data" produced "about 88,700,000 results in 0.19 seconds." A second query of "lady gaga" produced 661,000,000

Level	Description	Source of Business Value
Level 1: Reporting	Answers "**What** happened?" by creating batch and ad hoc reports that summarize historical data; data across functions may not be consistent or well integrated.	Reduction in costs of report generation and printing
Level 2: Analyzing	Answers "**Why** did it happen?" by using ad hoc, real-time reports, and business intelligence tools to understand root causes.	Value associated with understanding root causes
Level 3: Predicting	Answers "**What** will happen?" by using predictive models that extrapolate from data to enable possible scenarios for the future; may be used to see potential for strategic advantage to business.	Value from being able to take action on predictions to help the business
Level 4: Operationalizing	Answers "**What** is happening now?" by linking business intelligence tools with operational systems to provide instantaneous views and updated predictions; data is integrated and accurate and viewed from enterprise perspective.	Value from real-time understanding of action/reaction and course correction instantly to improve operations
Level 5: Activating	Answers "**How** should we respond?" by automatically linking analytics with other systems, creating continuous updates from business intelligence tools that automatically are understood by operational tools and trigger events as needed.	Value from automated reactions based on real-time data stream. Value from dynamic process that "learns and corrects" automatically.

FIGURE 11.7 Analytical capabilities maturity levels.

Sources: Adapted from S. Brobst and J. Rarey, "Five Stages of Data Warehouse Decision Support Evolution," DSSResources.COM (January 6, 2003); and conversations with Farzad Shirzad, leader of Teradata's Center for Excellence in Analytics in 2011.

results in 0.13 seconds. Google's Web site claims to look at billions of sites with a choice of 46 languages to conduct the search.

Big data is the term used to describe techniques and technologies that make it economical to deal with very large datasets at the extreme end of the scale. According to Wikipedia, big datasets are on the order of exabytes (10^{18} bytes, abbreviated as EB) and zettabytes (10^{21} bytes, abbreviated as ZB) of data. A megabyte, abbreviated MB, is 10^6 bytes. Extreme datasets get that big because volumes of information are created, usually quickly, and stored for analysis. These extreme datasets create difficulties in storing, searching, sharing and analyzing; the size just cannot be handled by traditional data management tools or techniques. Having large data sets is desirable because of the potential trends and analytics that can be extracted, but when the dataset is so large that the information system cannot manage it, it's considered the "big data problem." In those cases, specialized computers and tools are needed to help managers mine the data.

Gary King, director of Harvard's Institute for Quantitative Social Science claims that big data: ". . . is a revolution. We're really just getting under way. But the march of quantification, made possible by enormous new sources of data, will sweep through academia, business and government. There is no area that is going to be untouched."[21]

Big data is increasingly common in part because of the rich, unstructured data streams that are created by social IT. Other examples of areas where big data problems typically occur are areas like simulations, scientific research, Internet searches, customer data management, and financial market analytics. Sensors that gather information for surveillance and sense-and-respond situations commonly create big data problems. With the growth of social IT, managers are increasingly finding that gathering all the information about their company and their customers from all the social sites available creates a data set that has the potential supply unique customer intelligence. Finding ways to manage and use the data, however, is significantly more difficult than managing more structured data sets.

Database warehouse vendors, such as Teradata. IBM and Oracle, have specially built tools for customers with big data problems. Data warehouses must be *scalable*, to allow capture and storage of all the data, *agile*, to accommodate changing requirements, mixed types of work, and quick turnaround of queries and reports, and *compatible* with the enterprise infrastructure to integrate with business applications and provide appropriate accessibility, backup and security.

There is a "dark side" to big data. The intense number crunching is likely to yield a number of "false discoveries." Any results should be questioned before they are applied. Further, extensive analysis might yield a correlation and lead to a statistical inference that is unfair or discriminatory. Finally, Big Data might offer a high tech twist to an old practice "I know what the facts are—now let's find the ones we want." Here again, care must be applied when using powerful tools.[22]

▶ SOCIAL ANALYTICS

In 2011, managers saw a rise in interest in using social IT as long as there was some way to measure the value gained from the invested time and resources. A class of tools called **social analytics**, or social media analytics were created to address this issue, and as expected, many vendors began offering packages that provided these tools. The

[21] S. Lohr, "The Age of Big Data," *The New York Times* (February 12, 2012), SR1.
[22] Ibid.

goal of social analytics is to measure the impact of social IT investments on the business. At issue, however, is how to analyze conversations, tweets, blogs, and other social IT data to create meaningful, actionable facts. For example, it might be relatively easy to measure the number of *hits* on a Web site or the number of *click-throughs* from a link. But what does that information really tell a manager? What action would the manager consider taking based on this type of data? *Hits* and *click-throughs* are only meaningful in context and with other data that indicate if business value was achieved. That is, they only become information when they are processed to become relevant and purposeful.

As of the writing of this chapter, social analytics is one of the key topics discussed by managers seeking to incorporate social IT into their business. Vendors such as Google Analytics and Radian6 (acquired by Salesforce.com) offer platforms with social analytics tools. For example, Radian6's platform includes tools that enable:

- Listening to the community—identify and monitor all conversations in the social Web on a particular topic or brand.

- Learning who is in the community—learn customer demographics such as age, gender, location, and other trends to foster closer relationship with community.

- Engaging people in the community— communicate directly with customers on social platforms such as Facebook, YouTube, LinkedIn, and Twitter using a single app.

- Tracking what is being said—measure and track demographics, conversations, sentiment, status, and customer voice using a dashboard and other reporting tools.

UPS, Pizza Hut, Pepsi, AMD, and Dell Computers are examples of companies with well-know case studies about their use of social analytics and monitoring tools like Radian6 for engaging and encouraging collaboration among their customers. For example, in a presentation to the Blogwell community in 2011, a UPS manager described how the company turned around its customer service efforts using social IT and social analytics.[23] UPS studied their customer service process and monitored the social Web for comments. They noticed that some customers loved them, but others had a bad experience and wrote about it on sites like Twitter and Facebook. By using social analytics platform, they identified dissatisfied customers and addressed their problems on the social platform used by the customer. This resulted in more than 1 million positive tweets about UPS and lots of public recognition for turning around their customer service process.

Google Analytics, on the other hand, is a set of social analytics tools that enable organizations to analyze their Web site. The Google Analytics site thoroughly analyses the key words used by visitors to reach a Web site, and provides statistics to help managers understand the searches potential customers use. Some features are:

- Web site testing and optimizing—to understand traffic to Web sites and to optimize the site's content and design for increasing traffic.

- Search optimization—to understand how Google sees an organization's Web site, how other sites link to the organization's site, and how specific search queries drive traffic to the organization's site.

---

[23] socialmedia.org/blogwell (November 8, 2011).

Social Business Lens: Social Graphs

Ever wonder who your connections are connected to? A social graph is a pictorial representation of relationships. Tools that create social graphs look at the network of people in a community and draw a map showing all the connections. Today it has come to mean the networks of everyone on the Web.

While social scientists created the term long ago, Facebook made it part of the popular lexicon when CEO, Mark Zuckerberg referred to it in describing his platform. Facebook is an application built on the concept that there is value connecting the social graphs of individuals to create a large, global social graph.

Typically the diagram uses individuals as the notes of the graphs, and lines between them to indicate some type of relationship. I might be that they 'know' each other or 'work at the same place' or 'are connected on Facebook". Relationships can be strong, such as a close friend, or weak, such as an acquaintance. When analyzing a social graph, understanding what the lines are depicting is important.

Social graphs are useful for applications like Facebook and LinkedIn, who utilize the connections to help individuals grow their networks. But there are many other uses for this type of analytics. Do leaders have different social graphs than those they lead? Want to effect change? Then you want to know who the influencer is in an organization or community. Need to find expertise that is outside your network? Perhaps the extended social graph of your connections has such a person. There are ways to monetize this too. Zuckerberg shared his vision "Yelp maps out the part of the graph that relates to small businesses. Pandora maps the part that relates to music. If we can take these separate maps and pull them all together, then we can create a Web that's smarter, more social, more personalized, and more semantically aware."

Source: Facebook: One Social Graph to Rule Them All? (April 21, 2010), http://www.cbsnews.com/stories/2010/04/21/tech/main6418458.shtml.

- Search term interest and insights—to understand the interest over time of a search term, regional interest in the term, top searches for terms of similar category, and popularity of similar terms.
- Advertising support and management—to identify the best ways to spend advertising resources for online media.

Re/Max real estate franchise network is an example of a company using social analytics like Google analytics. With franchises in 62 countries, Re/Max is a leading provider of residential, commercial, referral, relocation, and asset management. As part of their online strategy, Re/Max created a site that listed all properties available, whether listed by Re/Max agents or others, and made it available to anyone accessing the site. They then used Google Analytics to understand consumer behavior on the site and to drive leads to agents in their franchises. Prior to this strategy, they used focus groups to understand consumer behavior, but they were expensive, limited in scope, and lacking in real data. The site gets more than 2 million hits a month, mostly from visitors who searched for "remax" in their query. Google Analytics helped managers redesign the Web site so the most used tools were on the home page, further providing value to potential customers. Ultimately, Google Analytics helped Re/Max drive more leads to agents, reducing the cost agents were used to paying for leads.[24]

► CAVEATS FOR MANAGING KNOWLEDGE AND BUSINESS INTELLIGENCE

Following such a broad survey, it seems appropriate to conclude with a few caveats. First, recall that knowledge management and business intelligence continue to be emerging disciplines. Viewing business intelligence as a process rather than an end by itself requires managers to remain flexible and open-minded.

Second, the objective of knowledge management is not always to make knowledge more visible or available. Like other assets, it is sometimes in the best interests of the firm to keep knowledge tacit, hidden, and non-transferable. Competitive advantage increasingly depends on knowledge assets that are difficult to reproduce. Retaining knowledge is as much a strategic issue as sharing knowledge. Business intelligence, on the other hand, is designed to make knowledge visible, at least inside the enterprise, so it can be analyzed and acted upon to meet business objectives.

Third, knowledge can create a shared context for thinking about the future. If the purpose of knowledge management and business intelligence is to help make better decisions, then it must provide value for future events, not just views of the past history. The goal is to use data to identify trends and environmental changes, then create predictions that help inform business strategy and long-term goal setting.

Finally, people lie at the heart of knowledge management and business intelligence. Establishing and nurturing a culture that values learning and sharing of knowledge enables effective and efficient knowledge management. Knowledge sharing—subject, of course, to the second caveat already described—must be valued and practiced by all employees for knowledge management to work. The success of knowledge management ultimately depends on a personal and organizational willingness to learn.

► SUMMARY

- Knowledge management includes the processes necessary to generate, capture, codify and transfer knowledge across organizations. Business intelligence is the set of technologies and practices used to analyze and understand data and to use it in making decisions about future actions. Business analytics is the set of quantitative and predictive models used to drive decisions.

- The four main types of intellectual property are patents, trademarks, designs, and copyrights.

- Data, information, and knowledge should not be viewed as interchangeable. Knowledge is more valuable than information, which is more valuable than data because of the human contributions involved.

---

[24] www.google.com/analytics/case_study_remax.html (accessed on February 20, 2012).

- The two kinds of knowledge are tacit and explicit. Tacit knowledge is personal, context-specific, and hard to formalize and communicate. Explicit knowledge is easily collected, organized, and transferred through digital means.

- Knowledge management is a dynamic and continuously evolving process that involves knowledge generation, capture, codification, and transfer. Traditional business intelligence includes reporting, querying, dashboards and scorecards.

- Business intelligence 2.0 integrates Web 2.0 capabilities and features into traditional BI systems and creating instant access to real-time information and data.

- Successfully competing with business analytics means that an organization has these five capabilities: hard to duplicate, uniqueness, adaptability, better than competition, and renewability.

- There are five levels of analytics maturity: reporting, analyzing, predicting, operationalizing, and activating.

- Big data refers to very large data repositories often found in environments where information is created quickly. Tools for managing big data sets are different than those for other data sets.

- Social analytics provide companies with tools to monitor and engage their communities and to evaluate the success of their investment in social IT.

▶ KEY TERMS

big data (p. 341)
business analytics (p. 327)
business intelligence (p. 327)
data (p. 330)
data mining (p. 339)
data warehouses (p. 338)
explicit knowledge (p. 334)
externalization (p. 334)
evidence-based
   management (p. 340)

folksonomy (p. 335)
information (p. 330)
intellectual capital (p. 328)
intellectual property (p. 328)
knowledge (p. 331)
knowledge capture (p. 335)
knowledge
   codification (p. 335)
knowledge
   generation (p. 335)

knowledge
   management (p. 327)
knowledge transfer (p. 335)
social analytics (p. 342)
socialization (p. 335)
tacit knowledge (p. 332)
tagging (p. 335)

▶ DISCUSSION QUESTIONS

1. The terms *data*, *information*, and *knowledge* are often used interchangeably. But as this chapter discussed, they can be seen as three points on a continuum. What, in your opinion, comes after knowledge on this continuum?

2. What is the difference between tacit and explicit knowledge? From your own experience, describe an example of each. How might an organization manage tacit knowledge?

3. What does it take to be a successful competitor using business analytics? What is IT's role in helping build this competence for the enterprise?

4. How do social analytics aid an organization?

5. Why is it so difficult to protect intellectual property? Do you think that the Digital Millennium Copyright Act is the type of legislation that should be enacted to protect intellectual property? Why or why not?

6. PricewaterhouseCoopers has an elegant, powerful intranet knowledge management system called Knowledge Curve. Knowledge Curve makes available to its consultants and auditors a compendium of best practices, consulting methodologies, new tax and audit insights, links to external Web sites and news services, online training courses, directories of in-house experts, and other forms of explicit knowledge. Yet, according to one of the firm's managing partners, "There's a feeling it's underutilized. Everybody goes there sometimes, but when they're looking for expertise, most people go down the hall."[25] Why do you think that Knowledge Curve is underutilized?

CASE STUDY 11-1

STOP & SHOP'S SCAN IT! APP

The grocery store and supermarket shopping industries have combined annual revenues in the hundreds of billions of dollars. Industry guru Phil Lembert, estimated that by 2015, $706 billion dollars will be spent on groceries annually. Grocery shopping was a highly commoditized industry with over 85,000 stores in the United States. With little variation in available item selection and less money being spent on groceries in the down economy, competition for customer loyalty was at an all time high in 2012. By using business analytics to help process buying habits of its customers, Stop & Shop, a Quincy, Massachusetts-based grocer, tried to get a better grasp on the hard-to-understand concept of customer loyalty in grocery shopping.

In 2009, Stop & Shop introduced Scan It!, a portable electronic device for customers shopping in their stores. The device allowed customers to "scan and bag" products, expediting check out times at the end of their shopping trip. Additionally, the device offered deals based on the location of the scanner (and therefore the customer) in the store. Location-specific discounts in real time became increasingly popular to customers, as usage of Scan It! grew by 10% in both the first and second quarters of 2009. The most beneficial aspect of the Scan It!, however, came with the powerful analytics software built into the device by Modiv Media, in which Stop & Shop owns a minority interest. The software kept track of each customer's purchasing habits both past and present, to individualize coupons in real time for the customer.

The scanner resulted in three positive trends for Shop & Stop. Customer loyalty grew, which allowed Stop & Shop to secure a greater customer base than area demographics would predict. Additionally, each shopper's basket size increased as individually tailored coupons enticed customers to buy more. Lastly, Stop & Shop saw its customer base grow, as word of mouth marketing brought in more customers to try the state of the art device.

Stop & Shop saw customer adoption plateau, however, as a couple of years passed, and the age of mobile apps increased ease of use. In October 2011, the grocer created the Scan It! app for the iPhone and Android. By eliminating the need to sign in and retrieve a scanner at the store, customer adoption continued its upward climb. Additionally, as customers became increasingly concerned about saving money while shopping, Stop & Shop built in budgeting software to allow customers to track their spending more effectively. Ads for the new app proclaimed, "New Mobile App Allows Customers to Shop, Bag, and Tally Their Grocery Order with Their Personal iPhone® and Android™ Devices". Scan It! was heralded as "a first of its kind grocery app that allows customers to use their personal mobile device to scan, tally, and bag their groceries while they shop."[26]

[25] Thomas Stewart, "The Case Against Knowledge Management," *Business 2.0* (February 2002), 81.
[26] Adapted from http://www.internetretailer.com/2011/10/20/stop-shop-expands-availability-scan-it-mobile-app; http://www.stopandshop.com/our_stores/tools/scan_it_mobile.htm; and http://southeastfarmpress.com/vegetables/supermarket-guru-seeking-next-big-trend.

Stop & Shop bundled an app that not only rewarded customers who shopped at their stores by helping them save money, but it provided additional functionality to the customers and tracked information on sales, which Stop & Shop loaded into its data warehouse and used to understand its customers. Analytics then helped Stop & Shop put the right items on its shelves to maximize sales and create customer loyalty.

Discussion Questions

1. What is the benefit of the Scan It! data to Stop & Shop? What are some of the questions can they now answer about their customers?

2. How would you assess the level of maturity of Stop & Shop's use of analytics? What might they do differently with the data to gain more value?

3. What concerns might shoppers have about their privacy? How would you advise Stop & Shop management to respond to these concerns?

CASE STUDY 11-2

BUSINESS INTELLIGENCE AT CKE RESTAURANTS

At a time when most fast-food restaurants were touting nutrition, Hardee's proudly introduced the Monster Thickburger. This burger boasts a phenomenal 1,420 calories and 107 grams of fat. It consists of two, one-third-pound charbroiled 100% Angus beef patties, three slices of American cheese, a dollop of mayonnaise, and four crispy strips of bacon on a toasted buttery sesame seed bun. What on earth was CKE Restaurants, the owners of the Hardee's chain, thinking?

Because of its Business Intelligence System (BIS), CKE was confident about introducing the Monster Thickburger across the United States. A BIS uses data mining, analytical processing, querying, and reporting to process a business's data and derive insights from it. CKE's BIS, known ironically inside the company as CPR (CKE Performance Reporting) monitored the performance of its Monster Thickburger in test markets to ensure that the burger contributed to increases in sales and profits at restaurants without cannibalizing sales of other more modest burgers. To do so, CKE's BIS studied a variety of factors—such as menu mixes, Monster Thickburger production costs, average unit volumes for the Monster Thickburger compared with other burgers, gross profits and total sales for each of the test stores, and the contribution that each menu item (including the Monster Thickburger) made to total sales. Because the sales of Monster Thickburger exceeded expectations in the test markets, CKE developed a $7 million dollar advertising campaign to launch its nationwide introduction. Monster Thickburger sales exceeded expectations, and Hardee's sales revenues increased immediately, eventually growing by 8%. "The Monster Thickburger was directly responsible for a good deal of that increase," says Brad Haley, Hardee's Executive Vice President of Marketing.

CKE, partially because of its reliance on CPR, was rescued from the brink of bankruptcy. It increased sales at restaurants open more than a year, narrowed its overall losses, and finally turned a profit after three years. CPR, its proprietary system, consists of a Microsoft SQL server database and uses Microsoft development tools to parse and display analytical information. It uses econometric models to provide context and to explain performance. The company reviews and refines these models each month. The econometric models take into consideration 44 factors, including the weather, holidays, coupon activity, discounting, free giveaways, and new products.

With the click of a button, for example, a sales downturn can be explained on a screen that shows that 5% of the 8% decrease was due to torrential rain in the Northeast and 2% was due to free giveaways.

In the competitive restaurant chain industry, companies have to be agile and responsive to the dynamic environment that they face. They must match their BIS initiatives to their business strategies in order to improve operations and their bottom lines. BISs assist them in making strategic decisions about menu items and closures of underperforming stores, as well as tactical matters such as renegotiating contracts with food suppliers, monitoring food costs, and identifying opportunities to improve inefficient processes. To derive value from their BISs, many restaurant chains have successfully reduced the three biggest barriers to BIS success: voluminous amounts of irrelevant data, poor data quality, and user resistance.

CKE's CIO and Executive Vice President of Strategic Planning, Jeff Chasney, states: "If you're just presenting information that's neat and nice but doesn't evoke a decision or impart important knowledge, then it's noise. You have to focus on what are the really important things going on in your business."

Chasney stresses a BIS should be different from the plain-vanilla standard corporate reporting tools of old. Rather, a BIS should provide managers with insights rather than just data. He believes that the context from which the data was collected significantly impacts how that data should be interpreted. Systems that just report changes without enough background or information on what caused those changes are not very useful. Managers don't know what data to trust. Chasney explained: "If your business intelligence system is not going to improve your decision making and find problem areas to correct and new directions to take, nobody's going to bother to look at it."

The first step to developing a BIS is to understand the company's decision-making processes. Before information is collected, analyzed and used in the BIS, someone has to identify what information is needed to confidently make decisions. For instance, the CEOs of CKE's three restaurant chains wanted to understand what made sales fluctuate, while the COOs wanted to know how to recognize good business opportunities as well as underperforming properties. Then the BIS designer must determine the appropriate presentation format, be it a report, a chart, or a Web site.

BIS must add value to the executive's decision-making processes. To do that, attention must be paid to the critical performance indicators. For CKE, as Chasney learned, those are sales, cost of sales, exceptions (such as high-performing or underperforming areas), and business trends.

Discussion Questions

1. How does the Business Intelligence System (BIS) at CKE add value to the business?
2. What are some tips for developing and using the BIS described in this case?
3. Was the introduction of the Monster Thickburger a good idea or an example of information leading to a wrong decision?

Sources: Christine Lagorio, "Man vs. Monster Thickburger," CBS News (February 11, 2009), http://www.cbsnews.com; and Meredith Levinson, "The Brain Behind the Big, Bad Burger and Other Tales of Business Intelligence," *CIO Magazine* (May 15, 2007), http://www.cio.com/article/109454/The_Brain_Behind_the_Big_Bad_Burger_and_Other_Tales_of_Business_Intelligence.

CHAPTER 12

USING INFORMATION ETHICALLY

IT has created a unique set of ethical issues related to the use and control of information. This chapter addresses those issues from various perspectives using three normative theories (stockholder, stakeholder, and social contract) to understand the responsible use and control of information by business organizations. Social contract theory is extended to evolving issues such as green computing and responsiveness to foreign governments when ethical tensions emerge. At the individual and corporate level, Mason's PAPA (Privacy, Accuracy, Property, Accessibility) framework is applied to information control. The chapter concludes with discussions of the ethical role of managers in today's dynamic world of social business and security controls to keep information safe and accurate.

When TJX Co. found the largest data security breach in the history of retailing, it faced a serious ethical dilemma not faced by many companies. It originally estimated that the credit card accounts of 45.6 million customers worldwide were affected (though that number has been updated to 94 million). Given the extent of the breach, multiple state, federal, and foreign jurisdictions dictated how and when it must inform affected customers and what corrective steps it must take. Most jurisdictions allowed 45 days for it to act following the determination of the breach. Any extension beyond 45 days would incur heavy fines. However, on the ethical side it became an even more pressing issue. Should TJX inform the affected customers immediately or wait till the breach was secured and all remedial steps were undertaken, which may take weeks?

As a socially responsible company, TJX makes its obligations to customers a priority. If it informed the customers immediately, the customers could start taking preventive steps to protect themselves from the identity theft and avoid any resulting financial and psychological losses. However, this means the breach would become public knowledge before the remedial steps were taken. More hackers would learn about it and possibly exploit the weakness in its IT infrastructure. Additionally, the financial markets would lose confidence in the company and severely punish shareholders. Such loss of image would also affect its ability to attract and retain high-quality employees in the long run. On the other hand, if it waited for 45 days, financial stability of many customers would be compromised through misuse of their credit card and other private records. This could result in a major class-action litigation, which might permanently affect the company.

350

As in the case of TJX, information collected in the course of business is important for the conduct of business and can even create valuable competitive advantage. But managers must ask ethical questions concerning just how that information will be used and by whom, whether they arise inside or outside the organization. Failing to do so can carry serious consequences. Failing to protect consumer information ultimately can hurt shareholder relationships if costs associated with a breach have a negative impact on the bottom line. Acting responsibly is likely to gain legitimacy in the eyes of key stakeholders. Further, failure to adequately control information can cause spillover effect with repercussions for an entire industry. For example, following the TJX breach, Massachusetts passed legislation with stringent requirements for any organization maintaining information about its citizens.[1] As computer networks and their products come to touch every aspect of people's lives, and as the power, speed, and capabilities of computers expand, managers are increasingly challenged to govern their use and protect information residing on them in an ethical manner.

In such an environment, managers are called on to manage the information generated and contained within those systems for the benefit not only of the corporation, but also of society as a whole. The predominant issue, which arises due to the omnipresence of corporate IS, concerns the just and ethical use of the information companies collect in the course of everyday operations. Without official guidelines and codes of conduct, who decides how to use this information? More and more, this challenge falls on corporate managers. Managers need to understand societal needs and expectations to determine what they ethically can and cannot do in their quest to learn about their customers, suppliers, and employees, and to provide greater service.

Before managers can deal effectively with issues related to the ethical and moral governance of IS, they need to know what these issues are. Unfortunately, as with many emerging fields, well-accepted guidelines do not exist. Thus, managers bear even greater responsibility as they try to run their businesses and simultaneously develop control methods that meet both corporate imperatives and the needs of society at large. If this challenge appears to be a matter of drafting operating manuals, nothing could be further from the truth.

In a society whose legal standards are continually challenged, managers must serve as guardians of the public and private interest, although many may have no formal legal training and, thus, no firm basis for judgment. This chapter addresses many such concerns. It begins by expanding on the definition of ethical behavior and introduces several heuristics that managers can employ to help them make better decisions. Next this chapter elaborates on the most important issues behind the ethical treatment of information and some newly emerging controversies that will surely test society's resolve concerning the increasing presence of IS in every aspect of life.

This chapter takes a high-level view of ethical issues facing managers in today's environment. It focuses primarily on providing a set of frameworks the manager can apply to a wide variety of ethical issues. Outside the scope of this chapter are several important issues such as the digital divide (the impact of computer technology on

---

[1] M. Culnan and C. Williams, "How Ethics Can Enhance Organizational Privacy: Lessons from the ChoicePoint and TJX Data Breaches," *MIS Quarterly* (2009), 33(4), 673–687.

the poor or "have-nots," racial minorities, and third world nations), cyberwar (politically motivated hacking to conduct sabotage and espionage), or social concerns that arise out of artificial intelligence, neural networks, and expert systems. Although these are interesting and important areas for concern, the objective in this chapter is to provide managers with a way to think about the issues of information ethics and corporate responsibility.

▶ RESPONSIBLE COMPUTING

The technological landscape is changing daily. Increasingly, however, technological advances come about in a business domain lacking ethical clarity. Because of its newness, this area of IT often lacks accepted norms of behavior or universally accepted decision-making criteria. Daily companies encounter ethical dilemmas as they try to use their IS to create and exploit competitive advantages. These ethical dilemmas arise whenever a decision or an action reflects competing moral values that may impair or enhance the well-being of an individual or a group of people. They arise when there is no one clear way to deal with the ethical issue.

Managers must assess current information initiatives with particular attention to possible ethical issues. Because so many managers have been educated in the current corporate world, they are used to the overriding ethical norms present in their traditional businesses. Managers in the information age need to translate their current ethical norms into terms meaningful for the new electronic corporation. Clearly they need to consider **information ethics**, or the "ethical issues associated with the development and application of information technologies."[2]

Consider three theories of ethical behavior in the corporate environment that managers can develop and apply to the particular challenges they face. These normative theories of business ethics—stockholder theory, stakeholder theory, and social contract theory—are widely applied in traditional business situations. They are "normative" in that they attempt to derive what might be called "intermediate-level" ethical principles: principles expressed in language accessible to the ordinary businessperson, which can be applied to the concrete moral quandaries of the business domain.[3] Following is a description of each theory accompanied by an illustration of its application using the TJX example outlined at the beginning of this chapter.

Stockholder Theory

According to **stockholder theory**, stockholders advance capital to corporate managers, who act as agents in furthering their ends. The nature of this contract binds managers to act in the interest of the shareholders (i.e., to maximize shareholder value). As Milton Friedman wrote, "There is one and only one social responsibility of business: to use its resources and engage in activities designed to increase its profits so long as it stays within

---

[2] M. G. Martinsons and D. Ma, "Sub-cultural Differences in Information Ethics across China: Focus on Chinese Management Generation Gaps," *Journal of AIS* (2009), 10(Special Issue).

[3] Hasnas and Smith, "Ethics and Information Systems," 5.

the rules of the game, which is to say, engages in open and free competition, without deception or fraud."[4]

Stockholder theory qualifies the manager's duty in two salient ways. First, managers are bound to employ legal, non-fraudulent means. Second, managers must take the long-term view of shareholder interest (i.e., they are obliged to forgo short-term gains if doing so will maximize value over the long term).

Managers should bear in mind that stockholder theory itself provides a limited framework for moral argument because it assumes the ability of the free market to fully promote the interests of society at large. Yet the singular pursuit of profit on the part of individuals or corporations cannot be said to maximize social welfare. Free markets can foster the creation of monopolies and other circumstances that limit the ability of members of a society to secure the common good. A proponent of stockholder theory might insist that, as agents of stockholders, managers must not use stockholders' money to accomplish goals that do not directly serve the interests of those same stockholders. A critic of stockholder theory would argue that such spending would be just if the money went to further the public interest.

The stipulation under stockholder theory that the pursuit of profits must be legal and non-fraudulent would not limit TJX from waiting to announce the security breach until it had taken corrective action. The delay allowed by law might also have a positive impact on TJX's stock price. The delay would satisfy the test of maximizing shareholder value because it would help keep the price of its stock from dropping. Further, a recent survey has shown that customers are reluctant to shop in stores once data breaches have been announced, so delaying may be important for maintaining a steady stream of revenues for as long as possible. On the other hand, disgruntled customers would definitely stop shopping at its stores if TJX waited too long.[5] Any lost revenues would weigh against managers' success in meeting the ethical obligation to work toward maximizing value. In the end it appears that TJX only took the actions necessary to bring its practices in line with those expected in industry.[6]

Stakeholder Theory

Stakeholder theory holds that managers, although bound by their relation to stockholders, are entrusted also with a responsibility, fiduciary or otherwise, to all those who hold a stake in or a claim on the firm.[7] The term "stakeholder" is currently taken to mean any group that vitally affects the survival and success of the corporation or whose interests the corporation vitally affects. Such groups normally include stockholders, customers, employees, suppliers, and the local community, though other groups may also be considered stakeholders, depending on the circumstances. At its most basic level,

[4] M. Friedman, *Capitalism and Freedom* (Chicago, IL: University of Chicago Press, 1962), 133.

[5] There is an interesting presentation of a similar breach with commentaries from the CIOs of ChoicePoint, Motorola, Visa International, and Theft Resource Center in Eric McNulty's "Boss I Think Someone Stole Our Customer Data," *Harvard Business Review* (September 2007), 37–50.

[6] M. Culnan and C. Williams, "How Ethics Can Enhance Organizational Privacy: Lessons from the ChoicePoint and TJX Data Breaches," *MIS Quarterly* (2009), 33(4), 673–687.

[7] Hasnas and Smith, "Ethics and Information Systems," 8.

stakeholder theory states that management must enact and follow policies that balance the rights of all stakeholders without impinging on the rights of any one particular stakeholder.

Stakeholder theory diverges most consequentially from stockholder theory in affirming that the interests of parties other than the stockholders also play a legitimate role in the governance and management of the firm. As a practical matter, it is often difficult, if not impossible to figure out what is in the best interest of each stakeholder group and then balance their conflicting interests.

When stakeholders feel that their interests haven't been considered adequately by the managers making the decisions, their only recourse may be to stop participating in the corporation: Customers can stop buying the company's products, stockholders can sell their stock, and so forth. But some stakeholders are not in a position to stop participating in the corporation. In particular, employees may need to continue working for the corporation, even though they dislike practices of their employers, or experience considerable stress due to their jobs.

Viewed in light of stakeholder theory, the ethical issue facing TJX presents a more complex dilemma. John Philip Coghlan, CEO of Visa USA noted, "A data breach can put an executive in an exceedingly complex situation, where he must negotiate the often divergent interests of multiple stakeholders."[8] TJX's shareholders stand to gain in the short-term, but what would be the effects on other stakeholders? One stakeholder group, the customers, definitely could benefit from knowing about the breach as soon as possible because they could take steps to protect themselves. Customers could be informed of the severity of the breach and protective actions that they could take through a special Web page, toll-free information hotlines, or Webcasts. TJX could also offer them free credit-monitoring service and compensate those who are injured. Research has shown that customers who receive adequate compensation after making a complaint are actually more loyal than those without complaints.[9] On the other hand, if the breach were not announced, fewer hackers might attempt to break into the systems. Nonetheless, it probably could be shown that the costs to customers outweighed the benefits within the larger stakeholder group.

Social Contract Theory

Social contract theory places social responsibilities on corporate managers to consider the needs of a society. Social contract theorists ask what conditions would have to be met for the members of society to agree to allow the corporation to be formed. Thus, society bestows legal recognition on a corporation to allow it to employ social resources toward given ends that create more value to the society than the corporation consumes. Thus, society charges the corporation to enhance its welfare by satisfying particular interests of consumers and workers in exploiting the advantages of the corporate form.[10]

---

[8] McNulty, "Boss I Think Someone Stole Our Customer Data."

[9] Ibid.

[10] Hasnas and Smith, "Ethics and Information Systems," 10.

The social contract comprises two distinct components: social welfare and justice. The former arises from the belief that corporations must provide greater benefits than their associated costs, or society would not allow their creation. Thus, the social contract obliges managers to pursue profits in ways that are compatible with the well-being of society as a whole. Similarly, the justice component holds that corporations must pursue profits legally, without fraud or deception, and avoid activities that injure society.

Social contract theory meets criticism because no mechanism exists to actuate it. In the absence of a real contract whose terms subordinate profit maximization to social welfare, most critics find it hard to imagine corporations losing profitability in the name of altruism. Yet, the strength of the theory lies in its broad assessment of the moral foundations of business activity.

Applied to the TJX case, social contract theory would demand that the manager ask whether the delay in notifying customers about the security breach could compromise fundamental tenets of fairness or social justice. If customers were not apprised of the delay as soon as possible, TJX's actions could be seen as unethical because it would not seem fair to delay notifying them. If, on the other hand, the time prior to notification were used to take corrective action with the consequence of limiting not only hackers from stealing confidential customer information but also of forestalling future attacks that would impact society as a whole, the delay conceivably could be considered ethical.

Although these three normative theories of business ethics possess distinct characteristics, they are not completely incompatible. All offer useful metrics for defining ethical behavior in profit-seeking enterprises under free market conditions. They provide managers with an independent standard by which to judge the ethical nature of superiors' orders as well as their firms' policies and codes of conduct. Upon inspection, the three theories appear to represent concentric circles, with stockholder theory at the center and social contract theory at the outer ring. Stockholder theory is narrowest in scope, stakeholder theory encompasses and expands on it, and social contract theory covers the broadest area. Figure 12.1 summarizes these three theories.

What, ultimately, did TJX do? TJX disclosed the breach in January 2007, but did not release a comprehensive executive summary of the attack until March 2007, when it made a regulatory filing. The preceding December TJX had actually noticed suspicious software, at which point it hired IBM and General Dynamics to investigate. Three days later, these investigators determined that TJX's systems had been compromised due to its failure to implement adequate information security procedures and detect and limit unauthorized access.[11] Further, the attacker still had access. Unfortunately, it took TJX 17 months to find out that their computer systems had been breached on numerous occasions on a colossal scale.[12] It was over a year later, on February 29,

[11] M. Culnan and C. Williams, "How Ethics Can Enhance Organizational Privacy: Lessons from the ChoicePoint and TJX Data Breaches," *MIS Quarterly* (2009), 33(4), 673–687.

[12] Kevin Murphy, "TJX Hack Is Biggest Ever," *Computer Business Review* (March 30, 2007), http://www.cbronline.com/article_news.asp?guid=0EFDDC37-4EA7-4A78-9726-E6F63C86234D.

Theory	Definition	Metrics
Stockholder	Maximize stockholder wealth, in legal and non-fraudulent manners.	Will this action maximize long-term stockholder value? Can goals be accomplished without compromising company standards and without breaking laws?
Stakeholder	Maximize benefits to all stakeholders while weighing costs to competing interests.	Does the proposed action maximize collective benefits to the company? Does this action treat one or more of the corporate stakeholders unfairly?
Social contract	Create value for society in a manner that is just and non-discriminatory.	Does this action create a "net" benefit for society? Does the proposed action discriminate against any group in particular, and is its implementation socially just?

FIGURE 12.1 Three normative theories of business ethics.

2008, when the President and CEO, Carol Meyrowitz, wrote a letter to "valued customers" about the breach that had been announced on January 2007. The TJX retail chain agreed to pay $24 and $41 million in restitution to MasterCard and Visa issuing lenders, respectively, who were affected by the breach. TJX also offered free credit monitoring for cardholders and a $30 store voucher.[13] It wasn't until June 2009 that TJX finally reached a settlement of US$9.75 million with 41 states to compensate them for their investigations of the breach.[14] Based on the newspaper accounts, one could surmise that TJX's overriding approach was more consistent with the stockholder theory than social contract theory. At least one stakeholder group, the customers, were not well-served.

▶ CORPORATE SOCIAL RESPONSIBILITY

Application of social contract theory helps companies adopt a broader perspective. In this section we adopt a "big picture" by exploring two types of corporate social responsibility. We look at a new way of doing business, green computing. We also consider an ethical dilemma that more and more corporations are facing in our flattening world.

---

[13] Martin Bosworth, "TJX to Pay Mastercard $24 Million for Data Breach," ConsumerAffaris.com (April 6, 2008), http://www.consumeraffairs.com/news04/2008/04/tjx_mc.html (accessed on July 29, 2008).

[14] J. Vijayan, "TJX Reaches $9.75 Million Breach Settlement with 41 States," *Computerworld*, (June 24, 2009), http://www.computerworld.com/s/article/9134765/TJX_reaches_9.75_million_breach_settlement_with_41_states (accessed on January 28, 2012).

Green Computing

Gartner Inc. continues to put green computing at the top of its list of upcoming strategic technologies, signaling that more and more companies are becoming socially responsible.[15] **Green computing** is concerned with using computing resources efficiently. The need for green computing is becoming more obvious when considering the amount of power needed to drive the world's PCs, servers, routers, switches, and data centers. Consider, for example, the computing power consumed by the five largest search companies at the peak of energy consumption in 2007. The five companies used about 2 million servers that needed approximately 2.4 gigawatts to run. By comparison, the massive Hoover Dam at a maximum only generates about 2 gigawatts. The situation was exacerbated by the cooling systems that companies added to combat the heat generated by the highest-performing systems. The usage patterns dropped since 2007, most likely because the financial crisis of 2008, a greater focus on sustainability and the use of more energy-saving technologies.[16] However, the use is still substantial.

Companies are working in a number of ways to adopt more socially responsible approaches to energy consumption. In particular they are replacing older systems with more energy-efficient ones, moving workloads based on energy efficiency, using the most power-inefficient servers only at times of peak usage, improving air flows in data centers, and turning to cloud computing, as well as virtualization. As introduced in Chapter 6, virtualization lets a computer run multiple operating systems or several versions of the same operating system at the same time. SAP improved its data center efficiency on the computing through its continued investments in virtualization. Energy consumption dropped and they were able to eliminate 1,400 servers. SAP increased the number of virtual servers from 37% in 2009 to 49% in 2010. The virtualization rate of new servers grew from around 80% to 83%.[17] On their Web site, SAP notes the value of green IT which in terms of energy usage "presents some of the greatest opportunities to increase our efficiency, improve our operations and reach our sustainability goals. It is one of the best examples of how creating positive impact also benefits our business. By reducing our total energy consumption, we can be both sustainable and profitable."[18]

An especially creative green approach is the one contemplated by Google to cool the computers that power its search engine. Google's management is considering placing the computers in a fleet of barges anchored approximately seven miles (11 km) offshore. This would allow Google to turn tidal power, a continuous uninterruptible power source, into electricity. The sea could also be used to power a cooling pump to

[15] Hype Cycle for Sustainability and Green IT (2011), Gartner, Inc., http://www.gartner.com/DisplayDocument?doc_cd=214739&ref=g_noreg (accessed on February 28, 2012).

[16] These two articles contrast energy use in 2007 and 2011: G. Lawton, "Powering Down the Computing Infrastructure," *Computer* (February 2007), 16–19; and J. Markoff, "Data Centers' Power Use Less Than Was Expected, *The New York Times* (July 31, 2011), http://www.nytimes.com/2011/08/01/technology/data-centers-using-less-power-than-forecast-report-says.html?_r=2 (accessed on February 28, 2012).

[17] Data Center Energy, SAP Sustainability Report, http://www.sapsustainabilityreport.com/data-center-energy (accessed on January 30, 2012).

[18] "Total Energy Consumed", SAP Sustainability Report, http://www.sapsustainabilityreport.com/total-energy-consumed (accessed on January 30, 2012).

carry away the considerable heat generated by its computers.[19] Or the sea could be used to power servers in an abandoned paper mill built more than half a century ago. Google transformed the mill in Hamina, Finland, into a data center with massive computing facilities. Part of the appeal of the mill was its underground tunnel system that was designed to pull water from the Gulf of Finland. Originally, that frigid Baltic water cooled a steam generation plant at the mill, but Google saw it as a way to cool its servers.[20]

Green programs can have a triple bottom line (TBL): economic, environmental, and social. That is, green programs create economic value while being socially responsible and sustaining the environment. Thus, they create a triple bottom line that is also known as "3BL," or "People, Planet, Profit."

Green computing can be considered from the social contract theory perspective: managers benefit society by conserving global resources when they make green, energy-related decisions about their computer operations. These are the "people" and "planet" motivations. However, their actions may also be evaluated from the stockholder theory perspective. Energy-efficient computers reduce not only the direct costs of running the computing-related infrastructure, but also the costs of complementary utilities, such as cooling systems for the infrastructure components. This creates a huge "profit" motivation for companies to turn "green." The companies can become more environmentally friendly and reduce their energy costs at the same time.

Ethical Tensions with Governments

Organizations are also facing a dilemma reconciling their corporate policies with regulations in countries where they want to operate. "Managers may need to adopt much different approaches across nationalities to counter the effects of what they perceive as unethical behaviors."[21] For example, the United Arab Emirates threatened to shut off BlackBerry messaging, e-mail and Web browsing services if the device's maker, Research in Motion (RIM) did not provide certain information necessary for national security. RIM managers did not want to disclose confidential information. But they also didn't want to endanger UAE's national security. Even though a compromise was reached shortly before the shutdown was to go into effect, the case reflects the challenges of dealing with foreign governments.[22]

Censorship posed an ethical dilemma for Google. Enticed by the lure of a gigantic market, Google tried to set up business in China. The Chinese government that is quite use to developing and enforcing regulations, wanted to limit the overseas Web sites that Google's search engine could retrieve when operating in China. The Chinese

---

[19] J. Mick, "Google Looks at Floating Data Centers for Energy," *Daily Tech* (September 16, 2008), http://www.dailytech.com/Google+Looks+to+Floating+Data+Centers+for+Energy/article12966.htm (accessed on October 1, 2008).

[20] Cade Metz, "Google Reincarnates Dead Paper Mill as Data Center of Future," *Wired Enterprise* (January 26, 2012), http://www.wired.com/wiredenterprise/2012/01/google-finland/ (accessed on January 28, 2012).

[21] Leidner and Kayworth (2006), 368.

[22] "For Data, Tug Grows Over Privacy vs. Security," *The New York Times* (August 3, 2010), http://query.nytimes.com/gst/fullpage.html?res=9504E4D6113CF930A3575BC0A9669D8B63 (accessed on January 28, 2012).

government also interfered with Google's e-mail services, making it difficult for users to gain access to Gmail. Google faces the dilemma of how to deliver the level of services it deems appropriate in the face of stiff government regulation. It is a dilemma that is likely to become very common with increased globalization. In this case, the balancing act is at a national level.

▶ PAPA: PRIVACY, ACCURACY, PROPERTY, AND ACCESSIBILITY

In an economy that is rapidly becoming dominated by knowledge workers, the value of information is tantamount. Those who possess the "best" information and know how to use it, win. The recent trend in cloud computing permits high levels of computational power and storage to be purchased for relatively small amounts of money. Although this trend means that computer-generated or stored information now falls within the reach of a larger percentage of the populace, it also means that collecting and storing information is becoming easier and more cost effective. This circumstance certainly affects businesses and individuals for the better, but it also can affect them substantially for the worse.

Consider several areas of information ethics in which the control of information is crucial. Richard O. Mason[23] identified four such areas, which can be summarized by the acronym PAPA: privacy, accuracy, property, and accessibility (see Figure 12.2). Mason's framework has limitations in terms of accommodating the range and complexity of ethical issues encountered in today's information intensive world. However, this framework helps to understand information ethics because it is both popular and simple.

Privacy

Many consider privacy to be the most important area in which their interests need to be safeguarded. **Privacy** has long been considered "the right to be left alone."[24] While it has been argued that so many different definitions exist that it is hard to satisfactorily define the term,[25] it is "fundamentally about protections from intrusion and information gathering by others."[26] Typically, it has been defined in terms of individuals' ability to personally control information about themselves. But requiring individuals to control their own information would severely limit what is private. In today's information-oriented world, individuals really have so little control.

Though total control is difficult in today's digital world, individuals do have control to manage their privacy through *choice, consent* and *correction*. In particular, individuals can choose situations that offer the desired level of access to their information ranging

---

[23] Richard O. Mason, "Four Ethical Issues of the Information Age," *MIS Quarterly* (March 1986), 10(1).

[24] Samuel D. Warren and Louis D. Brandeis, "The Right to Privacy," *Harvard Law Review* (December 1890), 4(5), 193–200.

[25] Paul Pavlou, "State of the Inform Privacy Literature: Where Are We Now and Where Should We Go?" *MIS Quarterly* (2011), 35(4), 977–985.

[26] E. F. Stone, D. G. Gardner, H. G. Gueutal, and S. McClure, "A Field Experiment Comparing Information-Privacy Values, Beliefs, and Attitudes Across Several Types of Organizations," *Journal of Applied Psychology* (August 1983), 68(3), 459–468.

Area	Critical Question
Privacy	What information must people reveal about themselves to others? Are there some things that people do not have to reveal about themselves? Can the information that people provide be used to identify their personal preferences or history when they don't want those preferences to be known? Can the information that people provide be used for purposes other than those for which they were told that it would be used?
Accuracy	Who is responsible for the reliability, authenticity, and accuracy of information? Who is accountable for errors in the information?
Property	Who owns information? Who owns the channels of distribution, and how should they be regulated? What is the fair price of information that is exchanged?
Accessibility	What information does a person or organization have a right to obtain, with what protection, and under what conditions? Who can access personal information in the files? Does the person accessing personal information "need to know" the information that is being accessed?

FIGURE 12.2 Mason's areas of managerial control.
Source: Adapted from Richard O. Mason, "Four Ethical Issues of the Information Age," *MIS Quarterly* (March 1986), 10(1), 5.

from "total privacy to unabashed publicity."[27] Many are finding out that talking about their latest bashes in detail on Facebook does not go over very well with potential employers who access their pages. A recent study reported that 70% of U.S. recruiters and human resource professionals have rejected candidates based on data found online.[28] Less than 20% of Facebook's members had adjusted the default privacy settings prior to Facebook's change in policy (when it came under fire) to enhance customer privacy.[29] The concern about privacy on Facebook (and other Internet sites) varies across the globe; for example, it is greater in Europe than in the United States.

Individuals may also exert control when they manage their privacy through consent. When they give their consent, they are granting access to otherwise restricted information and they are specifying the purposes for which it may be used. In granting access, they should recognize that extensive amounts of data that can personally identify them are being collected and stored in databases and this data can be used in ways that they had not intended. When giving their consent, individuals should try to anticipate how their information might be reused as a result of data mining or aggregation. They should also try to anticipate unauthorized access through security breaches or internal browsing in companies whose security is lax. Finally, individuals should have control in managing

[27] H. T. Tavani and James Moore, "Privacy Protection, Control of Information, and Privacy-Enhancing Technologies," *Computers and Society* (March 2001), 6–11.
[28] Andrew LaVallee, "Facebook Outlines Privacy Changes," *Wall Street Journal* (December 9, 2009), http://blogs.wsj.com/digits/2009/12/09/facebook-outlines-privacy-changes/ (accessed on May 11, 2011).
[29] Lori Andrews, "Facebook is Using You," *The New York Times* (February 5, 2012), SR7.

their privacy by being able to access their personal information and correct it if it is wrong. To protect the integrity of information collected about them, federal regulators have recommended allowing consumers limited access to corporate information databases. Consumers thus could update their information and correct errors.

For organizations, the tension between the proper use of personal information and information privacy is considered to be one of the most serious ethical debates of the information age.[30] One of the main organizational challenges to privacy is surveillance of employees.[31] For example, to ensure that employees are productive, employers can monitor their employees' e-mail and computer utilization while they are at work, even though they have not historically monitored telephone calls.

Individuals are also facing privacy challenges from organizations providing them with services. Their actions are being traced not only with cookies, but maybe also with "beacons," "Flash cookies," and even "supercookies" that can follow individuals' surfing behaviors without them knowing it. Every time someone logs onto one of the main search engines, a "cookie" is placed in their hard drive so that these companies can track their surfing habits. A simple "**cookie**," which is a text message given to a Web browser by a Web server, has been ruled to be legal by the U.S. courts. The browser stores the cookie's message with user identification codes in a tracking file that is sent back to the server each time the browser requests a page from the server.[32] A recent examination of the 50 most popular American Web sites determined that over two-thirds of the over 3,000 tracking files installed by a total of 131 companies after people visited these Web sites were used to create rich databases of consumer profiles that can be sold.[33]

Apple and Google recently came under fire for collecting and storing unencrypted location information from both personal computers and mobile devices. The information was obtained after the computer or mobile searched for available wireless networks that were nearby. Typically the users gave permission to the companies to determine the computer's approximate location, but many did not know that the information was being stored. Going against previous policy about keeping information about Internet searches sacrosanct, Google now combines user information from its sister sites, Gmail, Google+, and YouTube, to direct user searches.[34]

Do customers have a right to privacy while searching the Internet? Courts have decided that the answer is no, but as society moves ahead, the right to monitor customer habits in terms of their phone usage, location, emailing behaviors, and a myriad of other

[30] Paul Pavlou, "State of the Inform Privacy Literature: Where Are We Now and Where Should We Go?" *MIS Quarterly* (2011), 35(4), 977–985.

[31] B. C. Stahl, "The Impact of UK Human Rights Act 1998 on Privacy Protection in the Workplace," *Computer Security, Privacy, and Politics: Current Issues, Challenges, and Solutions* (Hershey, PA: Idea Group Publishing), 55–68.

[32] Webopedia, http://www.webopedia.com/TERM/c/cookie.html (accessed on June 28, 2002).

[33] Julia, Angwin, "The Web's New Gold Mine: Your Secrets," *Wall Street Journal* (July 30, 2010), http://online.wsj.com/article/SB10001424052748703940904575395073512989404.html (accessed on January 28, 2010).

[34] Julia Angwin, "Google Widens Its Tracks," *Wall Street Journal* (July 30, 2010), http://online.wsj.com/article/SB10001424052970203806504577181371465957162.html?mod=djem_jiewr_IT_domainid (accessed on January 28, 2012).

behaviors will be affected by how managers decide to use the information that they have collected.

Why would people be willing to give up this privacy? First, by supplying the information to vendors, they can receive personalized services in return. For example, the location device on their mobile might alert them that the restaurant that they are just walking by has a special off on one of their favorite foods—sushi. Second, they might actually be paid for the information at a price that exceeds what they are giving up. Third, they might see providing information, such as that contained on many Facebook pages, as something that everybody is doing. Some individuals, especially younger individuals, share information that would otherwise be considered private simply because they view it as a way to have their friends know them and as a way to get to know their friends. Social interaction among "digital native" individuals who have grown up in the Internet age, do not know about society without the Web. They are comfortable building relationships, and consequently sharing information, on the Web that others might consider private. Unfortunately, what's posted on the Web is there forever, and while it may be fun to share it now, there may be unintended consequences in the future.

Governments around the world are grappling with privacy legislation. Not surprisingly, they are using different approaches for ensuring the privacy of their citizens. The United States' sectoral approach relies on a mix of legislation, regulation, and self-regulation. It is based upon a legal tradition with a strong emphasis on free trade. In the United States, privacy laws are enacted in response to specific problems for specific groups of people or in specific industries. Examples of the United States' relatively limited privacy legislation include the 1974 Privacy Act that regulates the U.S. government's collection and use of personal information and the 1998 Children's Online Privacy Protection Act that regulates the online collection and use of children's personal information.

The Gramm–Leach–Bliley Act of 1999 applies to financial institutions. It followed in the wake of banks selling sensitive information, including account information, Social Security numbers, credit card purchase histories, and so forth to telemarketing companies. This U.S. law somewhat mitigates the sharing of sensitive financial and personal information by allowing customers of financial institutions the limited right to "opt-out" of the information sharing by these institutions with non-affiliated third parties. This means that the financial institution may use the information unless the customer specifically tells the institution that his or her personal information cannot be used or distributed.

The Health Insurance Portability and Accountability Act (HIPAA) of 1996 is designed to safeguard the electronic exchange privacy and security of information in the health care industry. Its Privacy Rule ensures that patients' health information is properly protected while allowing its necessary flow for providing and promoting health care. HIPAA's Security Rule specifies national standards for protecting electronic health information from unauthorized access, alteration, deletion, and transmission.

The Fair Credit Reporting act limits the use of consumer reports provided by consumer reporting agencies to "permissible purposes" and grants individuals the right to access their reports and correct errors in them.

Social Business Lens: Personal Data

Social IT, especially Facebook, is redefining how people think about themselves and define themselves to others. Sherry Turkle, the author of *Home Alone* and a professor at Massachusetts Institute of Technology, says about Facebook and the new marketplace for personal data: "I can't think of another piece of passive software that has gotten so embedded in the cultural conversation. . . . It crystallized a set of issues that we will be defining for the next decade—self, privacy, how we connect and the price we are willing to pay for it."

What many people who supply this data about themselves may not realize is that that data may exist indefinitely in the ether. Furthermore, that data about personal lives and wants may be mined indefinitely by technology companies. Lori Andrews, in her book *I Know Who You Are and I Saw What you Did: Social Networks and the Death of Privacy*, is concerned that the Internet companies are in business for the money and hence they really would prefer to keep their customers in the dark about how their personal data is being used to generate profits.

And what is Andrews' solution? She proposes a social network constitution that can be used to judge the activities of social networks. Her constitution has ten articles and begins with: "We the people of Facebook nation." Articles like "No person shall be discriminated against based on his or her social network activities or profile" or "Each individual shall have control over his or her image from a social network, including over the image created by data aggregation" point to the need for people who supply data to social networks to demand respect for the data. Her focus is on rights, but not individuals' responsibilities in keeping private information private.

Some suggest that reputation management is destined to be big business in the future, given the amount of personal data on the Web. *BusinessWeek* noted that online reputation management is booming. Companies such as Reputation.com and Elixir offer services to help individuals, and companies, clean up their online presence so that searches for their name produce mostly positive references.

It could be argued that individuals need to recognize that surrendering their privacy in change of coupons, free music, and videos or customized products and services may lead to the loss of something of value. . . And that the data may remain accessible far longer than they want it to be.

Sources: J. Wortham, "It's Not About You, Facebook. It's About Us," *The New York Times* (February 12, 2012), BR3; E. Morozov, "Sharing it All," *New York Times Book Review* (January 29, 2012), 18; and T. McNichol, "Fixing the Reputation of Reputation Managers," *BusinessWeek* (February 2, 2012), http://www.businessweek.com/magazine/fixing-the-reputations-of-reputation-managers-02022012.html (accessed on April 5, 2012).

In contrast to the United States' sectoral approach, and with strong encouragement of self-regulation by industry, the European Union relies on omnibus legislation that requires creation of government data protection agencies, registration of databases with those agencies, and in some cases prior approval before processing personal data. It is linked with the continental European legal tradition where privacy is a well-established right.[35] Because of pronounced differences in governmental approaches, many U.S. companies were concerned that they would be unable to meet the European "adequacy" standard for privacy protection specified in the European Commission's Directive 95/46/EC on Data Protection that went into effect in 1998. This directive sets standards for the collection, storage, and processing of personal information. It prohibits the transfer of personal data to non-European Union nations that do not meet the European privacy standards. Many U.S. companies believed that this directive would significantly hamper their ability to engage in many trans-Atlantic transactions. However, the U.S. Department of Commerce (DOC), in consultation with the European Commission, developed a "safe harbor" framework in 2000 that allows U.S. companies to be placed on a list maintained by the DOC. The U.S. companies must demonstrate through a self-certification process that they are enforcing privacy at a level practiced in the European Union.[36]

Accuracy

The **accuracy**, or the correctness, of information assumes real importance for society as computers come to dominate in corporate record-keeping activities. When records are inputted incorrectly, who is to blame? Recently, a couple was told by Bank of America, their mortgage holder, that they would have to vacate their house by Christmas Eve unless they put their house up for forced sale. The couple was flabbergasted because they had never missed making a house payment. They had, however, refinanced their home less than a year earlier. Although they used a conventional mortgage, they had checked out loan rates on the Make Home Affordable Program. Unbeknownst to them, the mere initiation of this type of loan application triggers to the credit world that the applicant is in bad financial straits. A comedy of errors ensued in which the limit on a credit card was reduced, their good accounts were cancelled, and their credit score was ruined. Another unit of Bank of America admitted to erroneously reporting to credit agencies that the couple was seeking a loan modification, ruining their credit rating and as the result putting their mortgage into default. This unit sent a letter of apology in September and turned the case over to a special unit at Bank of America that is charged with dealing with severe customer issue. The special unit was supposed to notify the credit reporting agencies that the couple was a good credit risk. Unfortunately, it didn't

---

[35] B.C. Stahl, "The Impact of UK Human rights Act 1998 on Privacy Protection in the Workplace," *Computer Security, Privacy, and Politics: Current Issues, Challenges, and Solutions* (Hershey, PA: Idea Group Publishing), 55–68.

[36] U.S. Department of Commerce, "Safe Harbor Overview," http://export.gov/safeharbor/eu/eg_main_018476.asp (accessed on January 28, 2012).

do so, costing the couple much anxiety and financial loss.[37] Although this incident may highlight the need for better controls over the bank's internal processes, it also demonstrates the risks that can be attributed to inaccurate information retained in corporate systems. In this case, the bank was responsible for the error, but it paid little—compared to the family—for its mistake. Although they cannot expect to eliminate all mistakes from the online environment, managers must establish controls to ensure that situations such as this one do not happen with any frequency.

Over time it becomes increasingly difficult to maintain the accuracy of some types of information. Although a person's birth date does not typically change (my grandmother's change of her birth year notwithstanding), addresses and phone numbers often change as people relocate, and even their names may change with marriage, divorce, and adoption. The European Union Directive on Data Protection requires accurate and up-to-date data and tries to make sure that data is kept no longer than necessary to fulfill its stated purpose. Keeping data only as long as it is necessary to fulfill its stated purpose is a challenge many companies don't even attempt to meet.

Property

The increase in monitoring leads to the question of **property**, or who owns the data. Now that organizations have the ability to collect vast amounts of data on their clients, do they have a right to share data with others to create a more accurate profile of an individual? Consider what happens when a consumer provides information for one use, say a car loan. This information is collected and stored in a data warehouse and then "mined" to create a profile for something completely different. And if some other company creates such consolidated profiles, who owns that information, which in many cases was not divulged willingly for that purpose? Who owns images that are posted in cyberspace? With ever more sophisticated methods of computer animation, can companies use newly "created" images or characters building on models in other media without paying royalties? Mason suggests that information, which is costly to produce in the first place, can be easily reproduced and sold without the individual who produced it even knowing what is happening—and certainly not being reimbursed for its use. In talking about this information that is produced Mason notes:

> . . . information has the illusive quality of being easy to reproduce and to share with others. Moreover, this replication can take place without destroying the original. This makes information hard to safeguard since, unlike tangible property, it becomes communicable and hard to keep it to one's self.[38]

Accessibility

In the age of the information worker, **accessibility**, or the ability to obtain the data, becomes increasingly important. Would-be users of information must first gain the

---

[37] G. Gombossy, "Bank Of America's Christmas present: Foreclose Even Though Not A Payment Missed" (December 24, 2010), http://ctwatchdog.com/finance/bank-of-americas-christmas-present-foreclose-even-though-not-a-payment-missed (accessed on February 27, 2012).

[38] Richard O. Mason, "Four Ethical Issues of the Information Age," *MIS Quarterly* (March 1986), 10(1), 5.

physical ability to access online information resources, which broadly means they must access computational systems. Second and more important, they then must gain access to information itself. In this sense, the issue of access is closely linked to that of property. Looking forward, the major issue facing managers is how to create and maintain access to information for society at large without harming individuals who have provided much, if not all, of the information.

Today's managers must ensure that information about their employees and customers is accessible only to those who have a right to see and use it. They should take active measures to see that adequate security and control measures are in place in their companies. It is becoming increasingly clear that they also must ensure that adequate safeguards are working in the companies of their key trading partners. The managers at TRICARE, a military health provider, were no doubt embarrassed when they reported to 4.9 million active and retired military personnel and their families that their personal and medical records were compromised. Back-up tapes containing records back to 1992 had been left in care of an employee of TRICARE's data contractor, Science Applications International Corp. The tapes were stolen from the car in San Antonio, Texas, while they were being transferred from one federal facility to another.[39] Accessibility clearly is an issue that extended beyond TRICARE's internal systems.

Accessibility is becoming increasingly important with the surge in **identity theft**, or "the taking of the victim's identity to obtain credit, credit cards from banks and retailers, steal money from the victim's existing accounts, apply for loans, establish accounts with utility companies, rent an apartment, file bankruptcy or obtain a job using the victim's name."[40] In short, identity theft is a crime in which the thief uses the victim's personal information (such as driver's license number or Social Security number) to impersonate the victim. In TJX's case, the security breach made its customers vulnerable to identity theft.

According to subject matter experts, identity theft is categorized in two ways: true name and account takeover. True name identity theft means that the thief uses personal information to open new accounts. The thief might open a new credit card account, establish cellular phone service, or open a new checking account to obtain blank checks. Account takeover identity theft means the imposter uses personal information to gain access to the person's existing accounts. Typically, the thief will change the mailing address on an account and run up a huge bill before the person whose identity has been stolen realizes there is a problem.

Identity theft is a problem for both individuals and businesses. The U.S. government keeps statistics on reported cases of identity theft.[41] The incidence of identity theft had been growing at an amazing rate during the early part of this century. A total of

---

[39] Jim Forsyth, "Records of 4.9 mln stolen from car in Texas data breach," *Reuters* (September 29, 2011), http://www.reuters.com/article/2011/09/29/us-data-breach-texas-idUSTRE78S5JG20110929 (accessed on February 28, 2012).

[40] Identity Theft Organization, Frequently Asked Questions, http://www.identitytheft.org (accessed on April 5, 2012).

[41] http://www.consumer.gov/sentinel/pubs/Top10Fraud2004.pdf (accessed on August 4, 2005).

8.6 million households experienced identity theft in 2010[42] and American businesses and individuals experienced losses to the tune of $54 billion a year earlier because of identity theft.[43] The most victimized tend to be college students and young adults who have not learned to use security software or shred documents.

Although some cases of individual identity theft can be traced to carelessness on the part of victims, some may also be credited to the failure of businesses to limit accessibility to their databases. Businesses are also subject to significant losses due to identity theft. Illegitimate e-mail messages that solicit personal information for the thief can ruin a business's hard-won reputation. Purchases made by the thief must be paid for, and often that loss is covered by the business. The U.S. Federal Trade Commission (FTC) maintains a Web site to help both individuals and businesses manage identity theft.[44]

Managers' Role in Ethical Information Control

Managers must work to implement controls over information highlighted by the PAPA principles. Not only should they deter identity theft by limiting inappropriate access to customer information, but they should also respect their customers' privacy. Three best practices can be adopted to help improve an organization's information control by incorporating moral responsibility:[45]

- **Create a Culture of Responsibility.** CEOs and top-level executives should lead in promoting responsibility for protecting both personal information and the organization's information systems. Internet companies should post their policies about how they will use private information and make a good case as to why they need the personal data that they gather from customers and clients. Mary Culnan noted in *CIO* magazine about customers providing information: "If there are no benefits or if they aren't told why the information is being collected or how it's being used, a lot of people say 'Forget it.' "[46] The costs of meaningfully securing the information may outweigh the obvious benefits. . . unless there is a breach. Thus, it is unlikely that an organization can create a culture of integrity and responsibility unless there is a moral commitment form the CEO.

- **Implement Governance Processes for Information Control.** In Chapter 8 we discuss the importance of mechanisms to identify the important decisions that need to be made and who would make them. Further, control governance structures such as COBIT and ITIL can help identify risks to the information

---

[42] L. Langton, "Identity Theft Reported by Households, 2005–2010," Bureau of Justice Statistics (November 30, 2012), http://www.bjs.gov/index.cfm?ty=pbdetail&iid=2207 (accessed on February 28, 2012).

[43] PR Web, "79% of U.S. Citizens Concerned About Identity Theft Yet Just 12% Enrolled in An Identity Theft Protection Program" (February, 28, 2012), http://www.prweb.com/releases/identity-theft/statistics2011/prweb4907404.htm (accessed on February 28, 2012).

[44] Welcome to the FTCs Identity Theft Site, http://www.ftc.gov/bcp/edu/microsites/idtheft/ (accessed on April 5, 2012).

[45] M. Culnan and C. Williams, "How Ethics Can Enhance Organizational Privacy: Lessons from the ChoicePoint and TJX Data Breaches," *MIS Quarterly* (2009), 33(4), 673-687.

[46] "Saving Private Data," *CIO Magazine*, (October 1, 1998).

> **Geographic Lens: Should Subcultures be Taken into Account When Trying to Understand National Attitudes Toward Information Ethics?**
>
> Ethics can naturally be expected to vary across countries. An interesting study of 1,100 Chinese managers showed that it can also vary depending upon subcultures resulting from major events within a country. Maris Martinsons and David Ma studied the responses to PAPA-based ethical situations made by three different Chinese generations: *Republican*—people born before the People's Republic of China was established in 1949; *Revolution*—people born between 1950 and 1970 under Communist rule. This generation lived during Mao Zedong's Cultural Revolution in 1966 and the Great Leap Forward (1958–1961); *Reform*—people born after 1970 when Deng Xiaoping's government introduced Open Door Policy and a One Child Policy as part of economic and social reforms.
>
> Survey results indicate that there are significant differences in information ethics across generations. The Revolution Generation experienced a profound event that appears to have increased its ethical acceptance of both inaccurate information and intellectual property violations. The Reform generation is much less accepting of privacy violations than older generations of Chinese managers. They are more conscious of the right to privacy and less inclined to compromise the privacy of others.
>
> Source: M. G. Martinsons and D. Ma, "Subcultural Differences in Information Ethics across China: Focus on Chinese Management Generation Gaps," *Journal of AIS* (2009), 10(Special Issue), 816–833.

and behaviors to promote information control. These concepts of governance also apply to information control. Organizations need governance to make sure that their information control behaviors comply with the law and reflect their risk environment.

- **Avoid Decoupling.** Often organizations use complex processes to treat rather personal privacy issues. Should an apparent conflict appear, managers can decouple the impact to individuals from institutional processes and mechanisms. In that way, they can shift the responsibility away from themselves and onto the institution. It would be much better if the managers were to act as if the customer's information were actually their own. This would mean that in delicate situations involving privacy or other issues of information control, managers would ask themselves "How would I feel if my information was handled in this way?"[47]

---

[47] M. Culnan and C. Williams, "How Ethics Can Enhance Organizational Privacy: Lessons from the ChoicePoint and TJX Data Breaches," *MIS Quarterly* (2009), 33(4), 685.

► SECURITY AND CONTROLS

It should be clear from the earlier discussion that the PAPA principles work hand-in-hand with security. Unfortunately, organizations more often than not may rely on luck rather than on proven information systems controls, at least according to an Ernst & Young survey.[48] More than half of the high-level executives responding to the survey reported that hardware, telecommunications, and software failures, as well as major viruses, Trojan horses, or Internet worms, had resulted in unexpected or unscheduled outages of their critical business systems. The survey confirmed that companies turn to technical responses to deal with these and other threats. In particular considerable emphasis is placed on using technology (i.e., antivirus countermeasures, spam-filtering software, intrusion detection systems) to protect organizational data from unauthorized hackers and undesirable viruses. Managers go to great lengths to make sure their computers are secure from outsider access, such as a hacker who seeks to enter a computer for sport or for malicious intent. They also try to safeguard against other external threats such as telecommunications failure, service provider failure, spamming, or distributed denial of service (DDoS) attacks.

Technologies have been devised to manage the security and control problems. Figure 12.3 summarizes three types of tools (e.g., firewalls, passwords, and filtering tools) that restrict access to information on a computer by preventing access to the server on the network. They provide warning for early discovery of security breaches, limit losses suffered in case of security breaches, analyze and react to security breaches (and try to prevent them from reoccurring), and recover whatever has been lost from security breaches.[49]

As the physical corporate walls are torn down and more workers work from remote locations, enterprises use technological advances to keep up with their business and network security needs. Some of these technologies include antivirus and antispyware, desktop firewalls, devices that can trace stolen laptops, devices that prevent USB mass-storage devices or iPods from accessing data on home-based computers, or data-leak prevention technology that keeps sensitive corporate data from being printed out, e-mailed, or saved to removable media without the proper authorization, even on remote endpoints.[50]

Additional technological approaches to security and privacy may include a combination of software and hardware. For example, some of today's laptop computers have built-in fingerprint identification pads to prevent unauthorized use. Biometrics are also being considered for security purposes at national levels. For example, the United Kingdom passed the Identity Cards Act in 2006 that required nationals to obtain a compulsory national identity card that contained 50 different types of information, including name, birth date and place, current and past addresses, a head and shoulders photograph, fingerprints, an iris scan and other biometric information, personal

[48] Ernst & Young, Global Information Survey, 2004.

[49] J. Berleur, P. Duquenoy, and D. Whitehouse, "Ethics and the Governance of the Internet," IFIP SIG 9.2.2, White paper (September 1999).

[50] Cara Garretson, "Heightened Awareness, Reinforced Products Advance Teleworker's Security," *Network World* (February 20, 2007), http://www.networkworld.com/news/2007/022007-heightened-awareness.html?ap1=rcb (accessed on April 12, 2012).

Security Category	Security Tools	Definition
Hardware system security and control	Firewalls	A computer set up with both an internal network card and an external network card. This computer is set up to control access to the internal network and only lets authorized traffic pass the barrier.
	Encryption and decryption	Cryptography or secure writing ensures that information is transformed into unintelligible forms before transmission and intelligible forms when it arrives at its destination to protect the informational content of messages.
	Anonymizing tools and Pseudonym agents	Tools that enable users to navigate the Internet either anonymously or pseudonymously to protect the identity of individuals.
Network and software security controls	Network operating system software	The core set of programs that manage the resources of the computer or network often have functionality such as authentication, access control, and cryptology.
	Security information management	A management scheme to synchronize all mechanisms and protocols built into network and computer operating systems and protect the systems from unauthorized access.
	Server and browser software security	Mechanisms to ensure that errors in programming do not create holes and trapdoors that can compromise Web sites.
Broadcast medium security and controls	Labeling and rating software	The software industry incorporates Platform for Internet Content Selection (PICS) technology, a mechanism of labeling Web pages based on content. These labels can be used by filtering software to manage access. Also online privacy seal programs such as Truste that inform users of online vendor's privacy policies and ensures that policies are backed and enforced by reputable third parties.
	Filtering/blocking software	Software that rates documents and Web sites that have been rated and contain content on a designated filter's "black list" and keeps them from being displayed on the user's computer.

FIGURE 12.3 Security and control tools.

Sources: Adapted from J. Berleur, P. Duquenoy, and D. Whitehouse, "Ethics and the Governance of the Internet," IFIP-SIG9.2.2, White paper (September 1999); and Tavani and Moor, "Privacy Protection, Control of Information and Privacy-Enhancing Technologies," *Computers and Society* (March 2001), 6–11.

reference information, and registration and record histories. The British government argued that the card would give people a convenient way to prove their identity and prevent identity theft by providing a unique individual identifier. It also would offer a secure way of identifying people for national security, detect crime, aid in enforcing immigration controls, prevent illegal workers, and assist in providing public services. Opponents feared the card would create a "Big Brother" world and the unique identifier, ironically, would increase identity theft because all necessary information was contained in one central location. After much public debate, the Identity Cards Act was repealed in 2010 and the card was scrapped for nationals.

Technological security controls extends beyond dealing with external threats; managers must also guard against potentially more lethal threats—threats that originate from within the company. Internal threats include operational errors (i.e., loading the wrong software) and former or current employee misconduct involving information systems, as well as hardware or software failure. Managers from the highest echelons down must champion the human aspect of protecting information. This means that they must be supportive of efforts to develop employees into the company's strongest layer of defense. These efforts include training and awareness programs to alert employees to risks, make them aware of countermeasures that exist to mitigate these risks, and drill into them the importance of security, as well as awareness programs. Buttressing the technological controls, training, and awareness programs with a good governance structure reflecting security procedures and policies and an overall information security strategy can help round out a company's security efforts.

▶ SUMMARY

- Due to the asymmetry of power relationships, managers tend to frame ethical concerns in terms of refraining from doing harm, mitigating injury, and paying attention to dependent and vulnerable parties. As a practical matter, ethics is about maintaining one's own, independent perspective about the propriety of business practices. Managers must make systematic, reasoned judgments about right and wrong and take responsibility for them. Ethics is about decisive action rooted in principles that express what is right and important, and about action that is publicly defensible and personally supportable.

- Three important normative theories describing business ethics are (1) stockholder theory (maximizing stockholder wealth), (2) stakeholder theory (maximizing the benefits to all stakeholders while weighing costs to competing interests), and (3) social contract theory (creating value for society that is just and non-discriminatory).

- Social contract theory offers the broad perspective to display corporate responsibility in such areas as green computing and dealing with ethical issues in tensions with foreign governments about IT and its use.

- PAPA is an acronym for the four areas in which control of information is crucial: privacy, accuracy, property, and accessibility.

- To enhance ethical control of information systems companies should create a culture of responsibility, implement governance processes, and avoid decoupling

- Security looms as a major threat to Internet growth. Businesses are bolstering security with hardware, software, and communication devices.

▶ KEY TERMS

accessibility (p. 365)
accuracy (p. 364)
cookie (p. 361)
green computing (p. 357)

identity theft (p. 366)
information ethics (p. 352)
privacy (p. 359)
property (p. 365)

social contract
  theory (p. 354)
stakeholder theory (p. 353)
stockholder theory (p. 352)

▶ DISCUSSION QUESTIONS

1. Private corporate data is often encrypted using a key, which is needed to decrypt the information. Who within the corporation should be responsible for maintaining the "keys" to private information collected about consumers? Is that the same person who should have the "keys" to employee data?

2. Check out how Google has profiled you. Using your own computer, go to Ad Preferences: www.google.com/ads/preferences. How accurate is the picture Google paints about you in your profile?

3. Consider arrest records, which are mostly computerized and stored locally by law enforcement agencies. They have an accuracy rate of about 50%—about half of them are inaccurate, incomplete, or ambiguous. These records often are used by others than just law enforcement. Approximately 90% of all criminal histories in the United States are available to public and private employers. Use the three normative theories of business ethics to analyze the ethical issues surrounding this situation. How might hiring decisions be influenced inappropriately by this information?

4. The European Community's Directive on Data Protection strictly limits how database information is used and who has access to it. Some of the restrictions include registering all databases containing personal information with the countries in which they are operating, collecting data only with the consent of the subjects, and telling subjects of the database the intended and actual use of the databases. What effect might these restrictions have on global companies? In your opinion, should these types of restrictions be made into law? Why or why not? Should the United States bring its laws into agreement with the EU directive?

5. Should there be a global Internet privacy policy?

6. Is sending targeted advertising information to a computer using cookies objectionable? Why or why not?

7. What is your opinion of the British Identity Card discussed in this chapter?

CASE STUDY 12-1

ETHICAL DECISION MAKING

Situation 1

The help desk is part of the group assigned to Doug Smith, the manager of office automation. The help desk has produced very low quality work for the past several months. Smith has access to the passwords for each of the help desk members' computer accounts. He instructs the help desk supervisor to go into each hard drive after hours and obtain a sample document to check for quality control for each pool member.

Discussion Questions

1. If you were the supervisor, what would you do?
2. What, if any, ethical propositions have been violated by this situation?
3. If poor quality was found, could the information be used for disciplinary purposes? For training purposes?
4. Apply PAPA to this situation.

Situation 2

Kate Essex is the supervisor of the customer service representative group for Enovelty.com, a manufacturer of novelty items. This group spends its workday answering calls, and sometimes placing calls, to customers to assist in solving a variety of issues about orders previously placed with the company. The company has a rule that personal phone calls are only allowed during breaks. Essex is assigned to monitor each representative on the phone for 15 minutes a day, as part of her regular job tasks. The representatives are aware that Essex will be monitoring them, and customers are immediately informed when they begin their calls. Essex begins to monitor James Olsen, and finds that he is on a personal call regarding his sick child. Olsen is not on break.

Discussion Questions

1. What should Essex do?
2. What, if any, ethical principles help guide decision making in this situation?
3. What management practices should be in place to ensure proper behavior without violating individual "rights"?
4. Apply the normative theories of business ethics to this situation.

Situation 3

Jane Mark was the newest hire in the IS group at We_Sell_More.com, a business on the Internet. The company takes in $30 million in revenue quarterly from Web business. Jane reports to Sam Brady, the VP of IS. Jane is assigned to a project to build a new capability into the company Web page that facilitates linking products ordered with future offerings of the company. After weeks of analysis, Jane concluded that the best way to incorporate that capability is to buy a software package from a small start-up company in Silicon Valley, California. She convinces Brady of her decision and is authorized to lease the software. The vendor e-mails Jane the software in a ZIP file and instructs her on how to install it. At the initial installation, Jane is asked to acknowledge and electronically sign the license agreement. The installed system does not ask Jane if she wants to make a backup copy of the software, so as a precaution, Jane takes it on herself and copies the ZIP files sent to her onto a thumb drive. She stores the thumb drive in her desk drawer.

A year later, the vendor is bought by another company, and the software is removed from the marketplace. The new owner believes this software will provide them with a competitive advantage they want to reserve for themselves. The new vendor terminates all lease agreements and revokes all licenses on their expiration. But Jane still has the thumb drive she made as backup.

Discussion Questions

1. Is Jane obligated to stop using her backup copy? Why or why not?
2. If We_Sell_More.com wants to continue to use the system, can they? Why or why not?
3. Does it change your opinion if the software is a critical system for We_Sell_More.com? If it is a non-critical system? Explain.

Situation 4

Some of the Internet's biggest companies (i.e., Google, Microsoft, Yahoo, IBM, and Verisign) implemented a "single sign-on" system that is now available at more than 50,000 Web sites. As corporate members of the OpenID Foundation, they developed a system that is supposed to make it easier for users to sign on to a number of sites without having to remember multiple user IDs, passwords, and registration information. Theoretically, users also have a consistent identity across the Web. Under OpenID, the companies share the sign-on information for any Web user who agrees to participate. They also share personal information such as credit card data, billing addresses, and personal preferences.

Discussion Questions

1. Discuss any threats to privacy in this situation.
2. Who would own the data? Explain.
3. Who do you think should have access to the data? How should that access be controlled?

Situation 5

SpectorSoft markets eBlaster as a way to keep track of what your spouse or children are doing online. Operating in stealth mode, eBlaster tracks every single keystroke entered into a computer, from instant messages to passwords. It also records every e-mail sent and received and every Web site visited by the unsuspecting computer user. The data is sent anonymously to an IP address of the person who installed eBlaster. eBlaster could also be installed onto a business's computers.

Discussion Questions

1. Do you think it would be ethical for a business to install eBlaster to ensure that its employees are engaged only in work-related activities? If so, under what conditions would it be appropriate? If not, why not?
2. Apply the normative theories of business ethics to this situation.

Situation 6

Google, Inc. had a unique advantage as of March 2012. By combining information about user activity from its many popular applications (such as Gmail, Google+ and YouTube), Google algorithms were able to alert users when things might be of interest. This vast amount of information, analyzed properly, gave Google a way to compete. By combining data with information from Internet searches, Google could better compete against applications such as Facebook.

But this was a departure from its earlier privacy policy. In June 2011, the Executive Chairman of Google had declared, "Google will remain a place where you can do anonymous searches [without logging in]. We're very committed to having you have control over the information we have about you."

This may be possible for users who don't login to a Google account, but for those with Gmail or other personal accounts or an Android mobile phone, it's more difficult to remain anonymous. Offering a counter viewpoint, Chirstopher Soghoian, an independent privacy and security researcher said, "Google now watches consumers practically everywhere they go on the Web [and anytime they use an Android phone]. No single entity should be trusted with this much sensitive data."

Discussion Questions

1. Do you see any ethical issues involved in Google's new approach to combining information from a particular user? Why or why not?
2. How might users change their behaviors if they were aware of this new approach?
3. How is Google's combining data about individuals in one central location any different ethically from the United Kingdom placing all individual's necessary information on an identity card?
4. Apply the normative theories of business ethics to Google's new policy about combining user information?

Situation 7

Spokeo is a company that gathers online data for employers, the public or anybody who is willing to pay for their services. Clients include recruiters and women who want to find out if their boyfriends are cheating on them. Spokeo recruits via ads that urge "HR-Recruiters—Click Here Now."

Discussion Questions

1. Do you think it would be ethical for a business to hire Spokeo to find out about potential employees? If so, under what conditions would it be appropriate? If not, why not?
2. Do you think it is ethical for women to hire Spokeo to see if their boyfriends are cheating on them? Why or why not?

Sources: Situations 1 to 4 adapted from short cases suggested by Professor Kay Nelson, Southern Illinois University—Carbondale. The names of people, places, and companies have been made up for these stories. Any similarity to real people, places, or companies is purely coincidental. Situation 6 is from Julia Angwin, "Google Widens Its Tracks," *Wall Street Journal* (July 30, 2010), http://online.wsj.com/article/ SB10001424052970203806504577181371465957162.html?mod=djem_jiewr_IT_domainid (accessed on January 28, 2010). Situation 7 is from Lori Andrews, "Facebook is Using You," *The New York Times* (February 5, 2012), SR7.

CASE STUDY 12-2

MIDWEST FAMILY MUTUAL GOES GREEN

Midwest Family Mutual Insurance Co., an insurance company with nearly 100 million in written premiums in 2011, considers itself to be "operationally green." Through a variety of initiatives it has reduced its annual energy, natural gas, and paper consumption by 63%, 76%, and 65%, respectively. Ron Boyd, the carrier's CEO, attributes most of the improvements in energy usage to creating a virtual work- from- home office environment. As a result of implementing a series of electronic processes and applications. These include imaging and workflow technology, networking technology, and a VoIP network. In 2006, the year these savings were reported, all but two of Midwest Family Mutual's 65 employees worked from home. In addition to the energy savings that Midwest Family Mutual has directly experienced, Boyd estimates that the company's telecommuting policy has resulted in fuel savings of at least 25,000 gallons.

Though green computing was a commendable goal in itself, Midwest Family Mutual's bottom line also has benefitted from the company's socially responsible approach. Over a five year period Midwest Family Mutual's was able to shave its expense ratio to 29.9% from 33%. Boyd states: "Being environmentally green can equate to financial green."

Green computing grew out of Midwest Family Mutual's IT successes, according to Boyd. AS the company started realizing saving from the electronic processes it implemented, it started thinking about telecommuting arrangements that allowed its employees to work from home. He adds, "It became obvious that many of our jobs could be done wherever a high-speed connection existed. . . VOIP completed the technology requirements for all [employees] to work from home."

Boyd summarizes: "We became green as a side benefit of saving resources and cost." The company continued its green policy with its decision to sell its 24,000-square-foot office building in Minnetonka, Minnesota. However, in order to provide more centralized regional service to agents in the new states in which it was recently licensed (i.e., Arizona, Nevada, Utah, Colorado, Idaho, Washington, and Oregon), the company built a new home domicile in Chariton, Iowa, in 2012.

Discussion Questions

1. Do you think that the economic benefits that Midwest Family Mutual realized as a result of green computing are unusual? Do you think most companies can see similar types of economic gains? Explain.

2. What are some possible disadvantages the employees of Midwest Family Mutual may be experiencing as a result of their new virtual "work from home" office environment?

3. Apply the normative theories of business ethics to this situation.

Sources: Adapted from Anthony O'Donnell, "Plymouth, Minnesota-based Midwest Family Mutual's Move to a Paperless, Work-at-Home Operational Paradigm Has Yielded Both Environmental and Bottom-Line Benefits," *Insurance & Technology* (February 24, 2008), http://www.insurancetech.com/resources/fss/showArticle.jhtml;jsessionid=AYMVWDKZBGIFIQSNDLOSKHSCJUNN2JVN?articleID=206801556 (accessed on April 23, 2008); and Midwest Family Mutual News Archive, MFM Announces 2011 Results and Plans for 2012, https://midwestfamily.com/news.php?detail=589 (accessed on April 14, 2012).

Glossary

Accessibility: Area of information control involved with the ability to obtain data.

Accuracy: Area of information control dealing with the correctness of information or lack of errors in information.

Activity-based Costing: Costing method that calculates costs by counting the actual activities that go into making a specific product or delivering a specific service.

Agile Development: System development methodologies used to deal with unpredictability. They adapt to changing requirements by iteratively developing systems in small stages and then testing the new code extensively. They include XP (Extreme Programming), Crystal, Scrum, Feature-Driven Development, and Dynamic System Development Method (DSDM).

Allocation Funding Method: Method for funding IT costs which recovers costs based on something other than usage, such as revenues, login accounts, or number of employees.

Application: A software program designed to facilitate a specific practical task, as opposed to controlling resources. Examples of application programs include Microsoft Word, a word processing application; Lotus 1-2-3, a spreadsheet application; and SAP R/3, an enterprise resource planning application. Contrast to *operating system*.

Archetype: A pattern from decision rights allocation.

Architecture: Provides a blueprint for translating business strategy into a plan for IS.

ASP (Application Service Provider): An Internet-based company that offers a software application used through their Web site. For example, a company might offer small business applications that a small business owner could use on the Web, rather than buying software to load on their own computers.

Assumptions: Deepest layer of culture or the fundamental part of every culture that helps discern what is real and important to a group; They are unobservable since they reflect organizational values that have become so taken for granted that they guide organizational behavior without any of the groups thinking about them.

Backsourcing: A business practice in which a company takes back in-house assets, activities, and skills that are part of its information systems operations and were previously outsourced to one or more outside IS providers.

Balanced Scorecard: Method which focuses attention on the organization's value drivers (which include, but are not limited to, financial performance). Companies use it to assess the full impact of their corporate strategies on their customers and workforce, as well as their financial performance.

Beliefs: Perceptions that people hold about how things are done in their community.

Big Data: Term used to describe techniques and technologies that make it economical to deal with extremely large datasets at the extreme end of the scale.

Bring Your Own Device (BYOD): The scenario when employees bring their own devices to work and connect to enterprise systems. This is commonly used to mean devices such as smart phones, tablets and laptops.

Business Analytics: The use of data, analysis, and modeling to arrive at business decisions. Some organizations use business analytics to create new innovations or to support the modification of existing products or services.

Business Case: A structured document that lays out all the relevant information needed to make a go/no go decision. It contains an executive summary, overview, assumptions, program summary, financial discussion and analysis, discussion of benefits and business impacts, schedule and milestones, risk and contingency analysis, conclusion and recommendations.

Business Continuity Plan: An approved set of preparations and sufficient procedures for responding to a variety of disaster events.

Business Diamond: A simple framework for understanding the design of an organization, linking together the business processes, its values and beliefs, its management control systems, and its tasks and structures.

Business Intelligence: This term refers to the broader practice of using technology, applications, and processes to collect and analyze data to support business decisions.

Business-IT Maturity Model: Framework that displays the demands on the business side and the IT offerings on the supply side to help understand differences in capabilities.

Business Process Management (BPM): A well-defined and optimized set of IT processes, tools, and skills used to manage business processes.

Business Process Reengineering (BPR): Radical change approach which occurs over a short amount of time.

Business Strategy: A plan articulating where a business seeks to go and how it expects to get there.

Business Technology Strategist: The strategic business leader who uses technology as the core tool in creating competitive advantage and aligning business and IT strategies.

Capacity-on-demand: The availability of additional processing capability for a fee.

Captive Center: An overseas subsidiary that is set up to serve the parent company. Companies set up captive centers as an alternative to offshoring.

Centralized Architecture: Architecture where everything is purchased, supported and managed centrally usually in a data center.

Centralized IS Organization: Organization structure that brings together all staff, hardware, software, data, and processing into a single location.

Chargeback Funding Method: Method for funding IT costs in which costs are recovered by charging individuals, departments, or business units based on actual usage and cost.

CIO (Chief Information Officer): The senior-most officer responsible for the information systems activities within the organization. The CIO is a strategic thinker, not an operational manager. The CIO is typically a member of the senior management team and is involved in all major business decisions that come before that team, bringing an information systems perspective to the team.

Client: A software program that requests and receives data and sometimes instructions from another software program, usually running on a separate computer.

Cloud Computing: A style of infrastructure where capacity, applications, and services (such as development, maintenance, or security) are provided by a third-party provider over the Internet often on a "fee for use" basis.

COBIT (Control Objectives for Information and Related Technology): IT governance framework for decision controls that is consistent with COSO and that provides systematic rigor needed for the strong internal controls and Sarbanes-Oxley compliance.

Collaboration: Using social IT to extend the reach of stakeholders, both employees and those outside the enterprise walls. Social IT such as social networks enable individuals to find and connect with each other to share ideas, information and expertise.

Complementor: One of the players in a co-opetitive environment. It is a company whose product or service is used in conjunction with a particular product or service to make a more useful set for the customer. (See Value Net.)

Community Manager: The person who helps build, grow, and manage a community.

Cookie: A text message given to a Web browser by a Web server that is used to follow a person's surfing habits.

Co-opetition: A business strategy whereby companies cooperate and compete at the same time.

Consumerization of IT: The drive to port applications to personal devices and the ensuing issues to make them work.

Corporate Budget Funding Method: Method for funding IT costs in which the costs fall to the corporate bottom line, rather than being levied to specific users or business units.

Cost Leadership Strategy: A business strategy where the organization aims to be the lowest-cost producer in the marketplace. (See Differentiation Strategy; Focus Strategy.)

CRM (Customer Relationship Management): The management activities performed to obtain, enhance, and retain customers. CRM is a coordinated set of activities revolving around the customer.

Crowdsourcing: The act of taking a task traditionally performed by an employee or contractor and outsourcing it to an undefined, generally large group of people, in the form of an open call.

Cycle Plan: A project management plan that organizes project activities in relation to time. It identifies critical beginning and end dates and breaks the work spanning these dates into phases. The general manager tracks the phases to coordinate the eventual transition from project to operational status, a process that culminates on the "go live" date.

Culture: A set of shared values and beliefs that a group holds and that determines how the group perceives, thinks about and appropriately reacts to its various environments; A collective programming of the mind that distinguishes not only societies (or nations), but also industries, professions and organizations.

Dashboard: Common management monitoring tool which provides a snapshot of metrics at any given point in time.

Data: Set of specific, objective facts or observations that standing alone have no intrinsic meaning.

Data Mining: The process of analyzing databases for "gems" that will be useful in management decision making. Typically, data mining is used to refer to the process of combing through massive amounts of customer data to understand buying habits and to identify new products, features, and enhancements.

Database: A collection of data that is formatted and organized to facilitate ease of access, searching, updating, addition, and deletion. A database is typically so large that it must be stored on disk, but sections may be kept in RAM for quicker access. The software program used to manipulate the data in a database is also often referred to as a "database."

DBA (Database Administrator): The person within the information systems department who manages the data and the database. Typically, this person makes sure that all the data that goes into the database is accurate and appropriate, and that all applications and individuals who need access have it.

Debugging: The process of examining and testing software and hardware to make sure it operates properly under every condition possible. The term is based on calling any problem a "bug"; therefore, eliminating the problem is called "debugging."

Decentralized Architecture: Architecture in which the hardware, software, networking and data are arranged in a way that distributes the processing and functionality between multiple small computers, servers, and devices and they rely heavily on a network to connect them together.

Decentralized IS Organization: IS organization structure that scatters hardware, software, networks and data components in different locations to address local business needs.

Decision Models: Information systems-based model used by managers for scenario planning and evaluation. The information system collects and analyzes the information from automated processes and presents them to the manager to aid in decision making.

Decision Right: Indicates who in the organization has the responsibility to initiate, supply information for, approve, implement and control various types of decisions.

Differentiation Strategy: A business strategy where the organization qualifies its product or service in a way that allows it to appear unique in the marketplace. (See Cost Leadership Strategy; Focus Strategy.)

Digital Native: An individual who has grown up completely fluent in the use of personal technologies and the Web.

Digital Signature: A digital code applied to an electronically transmitted message used to prove that the sender of a message (e.g., a file or e-mail message) is truly who he or she claims to be.

Direct Cutover: Conversion in which the new system may be installed in stages across locations, or in phases.

Dynamic Business Process (also called agile business process): Agile process that iterates through a constant renewal cycle of design, deliver, evaluate, redesign and so on.

Economic Value Added (EVA): Valuation method which accounts for opportunity costs of capital to measure true economic profit and revalues historical costs to give and accurate picture of thrue market value of assets.

E-mail (electronic mail): A way of transmitting messages over communication networks.

Enacted Values: Value and norms that are actually exhibited or displayed in employee behavior.

Encryption: The translation of data into a code or a form that can be read only by the intended receiver. Data is encrypted using a key or alphanumeric code and can be decrypted only by using the same key.

Engagement: Using social IT to involve stakeholders in the traditional business of the enterprise Social IT such as communities and blogs provide a platform for individuals to join in conversations, create new conversations, offer support to each other, and other activities that create a deeper feeling of connection to the company, brand or enterprise.

Enterprise 2.0: A term used to describe a company using the technologies and practices resulting from Web 2.0 architectures, applications, and services. Enterprise 2.0 typically means a flat organization with unimpeded information flows between all levels and individuals in the organization. Companies adopting these practices seek to be agile, flexible, user driven, on-demand, and transparent.

Enterprise Architecture: The term used for a "blueprint" for the corporation that includes the business strategy, the IT architecture, the business processes, and the organization structure and how all these components relate to each other. Often this term is IT-centric, specifying the IT architecture and all the interrelationships with the structure and processes.

Enterprise System: A set of information systems tools that many organizations use to enable this information flow within and between processes across the organization.

ERP (Enterprise Resource Planning Software): A large, highly complex software program that integrates many business functions under a single application. ERP software can include modules for inventory management, supply chain management, accounting, customer support, order tracking, human resource management, and so forth. ERP software is typically integrated with a database.

Espoused Values: Explicitly stated, preferred organization values.

Explicit Knowledge: Objective, theoretical, and codified for transmission in a formal, systematic method using grammar, syntax, and the printed word. (See Tacit Knowledge.)

Extranet: A network based on the Internet standard that connects a business with individuals, customers, suppliers, and other stakeholders outside the organization's boundaries. An extranet typically is similar to the Internet; however, it has limited access to those specifically authorized to be part of it.

Farshoring: Form of offshoring that involves sourcing service work to a foreign lower-wage country that is relatively far away in distance or time zone (or both).

Federalism: Organization structuring approach that distributes power, hardware, software, data, and personnel between a central IS group and IS in business units.

File Transfer: Means of transferring a copy of a file from one computer to another over the Internet.

Firewall: A security measure that blocks out undesirable requests **for** entrance into a Web site and keeps those on the "inside" from reaching outside.

Flat Organization Structure (also called horizontal organization structure): Organization structure with less well-defined chain of command and with ill-defined, fluid jobs.

Focus Strategy: A business strategy where the organization limits its scope to a narrower segment of the market and tailors its offerings to that group of customers. This strategy has two variants: *cost focus*, in which the organization seeks a cost advantage within its segment, and *differentiation focus*, in which it seeks to distinguish its products or services within the segment. This strategy allows the organization to achieve a local competitive advantage, even if it does not achieve competitive advantage in the marketplace overall. (See Cost Strategy, Differentiation Strategy.)

Folksonomy: Collaboratively creating and managing a structure for any type of collection, such as a collection of ideas, data, or documents. The term is the merger of "folk" and "taxonomy," meaning that it is a user-generated taxonomy.

Full Outsourcing: Situation in which an enterprise outsources all its IS functions from desktop services to software development.

Functional View: The view of an organization based on the functional departments, typically including manufacturing, engineering, logistics, sales, marketing, finance, accounting, and human resources. (See Process View.)

Governance (in the context of business enterprises): Making decisions that define expectations, grant power, or verify performance.

Green Computing: An upcoming technology strategy in which companies become more socially responsible by using computing resources efficiently.

Groupware: Software that enables a group to work together on a project, whether in the same room, or from remote locations, by allowing them simultaneous access to the same files. Calendars, written documents, e-mail messages, discussion tools, and databases can be shared.

GUI (Graphical User Interface): The term used to refer to the use of icons, windows, colors, and text as the means of representing information and links on the screen of a computer. GUIs give the user the ability to control actions by clicking on objects rather than by typing commands to the operating system.

Hierarchical Organization Structure: An organization form or structure based on the concepts of division of labor, specialization, spans of control and unity of command.

Hypercompetition: A theory about industries and marketplaces that suggests that the speed and aggressiveness of moves and countermoves in any given market create an environment in which advantages are quickly gained and lost. A hypercompetitive environment is one in which conditions change rapidly.

Identity Theft: The taking of the victim's identity to obtain credit, credit cards from banks and retailers, steal money from the victim's existing accounts, apply for loans, establish accounts with utility companies, rent an apartment, file bankruptcy or obtain a job using the victim's name.

Information: Data endowed with relevance and purpose; data in a context.

Information Ethics: Ethical issues associated with the development and application of information technologies.

Information Integration: Involved with determining information to share, the format of that information, the technological standards they will both use to share it, and the security they will use to ensure that only authorized partners access it.

Information Model: A framework for understanding what information will be crucial to the decision, how to get it, and how to use it.

Information Resource: The available data, technology, people, and processes within an organization to be used by the manager to perform business processes and tasks.

Information System: The *combination* of technology (the "what"), people (the "who"), and process (the "how") that an organization uses to produce and manage information.

Information Systems (IS) Strategy: The plan an organization uses in providing information services.

Information Systems Strategy Triangle: The framework connecting business strategy, information system strategy, and organizational systems strategy.

Information Technology: All forms of technology used to create, store, exchange, and use information.

Infrastructure: Everything that supports the flow and processing of information in an organization, including hardware, software, data and network components. It consists of components, chosen and assembled in a manner that best suits the plan and enables the overarching business strategy.

Innovation: Using social IT to identify, describe, prioritized and create new ideas for the enterprise. Social IT offer the community members a forum to suggest new ideas, comment on other ideas, and vote for their favorite idea, giving managers a new way to generate and decide on products and services.

Insourcing: The situation in which a firm provides IS services or develop IS from its own in-house IS organization.

Instant Messaging (IM): Internet protocol (IP)-based application that provides real-time text-based communication between people using a variety of different device types, including computer-to-computer and movile devices.

Integrated Supply Chain: An enterprise system that crosses company boundaries and connects vendors and suppliers with organizations to synchronize and streamline planning and deliver products to all members of the supply chain.

Intellectual Capital: The knowledge that has been identified, captured, and leveraged to produce higher-value goods or services or some other competitive advantage for the firm.

Internet: The system of computers and networks that together connect individuals and businesses worldwide. The Internet is a global, *inter*connected *net*work of millions of individual host computers.

Intranet: A network used within a business to communicate between individuals and departments. An intranet is an application on the Internet, but limited to internal business use. It is a password-protected set of interconnected nodes that is under the company's administrative control. (See Extranets.)

IS (Information Systems): The technology (hardware, software, networking, data), people, and processes that an organization uses to manage information.

ISP (Internet Service Provider): A company who sells access to the Internet. Usually, the service includes a direct line or dial-up number and a quantity of time for using the connection. The service often includes space for hosting subscriber Web pages and e-mail.

IT (Information Technology): The technology component of the information system, usually consisting of the hardware, software, networking, and data.

IT Asset: Anything, tangible or intangible, that can be used by a firm in its processes for creating, producing, and/or offering its products (goods or services).

IT Capability: Something that is learned or developed over time for the firm to create, produce or offer its products.

IT Governance: Specifying the decision rights and accountability framework to encourage desirable behavior in using IT.

IT Portfolio Management: Evaluating new and existing applications collectively on an ongoing basis to determine which applications provide value to the business in order to support decisions to replace, retire, or further invest in applications across the enterprise.

ITIL (Information Technology Infrastructure Library): Control framework that offers a set of concepts and techniques for managing information technology infrastructure, development and operations that was developed in United Kingdom.

Joint Applications Development (JAD): A version of RAD or prototyping in which users are more integrally involved, as a group, with the entire development process up to and, in some cases, including coding.

Knowledge: Information synthesized and contextualized to provide value.

Knowledge Management: The processes necessary to capture, codify, and transfer knowledge across the organization to achieve competitive advantage.

Knowledge Repository: A physical or virtual place where documents with knowledge embedded in them, such as memos, reports, or news articles, are stored so they can be retrieved easily.

LAN (Local Area Network): A network of interconnected (often via Ethernet) workstations that reside within a limited geographic area (typically within a single building or campus). LANs are typically employed so that the machines on them can share resources such as printers or servers and/or so that they can exchange e-mail or other forms of messages (e.g., to control industrial machinery).

Legacy System: Older, mature information system (often 20 to 30 years old).

List Server: A type of e-mail mailing list where users subscribe, and when any user sends a message to the server, a copy of the message is sent to everyone on the list. This allows for restricted-access discussion groups: Only subscribed members can participate in or view the discussions because they are transmitted via e-mail.

Mainframe: A large, central computer that handles all the functionality of the system.

Managerial Levers: Organizational, control, and cultural variables that are used by decision makers to effect changes in their organizations.

Mashup: A term used in the Web 2.0 community to mean the combination of data from multiple sources into one Web page, for example, combining Google Maps with real estate data to produce a diagram showing home price ranges for certain neighborhoods.

Matrix Organization Structure: An organizational form or structure in which workers are assigned two or more supervisors, each supervising a different aspect of the employee's work, in an effort to make sure multiple dimensions of the business are integrated.

Middleware: Software used to connect processes running in one or more computers across a network.

Mission: A clear and compelling statement that unifies an organization's effort and describes what the firm is all about (i.e., its purpose).

Mobile Workers: Individuals who work wherever they are physically located.

Nearshoring: Sourcing service work to a foreign, lower-wage country that is relatively close in distance or time zone (or both).

Net Present Value (NPV): Valuation method that takes into account the time value of money in which cash inflows and outflows are discounted.

Network Effect: The value of a network node to a person or organization in the network increases when another joins the network.

Networked Organization Structure: Organization form or structure where rigid hierarchies are replaced by formal and informal communication networks that connect all parts of the company; Organization stucture known for it flexibility and adaptiveness.

Newsgroup: A type of electronic discussion in which the text of the discussions typically is viewable on an Internet or intranet Web page rather than sent through e-mail. Unless this page is shielded with a firewall or password, outsiders are able to view and/or participate in the discussion.

Object: Encapsulates both the data stored about an entity and the operations that manipulate that data.

Observable Artifacts: Most visible layer of culture that includes physical manifestations such as traditional dress, symbols in art, acronyms, awards, myths and stories about the group, rituals and ceremonies, etc.

Offshoring (short for outsourcing offshore): Situation in which IS organization uses contractor services, or even builds its own data center, in a distant land.

Onshoring (also called inshoring): Situation in which outsourcing work is performed domestically.

Open Source Software (OSS): Software released under a license approved by the Open Source Initiative (OSI).

Open Sourcing: A development approach called the process of building and improving "free" software by an Internet community.

Operating System (OS): A program that manages all other programs running on, as well as all the resources connected to, a computer. Examples include Microsoft Windows, DOS, and UNIX.

Oracle: A widely used database program.

Organizational Strategy: A plan that answers the question: "How will the company organize to achieve its goals and implement its business strategy?; includes the organization's design as well as the choices it makes to define, set up, coordinate, and control its work processes.

Organizational Systems: The fundamental elements of a business including people, work processes, structure, and the plan that enables them to work efficiently to achieve business goals.

Outsourcing: The business arrangement where third-party providers and vendors manage the information systems activities. In a typical outsourced arrangement, the company finds vendors to take care of the operational activities, the support activities, and the systems development activities, saving strategic decisions for the internal information systems personnel.

Parallel Conversion: Conversion in which the old system stops running as soon as the new system is installed.

Peer-to-Peer: Infrastructure that allows networked computers to share resources without a central server playing a dominant role.

Platform: The hardware and software on which applications are run. For example, the iPhone is considered a platform for many applications and service that can be run on it.

Portal: Easy-to-use Web sites that provide access to search engines, critical information, research, applications, and processes that individuals want.

Privacy: Area of information control involved with the right to be left alone; involved with the protections from intrusion and information gathering by others; an individuals' ability to personally control information about themselves.

Process: An interrelated, sequential set of activities and tasks that turn inputs into outputs and has a distinct beginning, a clear deliverable at the end, and a set of metrics that are useful to measure performance.

Process View: The view of a business from the perspective of the business processes performed. Typically the view is made up of cross-functional processes that transverse disciplines, departments, functions, and even organizations. (See Functional View.)

Project: A temporary endeavor undertaken to create a unique product, service or result. Temporary means that every project has a definite beginning and a definite end.

Project Manager: Person who makes sure that the entire project is executed appropriately and coordinated properly; defines project scope realistically and manages project so that it can be completed on time and within budget.

Project Management: An application of knowledge, skills, tools, and techniques to project activities to meet project requirements.

Project Management Office (PMO): The organizational unit within which resides the expertise for managing projects.

Project Stakeholder: Individual or organization that is actively involved in the project, or whose interests may be affected as a result of project execution or project completion.

Property: Area of information control focused on who owns the data.

Protocol: A special, typically standardized, set of rules used by computers to enable communication between them.

Prototyping: An evolutionary development method for building an information system. Developers get the general idea of what is needed by the users, and then build a fast, high-level version of the system as the beginning of the project. The idea of prototyping is to quickly get a version of the software in the hands of the users, and to jointly evolve the system through a series of cycles of design and build, then use and evaluate.

RAD (Rapid Application Development): This process is similar to prototyping in that it is an interactive process, where tools are used to speed up development. RAD systems typically have tools for developing the user, reusable code, code generation, and programming language testing and debugging. These tools make it easy for the developer to build a library of a common, standard set of code that can easily be used in multiple applications.

Resource-Based View (RBV): A view that attaining and sustaining competitive advantage comes from creating value using information and other resources of the firm.

Reengineering: The management process of redesigning business processes in a relatively radical manner. Reengineering traditionally meant taking a "blank piece of paper" and designing (then building) a business process from the beginning. This was intended to help the designers eliminate any blocks or barriers that the current process or environment might provide. This process is sometimes called BPR, Business Process Redesign or Reengineering or Business Reengineering.

Return on Investment: Valuation method which calculates the percentage rate that measure the relationship between the amount the business gets back from an investment and the amount invested.

Review Board: A committee that is formally designated to approve, monitor, and review specific topics.

Reuse: Relatively small chunks of functionality are available for many applications.

RSS or Really Simple Syndication (also called Web feeds): Refers to a structured file format for porting data from one platform or information system to another.

SAP: The company that produces the leading ERP software. The software, technically named "SAP R/3," is often simply referred to as SAP.

Sarbanes-Oxley (SoX) Act of 2002: United States federal statute increasing regulatory visibility and accountability of public companies and their financial health.

Scalable: Refers to how well an infrastructure component can adapt to increased, or in some cases decreased, demands.

Selective Outsourcing: The situation when an enterprise chooses which IT capabilities to retain in-house and which to give to an outsider.

Server: A software program or computer intended to provide data and/or instructions to another software program or computer. The hardware on which a server program runs is often also referred to as "the server."

Service-Level Agreement (or SLA): Formal service contract between clients and outrsourcing providers that describes level of service including deliveray time and expected service performance.

Service-Oriented Architecture (SOA): This is the term used to describe the architecture where business processes are built using services delivered over a network (typically the Internet). Services are software that are distinct units of business functionality residing on different parts of a network and can be combined and reused to create business applications.

Silos: Self-contained functional units.

Six Sigma: An incremental data-driven approach to quality management for eliminating defects from a process. The term "Six Sigma" comes from the idea that if the quality of all output from a process were to be mapped on a bell-shaped curve, the tail of the curve, six sigma from the mean, would be where there were less than 3.4 defects per million.

Social Business: An enterprise whose basic business model engages communities as a core competency and builds processes based on capabilities only available through the use of social IT.

Social Business Strategy: A plan of how the firm will use social IT to engage, collaboration and innovate. The social business strategy is aligned with organization strategy and IS strategy; includes a vision of how the business would operate if it seamlessly and thoroughly incorporated social and collaborative capabilities throughout the business model.

Social Contract Theory: A theory used in business ethics to describe how managers should act. Social contract theorists ask what conditions would have to be met for the members of such a society to agree to allow a corporation to be formed. Thus, society bestows legal recognition on a corporation to allow it to employ social resources toward given ends.

Social IT: The technologies used for collaboration, engagement and innovation over the Web. Typically these tools enable communities of people to chat, network, and share information. Common applications are social networks such as Facebook and LinkedIn, crowdsourcing, blogs, microblogs such as Twitter, and location-based such as Foursquare.

Social Media: The marketing and sales applications of social IT.

Social Networking Site: A Web site available from a Web-based service that allows members of the service to create a public profile within a bounded system, list other users with whom they share a connection, and view and interact with their list of connections and those made by others within the system. Examples are MySpace, Facebook, and LinkedIn.

Software-as-a-Service (SaaS): This term is used to describe a model of software deployment that uses the Web to deliver applications on an "as-needed" basis. Often when software is delivered as a service, it runs on a computer on the Internet, rather than on the customer's computer, and is accessed through a Web browser.

Stakeholder Theory: A theory used in business ethics to describe how managers should act. This theory suggests that managers, although bound by their relation to stockholders, are entrusted also with a fiduciary responsibility to all those who hold a stake in or a claim on the firm, including employees, customers, vendors, neighbors, etc.

Standardization: The process of agreeing on technical specifications that will be followed throughout the infrastructure. Often standards are agreed on for development processes, technology, methods, practices, and software.

Steering Committee: IT governance mechanism which calls for joint participation of IT and business leaders in making decisions about IT as a group.

Stockholder Theory: A theory used in business ethics to describe how managers should act. Stockholders advance capital to corporate managers who act as agents in advancing their ends. The nature of this contract binds managers to act in the interest of the shareholders (i.e., to maximize shareholder value).

Strategic Alliance: An interorganizational relationship that affords one or more companies in the relationship a strategic advantage.

Strategic Network: A long-term purposeful arrangement by which companies set up a web of close relationships to provide product or services in a coordinated way to those companies in the system of relationships.

Strategy: A coordinated set of actions to fulfill objectives, purposes, and goals.

Supply Chain Management (SCM) System: System that manages the integrated supply chain; processes are linked across companies with a companion process at a customer or supplier.

Synchronized Planning: Partners agree on a joint design of planning, forecasting, replenishment and what to do with the information.

Systems Development Life Cycle (SDLC): The process of designing and delivering the entire system. SDLC usually means these seven phases: initiation of the project, requirements definition phase, functional design phase, technical design and construction phase, verification phase, implementation phase, and maintenance and review phase.

Tacit Knowledge: Personal, context-specific, and hard to formalize and communicate. It consists of experiences, beliefs, and skills. Tacit knowledge is entirely subjective and is often acquired through physically practicing a skill or activity. (See Explicit Knowledge.)

Tagging: Process in which users themselves list key words that codify the information or document at hand, creates an ad-hoc codification system, sometimes referred to as a folksonomy.

Telecommuting: Combining telecommunications with commuting. This term usually means individuals who regularly work from home instead of commuting into an office. However, it is often used to mean anyone who works regularly from a location outside their company's office.

TOGAF (also called The Open Group Architecture Framework): Includes a methodology and set of resources for developing an enterprise architecture based on the idea of an open architecture, an architecture whose specifications are public (as compared to a proprietary architecture, where specifications are not made public).

Total Cost of Ownership (TCO): Costing method that looks beyond initial capital investments to include costs associated with technical support, administration, training, system retirement, etc.

Total Quality Management (TQM): A management philosophy in which quality metrics drive performance evaluation of people, processes, and decisions. The objective of TQM is to continually, and often incrementally, improve the activities of the business toward the goal of eliminating defects (zero defects) and producing the highest quality outputs possible.

Unified Communications (UC): An evolving communications technology architecture that automates and unifies all forms of human and device communications in context and with a common experience.

Utility Computing: Purchasing entire computing capability on an as-needed basis.

Value: Reflects the community's aspirations about the way things should be done.

Value Net: The set of players in a co-opetitive environment. It includes a company and its competitors and complementors, as well as their customers and suppliers, and the interactions among all of them. (See Complementor.)

Video Teleconference (also called videoconference): A set of interactive telecommunication technologies that allow two or more locations to interact via two-way video and audio transmissions simultaneously.

Virtual Corporation: A temporary network of companies who are linked by information technology to exploit fast-changing opportunities.

Virtual Private Network (VPN): A private network that uses a public network such as the Internet to connect remote sites or users. It maintains privacy through the use of a tunneling protocol and security procedures.

Virtual Team: Two or more people who (1) work together interdependently with mutual accountability for achieving common goals, (2) do not work in either the same place and/or at the same time, and (3) must use electronic communication technology to communicate, coordinate their activities and complete their team's tasks.

Virtual World: A computer-based simulated environment intended for its users to inhabit and interact via avatars.

Virtualization: Allows a computer to run multiple operating systems or several versions of the same operating system at the same time; virtual infrastructure where software replaced hardware in a way that a 'virtual machine' or a 'virtual desktop system' was accessible to provide computing power.

Voice over Internet Protocol (VoIP): A method for taking analog audio signals, like the kind you hear when you talk on the phone, and turning them into digital data that can be transmitted over the Internet.

Web 2.0: The term given to the Internet and its applications that support collaboration, social networking, social media, RSS, mashups, and a number of other information sharing tools. The term is used to distinguish it from Web 1.0, which was mostly used for transactions and information dissemination. Web 2.0 is not about different technical specifications, but about using the Internet in different ways from Web 1.0.

Web-based Architecture: Architecture in which significant hardware, software, and possibly even data elements reside on the Internet.

Web Logs (Blogs): Online journals that link together into a very large network of information sharing.

Web Services: The software systems that are offered over the Internet and executed on a third party's hardware. Often Web services refer to a more fundamental software that use XML messages and follow SOAP (simple object access protocol) standards.

Wide Area Network (WAN): A computer network that spans multiple offices, often dispersed over a wide geographic area. A WAN typically consists of transmission lines leased from telephone companies.

Wiki: Software that allows users to work collaboratively to create, edit, and link Web pages easily.

Wireless (Mobile) Infrastructure: Infrastructure that allows communication from remote locations using a variety of wireless technologies (e.g., fixed microwave links, wireless LANs, data over cellular networks, wireless WANs, satellite links, digital dispatch networks, one-way and two-way paging networks, diffuse infrared, laser-based communications, keyless car entry, and global positioning systems).

Wisdom: Knowledge fused with intuition and judgment that facilitates the ability to make decisions.

Workflow: Describes activities that take place in a business process.

Zachman Framework: Enterprise architecture that determines architectural requirements by providing a broad view that helps guide the analysis of the detailed view.

Zero Time Organization: An organization designed around responding instantly to customers, employees, suppliers, and other stakeholder demands.

Index